HARDPRESS.NET
HOME OF HARD-TO-FIND BOOKS

Letters Written by His Excellency Hugh Boulter...To Several Ministers of State in England, and Some Others
by Hugh Boulter

Address:
HardPress
8345 NW 66TH ST #2561
MIAMI FL 33166-2626
USA
Email: info@hardpress.net

BOULTER

CSA

INDIGNANTE JUSTUS INVIDIA FLOREBIT

LETTERS

WRITTEN BY

HIS EXCELLENCY

HUGH BOULTER, D.D.

Lord PRIMATE of All IRELAND, &c.

TO

Several Miniſters of State in England,

AND SOME OTHERS.

CONTAINING,

An Account of the moſt intereſting Tranſactions
which paſſed in IRELAND from 1724 to 1738.

VOLUME THE FIRST.

DUBLIN:

Printed for GEORGE FAULKNER and JAMES WILLIAMS.

MDCCLXX.

TO THE

HONOURABLE AND REVEREND

GEORGE TALBOT,

BY DIPLOMA, D. D.

THESE LETTERS

ARE INSCRIBED,

WITH ALL THE RESPECT

AND DEFERENCE

DUE TO A CHARACTER

OF SUCH EMINENT WORTH,

BY HIS AFFECTIONATE,

AND EVER OBLIGED SERVANT,

THE EDITOR.

Advertiſement.

THE Letters from which theſe are printed, are depoſited in the library of *Chriſt Church* in *Oxford*; they are intirely letters of buſineſs, and were collected by the late *Ambroſe Philips*, Eſq; who was ſecretary to his Grace, and lived in his houſe during that ſpace of time in which they bear date; they are all in the hand-writing of his Excellency, except ſome few marked thus †, which are fair copies by his ſecretary; and they are now firſt publiſhed as they were received from Mr. *Philips*, without any the leaſt material alteration or omiſſion whatever.

As to the merit of theſe Letters, the impartial publick will form ſuch a judgment of them as they ſhall be found to deſerve; it is paſt all doubt that they could not be intended for publication by his Grace, and therefore it ſhould ſeem fortunate that they have been preserved;

of which grievances this good Prelate lived to fee redreffed, particularly the regulation of the different fpecies of money, by which Commerce hath been carried on with more convenience. The character of his Grace was very unblemifhed, as he was pious and very charitable, having left a large part of his fortune for the latter good pur-pofes ; yet, with all thefe Virtues, he was too partially favourable to the people of England, and too much prejudiced againft the natives of Ire-land, who are moftly defcended from the Englifh.

G. F.

Dublin, March 22d.
    1770.

LETTERS

WRITTEN BY

His Excellency HUGH BOULTER

Lord Primate of all *Ireland,* &c.

---

† *To his Grace the Archbishop of* Canterbury.

My Lord,   *Dublin, Nov.* 28. 1724.

YOUR Grace will have the goodness to excuse my not writing sooner, considering the perpetual hurry I have been in here since my arrival, with receiving and paying compliments, and trying to settle a little in the lodgings I am in, 'till I can find a house to fix in. I had, I thank God, a very good journey and a quick passage hither, and can complain of no inconveniency I suffered, but the weakening of my arm, which obliges me to use another hand to write to my friends. My family have had their health very well here, and the weather has been what I should have counted good in *England.* I miss little here but my friends and acquaintance; and I have little to complain of but that too many of our own original esteem us *Englishmen,* as intruders.

At my coming away from *England,* I was very much straitened in my time, or I had crossed to *Lambeth* to take leave of your Grace, when I should have recommended to your favour Mr. *Blenner-Hasset*

VOL. I   A   for

for his Doctor's degree, I have known him for many years to be well-affected to his Majesty's family, and he was my chaplain all the time I was Bishop of *Briftol*, and his circumstances and family are such that a good living here will make him easier than any thing he has hopes of in *England*: and as I have given him hopes of doing somewhat for him, he thinks he shall command the more respect if he comes over a Doctor. I have not yet heard whether my predeceffors have claimed a right of giving degrees; but if they have, in the prefent ferment here againft the *English*, it would be very unpopular in me to exercife fuch a power in favour of one of my countrymen, nor would it anfwer the end he propofes. He will speedily wait upon your Grace in hopes of obtaining this favour at your hands. I am glad to find, by the King's fpeech and the addreffes of both houfes, which is the laft news we have had, that you are likely to have a quiet feffions in *England*, and wifh, when our turn comes, we may have as eafy a one here. I fhall always be proud of receiving your Grace's commands, and am, my Lord,

Your Grace's moft humble, and
Moft obedient Servant,
Hu. Armagh.

† *To the Duke of* Newcaftle, *Secretary of State.*

My Lord, *Dublin, Dec.* 3. 1724.

IT was Sunday laft before I had the honour of your Grace's of the 17th paft : I am very glad to find his Majefty's affairs go fo fmoothly in the Parliament in *England*; I could heartily wifh every thing was fo eafy here.

I have not troubled your Grace with an account of the behaviour of the old grand jury, and the prefentment of the new ; becaufe I did not queftion your
having

having an immediate account of both from better hands.

We are at prefent in a very bad ftate, and the people fo poifoned with apprehenfions of *Wood's* half-pence, that I do not fee there can be any hopes of juftice againft any perfon for feditious writings, if he does but mix fomewhat about * *Wood* in them. I muft do the better fort of people here, the juftice to fay, they fpeak with great concern of the imprudence of the grand juries, and the ill ftop to juftice: but thofe who would hinder it now are unable. But all forts here are determinately fet againft *Wood's* half-pence, and look upon their eftates as half funk in their value, whenever they fhall pafs upon the nation.

Our pamphlets, and the difcourfes of fome people of weight, run very much upon the independency of this kingdom ; and, in our prefent ftate, that is a very popular notion. But others, (who poffibly have had a hand in raifing this ferment at firft) declare publickly againft all fuch notions, profeffing the ut-moft loyalty to his Majefty ; and are very uneafy at the ill humour, and infolent behaviour of the people. I am fatisfied, many here think ten or fifteen thoufand pounds worth of halfpence would be of fervice ; but they dare not fay fo to any *Irifhman*, nor at prefent does there feem to be any way of com-pofing matters ; all fearing or pretending to fear, the parliament ; and except things cool a little, I am apt to think the parliament would fear the madnefs of the people. Though all people are equally fet againft *Wood* here, yet many of the prefent madneffes are fuppofed to come from Papifts, mixing with, and

A 2

fetting

---

* Dr. *Swift*, D. S. P. D. overthrew this pernicious fcheme by writing the Drapier's letters, and other papers againft this bafe coin See *Swift's* works, vol. 4. printed by *George Faulkner*.

setting on others, with whom they formerly had no manner of correspondence.

I have been in such an unsettled state, that I have been less able to learn how things go, than I hope to do in some time. As I gain more knowledge my-self, I shall take care to give your Grace the best in-formation I can ; and shall always be ready to receive your Grace's commands.

I am, my Lord,

Your Grace's most humble,

And most obedient Servant,

HU. ARMAGH.

† *Circular Letter to the Lord Primate's Suffragan Bishops.*

My Lord,   *Dublin, Dec.* 24. 1724.

AS I am very desirous to serve the * Church, to which it has pleased God to call me ; I have, since my arrival, been enquiring into the wants of the Clergy here, and the produce of the fund given to supply those wants. And finding, that the fund will, probably raise but 300 *l. per annum, communibus annis* ; and, that this scanty fund is about 1500 *l.* in debt ; I have been talking with my brethren, the bishops, about encouraging a subscription among them and the inferior clergy, to bring the fund out of debt, and make a small beginning of a larger sup-ply to the wants of the Church ; in hopes, that we may (after having done somewhat ourselves) with the better grace apply to the laity for their assistance.

And the proposal at last agreed upon by the Arch-bishop of *Dublin,* the Bishops of *Meath, Dromore, Elphin,*

---

* His Grace left the whole of his fortune, which was very considerable, except some few legacies, to the charitable uses proposed in this letter.

Elphin, Clonfert, and myfelf, to be communicated to our brethren the bifhops; and (if approved by them) to be, by them, recommended to the inferior clergy in their refpective diocefes, for their concurrence, is this: That every archbifhop and bifhop would be pleafed to fubfcribe, at the rate of 2 *per cent. per annum,* for three years, out of his yearly income, to be rated by himfelf, *deductis oneribus:* and (in like manner, and for the fame term) that every clergyman, poffeft of above 100 *l. per annum,* fubfcribe at the rate of 1 *per cent.* And, that every clergyman, poffeft of preferment from 50 to 100 *l. per annum,* fubfcribe Ten Shillings. Any one, notwithftanding, to be at liberty to fubfcribe a larger proportion if he thinks fit.

This is defigned to be employed in aid of the fund of firft-fruits: the money fo gathered, to be lodged in the hands of Dr. * *Coghill;* and to be laid out in purchafing glebes, or impropriations, as the bifhops fhall direct. Several of the clergy, who have been talked with here, have expreffed a readinefs to come into the defign, if the bifhops would fubfcribe a double proportion of what the clergy were defired to fubfcribe, on this occafion. The whole is defired to be entirely voluntary. I have reafon to believe the Archbifhops of † *Cafhel* and § *Tuam* will chearfully come into the defign.

I doubt not of your Lordfhip's readinefs to concur with any thing, that may be of fervice to religion: but I muft defire your opinion concerning this propofal; as being fatisfied, you are a better judge of what may be done, in prudence to advance the worfhip of God

---

* The right honourable *Marmaduke Coghill,* a civilian, and afterwards a commiffioner of the revenue.
† Dr. *Palliſer.*
§ Dr. *Synge.*

God and the proteftant religion, in this nation, than myfelf, who am fo newly arrived here.

> I am, my Lord,
>> Your Lordfhip's very affectionate
>>> Brother, and humble Servant,
>>>> HU. ARMAGH.

† *Letter to the Bifhop of* * Waterford.

My Lord,   *Dublin, Jan.* 19. 1724.

I HAVE received your Lordfhip's of the 13th inftant, and I am very much furprized at the account it enclofes. I do not remember to have heard of any cafe like it in *England* The Dean feems to me not to have behaved himfelf with the refpect due to his Diocefan : and I could wifh your Lordfhip had put him more in the wrong, by fhewing a little more patience and temper on your fide. But, what provocations were firft given by the Dean ; or, what was the full ftate of the difpute in the morning, on which the quarrel in the afternoon was grounded, does not appear by the account your Lordfhip has enclofed.

I am not yet enough acquainted with the laws and conftitutions of this church, to be able to advife what is proper to be done by your Lordfhip in a legal way : but I could heartily wifh, that (for the prevention of fcandal) fome method could be found of adjufting the differences, between your Lordfhip and the Dean, (of which, I hear, this is but one branch) by an amicable arbitration.

If, upon talking with others, I meet with any advice, worth tranfmitting to your Lordfhip, you fhall not fail of hearing from, my Lord,

> Your Lordfhip's affectionate
>> Brother, and humble Servant,
>>> HU. ARMAGH.

† *To*

¶ Dr. *Milly*.

† *To the Duke of* Newcaſtle, *&c.*

My Lord,   *Dublin,* *Jan.* 19. 1724.

IT is now ſome weeks ſince I had the honour of writing to your Grace, as I was deſirous to learn as much as I could from all hands, before I gave your Grace the trouble of another letter : I have in the mean time, made it my buſineſs to talk with ſeveral of the moſt leading men in parliament ; and have employed others to pick up what they could learn from a variety of people : and I find by my own and others enquiries, that the people of every religion, country, and party here, are alike ſet againſt *Wood's* halfpence, and that their agreement in this has had a very unhappy influence on the ſtate of this nation, by bringing on intimacies, between Papiſts and Jacobites, and the Whigs, who before had no correſpondence with them : ſo that 'tis queſtioned, whether (if there were occaſion) juſtices of the peace could be found, who would be ſtrict in diſarming Papiſts.

The apprehenſion of the loſs they ſhall ſuffer if theſe halfpence are introduced, has too much cooled the zeal of numbers, that were before very well affected ; and it has appeared by ſome occurrences ſince my arrival, of which your Grace had (no doubt) a particular account at the time they happened : and I fear on any new occaſion, it would ſtill more appear, that the uneaſineſs againſt the halfpence is a protection for any ſedition, uttered or publiſhed, that has any thing againſt the halfpence intermixed with it. So that it is impoſſible for the government, in our preſent ſtate, to have juſtice againſt any ſuch delinquents, nor do I believe, that any witneſſes in ſuch a proſecution, could be ſafe in their perſons.

That there has been a great deal of art uſed to ſpread this general infection, and that the Papiſts and Jacobites have been very induſtrious in this affair for
very

very bad ends, I find moſt of the men of ſenſe here will allow. It is likewiſe certain, that ſome fooliſh and other ill-meaning people, have taken this opportunity of propagating a notion of the independency of this kingdom on that of *England*, but I muſt, at the ſame time, do juſtice to thoſe of the beſt ſenſe and eſtates here, that they abhor any ſuch notion; and that they eſteem the great ſecurity of all they have here, to lie in their dependency on the kingdom as well as King of *England*. And I hope the folly of ſome, and the wickedneſs of others, in ſpreading ſuch pernicious principles, will not provoke any on the other ſide of the water, to take any angry ſteps, to diſtreſs a nation, where the Proteſtants are generally well affected to his Majeſty; and where the title to their eſtates is viſibly interwoven with that of his Majeſty to the Crown; and where no great damage can be done them, without ſenſibly hurting *England*: and I the rather hope ſo, becauſe there are other methods of preventing any ill conſequence of ſuch notions, which are very obvious, and of which I ſhall, if deſired, ſpeak more particularly another time.

At preſent I ſhall only proceed to acquaint your Grace, what are the apprehenſions people generally have here, of what they ſhall certainly ſuffer by the new halfpence being introduced, and which keep a ſpirit of uneaſineſs in them 'till the patent is abſolutely ſunk; for whilſt that ſubſiſts, though not puſhed into execution, 'tis conſidered here as a ſtorm, that will ſome day break over their heads.

By the beſt computations or conjectures here, the current coin of this nation, in gold, ſilver, and copper, is thought not to exceed 400,000 *l.* The addition of 40,000 *l.* in new copper, to the preſent copper-money, will make the copper-money of this nation, at leaſt, one eighth of their whole ſpecie. They think where the copper-money is ſo conſiderable a part of the whole ſpecie, it is impoſſible to keep

it

it from making a senfible part in all payments, whether of rents, debts, or the purchafe of goods : that if it be once admitted to have a currency, it will the more work its way into all payments ; as men of fubftance in trade will be tempted by a premium (from the patentee) of 20, 30, or 40, *per cent*. to force its currency among the meaner people ; and they again can only pay their landlords and others, in fuch as they receive : that (when, inftead of ferving for change, it enters into all payments) it will be impoffible to hinder the *Dutch* and others, from pouring in large quantities of counterfeit copper : that the confequence of this muft be the lofs of our filver and gold, to the ruin of our trade and manufactures, and the finking the rent of all the eftates here.

This is the fubftance of what the men of fenfe and eftates here, are fully poffeft with. And when I tell them the copper-money of *England* is confiderably fhort of the intrinfick worth of what it goes for ; and that yet I never could hear of any furmife of the *Dutch* pouring in any counterfeit copper there ; nor, was it ever attempted to make payments in copper there : what they anfwer is, that probably all the copper-money there, in being at once, feldom exceeds one hundredth part of the whole fpecie of money ; and fo is kept barely for ufe of change.

I have been talking with them, whether there could not be room for admitting from 10 to 20,000 *l*. in copper ? which I have reafon to believe they want ; or at leaft, that it would be a kindnefs to the nation if they had it. But they all agree, in the prefent ferment, it is impoffible to admit any : and they all exprefs a jealoufy, that the admitting any new copper would open a door for fuch a quantity, as would prove ruinous to this nation.

Thefe are the prefent notions of people here, which 'tis in vain to try to remove : and as long as
the

the fear of the new halfpence lasts, there is no hope
of any peace and quiet in people's minds : and much
less of any so much as decent proceedings, if a parliament were to sit.   This has made me talk further
with the same persons, what compromise can be offered to have *Wood's* patent sunk.   I have told them
there can be no doubt but *Wood* must have been a
very great sufferer by the obstructions he has already
met with ; and must be still a much greater, if his
patent be resigned : that I did not find any body in
England doubted of the legality of the grant : that
where the patentee was not proved to have contra-
vened the conditions of the grant, it could not in
justice be revoked ; [to this they unanimously reply,
that he has uttered worse than his patent allows] that
Wood could not be supposed willing to resign it, without a proper compensation ; and that the seditious and
clamorous behaviour of too many here, must rather
tend to provoke his Majesty and his ministry to support the patent, than to take any extraordinary steps
to sink it ; and that therefore the most proper way
seemed to be, the proposing some reasonable amends
to Mr. *Wood*, in order to his resigning the patent.

What those of sense and interest in parliament, and
that are well affected, all agree in, is, that, while
the fear of these halfpence hangs over this nation, it
is impossible to have things easy here, but that they
dare not offer any expedient, nor make any such
proposals to those on the other side of the water, for
fear of being fallen on, as undertaking for the parliament : but that if the ministry will please to make
a computation of what it may be reasonable to give
Mr. *Wood* for resigning his patent, and for his past
losses, and to send an order from his Majesty to pay
any body (really in trust for Mr. *Wood*, but without
mentioning his name in the order) such a sum *per
annum* for such a term of years, as they judge a reasonable

fonable equivalent, they do not doubt being able in parliament, to provide for fuch payment (if his patent has been firft refigned) whatever fufpicions there may be, that the payment is to Mr. *Wood*; or whatever oppofition is made to it in the houfe. And if the nation is gratified in this, they do not queftion, but by degrees publick juftice will again flourifh, and the former zeal for his majefty and his family revive. And I cannot but fay that without doing fomething like this, there is no profpect of any end of our prefent heats and animofities.

Your Grace will have the goodnefs to excufe the length and freedom of this letter, which nothing fhould have drawn from me but my concern for his Majefty's fervice, and a defire that your Grace fhould know the true ftate of affairs here.

The Archbifhop of * *Dublin* has of late been very ill, fo that his life was almoft defpaired of: but his illnefs has fince ended in a regular and painful fit of the gout, fo that I do not apprehend he is in any prefent danger. Your Grace had heard from me fooner on this fubject, if I had known his condition before the worft was over; all that I fhall fay now is, that I think his Majefty's fervice abfolutely requires, that whenever he drops, the place be filled with an *Englifhman*, and one with whom I may hope to have a very good agreement. But of this I fhall write further another time, as your Grace fhall give me encouragement.

I am, &c.

† *To*

* Dr. *King*.

† *To the same.*

My Lord,   *Dublin, Mar.* 4. 1724.

IT is now above a month ago, since I troubled your Grace with a very long letter, relating to the affairs of this nation : and I should not have written again on any of the subjects therein mentioned, till after receiving your Grace's commands, if there were not repeated advices from *England,* that upon the report of the Archbishop of *Dublin's* illness, there was a very great canvass on the bench about his successor, without the least regard to what might be represented from hence, as of service to his Majesty. Your Grace knows very well that I was very content with what I had in *England,* and my just expectations there ; and that it was purely in obedience to his Majesty's pleasure, that I came hither : and now I am here, the only thing that can make me uneasy, is, if I should not be enabled to carry on his Majesty's service here ; the prospect of doing which is the greatest comfort I have in my present station. But if the Bishopricks here, are to be disposed of elsewhere, without leaving me room for any thing more, than (as it may happen) objecting against a person, who may be sent over to the best promotions here, when I have done so ; and if I be not allowed to form proper dependencies here, to break the present *Dublin* faction on the bench, it will be impossible for me to serve his Majesty further than in my single capacity. I do not speak this, as if I did not think there are some on the *English* bench, that would do very well in *Dublin,* and would heartily join with me in promoting his Majesty's measures ; or that I do not esteem it wise gradually to get as many *English* on the bench here as can be decently sent hither ; but that I think being on the *English* bench alone, is not
a suffi-

a sufficient qualification for coming to the best promotions here ; and that an imprudent person may easily be tempted by *Irish* flattery, to set himself at the head of the Archbishop of *Dublin*'s party, in opposition to me. And besides, as there is a majority of the Bishops here that are natives, they are not to be disobliged at once.

I hope I shall never behave myself so as to be thought unfit to take care of his Majesty's interest on the bench here, and beg that, till it be found I am, I may be effectually supported in that authority and dependence, which I can assure your Grace I desire for no other end, than to be the more able to serve his Majesty.

I am, &c.

† To the same.

My Lord, Dublin, Mar. 9, 1724.

THERE has been a great deal of heat here, about an affair that has lately happened in the College, of which I had written sooner to your Grace, but that I hoped it might have been terminated here, as the statutes of the College direct, without giving any trouble at *London*. But as I hear from all hands, that very partial accounts of it have been sent over to *England*, and a great deal has been talked of it there among the Lords, and that great endeavours are using there to bring the matter before the Council, I think I should be wanting in my duty to his Majesty, if I did not give your Grace a short information of the case, which may prevent any hasty measures being taken through surprize.

Two Under-graduates of the College, one of them a scholar of the house, had company at their chambers till about an hour after the keys of the College
were

† *To the same.*

My Lord,   *Dublin, Apr.* 20, 1725.

I Had the honour of your Grace's of the firſt inſtant, and am very much obliged to you for making a favourable repreſentation to his Majeſty of the
advice I ſent relating to the College ; I am ſure I ſhall
always endeavour to ſhew the greateſt care and zeal
about his ſervice, and I hope his Majeſty will never
find me negligent in any thing of that nature.

The ſtand the Provoſt has made, has brought
others to reaſon ; and the lad, after having made
ſuch ſubmiſſion, as the Provoſt thinks reaſonable will
be re-elected ; and one of the ſenior fellows is to
make the Provoſt ſatisfaction for abuſing him in a
ſermon at the College chapel : I hope theſe two ſteps
will ſecure the Provoſt's authority for the future. I
ſhall always make it my buſineſs to ſend your Grace
whatever information I think may be of ſervice to
his Majeſty, and ſhall uſe my endeavours not to be
miſtaken in the characters of any perſons I have occaſion to mention.

I muſt again recommend Mr. *Stephens* to your
Grace's protection ; I would hope that (as he will
certainly be a promoter of polite learning) if he is
ſent to Chriſt-Church, and is willing to take the
Treaſury there, and employ under him a proper perſon, for whom he will be anſwerable, (which is as
much as half the Treaſurers there ſince the Reſtora-
tion have done) that my ſucceſſor cannot with juſtice complain, if he is made Canon there : But if it
be thought for his Majeſty's ſervice to have a more
active perſon there than the misfortune of his eyes
will permit him to be, I muſt entreat your Grace
that he may be provided for by ſomewhat that
is near an equivalent in ſome other Church, when-
                                                        ever

ever a vacancy happens at Chrift-Church; he is the only friend I have in *England* that I fhall trouble the Miniftry about there, and your Grace's kind care of him in this affair, fhall always be efteemed the higheft obligation by,

My Lord, &c.

† *To Lord* Townfhend, *Secretary of State.*

My Lord,   *Dublin, Apr.* 29, 1725.

I AM fenfible that I have been guilty of a very great omiffion, in not having fooner returned your Lordfhip my moft hearty thanks, for recommending me to his Majefty for fo great a poft, both for dignity and profit; I can affure your Lordfhip it has not been owing to want of either gratitude or duty to your Lordfhip: But whatever my poft is here, the only thing that can make it agreeable to me (who would have been very well content with a lefs ftation in my own country) is, if I may be enabled to ferve his Majefty and my country here, which it will be impoffible for me to do according to my wifhes, if the *Englifh* intereft be not thoroughly fupported from the other fide.   When I left *England,* I did not doubt but your Lordfhip was fufficiently fenfible how much this had been neglected for many years, and of the neceffity there was of taking other meafures for the future; but thofe of us from *England,* whofe hearts are ftill with our country, fear all this is forgotten, when we hear that the Mafterfhip of the Rolls (which as it is for life, is one of the greateft places in the law here) is permitted to be fold to a * native of this place; as I believe the

VOL. I.   B   thing

---

* *Thomas Carter,* Efq; who had alfo the *King's-Bench* office, and who was made a Privy-counfellor, on his being Mafter of the Rolls, which he purchafed from the Earl of *Berkely.* He was deprived of the laft employment in the year 1754, and foon after made Secretary of State for *Ireland.*

thing is paſt revoking. I ſhall trouble your Lordſhip no further about that affair. We ſhould likewiſe be very much alarmed (if we took it for any other than an idle report) that our Attorney-General is to be made Lord Chancellor here; againſt whom the *Engliſh* here have nothing to object, but that they think the only way to keep things quiet here and make them eaſy to the miniſtry, is by filling the great places with natives of *England*; and all we would beg is, where there is any doubt with your Lordſhip about the conſequence of a place here, that you would have the goodneſs to write hither to know its weight, before it be diſpoſed of. None of us deſire to recommend to any ſuch places; but we would entreat that in filling them up, a ſtrict regard may be had to the *Engliſh* intereſt; which if it be neglected in ſome more inſtances of conſequence, though I am effectually pinned down here, yet others (who are very able and thoroughly diſpoſed to ſerve their country) will think of returning thither again. I will only add, that (as all accounts from *England* are poſitive we are to have a new Chancellor) I heartily wiſh we had one ſent as ſoon as may be, that he may have time to look a little about him, and know ſomewhat of things and perſons here before the next ſeſſion of parliament is opened.

Your Lordſhip will have the goodneſs to excuſe theſe lines, which I have taken the freedom to trouble you with, purely out of my zeal for his Majeſty and his ſervice here.

I am, &c.

† *T.*

To the Duke of Newcaftle, *&c.*

My Lord,   *Dublin, Apr.* 29, 1725.

I HAVE by this poft, at the defire of fome of his Majefty's hearty friends here, written to my Lord *Townfhend* what a blow we think is given to the *Englifh* intereft, by the creation of a new Mafter of the Rolls, and the uneafinefs we are under at the report that a native of this place is like to be made Lord Chancellor. I muft requeft of your Grace, as I have of his Lordfhip, that you would both ufe your intereft to have none but *Englifhmen* put into the great places here for the future, that by degrees things may be put into fuch a way, as may be moft for his Majefty's fervice, and the eafe of his Miniftry. Your Grace will be fo good as to excufe this freedom from,

My Lord; &c.

To the fame.

My Lord,   *Dublin, May* 1, 1725.

AS I did myfelf the honour to write to your Grace the laft poft, I fhould not have given you the trouble of another letter fo foon, but that I fince underftand our Lord * Chancellor has defired leave to refign his place, and that the Lord Chief Baron here is recommended to fucceed him : Lord Chief Baron *Hale* is a worthy man, and heartily in the *Englifh* intereft, and I believe very capable of filling that poft ; but I muft entreat, in the name of all of us here, that if he is thought of, a proper perfon from *England* may be fent to fucceed him in his

B 2   pre-

---

* *Allen Broderick,* Lord Vifcount *Middleton.*

present post, or the *English* interest will go very much backward here, but as there has been so long a talk of a new Chancellor here, I almost take it for granted that the Ministry must have settled who is to fill that place from *England*, and all that I have to say on that supposition is, that as there is a deficiency of 100,000 *l*. to be supplied by the parliament, I should think it most adviseable, if there has been a necessity of promising an addition to the salary, to tempt a man of worth over, which has been much talked of here, the order should come over after the parliament is up, to pay him such addition from the date of his patent. I cannot help suggesting on this occasion, that one reason of our deficiency here, is the fall of the Customs by vast quantities of goods being run here from the *Isle of Man*, which is the great magazine of goods intended to be run, and from whence they are, as opportunity offers, transported hither in small vessels. I can hardly question but the Customs in *England* must suffer more this way than ours do in *Ireland:* And the only remedy we talk of here for this evil, is, if his Majesty were to buy the island of the Earl of *Derby*, and afterwards he may command the proper measures to prevent goods being lodged there for running *. I thought it my duty to mention this, though I do not question but your Grace knows more of the affair than I do.

I am, &c.

To

* This scheme was at last adopted, after about 40 Years deliberation.

To the same.

My Lord,   *Dublin, May* 8, 1725.

BY some letters from *Limerick* by yesterday's post, news is brought that the Bishop of *Limerick* is dead : on this occasion I find the Lord Lieutenant recommends his first Chaplain, Dr. *Buscough*, to succeed in that See. As Dr. *Buscough* is of some standing, and has supported a very good character, and is well affected to his Majesty and his family, and I am assured he will constantly concur with me in supporting his Majesty's interest here, I make bold likewise to recommend him to your Grace for his Majesty's favour for the said Bishoprick.

I am, my Lord, &c.

To Lord * Carteret.

My Lord,   *Dublin, May* 12, 1725.

I Heartily beg your Excellency's pardon that I have not sooner returned my thanks for the many favours and civilities received from your Lordship in this kingdom. I endeavour to go on as well as I can in the post your Excellency has left me in, and hope by degrees to grow so much master of the affairs of this nation, as to be able to give you a better account of things than I can at present.

By the last mail we have sent your Excellency an account of the several persons recommended for the chapel of *Rings-End*.

Mr. *Samson* is the person his Grace of *Dublin*, I believe, most wishes to succeed out of the three mentioned in his memorial ; and I have that charac-
tei

* *John*, Lord *Carteret*, afterwards Earl of *Granville* in right of his mother.

ter of his diligence in his prefent curacy, which is a
very great one, and which he has ferved about fix-
teen years, as well as of his good life and converfation, that I have no objection to him.

Your Excellency has a memorial in your packet
in behalf of Mr. *Vaughan*, curate of St. *John's*, and
he will do very well if your Excellency thinks proper.

Mr. *Whitcomb*, fellow of the College, is another
candidate, who has a very good character for morals, learning, and affection to his Majefty, and as this
preferment is confiftent with his fellowfhip, it would
be of more value to him than a living of perhaps double the value. The only objection I know againft
him is, that he muft refide in the College, and either
of the other two will go and live at *Ring's-End*; as I
think they are obliged to do by the foundation,
which requires that the curate there fhould not be abfent from the place above fixty days in the year.

We have not yet got an account from the Commiffioners of the arrears at *Lady-day* in the hands of
the Collectors, or then ftanding out; as foon as we
have we will tranfmit that to your Excellency, with
an account of what the government then owed.

As we have this day received orders for fending
four battalions to *England*, we fhall take the beft
meafures we can to have it done with fpeed. And I
find people are now fenfible of the difficulty the government would have been under on this occafion, if
you had not contrived to take off a year's arrears of
the army from the current fervice.

The army are mightily pleafed with the enlarge-
ment of their fubfiftence, as are all the tradefmen
who have dealings with the officers.

We have had ftrong rumours that Sir *J. St. Leger* * is to be turned out, and Mr. *Nutley* to fucceed
him;

---

* A Baron of the Exchequer.

him ; I have every where affirmed it is impoffible to be true ; fince your Excellency and every one in the fervice here knows how obnoxious the latter is to all of this country who wifh well to his Majefty, and that I believed no fuch thing would be done without, at leaft, confulting you before hand.

I fhall trouble your Excellency no further at prefent, but beg leave to fubfcribe myfelf,

My Lord, &c.

To the Archbifhop of Canterbury.

My Lord,   *Dublin, May* 22, 1725.

MR. *Blenner-Haffet* is very much obliged to your Grace for your great kindnefs to him in relation to his living in *Suffex*, and as I know his circumftances, I was very well difpofed to fecond your Grace's good intentions, by letting my living lapfe, not doubting by your Grace's intereft, if mine failed, of fecuring a prefentation from my Lord Lieutenant. But we have fince been fo continually alarmed with news of changes from *England*, that he was unwilling to run the hazard of a new Lord Lieutenant with a needy chaplain.

Your Grace will before this have heard that the Bifhop of *Limerick* is dead, and that Dr. *Bufcough* is recommended to fucceed him : I have likewife added my recommendations, but with what fuccefs I have not yet heard. Confidering the good character he has had for many years, and the little fuccefs he has had in *England*, I fhould think it hard if they refufe him this promotion in *England*.

Since my arrival here I have met with a practice in the Church, that to me feemed very odd, having heard of nothing like it in *England* ; which is of Prefbyters holding a fecond or third benefice in commendam, inftead of having a faculty : the practife

I be-

I believe was owing to my predeceſſour refuſing a
faculty where it might be thought reaſonable, which
made them look out for ſome ſtratagem to compaſs
the ſame thing ; and what they have pitched upon
and practiſed here, has been by granting the broad
ſeal to hold a ſecond or third, without inſtitution or
induction. That your Grace may the better underſtand the nature of this new tenure, I have here ſent
you the copy of a fiat of this ſort :

*This fiat containeth his Majeſty's grant and dona-
tion of the Deanery of the Cathedral Church of
Kilmacduach, &c. now void and in his Majeſty's diſpoſal, by the death of Stephen Handcock,
late Dean thereof unto Charles Northcote, Clerk,
Maſter of Arts, to have and to hold the ſaid
Deanery in commendam to him the ſaid Charles
Northcote, together with the Prebend of Kil-
macdonough, the Rectory and Vicarage of Kil-
maghan, the entire Rectory of Boughillane, and
the Vicarage of Clonfert, alias Sanctæ Trinitatis
Chriſt Church Newmarket, in the Dioceſe of
Cloyne, which he now holds and enjoys ; and al-
ſo to enter into the ſaid Deanery without inſtitution, inſtallation, or other ſolemnity ; and is done
according to his Grace's warrant, bearing date
The 19th day of Nov. 1719.*

I have enquired whether there is any act of parliament here, that gives the crown any ſuch power,
and am aſſured there is none, ſo that I think it
ſtands on the ſame bottom as a Biſhop taking a
commendam after conſecration. I have diſcourſed
with my Lord Lieutenant of the illegality, as I con-
ceive it, of this practiſe, and of the dangerous con-
ſequences of it, ſince I can apprehend it to be no
other than a ſequeſtration of a benefice, granted by
lay-powers, without being accountable for the profits

fits received, and without being charged with the cure of fouls ; and I do not fee but in time they may proceed to make fuch grants of benefices to laymen.   I told his Excellency if he pleafed to give the feveral perfons concerned in thefe extraordinary grants, which are, as far as I can learn, about half a dozen, legal grants of the fame preferments they now poffefs, I will readily grant them faculties for the holding them, that things may be brought into the legal way, and farther abufes may be prevented. His Excellency feemed very much furprized at this method of granting commendams to Prefbyters, and is very ready to put this affair into the right channel.   But before I proceed any further in this matter, I fhall be obliged to your Grace for your opinion, whether what has been done already is legal, that I may occafion no needlefs difturbance here, and I am fure your Grace's opinion of this matter will thoroughly fatisfy his Excellency.

I thank your Grace for your kind hints relating to the power I claim to grant faculties, and other extra-epifcopal powers, and I find it ftands upon a grant made by King *James* I. to the then Archbifhop of *Armagh*, and his fucceffors for ever, in virtue of a claufe in one of our *Irifh* acts of parliament, which they affure me is a legal grant, and fufficiently confirmed by above one hundred years poffeffion.

I thank your Grace for your kind prayers, and hope I fhall always make it my endeavour to promote the good of this Church, though I fear I fhall not always meet with the ready concurrence I could wifh for here *.   However, upon the encouragement your Grace gives me of your friendfhip, and your abilities to direct in any difficult cafe, I fhall
take

* His Grace's fcheme, recommended in his third letter, had then failed.

take the liberty to confult your Grace where I am in the leaft doubtful whether I am going upon fure grounds or not.

I am, &c.

To the Duke of Newcaftle, *&c.*

My Lord, *Dublin, June* 3, 1725.

BY the letters this day we have an account that my Lord Chief Baron *Hale* is to be removed to the Bench in *England*; I could heartily wifh, if it could have been without damage to him, who is a very deferving gentleman, that he might have continued here till *Michaelmas* term next, to have affifted at the next feffions of parliament. Your Grace is fenfible we have a new * Chancellor wholly unacquainted with *Irifh* affairs, and my Lord Chief Juftice *Windham* and myfelf, have not been long enough here, not to ftand in need of information on feveral occafions; and I can affure your Grace, it is very hard to rely on what thofe of this country advife in any difficult cafe. But whatever can be done in that affair, I do not queftion his Majefty's fending us a proper perfon from *England* to fucceed him.

Your Grace and the reft of the miniftry were fufficiently fenfible (when I left *England)* of the neceffity of filling the great pofts here with *Englifh*; and if the fame meafures be not followed, we that are here fhall have a bad time of it, and it muft prove of great prejudice to his Majefty's fervice. And on the other hand, if we are continued to be fupported, I do not fear but affairs will by degrees be brought to that ftate which the miniftry defire. I am fo fully fatisfied of the miniftry's prudent refolution on this point,

---

* Mr. *Weft*, who married a daughter of Dr. *Gilbert Burnet*, Bifhop of *Sarum.*

point, that I shall trouble your Grace no further, but subscribe myself,

My Lord, &c.

To the Bishop of Bristol.

My Lord,   *Dublin, June* 12, 1725.

SINCE your Lordship has not been pleased to write to me, as you promised my Lord Bishop of *London* some months ago, I think it proper to trouble your Lordship with a few lines. I cannot but think myself very ill used by your Lordship, by the violent pushes you have been pleased to make against Mr. *Stephens* coming to *Christ Church* upon a vacancy, when you know very well I had a positive promise of the next canonry there for him, some months before there were any thoughts of my removing hither: his merit for learning, and his affection to his Majesty and his family, you are no stranger to; and as I know the state of the College as well as your Lordship, I know his coming there can be of no disservice to his Majesty, or any ways distress the business of the College, since he is willing to be Treasurer. I find already you have been pleased to say that it is settled that Dr. *Foulkes* shall be Treasurer, and no doubt if Dr. *Terry* continues Sub-Dean, Dr. *Foulkes* is a very proper person, and there will then be no want of Mr. *Stephens* having any office at all; if Dr. *Terry* does not, Dr. *Foulkes* is a very proper Sub-Dean, and Mr. *Stephens* will discharge the office of Treasurer: and you cannot but know that if he supplies that office by a deputy at his own hazard, he does as much as most Treasurers there have done.

I understand you give out, that in the push you make against Mr. *Stephens*, you only consult his Majesty's service, but I know your only aim is serving a friend of your own; which I am not against your
doing,

doing, wherever any preferment is fairly open; but I desire it may not be at the expence of a friend of mine, who has had a positive promise of what you are labouring to get.

My behaviour to your Lordship in relation to your first coming to the College, and your being afterwards thought of for the Deanery, as well as upon your settling in the College, does not deserve such injurious treatment of me as you have been pleased to shew on this occasion. I find if my friend Mr. *Stephens* suffers in this point, it lies wholly at your door; and I hope though I am on this side of the water, I am not without friends, that may on a proper occasion remember any ill usage to me. I understand you have given out the Canons are against his coming thither: I know those on whose support you must very much depend, have that good opinion of his worth, and know my friendship for him so well, that they are far from being against his coming amongst them. I hope you will consider calmly whether you are using me and my friend as you would be willing to have others use you, or a friend of yours.

I am, &c.

To the Duke of Newcastle.

My Lord,   *Dublin, July* 3, 1725.

SINCE the honour of your Grace's of *June* 29, I have been employed on a visitation of my diocese, where I have by my charge to the clergy, made the Protestant Dissenters in those parts easy, and have, I hope, given some courage to his Majesty's friends. I met with all the civility I could desire, both from the gentry and clergy; and as the latter desired me to print my charge, and as some others think it may be of some service to the government, at least by giving me the more weight among the well-affected,

when

when they fee my fentiments in print, I have thoughts
of fpeedily putting it to the prefs.   I am fenfible
how much I am obliged to your Grace for favourably
reprefenting to his Majefty my attention to his
fervice.

My Lord Chancellor arrived here in my abfence,
but as I have been here now three or four days, we
have had fome conferences, and I am fure we fhall
both concur to the utmoft of our power in promoting
his Majefty's fervice.   I am glad to find by him that
we are to have a good Lord Chief Baron here ; and
it is fomewhat the greater pleafure to me that I had
fome knowledge of Mr. *Dalton* in *England.*

I am the more encouraged to continue any diligence I have hitherto ufed by the repeated affurances
your Grace is pleafed to give me of his Majefty's
gracious intention to fupport me here, and can promife his Majefty and affure your Grace that I fhall
make no other ufe of what fupport he is pleafed
to give me, than to maintain his intereft in this
kingdom.

As the feffions of parliament is now drawing near,
I hope my Lord Lieutenant will be impowered in his
fpeech to fpeak clearly as to the bufinefs of the half-
pence, and thoroughly rid this nation of their fear
on that head : I fhould hope if this is done, we fhall
have a pretty eafy feffion ; the manner that is moft
proper I fubmit to your Grace and others in the miniftry, who are beft judges how his Majefty's honour
may be beft preferved, and this nation at the fame
time made eafy.

As by examining into * *Pratt*'s accounts, it appears the nation is run above 100,000 *l.* in debt,
befides the 50,000 *l.* for the intereft of which provifion is made, it muft be expected that we fhall have
fome

* Deputy Vice Treafurer of *Ireland,* which place he loft, and
was fucceeded by *Luke Gardiner,* Efq;

some grumbling speeches in both houses ; but if the dread of *Wood*'s half-pence is effectually removed, I hardly doubt of a good issue of the sessions.

I am now come to continue at *Dublin* for the rest of the year, and shall be proud of receiving your commands.

I am, &c.

To the same.

My Lord, *Dublin, Aug.* 14, 1725.

AFTER having wrote so lately to your Grace, I should not have given you the trouble of these lines, if it were not out of the great concern I have that his Majesty's service may go on as smoothly as possible in the approaching parliament ; and this I would hope may be done, if my Lord Lieutenant is enabled to put an end to all fears about the half-pence in his speech : if he is not, there will certainly be a great heat in both houses, which it will be impossible to keep within any bounds of decency ; and this may give an advantage to those that will be glad of making a disturbance about Captain *Pratt*'s affair, or would appear some way considerable by raising a clamour. And I wish what favour his Majesty shall please to shew us about the half-pence, be not afterwards taken as an effect of their noise rather than his Majesty's goodness. But the whole I have written is submitted to your Grace's superior prudence.

My Lord Lieutenant and our new Lord Chancellor went yesterday to *Drogheda* to see the place of the action on the * *Boyne* ; at their return the proper pre-
parations

---

* On the first of *July*, 1690, a great battle was fought at this place between the armies of King *William* III. and *James* II. in which the former was victorious. In honour of which success, there is one of the finest obelisks in the world erected there to commemorate this event.

parations will be making for a good feffions, but moft will depend on what inftrudtions your Grace fhall tranfmit.

I am, &c.

To Lord Townfhend.

My Lord,   *Dublin, Sept.* 4, 1725.

A S I have been vifiting my diocefe this fummer, and have been perfuaded to print my charge to the clergy, in hopes it may be of fome fervice here, I have made bold to fend your Lordfhip fome copies; Mr. *Edgecombe* was fo kind as to undertake to deliver them to Sir *Robert Walpole,* with a defire to forward them to your Lordfhip : I muft beg of your Lord-fhip to prefent one to Prince * *Frederick* with my moft humble duty, to accept of another yourfelf, and to difpofe of the remaining four as your Lordfhip pleafes.

I cannot omit taking this opportunity of thanking your Lordfhip for all favours, and affuring your Lordfhip I fhall make the beft ufe I can of the great poft you have procured me, to his Majefty's fervice in this place ; and I am fure in fo doing I fhall beft anfwer your Lordfhip's expectation. I muft likewife acknowledge the obligations we all lie under here for your procuring fo great an inftance of his Majefty's goodnefs, as the revoking *Wood's* patent ; I cannot fay every body here is as thankful as they ought to be on this occafion, but do not doubt but both houfes will make the moft profound return of gratitude to his Majefty.

I am

---

* Eldeft Son of *George, Prince* of *Wales,* afterwards *George* II. who was fucceeded in the principality of *Wales,* by the faid prince *Frederick,* who died *March* 20, 1751. His prefent Majefty *George* III. is the eldeft fon of his Royal Highnefs.

I am glad it has lain in my power to provide for Mr. *Power* the clergyman, to his satisfaction, whom your Lordship was pleased to recommend to my care, before I left *England*; I have given him a living of about 150 *l. per ann.* I shall trouble your Lordship no longer, but beg leave to subscribe myself,

My Lord, &c.

To the Duke of Newcastle.

My Lord,   *Dublin, Sept.* 9, 1725.

I HAVE had the honour of your Grace's of the 26th ult. I can assure your Grace that it was with the greatest pleasure I saw the exemplification of the surrender of Mr. *Wood*'s patent at the council, because I am sure it will make his Majesty's business go on smoothly in parliament, and quiet the minds of all his Majesty's well-affected subjects here. His Majesty's enemies, and those who want to be considerable by making an opposition to his Majesty's business in parliament, could not disguise their looks enough not to shew their great disappointment by this great instance of his Majesty's goodness and condescension to this nation. And though some have laboured to disguise the fact and given out that the patent was surrendered to my Lord * *Abercorn*, yet when the sessions open on *Tuesday* se'nnight, there will be no more room for deceiving the people as to the fact, and I am satisfied his Majesty will then receive the utmost returns of gratitude from both houses, which will be no other than the sense and voice of all the people of this nation, that do not wish for disturbances. I have discoursed with several members of parliament, who all express the utmost thankfulness for this signal instance of his Majesty's favour, and give the greatest assurances,

* A *Scotch* Earl, and Lord Viscount *Strabane* in *Ireland*.

rances of an eafy feffions. I am fenfible I have had no other hand in this affair than reprefenting the true ftate of this nation to the miniftry, and am very glad his Majefty employs fuch as are willing to be informed of the truth, which I fhall always make it my endeavour to acquaint them with.

There is a perfect agreement betwixt me and my Lord Chancellor, and I dare fay will continue, not only on account of our old friendfhip, but out of the earneft defire we both have of promoting his Majefty's fervice; and I am thoroughly fenfible of what affiftance he will be to me in fo doing, and I fhall not be wanting in my endeavours to affift him in the fame.

I muft beg your Grace's acceptance of one of my charges, which I trouble Mr. *Edgecombe* to take with him to your Grace; and likewife the favour of fending a fmall parcel to my Lord *Townfhend* at *Hanover*.

I am, &c.

To the fame.

My Lord, *Dublin, Sept.* 11, 1725.

AS I had the honour of writing to your Grace by the laft poft, I fhould not fo foon have given you a new trouble, but for an accident that has fince happened to the Archbifhop of *Cafhel*. Whilft his lady was bathing his leg with brandy or fpirits, they unfortunately took fire, and his leg is fo hurt by it, that his life is thought to be in great danger. As his poft is the third in this Church, and has a good income belonging to it, I thought it my duty to give your Grace immediate notice of the danger he is in.

As foon as there is any decifive turn in his illnefs, I fhall inform your Grace of it; in the mean time I would fuggeft, that if he dies, as the parliament is now juft opening, I fhould rather think it moft advifeable for his Majefty's fervice, the better to prevent any uneafinefs in either houfe of parliament, to fill his place with fome *Englifhman* that is already on the bench here. And I muft entreat that no meafures may be taken on the other fide of the water in this affair, fo as not to leave full room for advice or a reprefentation from hence.

There has been fome time ago a great difcourfe here of a defign to remove the Provoft of this College to a Bifhoprick, not fo much out of good will to him, as to make way for another to fucceed him ; but as the perfon who it is fufpected will pufh for being his fucceffor, is one that in the opinion of his Majefty's friends here would be a very dangerous man in that ftation, I cannot but take this opportunity of begging, that your Grace and the reft of his Majefty's fervants would be upon your guard againft any hafty promife being obtained from his Majefty relating to the Provoftfhip here. The prefent Provoft is a very good man, but it is of the laft confequence here who fucceeds him, by whatever means there happens a vacancy in his place. I fhall trouble your Grace no more at prefent, but fubfcribe myfelf,

My Lord, &c.

To the fame.

My Lord,   *Dublin, Sept.* 21, 1725.

I HAVE had a pretty laborious day of it in the Houfe of Lords, where my Lord Lieutenant opened the feffions with a very good fpeech. Things went very well in the Houfe of Commons, where they came to a proper refolution for an addrefs without any thing worth calling oppofition ; but in our Houfe we fought through a refolution for an addrefs with great oppofition from the Archbifhops of *Dublin* and

Tuam,

Tuam, my Lord *Middleton* and others, and upon a division they carried the words *great wisdom* to be added to his Majesty's *goodness* and *condescension*, for which we were to thank his Majesty, in putting an end to *Wood's* patent ; but as this is no doubt meant as a reflection on what is past, or an insinuation of the weight of our clamours, I hope with my Lord Lieutenant's assistance to throw those words out, either in the committee, or when the address is reported to the House.

By the best accounts I can get, the Archbishop of *Cashel* has got over his late hurt, so that I shall trouble your Grace no more on that head, but subscribe myself,

Your Grace's, &c.

To the same.

My Lord,   *Dublin, Sept.* 23, 1725.

WE this day reported to the house the address to his Majesty, and after a long debate, threw out the words *great wisdom* before the words *royal favour and condescension,* so that when the address comes over to *England,* your Grace will see where it was to have come in, and will better judge of the impropriety of it, and that a reflection was designed by it on the ministry, as some of them plainly shewed in the debate it was intended for.

There were 21 against those words standing part of the address, and 12 for it. I am satisfied one thing aimed at by this push was to slur an *English* administration : but I hope by this majority we have pretty well discouraged all attempts of that kind, or any other to make an uneasy session.

I cannot help mentioning to your Grace that my Lord *Forbes* has been one of the most active and I think most peevish Lords here, after his Grace of

C 2

Dublin

Dublin and my Lord *Middleton*, of any concerned in this push. I must on the other side, do my Lord Lieutenant the justice to acquaint your Grace that he has been very industrious these two days to bring the Lords to a proper temper. As I have nothing farther to acquaint your Grace with, I shall beg leave to subscribe myself,

> My Lord, &c.

To the Archbishop of Canterbury.

My Lord,   *Dublin, Sept.* 24, 1725.

AS there is a perfect recess from business in *England*, and we are just entering upon it, by our session of parliament opening last *Tuesday*, I thought it might not be unacceptable to give your Grace some short account of what has passed here.

My Lord Lieutenant was pleased to appoint me to be the mover of an address to his Majesty upon his speech, and to prepare proper heads on that occasion; accordingly after his Excellency's speech from the throne, I proposed an address, and in a short speech run through the several heads I thought proper, and then gave in a written resolution to be an instruction to the committee, that were to draw up the address: upon reading the resolution, after some opposition to the offering such a resolution in writing, his Grace of *Dublin* proposed an amendment to the resolution, by inserting the words *great wisdom,* so that the part where they stood would have run thus, *and to express the grateful sense they have of his Majesty's great wisdom, royal favour and condescension, in putting so effectual an end to the patent formerly granted Mr.* Wood, *&c.* And the reason he gave was in effect, that the ministry had been the authors of that patent, but that his Majesty had been wise enough to see the ill consequences of it, and so had revoked it. This

I opposed,

I oppofed, as declared to be intended as a reflection on the miniftry, and fo a debate enfued ; but feveral of the houfe thinking it a compliment to his Majefty to own his wifdom, and not feeing the impropriety of it, where we were thanking him for what we ought to afcribe to nothing but his goodnefs, his amendment was carried.

On *Wednefday* I brought into the committee an addrefs fomewhat differing in form from the refolution of the houfe, and without the words *great wifdom*, but they infifting that the committee were bound down to thofe words as having been upon debate fettled by the houfe, I was forced to add them, but as it appeared more in the committee that they were intended to reflect on the miniftry, yefterday a motion was made in the houfe upon the report, to leave them out of the addrefs, and after a long debate (in which my Lord *Middleton* laboured to revive the former heat about *Wood*'s patent, and where he and others evidently fhewed thofe words were intended as a reflection) they were thrown out by 21 againft 12.

I have in thefe debates done my part according to my abilities, to fupport his Majefty's fervice. I am fenfible one thing that in part difpofed fome to be peevifh, was the feeing an *Englifh* * Primate here. My Lord Lieutenant was under great concern about this affair, that there fhould be an attempt againft thanking his Majefty in the moft decent manner, and fpoke to feveral of the Lay Lords to bring them to temper, without which we had been worfted.

The words *great wifdom* were to have ftood in the addrefs immediately before the words *royal favour*. I have fent your Grace one of my Lord Lieutenant's fpeeches, and fhall fend you this addrefs and that to
his

* This muft be an invidious reflection, as moft of the Primates of *Ireland*, fince the reformation have been from *England*. *February*, 1770.

his Excellency as foon as they are printed ; we prefented his Excellency with both to day. The Commons have gone on with great temper and unanimity.
Your Grace will excufe this long letter.

        I am, my Lord, &c.

To the Duke of Newcaftle, *&c.*

My Lord,   *Dublin, Oct.* 2, 1725.

I Received your Grace's obliging letter of the
 23d. paft, and before this your Grace will have
received two of mine, giving an account of what
happened in the Houfe of Lords laft week ; fince
which nothing has paft worth notice, except our ordering an impudent * poem on thofe debates to be
burned, and the printer to be taken into cuftody.

I find every body judges that the difficulty of the
feffion is over in our houfe, by our having had a fair
trial of our ftrength there ; and that the male-contents
of the Houfe of Commons will be lefs enterprizing
now they fee fo little profpect of any difturbance in
our houfe.

I can ftill affure your Grace the generality here are
very fenfible of his Majefty's goodnefs in procuring
the furrender of *Wood's* patent. I thank your Grace
for tranfmitting a copy of my laft letter to *Hanover*,
and am obliged to you for your approbation of what
I propofed.

The Archbifhop of *Cafbel* is in a declining condition ftill, and probably will fcarce outlive many
months ; whenever he drops I fhall immediately acquaint your Grace with it, and with what removes I
apprehend may be moft for his Majefty's fervice. I
am very fenfible of the great obligations I lye under
to his Majefty's minifters both in *England* and *Hano-*
                ver,

* Entitled, On Wifdom's Defeat,
    In a learned debate, &c.

ver, both before and since my tranflation hither, and
fhall on all occafions fhew that zeal for his Majefty's
fervice as may moft recommend me to the continuance of their efteem and friendfhip.

I muft take this occafion of reminding your Grace
of a paper fent from the Council here juft before his
Majefty left *England*, relating to the new gold fpecies
of *Portugal*: what we defired was that they might be
put on the fame foot with guineas, in proportion to
their weight and finenefs; the want of having their
value fettled by a proclamation is a great hindrance
to trade here, and leaves room for their being counterfeited with impunity. If there has been no report
yet made from the mint relating to them, I would
beg your Grace to call for one; if there has, I muft
entreat that we may have the neceffary orders fent us
for publifhing a proclamation here.

I am, &c.

† To the fame.

My Lord,   *Dublin, Oct.* 12, 1725.

I HAD the honour of your Grace's of the 30th
of the laft, and am very well pleafed that your
Grace approves of what I did at the opening of the
feffion, in the bufinefs of the addrefs, and that you
think it will be gracioufly accepted by his Majefty. I
thank your Grace for tranfmitting a favourable account of my actions to *Hanover*.

I believe the ftruggle in the Houfe of Lords is pretty
well over; but I find there will be fome contention
in the Houfe of Commons about paying the debts of
the nation; but as the management of that affair is
put into the hands of the fpeaker and the reft of his
Majefty's hearty friends, I do not doubt but all will
end well.

There

There are great endeavours ufed to miflead the country gentlemen, but there will be equal pains taken to fet them right. When any thing material occurs here, I fhall take the liberty to acquaint your Grace with it.

By the promotion of Dean *Percival* to the rectory of St. *Michan*'s in this city, the parifh of St. *John*'s (in this city too) is become vacant ; and the chapter of *Chrift Church* (who are the patrons) have prefented Dr. * *Delany* to it ; he is one of the fenior fellows of the College here, and their greateft pupil-monger ; what with his fellowfhip and pupils, he is thought to have fix or feven hundred pounds *per ann.* He is a great tory, and has a great influence in thefe parts ; and it were to be wifhed for his Majefty's fervice, that he might be tempted by fome good country living to quit the College ; but if he has St. *John*'s with his fellowfhip, there can be no hopes of his removal : but I am informed, that without a royal difpenfation, he cannot keep his fellowfhip with this new living ; I muft therefore defire your Grace, that if any application be made on the other fide of the water, for his Majefty's difpenfing with the ftatute of the College relating to the value of a living that may be held with a fellowfhip, that your Grace would get it ftopt,

I am, &c.

To the fame.

My Lord,   *Dublin,* *Oct.* 28, 1725.

I HAVE received the honour of your Grace's of the 14th and 21ft inftant, and am very glad to find my endeavours to ferve his Majefty, and to make the feffions eafy in our houfe are fo well accepted : I
fhall

---

* Afterwards preferred to the profitable Deanry of *Downe*.

shall always continue the same diligence, and as the affair of the debts of the nation and providing for them, has taken a different turn in the House of Commons from what was hoped, I perceive we must be the more vigilant in our house, for fear the success they have had in the commons should give new spirit to those who want to make disturbances. The tories have pushed very unanimously with the discontented whigs on this occasion, and I fear his Majesty's friends have not been so diligent in undeceiving the country gentlemen as might have been expected from them; but I hope in another session the debts may be provided for; though in the mean time great numbers must suffer very much by the slowness of the payments.

I have nothing new to send about the Archbishop of *Casbel*, beside my acknowledgments for your kind assurances on that head.

I thank your Grace for pressing the treasury for a report upon the *Portugal* coin, and hope we shall in a little time receive the necessary orders from *England*.

I likewise thank your Grace for the care you have already taken, and design for the future to take in Dr. *De any*'s affair, which his Majesty's friends here look upon as a piece of service to the government.

I am, &c.

To Lord Townshend.

My Lord,   *Dublin, Nov.* 4, 1725.

I HAVE had the honour of your Lordship's of the 15th of the last, and am very glad that my behaviour in the House of Lords, at the opening of the sessions was acceptable to his Majesty, and approved by your Lordship: I shall always esteem it my duty to serve his Majesty with the greatest zeal, and to the utmost of my abilities on all occasions that

offer

offer here ; and fhall do it with more chearfulnefs, as I find his Majefty is willing I fhould do fo.

I am fenfible of the hurry your Lordfhip muft have been in upon removing to the *Gohrde* *, and fhall never impute any delay in your Lordfhip's an-fwers, but to want of leifure.

As foon as any vacancy happens in the Church here, I fhall upon your Lordfhip's encouragement, trouble you with my opinion what may be moft for his Majefty's fervice.

I thank your Lordfhip for your kind acceptance of my charge, and your trouble in diftributing thofe I fent you. I am, with the greateft fincerity and refpect,

> My Lord, &c.

To the Duke of Newcaftle, *&c.*

My Lord, *Dublin, Nov.* 11, 1725.

I HAVE had the honour of your Grace's of the 4th inftant, and am concerned as well as your Grace, at the ungrateful return here made to his Majefty's late fignal favour to us ; but I hope all will end well, as the difcontented party feem every day to lofe ground in the Houfe of Commons : and I can affure your Grace no endeavours are wanting in his Majefty's friends and fervants to open the eyes of the honeft and well-meaning country gentlemen, who had been very much prepoffeffed by thofe that want to embarafs affairs here.

As to Dr. *Delany*'s affair ; when I was in *England*, and belonged to the Univerfity, I was always againft perfons holding any tolerable preferments with their fellowfhips, as being a hindrance to fucceffion in Colleges, and excluding fome or other, that may
want

---

* A hunting feat of the King's at *Hanover*.

want that help in their education, from getting upon a foundation ; and though a power is referved to the crown to difpenfe with the ftatutes of the College here, yet I would hope it will not be done merely for being afked for, where there is not fome very good motive befide : whereas in this cafe, his Majefty's friends here think it is certainly for his Majefty's intereft, that the Dr. fhould not be permitted to hold a preferment with his fellowfhip that will put him above the temptation of accepting a country living, in fome one of which they heartily wifh he was fettled.

I heartily thank your Grace for your promife not to forget Mr. *Stephens*, upon a vacancy at *Chrift Church*, and as the only thing that has been in earneft propofed by way of equivalent, is fcarce of half the value or dignity of a Canonry of *Chrift Church*, I fhould defire a fpecifick performance of the firft engagement, and muft in that as well as I fhall on all other occafions, depend upon your Grace's friendfhip and fupport. I am with the greateft fincerity and regard,

My Lord, &c.

✝ *To the fame.*

My Lord,   *Dublin, Nov.* 16, 1725.

I AM very forry that I muft fend your Grace word that yefterday the difcontented carried every thing before them, and have falfely ftated the debt of the nation, and (in effect) clofed the committee of fupply ; and I am the more troubled at this behaviour of the Commons, becaufe it is fo unworthy a return to his Majefty's late goodnefs to us. The army is like to be in great diftrefs by what they have done, to prevent which they talk of doing a moft unjuft and unreafonable thing, the voting that
the

the payments on the civil lift fhall be poftponed, to fupply the exigencies of the army.   Great pains have been taken by my Lord Lieutenant, and by all his Majefty's fervants and friends of confequence, to bring the members to reafon, and much has been faid in the houfe in debates on thefe occafions, on the fide of his Majefty's fervice ;   but it was only faying, that the carrying fuch a queftion would bring on new taxes, and the queftion however true or reafonable in itfelf, was fure of being loft.

My Lord, I muft take the liberty to acquaint your Lordfhip, that the ill fuccefs his Majefty's affairs have met with, is owing to the indefatigable induftry and art of two leading men in the Houfe of Commons :   the intereft of the firft of them muft every day decreafe, as the * father is now out of poft, and upon retiring to *England* ; and as the † fon himfelf is far from being beloved here : the other has no perfonal intereft ;   and if he has not the fupport of a new place, or new countenance, will foon fink in his weight.

Whatever uneafinefs is created here by any turbulent or defigning perfons, whilft his Majefty and his minifters think proper any ways to employ me in the public fervice, will at leaft light as heavy upon me as any body here :   but I am very willing to undergo my fhare of any fuch trouble at any time, if no new encouragement is given to fuch doings, by buying off any difcontented perfons here ;   for if any body is bought off, there will always arife a fucceffion of people to make a difturbance every feffion ;   and there wants no accident here to furnifh a bottom of popularity, every one having it always in his power to grow popular, by fetting up for the *Irifh*, in oppofition to the *Englifh* intereft.   And there is no doubt
but

---

* Lord Vifcount *Midleton.*
† The hon. *Sr. John Broderick.*

but some occasion of things going as they have, has been an unwillingness in too many to see an *English* adminiftration well eftablifhed here ; and an intention to make all the *English* already here, uneafy ; and to deter others from coming hither. But if thofe who have places here, and yet have joined in the late meafures, are remembered after the feffions ; and if nobody finds his account in having headed the oppofition made now to his Majefty's fervice, I do not doubt but the face of affairs will here gradually alter, and we may hope that the next feffions will be more eafy and fuccefsful.

I am, &c.

To the fame.

My Lord,   *Dublin, Nov.* 20, 1725.

I HAD yefterday the honour of your Grace's of the 13th inftant, with advice that their Excelcies the Lords Juftices * were pleafed to refufe the favour defired by Dr. *Delany.* I can affure your Grace, the oppofition I made to it was not from any pique to the Dr. but that I thought myfelf, and found his Majefty's friends here, were of opinion, that it was not for his Majefty's fervice that the Dr. fhould have a parifh in this city.

By his petition I perceive your Grace might apprehend that it was only a dignity, of the nature of a fine cure, that he defired to hold with his fellowfhip, as is the cafe of prebends in *England* ; but this prebend, as moft other dignities here, has a parifh with cure of fouls annexed to it.

I am very fenfible of the great regard fhewn to me on this occafion by their Excellencies ; and hope by degrees,

---

* In *England.*

degrees, with the affiftance I have from his Majefty's minifters, to fupport and encreafe his Majefty's friends in the College: I am fure it is my fettled purpofe, and fhall always be my endeavour to make no other ufe of the countenance I meet with from your Grace and the reft of the minifters, than the advancing his Majefty's fervice here.

I humbly thank your Grace for the particular care and concern you have been pleafed to fhew on this, as well as all other occafions, for my reprefentations and requefts.

I am, my Lord, &c.

To the Bifhop of London.

My Lord,   *Dublin, Nov.* 30, 1725.

THE prints, *as well as private letters*, by the laft mail, inform us that the Bifhop of *Chefter* is dead: as this makes a vacancy at *Chrift Church* that was not fo foon reckoned upon, I muft apply to your Lordfhip for your affiftance to get that canonry for Mr. *Stephens.* It is probable before long there will be another vacancy, to anfwer the fchemes of fome other perfons, which may make them lefs active on this occafion to oppofe me: and as your Lordfhip was an early witnefs of the promifes made me in favour of Mr. *Stephens*, upon my dropping all oppofition to Dr. *Foulkes*; you are beft able to be my follicitor in this affair; and the many proofs I have formerly had of your friendfhip make me not doubt but you will give me this further inftance of your kindnefs, by heartily ferving my friend Mr. *Stephens* on this occafion. I can affure your Lordfhip I fhall always efteem it one of the greateft obligations laid on,

My Lord, &c.

To

To the Duke of Newcaftle, *&c.*

My Lord   *Dublin, Nov.* 30, 1725.

SINCE I troubled your Grace laft, the prints inform us that the Bifhop of *Chefter* is dead, by which there is a canonry of *Chrift Church* become vacant : I would hope as there is ftill a probability of another vacancy before long by the death of Dr. *Burton*, that thofe who have been forming fchemes for fome friends of theirs againft that vacancy fhould happen, may be content to ftay for it, and that the promife made me that Mr. *Henry Stephens*, Vicar of *Malden* in *Surry*, fhould have the firft canonry that fell, may be performed. It is a favour I have often troubled your Grace about, and your fupporting my juft pretenfions on this occafion, will always be acknowledged as one of the greateft obligations, by

         My Lord, &c.

To the Archbifhop of Canterbury.

My Lord,   *Dublin, Dec.* 8, 1725.

I AM obliged to your Grace for your favour of the 17th ult. but it came not to hand till almoft a fortnight afterwards, nor have we had any mail fince that which brought the 25th ult.

I am very much obliged to your Grace and the other Lords Juftices, for rejecting Dr. *Delany*'s requeft for a faculty to hold a living with his fellowfhip. I can affure your Grace it was not out of any ill will to the perfon that I oppofed it, but that his Majefty's friends here think it would be very much for his Majefty's fervice, if he were removed from the College to fome other part of the kingdom, inftead of having a living here in town, and fuch an

           addition

addition to his fellowſhip, as may put him beyond any temptation but that of a wife, to quit it. This was my reaſon then, and ſtill continues ſo, but I am now a little ſurprized with what I did not then know, that his application was not to be diſpenſed with from the obligation of any ſtatute, but of an oath he had taken never to hold ſuch a benefice: this, where there is not an expreſs clauſe in the oath, *niſi tecum aliter diſpenſatum fuerit*, ſeems to me altogether new.

I can aſſure your Grace, whatever weight you and others in power on that ſide of the water are pleaſed to give to any repreſentations of mine, I ſhall make no other uſe of it than for the ſervice of his Majeſty, and the peace and quiet of the country I am placed in.

I am ſorry to hear your Grace has been diſordered with a cold, and hope it may be quite gone off before this. Now the Biſhop of *Cheſter* is gone off, the Biſhop of *Briſtol*, will, I hope, have an eaſy time of it at *Chriſt Church*.

If there had been any thing particular in our bills, eſpecially relating to the Church, I ſhould have given your Grace advice of it. We ſuppoſe here that the money bill has been ſome days at *Holyhead*, and ſhall be glad to ſee it, becauſe without it ſome of the duties expire at *Chriſtmas*. I ſhall in a little time have occaſion to give your Grace an account of a bill now drawing up relating to parſonage-houſes.

I hope his Majeſty may be ſafe landed in his dominions before this comes to your hands. I laſt week removed to a new houſe here, where I propoſe, God willing, to ſpend the reſt of my days. I am, with the greateſt reſpect,

　　　　　　My Lord, &c.

　　　　　　　　　　　　　　　　　　To

To the Duke of Newcaſtle.

My Lord,   *Dublin, Dec.* 23, 1725.

AS we are in hopes his Majeſty may now be upon the point of landing in *England,* and as probably the biſhoprick of *Cheſter* and canonry of *Chriſt Church* may be diſpoſed of ſoon after his arrival, your Grace will have the goodneſs to excuſe my putting you in mind of Mr. *Stephens* of *Malden,* for the canonry.   After what I have already wrote on this occaſion, I need ſay nothing farther than that in ſerving my friend, you will lay the greateſt obligation on,

My Lord, &c.

To the ſame.

My Lord,   *Dublin, Dec.* 30, 1725.

I HAVE lately had the honour of your Grace's of the 16th, and am glad my ſeveral dates of the laſt month have come ſafe to your hands.   I am very ſorry the endeavours of his Majeſty's ſervants and friends have had no better ſucceſs here, this ſeſſion of parliament, and that the people have ſo little conſulted their own true intereſt.   I would hope the reports we have here are groundleſs, that a certain Lord, who acted with as much peeviſhneſs as any body in our houſe, and had a great hand in animating the commons to their behaviour, is likely to be ſent in a great poſt to the *Weſt Indies.*

I ſhall always be ready to do my part in purſuing thoſe meaſures, which ſhall be thought proper by my ſuperiors, to break that ſpirit of oppoſition, which has of late exerted itſelf ſo much here.

I muſt beg leave to put your Grace in mind of the letter from the council here, relating to the new ſpecies of *Portugal* gold.   I muſt own we deſerve no favour * here, but as the parts of *England* we trade with, would find their advantage in having the value of thofe fpecies fettled by proclamation, as well as we of this nation ; and, as every body here muft be fenfible, that under our prefent behaviour, the granting us this favour muft be owing to the application of the *Englifh* from hence, I would hope that the fettling of that affair would be of fome fervice to his Majefty.

I thank your Grace for your kind promifes to ufe your beft endeavours to procure the canonry of *Chrift Church*, now vacant, for my friend Mr. *Stephens*. If his Majefty's fervice requires the making any perfon Bifhop of *Chefter*, who muft have that canonry to fupport his bifhoprick, I muft beg of your Grace, that at the fame time, it may be fettled, that Mr. *Stephens* fhall fucceed to the next vacancy there, by whatever means it fhall happen.

I have nothing to trouble your Grace with further at prefent, than my fincere wifhes that you may enjoy a great many years with the fame health and happinefs as you have gone through this, I am, with the greateft fincerity and refpect,

My Lord, &c.

To the fame.

My Lord,   *Dublin, Feb.* 10, 1725.

I AM forry to find by a letter I have received from the Bifhop of *London* that there has been a neceffity of putting my friend Mr. *Stephens* by the vacant canonry of *Chrift Church* ; however I learn by the Bifhop and others, that I was very much obliged to your Grace's friendfhip on that occafion, and that you have obtained an abfolute promife of the next vacancy that fhall happen there for my friend ;

I muft

---

* Is not this moft rafh, with regard to *Ireland* ?

·I muſt ſtill depend on your friendſhip for the per- formance of this new promiſe.

I hope our bills that we have ſent from hence will meet with all convenien: diſpatch at the council, that our ſeſſions may be brought to a concluſion. I do not deſpair of ſeeing a vote of credit carried in the Houſe of Commons at our next meeting, which will make things pretty eaſy. The poor oppoſi- tion that was made made here on occaſion of the laſt addreſs to his Majeſty by Mr. *Brodrick* and his friends, has given a new ſpirit to the Whigs, and Mr. Speaker and others have aſſured me, they will omit nothing in their power that may bring a good appearance of his Majeſty's friends together againſt the 17th of this month.

The general report is, that Dean *Swift* deſigns for *England* in a little time ; and we do not queſtion his endeavours to miſrepreſent his Majeſty's friends here, wherever he finds an opportunity : but he is ſo well known, as well as the diſturbances he has been the fomenter of in this kingdom, that we are under no fear of his being able to diſſerve any of his Majeſty's faithful ſervants, by any thing that is known to come from him : but we could wiſh ſome eye were had to what he ſhall be attempting on your ſide of the water.   I am, &c.

To the Archbiſhop of Canterbury.

My Lord,   *Dublin, Feb.* 24, 1725.

AS our bills arrived here on *Tueſday*, the parlia- ment met, according to their adjournment, on this day, to proceed on buſineſs, and the firſt thing done in both houſes, was acquainting them with his Majeſty's anſwers to their ſeveral addreſſes ; in our houſe nothing happened, as nothing was expected : but in the houſe of Commons (as his Majeſty in his anſwer expreſſed his hopes that they would take care to put the army in a condition for service, if there should be occasion) there came on a debate of several hours. What was designed to be carried there was an address to his Majesty, to apply so much of the money given this session of parliament as might pay two years interest at seven *per cent.* of the arrears of the army from *Midsummer* 1724, to *Midsummer* 1725 ; and likewise two years interest of the arrears due to the half-pay officers, from *Christmas* 1724, to *Midsummer* 1725. The arrears of the army for the time mentioned, amount to about 51000 pounds ; the arrears due to the half-pay officers. for the six months, amount to about 11,000 pounds, and there would then have been left due near nine months to both of them. But after great debates, it was found it would be but by a small majority things could be carried in that way, and that much the same thing could be compassed in another way, into which the house came at last without a division ; which was to address his majesty to apply 10,000 pounds for the use of the army in what manner he shall think proper ; so that what is understood here is, that their several debentures for the time mentioned, will be struck so as to carry interest for two years ; and there is no doubt but the officers will then be able to part with them as ready money. I think they have likewise engaged to provide for these 10,000 pounds, together with the arrears themselves that shall be found then standing out, at the next sessions of parliament.

I was willing to send your Grace an account of this, as being the best thing that has passed in the house this sessions, though with as ill a grace, and with as perverse an opposition, as such a thing could be done with.

As the house sat late on this occasion, and I have the account of what passed only by word of mouth, it is not so nicely exact as I could have wished to have

have fent it to your Grace. I am glad to find by the publick papers, that things go in your parliament with fuch zeal and affection to his Majefty, as we hope here will intimidate his enemies both at home and abroad. I am, with the trueft refpect, my Lord,

Your Grace's, &c.

To the Reverend Mr. Power.

S i r,   *Dublin, Feb.* 24, 1725.

I Received yours of the 24th of *November*, in anfwer to mine of the 20th, and delivered your prefent, which was kindly received.

What I write to you now is by the exprefs orders of my Lord Primate, to inform you that his Grace hears from perfons of credit fuch things of you as are highly difpleafing to him. You are reprefented as a perfon who have neither difcretion in your words and converfation, nor proper decency in your actions and conduct, nor a due regard to the offices of your function; and that the refult of your whole behaviour has given fuch offence to the generality of your parifhioners, that your congregation falls off daily from you. I am ordered to acquaint you, that my Lord is very much troubled to have fo indifferent a character of a clergyman, whom he has promoted; and that he will not reft fatisfied with fuch a behaviour as brings a fcandal on religion, and a difrepute on himfelf.

I am, Sir,
Your very humble fervant,

AMBR. PHILIPS.

To

To the Duke of Newcastle.

My Lord,　　　　　　　*Dublin, Mar.* 22, 1725:

I HAD the favour of your Grace's of the 10th inftant, and am very much obliged to you for your kind congratulations on my being made one of the Lords Juftices: I can affure your Grace I fhall in that ftation, as I have in what I already enjoy here by his Majefty's favour, moft faithfully endeavour to promote his Majefty's fervice.

I am very fenfible of the great hurry of important bufinefs there has been in *England,* fo as to hinder your regularly correfponding about our fmall affairs.

We have indeed at laft put a pretty good end to a troublefome feffion of parliament ; but without fomewhat done to fhew that the oppofing his Majefty's fervice here, is not the way to make court in *England,* we can hardly fail of having as uneafy a feffions the next.

In obedience to his Majefty's letter upon the addrefs of the Commons here, my Lord Lieutenant is iffuing the debentures of the army for one year, and of the half-pay officers for fix months, fo as to carry quarterly payments of intereft for two years from *Chriftmas* laft, till the parliament meets again to pay off the principal ; and I hope thofe arrears will by this method be circulated for thofe two years, whilft the current fervice is anfwered by the revenue coming in in the mean time.

But I cannot but obferve that thofe who have made the great difturbance in parliament, are as bufy now in frightning the bankers and other monied men from having any thing to do with thefe warrants, and advancing any money upon them, as they were in hindering the payment of our debts in

the

the houfe : I hope it will be without any effect, but I think their paft and prefent behaviour requires that the government fhould fhew their refentment of fuch proceedings ; and the more fo, becaufe one of the arts by which they have drawn too many well-meaning members to join with them in parliament, has been telling them that by their oppofition they were making court on the other fide of the water. I am very fenfible that by the language fome from hence, who talked in that way, have met with at their arrival in *England* from the miniftry, they know the contrary. But the country gentlemen here will never be perfuaded of this, but by feeing thofe men turned out of our privy council. And I would hope that the difobliging two or three members of the Houfe of Commons in *England*, will not be thought of greater confequence than the keeping things quiet here, by fhewing a juft difpleafure againft thofe who would embroil this kingdom.

There is another thing I muft beg leave to mention, and on which fubject I fhall fpeak my fentiments very freely to the miniftry, when I have the honour to wait upon them in *England* ; and that is the granting places for more than one life, or the reverfion of places now full. I fee plainly fo far as it has prevailed, or fhall hereafter prevail, it tends to loofen that fmall hold the crown ftill retains in this nation : as I fhall therefore always oppofe any applications of that nature from hence, fo I hope the miniftry will have the goodnefs to difcourage all follicitations of the like kind on the other fide of the water.

Here have been great complaints of the amendments and defalcations made in our bills by the Attorney General : I muft own I could wifh he would have confulted my Lord Chief Baron *Gilbert* or Baron *Hale*, before he had determined things to be

pro-

provided for by law here, which our judges affure us are not provided for; but on this fubject I may poffibly trouble your Grace fome other time.

I have formerly wrote about Mr. *Carter*, and I hope when the judges return from their circuits, to be able to point out fuch a way of dealing with him, as will make his oppofition in future feffions of little weight: I am fure the rudenefs with which he has, in his fpeeches in parliament, treated the *English* miniftry, not to fay the whole nation, as well as thofe of us who are fettled here, deferve that he fhould be made an example of.

Your Grace will have the goodnefs to excufe the liberty I have taken in this letter, in which I can affure you I have no other view than in the beft mann'r I can, to promote the intereft of *England* and his Majefty's fervice in this country.

I am very glad to find by your Grace's letter that things have fo good an afpect both at home and abroad, and heartily wifh they may go on with fuccefs.

I am, &c.

To the fame.

My Lord,   *Dublin, Apr.* 5, 1726.

HIS Excellency the Lord Lieutenant left the caftle about four in the afternoon laft *Friday*, and after fome ftay in the bay of *Dublin*, fet fail about ten that night: as the wind continued very fair that night and the next day, we had no doubt here but that on *Saturday* in the afternoon his Lordfhip muft be landed at *Hyle-lake*. It was then thought proper to have the commiffion for the Lords Juftices fealed that night, when we were fworn in council. Yefterday we received the ceremonious compliments of the city and univerfity in the prefence

fence chamber : what farther compliments are to be made on this occasion are to be received in the closet.   I do not question but there will be a good agreement amongst us ; but if by any accident there be not, I shall endeavour to take care that it may not be through any fault of mine.   When any thing of consequence occurs here, I shall be sure to acquaint your Grace with it ; in the mean time I beg leave to subscribe myself,

My Lord, &c.

To Lord Carteret.

My Lord,   *Dublin, Apr.* 16, 1726.

THE bearer is wife to Mr. *Cassel* ; he is the person who gave from time to time the best accounts of the popish priests, and what was doing amongst that party : he tells me his wife will have occasion to wait on your Excellency, to sollicit an affair of his, and desired I would give her a few lines to introduce her.   I hope your Lordship will be so good as to excuse this trouble, since it was a favour I could not well deny him.

I am, my Lord, &c.

To the Duke of Newcastle.

My Lord,   *Dublin, May* 14, 1726.

WE have from time to time transmitted to his Excellency the Lord Lieutenant an account of all we have learnt relating to the ship *Patience* seized at *Killybeg's,* and by this mail have sent the copy of a letter to one *Deaz,* a Jew, that probably discovers the truth of the captain's design.

I find the papists are in several parts here employed in fasting and prayers, by an order from the

pope,

pope, as they say, and a promise of indulgences, but on what occasion they do not own.

There seem likewise to be men lifting in several parts, but whether for *France* or *Spain* is uncertain, though they pretend for the former : but by the laws here it is capital to lift or be lifted in any foreign service, without leave from the crown.

We have had strong reports that Mr. *Nutley* is going to be made a judge here, but as he has had very severe censures past on him by the House of Commons, at the beginning of his Majesty's reign, and is counted one most in the secrets of the tories, I have ventured to say that I was sure there could be nothing in it.

Since my Lord Lieutenant's arrival at *London* nothing has happened that has required my writing to your Grace, nor should I give you any trouble at present, only to assure your Grace that as any thing of consequence happens, I shall be sure to inform your Grace of it.

I rely on your Grace's goodness for Mr. *Stephens*, whenever a canonry shall fall at *Christ Church*.

I am, &c.

To the same.

My Lord,   *Dublin, May* 19, 1726.

IN my last I gave your Grace a hint that numbers were lifting here for foreign service. We have daily new accounts from several parts that the lusty young fellows are quitting the country, on pretence that they are going to *England* for work. Such as have occasion to employ many hands, begin to feel the effects of this desertion, and nobody here questions but that all these really are going into foreign service.

We

We fhall not be wanting in our endeavours to keep every thing quiet here : but as accounts from all hands feem to forebode fome mifchievous defigns among the papifts, I am very apprehenfive that before fome months are paft, there will be a neceffity of putting the militia here in good order, to prevent any furprize, efpecially fince fix regiments have been drawn from hence. But of this affair I have not yet had an opportunity of talking with the other Lords Juftices ; nor fhall we attempt any thing of that nature till the defigns of the papifts here clear up farther, and we are able to make a proper reprefentation of the ftate of this nation, and receive his Majefty's commands what he will pleafe to have done.

We have given all poffible difpatch to the tranfportation of the forces, and in whatever elfe occurs, fhall ufe our beft endeavours to ferve his Majefty, and fecure the peace of this kingdom.

I am, in duty to his Majefty, obliged to acquaint your Grace that the new lift of privy counfellors has very much offended feveral that are beft affected to his Majefty here ; and that we of the *Englifh* nation think by this increafe our weight will grow lefs in the council than it was : and befides, we think it very much leffens that authority we imagine it is defigned we fhould have here, to have a thing of this moment fettled and finifhed, without our being in the leaft confulted * whether we were of opinion it would be for his Majefty's fervice to admit fuch a number and fuch perfons.

I am confident we fhall ferve his Majefty here to the utmoft of our power, but that power muft every day grow lefs, if it appears that things of the greateft

* My Lord Lieutenant had no regard to the Primate and the other Lords Juftices in this inftance.

eft confequence are fixed on the other fide of the water without our privity.

I am, &c.

To Lord Carteret.

My Lord,   *Dublin, May* 19, 1726.

I THINK it my duty to acquaint your Excellency, that every day frefh accounts come in to us that there are great numbers lifting here for foreign fervice ; the word given out in thefe parts is, that they are going over to *England* for work. Complaints come in daily from fuch as employ numbers of hands, that the lufty young fellows are quitting them upon this pretence.   There are likewife accounts from feveral parts that unufual faftings and devotions are fet on foot among the papifts, and very feditious fermons preached amongft them.

We have given the neceffary orders to all cuftom-houfe officers to have a watchful eye on all who attempt to leave the kingdom : and fhall as new informations come in, go on giving the beft orders we can.

But by the beft judgment I can make, in fome time we fhall be under a neceffity of putting the militia here in order, to prevent any furprize.   But of this we have not yet had time to confider maturely ; and as whenever it is done, it may caufe fome alarm, we fhall do nothing of that nature, without firft laying the ftate of affairs here before his Majefty, and receiving his commands.

I am very forry, my Lord, to be forced to acquaint your Lordfhip, that the new increafe of our privy council has given very great uneafinefs to feveral well-affected to his Majefty here, on account of the characters of feveral of the perfons.   And I cannot but fay that the *English* think it is a great

weak-

weakening to that weight we had in the privy council before.

When General *Macartney* arrives in *England*, I am confident he will report that we have ufed all poffible diligence in expediting the tranfport of the forces, which we hope, if the wind permits, will fail from *Cork* the middle of next week.

When we are mafters of any regular examinations relating to what is tranfacting among the papifts here, we fhall tranfmit them to your Excellency, to be laid before his Majefty. In the mean time I thought it proper to let your Lordfhip know in general what is doing here.

I am, &c.

To the Archbifhop of Canterbury.

My Lord,   *Dublin, May* 21, 1726.

THE encouragement your Grace has been pleafed to give me, to afk your advice in any difficulty I meet with here, occafions my giving you this trouble. I find myfelf very much aggrieved by the Archbifhop of *Dublin* in fome points, the which are of fuch a nature, that I cannot (without prejudice to my fucceffors) fuffer them to go on, without looking out for fome remedy. But I am unwilling to take any ftep, before I have the favour of your opinion and advice, as to what meafures are moft proper to be taken by me, or rather by the crown, which is, I think, at leaft as much concerned as I am, in the cafe I fhall now lay before you.

The power the Archbifhop of *Armagh* claims of granting licenfes for marriages, at uncanonical hours and places, is as follows:

In the 28th of *Hen.* VIII. there was a ftatute paft here, entitled, *the Act of Faculties*; which for the bulk

bulk of it, is only a recital of the *Englifh* ftatute of the 25th of *Hen.* VIII. concerning *peter-pence and difpenfations*; with an application at the end to the kingdom of *Ireland.* There is likewife another ftatute paft here 2ᵈᵒ. *Eliz.* entitled, *an act for reftoring to the crown the ancient jurifdiction over the eftate ecclefiaftical and fpiritual, and abolifhing all foreign authority repugnant to the fame*; which act is almoft verbatim the fame with the *Englifh* ftatute 10ᵐᵒ. *Eliz.* of the fame title, as to the general part; and as to the repealing and reviving part, repeals or revives fuch ftatutes of *Phil.* and *Mary,* or *Hen.* VIII. as were thought proper to be repealed or revived. And in both thefe acts, there is a power lodged in the crown, to authorize fuch perfon or perfons as the crown fhall think proper to exercife the feveral powers therein mentioned in this kingdom.

In virtue of thefe two ftatutes (which in the beginning of the grant are mentioned as the foundation of the feveral powers therein granted) King *James* the firft, by letters patent to *Chrift. Hampton,* Archbifhop of *Armagh,* (dated *April* 10. *anno regni* of *England* 20. and of *Scotland* 55.) did among other things, grant full power, authority, and jurifdiction to him the faid *Chrift. Hampton* and his fucceffors Archbifhops of *Armagh* for ever, from time to time and at all times requifite, to give, grant, and difpofe of all manner of fuch licenfes, difpenfations, compofitions, faculties, grants, refcripts, delegacies, inftruments, and all other writings (of what kind, nature, or quality foever they be) as by force of the faid Act of Parliament may be given and granted, in the moft large and ample manner : and did likewife by the fame letters patent, enable *Chrift. Hampton* and his fucceffors, &c. to appoint a commiffary or commiffaries, under them. In virtue of thefe letters patent, my predeceffors have from time to time appointed commiffaries, who as occafion has offered,

offered, have granted faculties for marriages at un-canonical hours and places, which are here ufually termed *prerogative licenfes.*

The authority of thefe licenfes never has (that I can learn) been difputed, nor is it now; but his Grace of *Dublin* is pleafed to fet up his licenfes as of equal force with the prerogative licenfes; which li-cenfes of his differ no farther from the common epifcopal licenfes in *England,* than what neceffarily follows from their being directed here, to the clergy-man who is to marry the parties; whereas in *Eng-land,* they are directed to the parties to be married. The canons indeed here are very fevere againft any clergyman marrying in uncanonical places or hours: the 52d. canon here punifhing the fo doing in a be-neficed clergyman, with deprivation; in a non-be-neficed clergyman, by degradation: whereas by the *Englifh* canon, the punifhment is only fufpenfion *per triennium.*

But to give a currency to the common epifcopal licenfes (which are all his Grace of *Dublin* even pre-tends to grant) he has been pleafed (both in private converfation, and at his publick vifitations) to en-courage his clergy to marry at any hour, and in pri-vate houfes, purely in virtue of one of his licenfes; affuring them they need not be afraid of the canon, fince he is the only perfon, who can call them to ac-count for breach of the canon, and that (they may depend upon it) he never will call them to fuch ac-count.

The ufe the Archbifhop of *Dublin* makes of his licenfes in this way (by making them ferve for mar-rying at uncanonical hours and places) is ufurping a power, which no ways belongs to him by any law or cuftom.   And as the power I claim entirely depends on the fupremacy given to the crown in fpiritual matters by thefe acts of parliament, and is derived to me (and my fucceffors) from the crown; I take
this

this proceeding of his Grace to be a direct invasion of the authority of the crown, as well as an injury to me. And therefore I think the crown as much concerned to stop these irregular proceedings as I am.

Now what I desire of your Grace is, to inform me, which is the most proper method for either the crown or myself, or both, to put a stop to this illegal practice: and likewise which is the best and easiest way of convicting and punishing any clergyman in the diocese of *Dublin*, who breaks the canon in this manner, though his proper ordinary will not meddle with him.

And as the ignorance I have observed in the most eminent common lawyers of *England* in ecclesiastical matters, persuades me that I can have very little help from consulting the lawyers of this country, who are much inferior to those of *England*, for skill and experience, I am the more desirous to have your Grace's advice in this matter: and the grievance I labour under on this head, is the greater here, because the people are more vain! than in *England*; and those of moderate fortunes in this country, think it beneath them to be married at the regular time and place. And in the way his Grace of *Dublin* has put this affair, the breaches of the canon relating to marriages, and the invasions of that power granted by the crown to the Archbishops of *Armagh*, are more numerous here than they would be, if any bishop made the like attempt in *England*.

I shall in a post or two send a copy of this case to the Bishop of *London*, to desire his opinion likewise: for I have a troublesome and perverse opponent to deal with; and cannot have too much assistance. I hope his lordship will wait upon your Grace to discourse over the subject with you, that upon any difficulties which either may offer, I may have your joint

joint-fenfe, or if opportunity fhould not offer of your confulting together, I fhall be very thankful for your Grace's advice fingly.

I am, my Lord, &c.

To the Duke of Newcaftle.

My Lord, *Dublin, June* 11, 1726.

AS we had fome difturbance in this town laft night, I thought it my duty to give your Grace a fhort account of it, to prevent its being taken for an affair of greater confequence than it proved.

As there had been various reports fpread about the town, that the papifts intended to make a rifing about the 10th of *June,* though we had no reafon to apprehend any fuch thing would be attempted, yet we thought ourfelves obliged in prudence to give the proper directions to the forces here to be in readi-nefs, if any thing fhould happen either on *Thurfday* night, yefterday, or laft night. All things were quiet till yefterday in the evening, when a very nu-merous rabble affembled in *Stephen's Green,* as they ufually have done on the 10th of *June,* and between eight and nine (upon a meffage to the Lord Mayor from fome of the inhabitants of the Green, com-plaining of fuch a riotous affembly) the Lord Mayor, Sheriffs, and fome aldermen, attended with a num-ber of conftables, came on the Green to difperfe the rabble, but meeting with oppofition, and being af-faulted with ftones, bricks, and dirt, the Lord Mayor fent for affiftance to the forces, and had firft a detachment of about 40 foot, and afterwards about the like number of horfe; at firft the rabble would not difperfe, but upon fome of the foot firing with ball, and wounding three or four of them, and the horfe appearing foon after, they difperfed, and about 30 of them are taken and imprifoned. They will very speedily be examined; and we are not without hopes of finding out some gentlemen, who by some circumstances are thought to have had a hand in occasioning this disturbance. If we are able to come at any design of importance, we shall send advice of it; but at present I do not find that there was much more in it than the popish rabble coming down to fight the whig mob, as they used to do on that day, only that upon the prospect of a war, the papists are better in heart, and so might come in greater numbers.

We have given the necessary orders without any noise or shew, to have every thing ready to prevent the prisoners being rescued, if any such attempt should be made. I am, with great sincerity and respect,

My Lord, &c.

To the Bishop of London.

My Lord,   *Dublin,* *June* 11, 1726.

THE bearer (*Hugh Tillam*) is a servitor-batchelor of *Trinity* College in *Dublin,* and is disposed to take orders and go to the *West Indies.* I have a certificate of his sobriety and studiousness from his tutor, Dr. *Delany*; he tells me he takes with him some recommendations to your Lordship, to which he desires I would add mine in this letter: your Lordship, upon examination, will be best able to judge whether he has learning sufficient; if he has, and you think it proper, I would recommend him to your Lordship to find some way of employing him in the Church in the *West Indies.*

I am, &c.

To

To Lord Carteret.

My Lord,   *Dublin, June* 16, 1726.

I HAVE received the honour of your Excellency's of the 19th paft. and am very much obliged
to your Lordfhip for the kind account I find you
have been pleafed to give his Majefty of my behaviour. It will always be a great pleafure to me, if
I have been any ways ufeful in affifting you to promote the King's fervice, which you have always at
heart.

I have taken what opportunities offered thoroughly to contradict the reports fpread here relating to
Sir *J. St. Leger* and Mr. *Nutley*, as I fhall all others
which tend to differve his Majefty.

I am afraid the hurry of bufinefs has made
your Excellency forget my Lord *Rofcommon*'s cafe.
As there are King's letters for giving a penfion
to fome other Lords, I was in hopes we fhould
have received one for encreafing his penfion, which
is lefs than what is allowed to others, and half
of it goes to his brother's widow, as I am informed.

Mr. *Philips* is extremely pleafed with the honour
you do him of fo kindly remembering him.

Dr. *Wye* of *Drogheda*, has wrote to me to recommend one of his fons to your Excellency, for
your intereft for a commiffion, if ten new regiments
are raifed, as has been rumoured.

I am, &c.

To the Duke of Newcaſtle.

My Lord,   *Dublin, June* 25, 1726.

I HAVE juſt now received the honour of your Grace's of the 21ſt, and am thoroughly ſenſible of the hurry you and the reſt of his Majeſty's ſervants muſt have been in, on account of the great affairs now tranſacting.

It is a great ſatisfaction to me that what I endeavour to do for his Majeſty's ſervice is well taken. Every thing here has been very quiet ſince the 10th of *June*.

As to the affair of the privy counſellors, your Grace may depend on my endeavouring to make that and whatever elſe is once over, as eaſy as I can; and that on all occaſions I ſhall be ready to ſuggeſt what I think may be moſt for the King's intereſt.

By letters that came to town yeſterday, there is advice that the Biſhop of *Cloyne* is in a very dangerous way; as ſoon as there is any farther advice about him, I ſhall communicate it to your Grace; but I thought proper to acquaint you with this at preſent, to prevent any ſurpriſe in naming his ſucceſſor, for ſome here are not without fears that intereſt may be made for a tory on this ſide, to ſucceed to that or the next vacancy on the bench.

                              I am, &c.

To the ſame.

My Lord,   *Dublin, June* 28, 1726.

I HAVE this day ſeen a letter from a good hand, that gives advice of the death of the Biſhop of *Cloyne:* I have by this poſt wrote to his Excellency on this affair about a ſucceſſor.

                                  The

The perfon I would recommend, if he is acceptable to your Grace and the miniftry, is Dr. *Skirret*, who has attended me hither as chaplain; but if your Lordfhip thinks he is not fo fit, I would recommend Dr. *Maule*, Dean of *Cloyne*, to fucceed to the bifhoprick; he is counted one well affected to his Majefty, and is very diligent in the difcharge of the cures he has at prefent, and has the honour of being known to feveral Bifhops in *England*.

I fhall trouble your Grace with no more at prefent, but fubfcribe myfelf,

My Lord, &c.

To the Bifhop of London,

My Lord,   *Dublin, June* 28, 1726.

SINCE my laft there is advice come by a good hand, that the Bifhop of *Cloyne* is dead. I have by this poft wrote to the Duke of *Newcaftle* and my Lord Lieutenant about this affair.

I muft beg the favour of your Lordfhip to learn on what terms Dr. *Skirret* ftands with the miniftry: if he is acceptable to them, I would willingly recommend him for a fucceffor to the Bifhop deceafed; if your Lordfhip finds they are prejudiced againft him, I think Dean *Maule*, who is Dean of *Cloyne*, would be one of the moft proper of this nation to fucceed.

As I am not prefent to talk with the miniftry, I cannot put the management of this affair into better hands than your Lordfhip's, who I am fure will be for what you think moft for the good of the Church, his Majefty's fervice, and my reputation.

I am, &c.

To

To Lord Carteret.

My Lord,   *Dublin, June* 28, 1726.

THERE is advice in town that the Bishop of *Cloyne* is dead, which by the accounts of last *Friday* is very likely to be true. On this occasion I must desire of your Excellency to recommend Dr. *Skirret* for his successor, if he be any ways acceptable to the ministry: and in that case, as your Excellency knows the great incumbrances on that bishoprick, I must beg the favour of your Excellency to reserve for him the other preferments in the gift of the crown, enjoyed by the late Bishop, that the Dr. may not be ruined by taking that bishoprick.

If Dr. *Skirret* is one the ministry are set against, I should willingly recommend Dean *Maule* for that bishoprick, who as I am assured is one well-affected to his Majesty, and is very diligent in the discharge of his present cures.

I have had the honour of your Excellency's of the 11th. I am,

My Lord, &c.

To the Duke of Newcastle.

My Lord,   *Dublin, June* 30, 1726.

YEsterday the Lords Justices met, and we wrote a common letter to my Lord Lieutenant relating to a successor to the late Bishop of *Cloyne*, in which three persons are named: Dr. *Maule*, Dean of *Cloyne*, Dr. *Howard*, Dean of *Ardagh*; and Mr. *Gore* *, Dean of *Down*. I have already wrote to your

---

* Chaplain to the House of Commons, and brother to Sir *Ralph Gore*, Bart.

your Grace my fentiments about Dean *Maule*, and give you this farther trouble only to do juftice to the other two gentlemen, that Dean *Howard* is accounted well affected to his Majefty, as is Dean *Gore*; but Dean *Maule* is fenior to them both.

I am, &c.

To the Bifhop of London.

My Lord, *Dublin, June* 30, 1726.

UPON the Lords Juftices meeting yefterday, we joined in a letter to my Lord Lieutenant, naming three candidates for the bifhoprick of *Cloyne*; Dean *Maule*, Dean *Howard* of *Ardagh*, and Dean *Gore* of *Down:* the laft two are counted well affected to his Majefty, but are juniors to Dean *Mau'e*; and the laft is not, that I can hear, in circumftances to afford to take the bifhoprick of *Cloyne*, which has a burthen of about 2500 *l.* on it; fo that I make no change in my recommendation by the laft.

I am, &c.

To Lord Carteret.

My Lord, *Dublin, July* 2, 1726.

SINCE the laft trouble I gave your Excellency, I have received a letter from Dr. *Wye* of *Drogheda* (whom your Lordfhip was fo kind as to make your chaplain, and to encourage him to hope for fomewhat in the church) to defire that if Dean *Howard* fhould be made Bifhop of *Cloyne*, your Excellency would be pleafed to beftow on him the deanery of *Ardagh*, and chanterfhip of *Chrift Church:* he has been a great many years minifter of *Drogheda*, which is a confiderable cure.

I have

I have likewise had a letter from the Bishop of *Meath*, the which I send enclosed to your Excellency: I suppose it is to desire you would be pleased to send an order to present his son to the living of *Moynet*, about which there may possibly be a lawsuit with Mr. *Carter*, who pretends to be patron of it. I shall in the mean time endeavour to learn what I can of the title of the crown, and what will be the best method to maintain it.

I am, &c.

P. S. Mr. *Daniel Pulteney* arrived here yesterday, and was admitted clerk of the council this day.

To Lord Townshend.

My Lord,   *Dublin, July* 2, 1726.

DR. *Rowan* fellow of the college here designs to wait on your Lordship with a petition to his Majesty, to appoint him Professor of the Law of Nature and Nations in this University, with a power of taking such gentlemen for pupils as are willing to put themselves under his care, and he will oblige himself to read such a number of lectures in a term as shall be thought proper, without any salary from the crown for the same, only on condition of enjoying his fellowship with all its emoluments, and the like privileges as are already granted to the professors established in this college.

He has always been well affected to his Majesty and his family, and is of abilities to fill the professorship he asks for with reputation. And I think it can be of no disservice to the College, that he should enjoy the same privileges as other professors enjoy; and hope that his being encouraged to continue in the college, may help to keep up there a good affection to his Majesty. I therefore take the
liberty

liberty to recommend him to your Lordſhip for your favour in promoting his requeſt.　I am,

My Lord, &c.

To Lord Carteret.

My Lord,　　　　　　　　　*Dublin, July* 6, 1726.

I HAVE the honour of your Excellency's of the 28th of the laſt, and humbly thank you for remembering the Earl of *Rofcommon*, and hope to hear after your Lordſhip's return to *London*, that his Majeſty is gracioufly pleaſed to make an addition to his former penſion.

The preſent vacancy of the biſhoprick of *Cloyne*, as it occaſions no doubt, very numerous applications to your Lordſhip, ſo it brings ſome upon me.

Mr. *Abbadie*, Dean of *Killaloo*, has been with me to deſire my recommendations to your Excellency to be thought of for ſome deanery which he ſuppoſes may happen to be vacant by promotion on this occaſion. He repreſents (and has ſhewn me papers from former governors here confirming) that he had a promiſe in King *William*'s time; of the firſt conſiderable preferment that fell, (which happened to be the deanery of St. *Patrick*'s) but that deanery being thought improper for one who could ſpeak no *Engliſh*, he was put off with that of *Killaloo*, with a farther promiſe of making him amends in ſomewhat better, which has never been performed. But his great uneaſineſs, is that many years ago, when there was an extreme ſcarcity of money here, he was obliged to let all his preferments *during his incumbency for about* 120 *l. per ann.* though now they would let for about 300 *l. per ann.* he would be glad to take a preferment of 200, or 250 *l. per ann.* for what he has, (which is the deanery of *Killaloo*, with four finecures, all

in

in the gift of the crown united by an epifcopal union *pro hac vice.)* Your Lordfhip knows him to have the character of a man of learning, and one well affected to his Majefty.

I have likewife received a letter from Dr. *Dongworth*, who would be thankful for either of Dean *Howard's* preferments in *Dublin*, if he fhould be removed to *Cloyne*; and another from Dr. *Tifdale* to the fame purpofe, who I perceive has wrote to your Excellency on this occafion. Your Lordfhip knows them both, and will have the goodnefs to excufe my giving you this trouble.

We had figned an order for paying the penfions recommended to me by your Excellency before the receipt of yours, and I fhall every quarter take care of their fpeedy payment. I am, my Lord, with the greateft refpect and fincerity,

Your Excellency's, &c.

To the Archbifhop of Canterbury.

My Lord,   *Dublin, July* 12, 1726.

I HAVE received your Grace's anfwer to mine about marriage licenfes, but I find I have expreffed myfelf fo obfcurely in the cafe as to be mifunderftood. The Archbifhop of *Dublin* does not pretend to have power to grant any other than epifcopal licenfes, nor does he grant any other; but what I complain of is, that he encourages his clergy to marry at uncanonical hours and in uncanonical places, though their licenfe contains no fuch power. I fhall follow your Grace's kind advice in not being too hafty to engage with fo litigious and obftinate a perfon, whatever my grievance may be.

On occafion of what your Lordfhip writes to me about my apparitor-general's patent, I have enquired of my commiffary how that affair ftands, who tells me me that my apparitor-general has nothing to do in, nor fee out of, the prerogative court, for any wills proved there. That the officer there anfwering to the apparitor, is called the marfhal of the court, and has twelve-pence fee for every will proved there, as the apparitor-general has for every will proved in the confiftory court: but that the two jurifdictions are kept as diftinct as they could be if they refided in two different perfons. As this is the cafe of my apparitor-general, I think it can be of no fervice in the controverfy depending before your Grace, to have a copy of the patent of my apparitor-general; but if you think it may, I fhall as foon as you are pleafed to intimate it, fend a copy of his patent.

My commiffary likewife tells me, he cannot by any writings now extant (though he has made a moft diligent fearch) trace the leaft foot-fteps of any extra-epifcopal power relating to faculties, grounded on prefcription, but that all fuch power refts here on the King's commiffion; fo that either the pope had more fully fwallowed up all metropolitical power here, than he was able to do in *England*, or thofe antient records, in which fomewhat would have appeared to the contrary, have been deftroyed in the wars.

I am, &c.

To the Duke of Newcaftle.

My Lord, *Dublin, July* 12, 1726.

I Underftand Sir *Hans Sloan* has waited upon your Grace to defire your favour in introducing Dr. *Welfted* to the King, with a book he has dedicated to his Majefty. As I believe Sir *Hans* has read the book, he will be able to give you an account of the nature and defign of it.

I can affure your Grace there are few in the kingdom of more learning than Dr. *Welfted*; and I believe

lieve but very few who have greater ſkill in phyſic than he has; and as I have intimately known him almoſt from the time of our firſt going to the univerſity of *Oxford*, I can aſſure your Grace on my perſonal knowledge, that he has been all along a hearty friend to, and advocate for, the revolution, and a ſteady adherent to the intereſts of the houſe of *Hanover* in the worſt times, for which I am ſatisfied he has been diſtreſſed in his buſineſs by the diſaffected. After what I have with the greateſt truth ſaid, it will be but a ſlight recommendation of him to your Grace, that he is one of the oldeſt and heartieſt of my friends, and that whatever countenance you give him, or favour you are pleaſed to ſhew him on this or any other occaſion, will be eſteemed a very particular obligation laid on me, who am with the greateſt reſpect and ſincerity *,

My Lord, &c.

To

* The reader hath already obſerved with pleaſure, what a ſteady friend his Grace ſhewed himſelf to be to Mr. *Stephens*; to Dr. *Welſted* he was ſtill more ſo, for that worthy gentleman having fallen into decay in the latter part of his life, my Lord Primate, though he was no relation, gave him two hundred pounds a year at the leaſt, during his life; nor was his friendſhip wanting to the Doctor's family after his deceaſe; the Primate then maintained a ſon of the Doctor's as a commoner at *Hart* hall in *Oxford*, with an intent of effectually providing for him, but the poor young gentleman died before he had taken a degree. Dr. *Welſted* was one of the editors of the *Oxford Pindar*, and eſteemed an excellent *Greek* ſcholar; he had been choſen immediately after the revolution, together with the Primate, Dr. *Wilcocks* Biſhop of *Rocheſter*, Dr. *Sacheverell*, and the incomparable Mr. *Addiſon*, a demy or fellow of *Magdalen* college, *Oxford*; and this went by the name of the golden election many years afterwards in that college: the moſt worthy Dr. *Hough* was Preſident of *Magdalen* college at this time, and was the cauſe of my Lord Primate's promotion afterwards, by recommending him to be chaplain to Sir *Charles Hedges*, then ſecretary of ſtate.

To Lord Carteret.

My Lord,   *Dublin, July* 14, 1726.

WHILST your Excellency was in this kingdom, I delivered you a petition from Mrs.
Pepper, widow to General *Pepper*. I remember your
Excellency was then of opinion, as the General had
fold out of the army, and died in good circumftances,
fhe could not without very great favour, obtain any
penfion as his widow : this makes me rather difcourage her from going to *England* to follicit for a penfion, which would engage her in a certain expence,
upon a very uncertain profpect ; but as the General
has left a fon behind him, for whom he made no
provifion, fhe is very defirous fomewhat may be done
for him in regard to his father's fervices : I find, as
he is in very indigent circumftances, he would be
very glad to ferve his Majefty in any capacity. His
mother fays he is very fober, and very well-affected
to his Majefty.

As he waits upon you perfonally with this, he can
beft fatisfy your Lordfhip as to his own character,
and what he would be thankful for. I take the liberty to recommend him to your Excellency's favour to
put him in fome way fit for a gentleman, if you
fhall find him fuch as Mrs. *Pepper* has reprefented
him to me.

I am, my Lord, &c.

To the Duke of Newcaftle.

My Lord,   *Dublin, July* 26, 1726.

I HAVE had the honour of your Grace's of the
9th, with the account of his Majefty's having
determined to give the bifhoprick of *Cloyne* to Dean
Maule,

Maule, and am very thankful to his Majefty for having that regard to my recommendation, and for his gracious intention to do fomething for my chaplain, Dr. *Skirret*, on a proper occafion. We have been expecting the two or three laft mails to receive his Majefty's commands by my Lord Lieutenant, about that bifhoprick, but we have not yet heard any thing from his Excellency *.

I am very much obliged to your Grace for taking in good part, the accounts I fend you of affairs here, and my opinion of them; I am fure they are by me entirely defigned for his Majefty's fervice.

The middle of next week I intend to fet out for the north upon my vifitation, which will occafion my abfence from *Dublin* for about a fortnight.

I am, &c.

To the Bifbop of London.

My Lord,   *Dublin, July* 30, 1726.

I AM very much obliged to your Lordfhip for the very diftinct advice you give me relating to the practice of the clergy of this city, in marrying at uncanonical hours and places, in virtue of the common licenfes : though it is a direct breach of the canon, without any pretence to fupport it, yet I fhall follow your advice, not to begin any information againft any offender, till I have thoroughly mooted the point here. My Lord Chancellor is entirely of your Lordfhip's opinion, as to the courfe to be taken in this affair.

I had anfwered your letter relating to the bifhoprick of *Cloyne* fooner, but that I have been every day expecting that we fhould receive his Majefty's commands
about

---

* His Excellency perhaps was not in hafte to give an account of a tranfaction he did not like.

about it ; but they are not yet a'rived, which (as I have had a letter from the Duke of *Newcaftle* with the fame advice as your Lordfhip fent me) I am a little furprized at, and fuppofe my Lord Lieutenant muft have kept the order till at his arrival in *London* he could endeavour to get it altered.

I underftand his Lordfhip came to *London* the end of laft week, fo that I fuppofe we fhall very fpeedily receive orders one way or another.

I am glad to find your Lordfhip has the fame good opinion of Dean *Mau'e* that I have ; and am obliged to you for the good advice you give me about my future recommendations. I have followed your Lordfhip's directions, and faid nothing of what you wrote about the bifhoprick, ftill waiting his Majefty's orders, and Dean *Maule* has ftill continued in the country.

I thank your Lordfhip for the account you give me of Dr. *Skirret's* uneafnefs for not being named fingly in my recommendation, and am glad you think I was in the right ; indeed what I proceeded upon was, that if I had named him fingly, and that nomination was not hearkened to, I did not doubt but the bifhoprick would be filled before I could have time to fend over another recommendation. I own if I had been upon the fpot to recommend by word of mouth, I need not have named a fecond, till I had found the firft I named was objected to, but in fo remote a fituation as I am in, I could not hope for time for a fecond nomination. I find by an angry letter I recei- ved from the Doctor, that you were pleafed to fhew him mine, which I could rather wifh had not been done.

As we Bifhops hold annual vifitations here, next *Wednefday* I intend to go on the vifitation of my dio- cefe, and fhall be abfent from *Dublin* about a fort- night.

I am, my Lord, &c.

To

To Lord Carteret.

My Lord,   *Dublin, Aug.* 20, 1726.

I HAD not the honour of your Excellency's of the 26th paſt, till I was upon my viſitation, which has been the occaſion I have anſwered it no ſooner. I have a very good opinion of Dean *Howard*, as likewiſe of Mr. *Synge* and Mr. *Ward* ; and ſhall be glad to ſee the firſt advanced, and the other two well provided for. Upon the receipt of your Lordſhip's, I wrote to have an account ſent you of Dean *Maule's* preferments, which I did not know, but Mr. * *Lingen* has, I am told, upon my writing, ſent your Lordſhip their ſeveral denominations. The living of *Mourn Abbey* has I believe, uſually gone with the deanery of *Cloyne*, which induced Dr. *Maule* to build a houſe there. The living of *Cork* is by act of parliament, upon the firſt vacancy, to be divided into the two pariſhes of St. *Mary Shandon*, and of St. *Paul :* the firſt will upon the diviſion be left worth better than 200 *l. per ann.* the latter worth near 100 *l.* the dean is not yet come to town, but on his arrival, if Mr. *Lingen's* account is any ways wrong, I will ſend a better. I find there is likewiſe fallen the deanery of *Clonfert*, about which the Lords Juſtices have written in my abſence. The Biſhop of *Clonfert* has deſired I would recommend Mr. *Forbes* to your Excellency for that deanery, as one who would be of great ſervice to him in the government of that dioceſe.

The late Dean of *Clonfert* held two or three little things in the dioceſe of *Kildare*, concerning which I find your Excellency has tranſmitted to you the Biſhop of *Kildare's* memorial, to deſire they may be diſpoſed

---

* *William Lingen,* Eſq; one of the ſecretaries to the Lords Juſtices.

poſed of to one who may reſide on them perſonally. I ſhould be glad if your Excellency would by them, or by St. *Paul's* at *Cork*, at preſent provide bread for poor Mr. *Horner*.

There has been a great miſtake committed in the King's letter relating to Dean *Maule*, by ordering him the ſame commendams his predeceſſor held ; this is contrary to what is practiſed commonly, which is where a biſhoprick wants a commendam, to find it in the preferments of the perſon promoted ; and beſides, I do not hear from any body that the crown has any pretence to the provoſtſhip of *Tuam*. But of this I ſhall write farther to your Excellency when Dean *Maule* comes to town. The affair of *Youghall* was over before my arrival, but I think it has gone as my Lord *Burlington* deſired. I humbly thank your Excellency for your care of my Lord *Roſcommon's* affair. I am,

Your Excellency's, &c.

To the Biſhop of London.

My Lord,   *Dublin, Sept.* 6, 1726.

THE bearer is Mr. *Abbadie*, Dean of *Killaloo*, one who for many years has made a figure in the world, by the writings he has publiſhed : I find upon enquiry, he was by King *William* recommended to the government here for ſomewhat conſiderable, and would have had the deanery of St. *Patrick's*, which fell ſoon after, but that having no knowledge of our language, it was thought improper to place him in the greateſt preferment in this city : However it was then fixed that he ſhould have the next deanery that fell, which happened to be that of *Killaloo*, which was given him with one or two little things to make him amends for its falling ſhort of the other deanery, and with thoſe helps he had but about half the value of what had been defigned him. At firft he made about 240 *l. per ann.* of his preferment, but afterwards, upon a great fcarcity of money here, was obliged to let his preferments during incumbency for about 120 *l per ann.* which I find was a pretty common cafe at that time with a great many other clergymen. He had afterwards repeated promifes of having fomewhat farther done for him, but nothing beyond promifes. As this is but a fmall income, and now he grows old he finds he wants an amanuenfis to affift him in his ftudies, he would gladly have fomewhat better either here or in *England.* He has firmly adhered to his Majefty's family here in the day of trial, and is every way a worthy man. I fhall do my endeavour to ferve him here, but as opportunities may not offer here fo foon, he defired I would recommend him to your Lordfhip, in hopes fomewhat might be done for him in *England.*

He would hope, if that confideration may be of fervice to him, that as his preferments are all in the gift of the government, they might eafily be obtained for fome friend of your Lordfhip's, if the Dean had fomewhat given him in *England.*

I take the liberty to recommend him to your Lordfhip's favour and countenance, and if it fhall lie in your way to help him to fomewhat in *England* that may be an honourable fubfiftance for him, the fmall remainder of life he is likely to live, you will do a kindnefs to a perfon of merit, and very much oblige,

My Lord, &c.

To the fame.

My Lord,   *Dublin, Sept.* 13, 1726.

I HAVE before me your Lordfhip's of the 10th paft, which I had anfwered fooner, if we had any thing ftirring here worth writing about.

I am

I am glad the miniftry were fo unanimous in fupporting the nomination of Dean *Maule* to the bifhoprick of *Cloyne*. His inftruments were paffed laft week, and he was laft *Sunday* confecrated by myfelf (at the defire of the Archbifhop of *Cafhel*) and the Bifhops of *Kildare* and *Fernes*. We are on thefe occafions forced to go to *Dunboyne*, the firft parifh in my province, to avoid a quarrel with his Grace of *Dublin*, who · expects any Archbifhop that confecrates in this town, fhould take a formal licence under hand and feal for fo doing.

There has been a miftake in granting a commendam to the Bifhop of *Cloyne*. As they followed the pattern of the grant to the late Bifhop of *Cloyne* at the fecretary's office, they have made the provoftfhip of *Tuam* part of his commendam, which we have no reafon as yet to believe to be in the King's gift.

I find by your Lordfhip's account that Dr. *Skirret* muft have placed himfelf fo as to overlook that part of my letter which your Lordfhip did not read to him, which I am fure was exceedingly rude in him. I thank your Lordfhip for your kind advice.

I have lately received a letter from Mr. *Pope*, (whom I recommended to your Lordfhip juft before I left *England)* to defire I would remind you of him, for fear he fhould be forgotten through the multiplicity of your bufinefs. As his behaviour deferves, and when your Lordfhip fhall find a proper occafion, I fhould be obliged to your Lordfhip to think of him.

I am, &c.

P. S. I have lately heard from Mr. *Stephens*, who is full of his acknowledgments of your Lordfhip's great civility, and the encouragement you give him.

To

To the Duke of Newcaſtle. ˙

My Lord,   *Dublin, Nov.* 12, 1726.

HAVING by a mail this day heard from *Eng-land,* that Dr. *Gilbert* is likely to be removed from *Chriſt Church* to the deanery of *Exeter,* I muſt beg leave to put your Grace in mind of Mr. *Stephens :* as he was put by that very canonry to prefer one juſt returned from ſerving at *Hanover,* I hope if this va-cancy ſhould happen, his Majeſty will be graciouſly pleaſed to beſtow on him what has been ſo long pro-miſed me on his account. I wholly depend on your Grace's friendſhip on this occaſion, and am, my Lord, in all ſincerity,

Your Grace's, &c.

To the ſame.

My Lord,   *Dublin, Nov.* 26, 1726.

WE continue ſo very quiet here, except on ac-count of the recruits for foreign ſervice, that I ſhould have nothing to inform your Grace of, if it were not for the preſent indiſpoſition of my Lord Chancellor * : he has been ill for four or five days with a great cold and fever ; he was bliſtered laſt night with little or no ſucceſs, but is ſo much mend-ed upon the bliſter running very well this afternoon, that he is thought to be out of danger.

I hope your Grace has received mine of the 12th inſtant, about Mr. *Stephens.*

I am, my Lord, &c.

To

* *Weſt.*

To Lord Carteret.

My Lord,   *Dublin, Dec.* 3, 1726.

AFTER about twelve days illnefs of a fever, my Lord Chancellor died this day about two in the afternoon: his death is very much lamented here by all, but efpecially by the lawyers, whofe good will and efteem he had entirely gained by his patience, civility, and great abilities. As he was an old friend and acquaintance of mine, I am very much troubled at this lofs, as well as I am heartily concerned for the terrible blow it is to his family.

I earneftly wifh his place may be filled by one that may give the fame fatisfaction he has given.

I take it for granted his fucceffor will be an *Englifhman*; but I cannot help fuggefting that I think it would be of fervice, and efpecially againft the next feffion of parliament, if either the Lord Chief Juftice *Windham*, or Lord Chief Baron *Dalton* were advanced to that ftation, and their vacant places fupplied from *England*.

They have both eftablifhed a very good character here, and are well fkilled in the affairs of *Ireland*, beyond what a new comer can hope for under a year at leaft; and I think fuch a promotion would be an encouragement to a perfon of fome worth to come over in one of their places, where they faw it was a ftep to the higheft poft in this country.

I am, &c.

To

To the Duke of Newcaftle.

My Lord,   *Dublin, Dec.* 3, 1726.

THE uncertain accounts I have fent your Grace of the health of my Lord Chancellor, have been owing to the various accounts we got here from his phyficians, and the turns in his diftemper ; but he this day died about two o'clock in the afternoon : he had by his abilities and humanity gained a gene- ral efteem here, and efpecially among the lawyers, with whom he was moft concerned.

I heartily wifh his place may be filled with one that may give equal fatisfaction. I take it for grant- ed that his fucceffor will be a native of *England*, who, befides his being duly qualified as a lawyer, muft be one of an undoubted whiggifh character, or it will give great uneafinefs in this country.

I cannot help fuggefting on this occafion that I think it might be for his Majefty's fervice to advance either the Lord Chief Juftice *Wyndham*, or my Lord Chief Baron *Dalton* to that poft. They have both a very good character, and are very well liked here : they both know the country, and the bufinefs very well, and are both very well known : fo that either of them will be capable of doing more fervice to his majefty next feffion of parliament among the mem- bers of both houfes, than a new comer will be capa- ble of doing : and I would hope it may be an in- ducement to fome perfon of worth to be willing to fucceed either of them from *England*, when they fee the rightly behaving themfelves as Judges a ftep to the higheft poft in the law here. They have both difcharged their places with that reputation, that I have no other reafon for recommending my Lord Chief Juftice *Wyndham* firft, but his being the fenior

of

of the two. If either of them be thought of for Lord Chancellor, we may foon have the place filled.

Your Grace will excufe what I have faid, as proceeding not fo much from friendfhip for thofe gentlemen, as a defire moft effectually and fpeedily to promote his Majefty's fervice here.

I am, &c.

To Lord Townfhend.

My Lord,   *Dublin, Dec.* 3, 1726.

THIS afternoon, about two o'clock, we loft my Lord Chancellor, after about twelve days illnefs. He has left behind him a very good character, and his death is very much regretted here.

I have no doubt but his place will be filled up with fome *Englifhman :* but whoever is thought of for it, befides a proper knowledge in his profeffion, ought to be one that has always been attached to the revolution and *Hanover* fucceffion, or it will create great uneafinefs here.

I hope your Lordfhip will have the goodnefs to forgive my fuggefting what I think would be for his Majefty's fervice on this occafion, which is the advancing either my Lord Chief Juftice *Wyndham,* or Lord Chief Baron *Dalton* to the chancellorfhip. They have already acquired a very great reputation by an able and impartial difcharge of their offices, and are very well beloved for their great civility to all who have had any affairs with them. They have a good knowledge of *Irifh* affairs, and are acquainted with a great number of both houfes of parliament. Nor do I think that it will be poffible for any new comer either to eftablifh fo good a character, or gain fo much efteem as they have, before next feffion of parliament; much lefs will fuch an one have that know-

knowledge, either of perfons or things here, againft
that feafon as they have.

Of the two, as my Lord Chief Juftice *Wyndham*
has been here longeft, I rather think him the moft
proper *.

If it be thought advifeable to advance one of
them, I hope his place will be fupplied from *England :*
and I fhould think that the preferring one of them to
be Chancellor, will not only be an encouragement to
English judges here to acquit themfelves well, but
be an inducement to perfons of worth to come over
hither, when they fee a judge's place a ftep towards
the higheft ftation in the law here.   But all this is
fubmitted to your Lordfhip's better judgment, by
My Lord, &c.

To the Duke of Newcaftle.

My Lord,   *Dublin, Dec.* 6, 1726.

IN my laft to your Grace, I gave you an account
of the death of my Lord Chancellor, and what
I thought might be for his Majefty's fervice on this
unhappy occafion.   I give your Lordfhip this farther
trouble, to defire your intereft with his fucceffor, to
make † Mr. *Philips* his fecretary : he is one who has
always been hearty in his Majefty's intereft, and that
of his family : he has the honour to be known to
your Grace, as having been fecretary to the *Hanover*
club

---

* He was foon after this recommendation appointed.
† Notwithftanding Mr. *Pope* hath faid, that
Still to one Bifhop Philips *feems a wit,*
and in another place,
— Ambrofe Philips *be preferr'd for wit :*
I do not find he is ever recommended on that account in thefe
letters ; he is recommended in this, for qualities Mr. *Pope* could
not well have been recommended for, *viz.* that he had been always in his Majefty's intereft, and that of his family.

club in the Queen's time.   He is at prefent with me in my family, and might officiate as fecretary to the Lord Chancellor without leaving me.   What fervice your Grace fhall pleafe to do him in this affair, will be efteemed a very great obligation laid on,

My Lord, ·&c.

To the fame.

My Lord,   *Dublin, Dec.* 20, 1726.

I HAVE juft now received the honour of your Grace's of the 13th.   I am too fenfible of the great hurry of your ftation, to expect an anfwer to every letter I trouble you with.

I am very glad to find the affair of giving us a new Lord Chancellor, has met with that difpatch ; and I can affure your Grace he is one who by his behaviour here has made himfelf very acceptable, and that his promotion will be very much liked ; and he has on all occafions been very diligent at the·council to advance his Majefty's fervice there.   And he and I have always had a perfect agreement together.   We are to have a council to-morrow, againft which time his patent will be got ready, and we fhall there deliver him the feals.

Since the arrival of this news my Lord Chief Juftice *Whitfhed* has been with me, to defire he may be recommended to fucceed Lord Chief Juftice *Wyndham* in the Common Pleas.   He complains, that he finds the bufinefs of his prefent ftation very fatiguing as he advances in life, and fays the two ftations are about the fame value ; but the Common Pleas is a place of lefs trouble : he reprefents that he has with great zeal and fidelity ferved his Majefty, and made himfelf many enemies by fo doing, and would hope for this favour as a reward of his fervices.

I muft

I muſt do him the juſtice to ſay, that he has certainly ſerved his Majeſty with great zeal and affection, and has drawn on himſelf the anger of the Jacobites by ſo doing, and the malice of other diſcontented perſons here, by diſcountenancing ſeditious writings in the affair of the half-pence : and if we may have another perſon of worth from *England* to ſucceed him, I think he may deſerve the favour he deſires. But I hope the filling up two of the Chief Juſtices places with perſons from *England*, is a point that will not be departed from notwithſtanding.

I thank your Lordſhip for the kind aſſurances you give me of ſupporting Mr. *Stephens* in the promiſe made me on his behalf.

I am, &c.

To Lord Carteret.

My Lord, *Dublin, Dec.* 21, 1726.

WE have at laſt gone through the affair of the coin, and ſent our deſire to his Majeſty, which we hope will ſomewhat alleviate our preſent calamity.

The ſubſtance is, putting gold coins and *Engliſh* ſilver on the current bottom they paſs for in *England*, ſo as to leave no temptation to any trader to carry out *Engliſh* ſilver from hence, or import gold hither preferably to ſilver. As to the advance made on foreign ſilver, it is but one half-penny in a piece of eight, above its current value in *Engliſh* money, and can be of no conſequence to any in *England*, but to ſuch as want to buy it up as bullion for exportation, and to them it will be no great matter. It has been with ſome difficulty that we have been able to manage things ſo well, and to keep off meddling with *Engliſh* ſilver, and trying to get the advantage of *England* ; as likewiſe to prevent the addreſſing for a mint

mint to be eftablifhed here. We have avoided any calculations, both to prevent our requeft-being fent to the officers of the mint, and running a length of time there ; and becaufe we were fatisfied no calculation of ours could give any light or be of any weight on your fide of the water. If in this particular we have not complied with the very words of your Excellency's letter to us, I am fure we have done our beft to anfwer your intentions, which were to affign the moft proper methods to remove the great want of filver here that were likely to be granted us from *England*.

Your Excellency knows very well the great fcarcity of filver here, when you left us, and I can affure you it has gone on increafing to the great detriment of trade, among the lower people and manufacturers, and to the putting all degrees under great difficulties to find money for common marketing ; and without fome fpeedy remedy the evil will be of dangerous confequence here. We muft therefore beg of your Excellency, out of your tender regard to this kingdom, to prefs for a fpeedy relief : your known goodnefs and your particular knowledge of our cafe, make it needlefs to add any thing farther, on this occafion. I am, with the greateft and moft fincere refpect,

My Lord, &c.

To the fame.

My Lord,   *Dublin, Dec.* 22, 1726.

I HAVE received the honour of your Excellency's of the 13th, and am very glad his Majefty has made fo good a choice of a new Chancellor, and do not doubt the public bufinefs being perfectly well carried on by him. I had great hopes when I wrote on that occafion, that my fentiments agreed with your

your Lordfhip's, as your Lordfhip had for fo long been an eye witnefs of my Lord Chief Juftice's be haviour, and of the fatisfaction he gave here. He was yefterday admitted Lord Chancellor in coun- cil.

Since the arrival of the meffenger, my Lord Chief Juftice *Whitfhed* has been with me, and defired I would write in his behalf, that he might fucceed Lord Chief Juftice *Wyndham* in the Common Pleas ; he thinks his prefent place is about the fame value, but complains of the great fatigue of it, as he ad- vances in years ; and he pleads his faithful fervices to the crown : your Lordfhip knows better than I that he has ferved his Majefty very faithfully, and that in fome very troublefome affairs ; and that he has by fo doing made himfelf many enemies here ; and if he could be made eafy, fo that we had an *Englifhman* of worth to fucceed him, it would be very well ; and what he defires is a reafonable com- penfation of his paft fervices. But I hope it will be a point ftill kept up to have two *Englifh* chiefs amongft the judges : the whole I fubmit to your Lordfhip's better judgment.

I have this day feen my Lord Chief Baron, who thanks your Excellency for your kind remembrance of him on the late remove, but is difpofed to keep in his prefent poft.

It is talked here that there is one folliciting for an advancement on this occafion, whofe fuccefs would not be pleafing here. I have this day feen the Attor- ney General, and find if there were to be a vacancy in the King's Bench, he would not care to remove thither.

I fhall fpeedily anfwer your Excellency's of the 17th.

I am, &c.

To

To the same.

My Lord,   *Dublin, Dec.* 26, 1726.

ON *Thursday* laft the meffenger brought me the honour of your Excellency's of the 17th, and I think not only myfelf but the generality here are very well pleafed with the choice his Majefty has made of a Chancellor and Lord Juftice. I believe Mr. *Wyndham* will give great fatisfaction in both pofts, and from the experience I have had of him already in public bufinefs, I am fatisfied we fhall act with a perfect agreement.

I am obliged to your Lordfhip for fetting the leaft value upon my friendfhip, and fhall always efteem it one of the happineffes of my life to continue in your Lordfhip's good graces.

I have been to wait on Mrs. *Weft,* to affure her of your Excellency's kind intentions to procure her fome favour from his Majefty : but as fhe fees no body, I was not admitted, but I have taken care to let her know how kind your Excellency is to her. We were all fworn Lords Juftices on *Friday* laft. Mr. *Conolly* is gone into the country for the holidays.

As *Chappel-izod* * is now at liberty, I have thoughts, with your Excellency's good liking, to borrow it for a country-houfe, as I cannot hope to make much ufe of my houfe at *Drogheda.* I heartily wifh your Excellency a happy new year, and many of them. I am, my Lord, with the utmoft truth and refpect,

                    Your Excellency's, &c.

                                        To

* A palace belonging to the King, adjoining to the *Phœnix* park near *Dublin.*

To the Duke of Newcastle.

My Lord,   *Dublin, Jan.* 1, 1726.

THE Archbifhop of *Cafhel* died this morning, about five o'clock, after a few days indifpofition from a cold. The perfon I would recommend to fucceed to *Cafhel,* and who is willing to remove is the * Bifhop of *Derry*; to whofe bifhoprick I would recommend the † Bifhop of *Meath* as a fucceffor; and to his bifhoprick the bifhop of *Dromore*; and to his Dr. *Cobb,* Bifhop of *Killala.* If the fcheme goes on thus far, I would recommend Dr. *Skirret* for the bifhoprick of *Killalla*; and if he is not pitched upon, Dr. *Howard,* Dean of *Ardagh.*

If it be thought proper to fend fome Bifhop from *England* to *Cafhel, Derry,* or *Meath,* I fhould be forry if any fhould be fent becaufe of his little worth or troublefomenefs there, for fuch an one will do the *Englifh* intereft a great deal of mifchief here, and I hope it will be confidered whether he be one that is likely to agree with me.

I am, &c.

P. S.   I have reafon to believe the Bifhop of *Derry* will not be fond of removing to *Cafhel,* if the Bifhop of *Meath* be not thought of for his fucceffor; and in that cafe the Bifhop of *Kilmore* and *Ardagh* § is a very proper perfon to remove to *Cafhel*; and either the Bifhop of *Dromore* or *Fernes,* to *Kilmore*; or in that cafe, *Kilmore* and *Ardagh* is worth the acceptance of an *Englifh* Bifhop, being reckoned at better than 2000*l. per annum.*

To

---

* Dr. *Nicholfon.*   † Dr. *Downes.*
§ Dr. *Godwin*; he was foon afterwards appointed, another vacancy having happened, by the unexpected death of Archbifhop *Nicholfon.*

To Lord Carteret.

My Lord,   *Dublin, Jan.* 2, 1726.

YEsterday morning died the Archbishop of *Cashel*, after a few days indisposition from a cold. Last winter I had the honour of talking over with your Excellency what removes on the Bench might be proper, in case of his death. As all then mentioned were approved by your Lordship, and are still alive, I would still recommend for the translations then talked of ; the Bishop of *Derry* to the Archbishoprick of *Cashel*, the Bishop of *Meath* to the bishoprick of *Derry* ; the Bishop of *Dromore* to the bishoprick of *Meath* ; and the Bishop of *Killala* to the bishoprick of *Dromore*.———If the scheme goes on thus far, I would recommend Dr. *Skirret* to succeed to the bishoprick of *Killala* ; and if he is not pitched upon, Dean *Howard* ; and if he has *Killalla*, I hope your Excellency will remember Mr. *Synge* for part of the Dean's preferments.

If it be thought proper to break this scheme, by sending some Bishop from the Bench in *England* to *Cashel, Derry,* or *Meath* ; I hope we shall not have one sent for being troublesome or good for nothing there ; and I hope, regard will be had to his being likely or unlikely to agree with me. I remember I have in conversation mentioned two that I should not desire to see here ; one for the restlessness of his temper, the other for the great liberties he was pleased to take with my character upon my being made Primate.

If it should not be thought proper to remove the Bishop of *Meath* to *Derry*, I am satisfied the Bishop of *Derry* had rather continue where he is ; and in that case the Bishop of *Kilmore* is a proper person to remove to *Cashel* ; and either the Bishop of *Dromore*

or

or *Fernes* to *Ki'more* ; and the Bishop of *Killalla* to *Dromore* or *Fernes :* I must own I think it would keep things more easy here, if the Archbishoprick should be bestowed on a Bishop here.

I heartily wish your Excellency many happy new years, and am,

My Lord, &c.

To Lord Carteret.

My Lord,   *Dublin, Jan.* 3, 1726.

I THIS day received your Excellency's of the 20th of *December*, and am entirely of your Lordship's opinion, that what his Majesty is graciously pleased to do for Mr. *West*'s family should be in trust for his widow and children : Mrs. *West*'s conduct since my Lord Chancellor's death, has so far given countenance to some whispers which went about before, that though his Lordship's death was very much lamented, it is not so popular here to do much for his widow.   His son I believe is pretty well secured by the marriage settlement, and by a voluntary settlement the late Chancellor told me his father had made on him and the grandson after his decease ; but I fear no provision at all is made for the daughter.   I shall talk with some others about the *quantum,* and the best method of doing it : and shall afterwards acquaint your Lordship with the result of their sentiments.

Colonel *Cornwallis* this day brought your Excellency's orders relating to the embarkation of the two regiments for *Gibraltar,* and we immediately gave all the necessary orders on that occasion, and have dispatched an express to Colonel *Parker,* with his orders and a letter of credit.   We are now expecting General *Macartney* with the orders relating to the other four regiments, till whose arrival we can do nothing

more

more than we have done, which is ftopping the ordinary payments in the treafury, that we may have money to clear the feveral regiments to be embarked, and anfwer what other difburfements this fervice may call for. As foon as he comes, we fhall haften all the proper orders.

The Archbifhop of *Cafbel* dying laft *Sunday* morning, we have by a meffenger yefterday, fent your Excellency what recommendations we thought proper on that occafion; and I trouble you with a letter in particular.

To the fame.

My Lord,   *Dublin, Jan. 5, 1726.*

SINCE I had the honour of writing laft to your Excellency, Mr. *Proby* a clergyman is dead, and the living of *Loughcrew* in the diocefe of *Meath*, being in the King's gift, is at the difpofal of your Excellency. My Lord Chancellor has a relation here a clergyman, one Mr. *John Willoughby*, in recommending whom we fhall join next *Saturday*. But as your Excellency might in the mean time have a letter from fome other hand, I give you the trouble of this, to prevent the effects of a more early application than we can make jointly.

I am, &c.

To the Duke of Newcaftle,

My Lord,   *Dublin, Jan. 5, 1726.*

AS we talk here that fome new regiments will be raifed, * Colonel *Cavalier* was with me to day, to

VoL. I.   G

* He was a *French* officer, who wrote his own Memoirs, and the Hiftory of the Civil Wars, in the *Cevennes*, in the reign of *Lewis* XIV.

to defire I would recommend him to be put in com=
miffion on this occafion.   I told him it was wholly out
of my way to recommend to the army, but as he
had very much diftinguifhed himfelf abroad in the
laft war, I would venture to take the liberty to acquaint your Grace that he is alive, and very willing
to ferve his Majefty if a war comes on.

I am, &c.

To *Lord* Carteret.

My Lord,   *Dublin, Jan.* 16, 1726.

I HAVE had the honour of your Excellency's of
the 7th, and I hope that if my Lord Chief Juftice *Whitfhed* is removed to the Common Pleas, we
fhall have one from *England* fent to the King's
Bench.

I am glad the Bifhops are likely to be made according to the fcheme fettled with your Excellency
when you was here.   I am obliged to your Excellency
for your kind manner of granting me the ufe of
Chappel-izod.

We have given the neceffary orders for making
the computation for filling the army, and fhall return
it with all poffible fpeed.

* Mr. *Williams* was with me laft night from Mrs.
Weft, to defire me to write to your Excellency to
forward the fettling fome penfion on her and her
children.   I am pretty well fatisfied all the effects
Mr. *Weft* has left, will do little more than anfwer his
debts on both fides of the water.   But as I am fettled
here, I do not care to meddle in any thing of a
penfion, that I apprehend will not be fo popular as I
could wifh, for the fake of my deceafed friend.   As
your Lordfhip cannot but be fenfible of the clamours
that

* Secretary to the late Chancellor *Weft.*

that will be raifed upon the *Englifh* here, if any of his *Irifh* creditors fhould go unpaid, I could wifh the truftees of the penfion may have a power of applying part of the penfion to pay thofe debts, if there fhould be any fear of thofe creditors being neglected.

I am, my Lord, &c.

To the fame.

My Lord,   *Dublin, Jan.* 17, 1726.

AS we are likely to have thirty-four new companies raifed upon this eftablifhment, I take this opportunity to put your Lordfhip in mind of Mr. *Hayward*, whom I recommended formerly to your Lordfhip for a lieutenant's or captain's commiffion. I know the new companies are to be fupplied with officers out of the half-pay lift here : but as feveral on that lift are too old to ferve, there may be room for him on this occafion : if there be, I fhall take it as a great obligation if your Lordfhip will be fo kind as to remember him.

I am, my Lord, &c.

To the Duke of Newcaftle.

My Lord,   *Dublin, Jan.* 21, 1726.

I *HAVE had the honour of your Grace's of the 12th, and am extremely obliged to his Majefty and the miniftry for the weight they have been pleafed to give my recommendations with his Majefty upon the vacancy of the Archbifhoprick of* Cafhel. *I* can affure your Grace I had no other view in the feveral parts of that fcheme, than promoting his Majefty's fervice, by obliging a number of perfons that are all very well affected,

G 2   and

and will, I doubt not fill their respective new stations, to the satisfaction of his Majesty's friends here.

I thank your Grace for recommending Dr. *Skirret* to my Lord Lieutenant for the deanery of *Ardagh* ; but nothing here that is not considerably better than what he enjoys in *England* can be of service to him, since by the laws of this country, he must quit whatever he has in *England*, to be capable of taking any thing here.

I am, &c.

To Lord Carteret.

My Lord,   *Dublin, Jan.* 21, 1726.

THERE is one Lieutenant *John Cunningham*, in Colonel *Haye*'s regiment, who was recommended to me by the Bishop of *Fernes*, to be my gentleman usher : I find he has been eighteen years a lieutenant, and has on all occasions shewn his zeal for his Majesty and his family : he is gone to *Gibraltar* with his regiment ; but as there are two companies to be added to that and the other regiments of foot left on our establishment, if the list of captains on the half-pay here should not furnish out captains enough that are proper for the thirty-four additional companies, I should be obliged to your Excellency to think of him for a captain's commission, in some of them, and his place may be filled by some lieutenant on the half-pay.

To the Archbishop of Canterbury.

My Lord,   *Dublin, Jan.* 24, 1726.

I THANK your Grace for your opinion about matrimonial cases, which I had done sooner, but that your letter has been mislaid.

I find

I find by the King's fpeech and addreffes of both houfes, with the other accounts of things, that it is very probable we fhall have a war, fince there feems to be nothing wanting on the part of our adverfaries, but money.   I muft own I am not fo angry on this occafion with the King of *Spain* for his breach of faith, as with the Emperor, who on account of the fervices done him in perfon and his family, lies under the greateft obligations poffible to the kingdom of *England.*

As it is poffible the prefent profpect of affairs may bring on a publick faft in *England*, which will likewife be attended with a faft here, I fhould be very glad in fuch a cafe to have the fame form of prayer ufed here as in *England*, as has been generally practifed ; but then it will be of fome confequence to have that form as foon as may be, that we may print it here, and have our faft as near the day appointed in *England* as we can.

I muft on this occafion defire the favour of your Grace to furnifh me with fuch a form, if there fhould be a faft, and to let me know before-hand in what time after the faft is once fixed, I may hope to receive it.   As what is particular on fuch occafions is only proper pfalms, leffons, collects, gofpel and epiftle, with fome few refponfes, an account of them may be eafily tranfmitted with a letter, as foon as they are fixed in *England*, without ftaying for a printed copy.

I am, &c.

To

To the Duke of Newcastle.

My Lord,   *Dublin, Jan.* 26, 1726.

AS his Grace of *Dublin* * has of late been pretty much out of order, though I cannot hear for certain that he is in any great danger, several letters may go from hence representing him as dying. That such accounts may not occasion any hasty measures being taken, I must beg leave to suggest, that the archbishoprick is a place of very great importance, and a good agreement betwixt the Primate and the Archbishop is of great consequence to the *English* interest here; I would therefore humbly intreat that no steps may be taken about appointing his successor, upon any rumours of his death, till my representations on that subject are considered, which I shall not fail to be speedy in sending, whenever it pleases God to remove his Grace.   I am,

Your Grace's, &c.

To Lord Carteret.

My Lord,   *Dublin, Jan.* 26, 1726.

I HAVE had the honour of your Excellency's of the 21st, and as far as I can hear, the late promotions on the Bishop's bench are very agreeable to the generality; I have not heard of any who has found fault with them but the Archbishop of *Dublin*.   As his Grace is at present very ill, it is possible there may be occasion for speedily thinking of a successor for him.   If it please God to remove him, your Excellency shall have my thoughts by the first opportunity.   I shall take the first time that offers to tell the

new

* Dr. *King*.

new Bifhop of *Meath* what your Excellency fays :
I believe he is very fenfible how very much he is
obliged to your Lordfhip for his tranflation, and that
if the recommendations or wifhes of fome in power
here could have prevailed, that bifhoprick had gone
another way.

I can guefs at the folicitations your Lordfhip muft
have about Dean *Howard's* preferments, by the fhare
I have had here to get me to write to your Excellency about them.

I have enquired about St. *Werburg's*, and am told
the value of it is about 250 *l. per ann.* and St.
Audoen's, which Mr *Synge* now has, is near 200 *l.
per ann.* But though the removing to St. *Werburg's*
without *Finglafs*, will be no great advancement in
point of profit, yet as it is a more creditable poft,
and has been ufually a ftep to a bifhoprick, and as
Mr. *Synge* is engaged in a great quarrel with his
prefent parifhioners, I believe he will hardly refufe
to remove to St. *Werburg's* alone ; and as your Excellency obferves, he may have it made up another
time : as to his living of St. *Audoen*, by his promotion it will come to the difpofal of the Archbifhop of
Dublin, and whether he will give it to Mr. *Ward* I
cannot tell ; indeed if his Grace fhould drop, and
Mr. *Synge* be removed during the vacancy, St.
Audoen's will come to your Excellency's difpofal.

I have not had an opportunity of enquiring of the
Bifhop of *Fernes* about Mr. *Saurin,* whom I do not
know, but have heard much of his brother at the
Hague.

I know Mr. *Mitchel* very well, and take him to be
a worthy gentleman, and think as he does, that fome
other truftee would be more proper than Mr.
Williams.

I am forry Mr. *Weft's* circumftances come out fo
bad, that his widow and children do certainly want
fome help ; but as we reckon he muft have received
above

above 6000 *l.* by his being Lord Chancellor, it is hardly believed here that he could worst his circumstances by coming hither.

Beside the parish of *Drogheda,* Dr. *Wye* who is lately dead, was possessed of the parish of *Dunleer* in that neighbourhood, and of two or three little parishes that were supposed to be united to *Dunleer,* which is in the gift of one Mr. *Tenison,* who derives his title from the Lord *Dartmouth :* upon Dr. *Wye*'s death it comes out that my Lord *Dartmouth* had only a grant of the patronage of *Dunleer* from the crown, and that the patronage of some or all the other parishes does not appear to have been granted away by the crown, in whom it was by the forfeiture of the old patrons ; that Dr. *Wye* was presented to *Dunleer* by my Lord *Dartmouth,* before he parted with the estate there, that the Dr. having no competitor, took the other parishes, which had been enjoyed by his predecessor, and held them till death : but as it does not appear that those parishes have ever been united as the law directs, or that the right of the crown, if any union was, has been considered and settled by having a proper share of turns, a caveat is entered with me, to institute nobody either to *Dunleer* or the supposed union, till enquiry is made what is the true state of this affair : and I would beg of your Excellency not to make any promise of the King's turn to the whole or any part of that supposed union, till the affair is better understood. As this discovery is made by Dr. *Wye*'s family, who has left eight or nine children unprovided for, and one of them a clergyman of sober life and good character, (who was his father's curate at *Dunleer)* your Excellency will be pleased to consider how far it may be proper to do somewhat for him, if those livings or some of them should appear to be in the gift of the crown.

I am, &c.

To

To the Duke of Newcastle.

My Lord,   *Dublin, Feb. 2,* 1726.

SINCE I had the honour of giving your Grace an account of the Archbishop of *Dublin*'s illness, he has been for some days thought past recovery, but is now looked upon by all to be out of danger for the present ; if any alteration should happen, I will give your Grace advice of it.

I am sorry that we had occasion to send off a flying packet last night to my Lord Lieutenant, with an account that the men of war and transports designed for *Gibraltar* are driven back to *Cork*, and that two of the transports are missing, and one of the men of war disabled for present service : I would hope by the news from *England* this day, that those forces will not be wanted at *Gibraltar* so soon as was apprehended.

I am, my Lord, &c.

To Lord Townshend.

My Lord,   *Dublin, Feb. 2,* 1726.

IT is a great pleasure to all his Majesty's friends here to hear what vigour and resolution both houses of parliament shew in defence of his Majesty, and the support of those wise measures he has taken in the perplexed state of affairs into which the union betwixt the Emperor and *Spain* has brought all *Europe.*

I am too sensible of the great load of business your Lordship must have on your hands at such a juncture, to trouble you about so small an affair as is the subject of this letter, without first begging your
pardon ;

pardon ; but I hope the concern I have for my friend will be thought a juft excufe.

I have advices from feveral hands, that fome are forming fchemes to put Mr. *Stephens* by the next canonry of *Chrift Church* which may become vacant, under the fpecious pretence of an equivalent.

As the firft promife was made me for him near three years ago, upon my giving way to Dr. *Foulkes* having the next turn there, which he has fince had, and was again renewed to me before I left *England*, I muft put myfelf under your Lordfhip's care for having a fpecifick performance of the canonry promifed Mr. *Stephens*.

Whoever they are that make a pufh for their friends in oppofition to him, I am fure they cannot have a greater zeal for his Majefty's fervice than I have ; and I queftion whether they are in pofts where they have greater opportunities of ferving his Majefty than the ftation his Majefty has been gracioufly pleafed to beftow on me ; and I hope I have not been behind them in the fuccefs I have had in my endeavours to promote his Majefty's fervice here. Mr. *Stephens* is the only clergyman I fhall defire to be provided for in *England* by his Majefty's favour ; and I intreat your Lordfhip to fupport the promife you was fo good as to make me.

I am, &c.

To Lord Carteret.

My Lord, *Dublin, Feb.* 9, 1726.

I Received your Excellency's kind letter of the 2d inftant, and am very much obliged to your Lordfhip for your friendfhip in relation to the filling up of the archbifhoprick of *Dublin* whenever it happens to be vacant : your Lordfhip was very good in the difcourfe you had with one of the minifters, and

I hope

I hope they will confider what you reprefented, that it will be for his Majefty's fervice to appoint fuch an Archbifhop as I can depend upon for acting in concert with me. I am entirely of opinion that the new Archbifhop ought to be an *Englifhman*, either already on the bench here, or in *England :* as for a native of this country, I can hardly doubt but whatever his behaviour has been or his promifes may be, when he is once in that ftation, he will put himfelf at the head of the *Irifh* intereft in the church at leaft ; and he will naturally carry with him the college and moft of the clergy here. I am fatisfied the perfon Mr. *Conolly* wants to have in that ftation, is the Bifhop of *Elphin*, whom your Excellency knows as well as I do. As for one on the bench in *England*, I hope the miniftry will never think of fending any body hither, becaufe he is reftlefs there, fince his reftleffnefs there will have no confequence to the publick, but he may here be fure of a diffatisfied party to head.

His Grace of *Dublin* tells every body the bifhop of *Briftol* has a promife of being his fucceffor, which I fhould be very forry to find true.

Since the Archbifhop's illnefs I have talked with the new Bifhop of *Derry* *, and acquainted him what your Excellency had told me formerly of your kind intentions in relation to him, for which he expreffed the greateft thankfulnefs, but faid, he was by his late tranflation made fo very eafy, that he fhould defire to be excufed from any farther remove ; which I find were your Lordfhip's thoughts about him.

About ten days ago I wrote to a Bifhop in *England*, and another in *Ireland*, to know their thoughts about removing to *Dublin*, if a vacancy fhould happen, but

---

* Dr. *Downes*, father of Dr. *Downes*, late Bifhop of *Raphoe*, a fon who even did honour to fuch a father.

but have not yet received any anfwer from either of them : what I propofed to myfelf was to be able to lay down two fchemes, either for one of the bench here or one in *England* to have *Dublin*, as foon as I could have fettled upon receiving their anfwers, and to leave it to the miniftry to judge which they thought moft proper : as foon as I hear from them, I fhall be able to write more explicitly to your Excellency, and do in the mean time defire your friendfhip, that nobody may be pitched upon who may make me uneafy, fince that cannot be done without differving his Majefty.

His Grace is rather better than he has been ; but it is very uncertain whether he may ever come abroad again.

I am fatisfied there will be a good deal of murmuring here to fee the archbifhoprick filled with an *Englifhman*, but I think it is a poft of that confe-quence, as to be worth filling aright, though it fhould occafion murmuring.

I thank your Lordfhip for keeping yourfelf on the referve about *Dunleer*, till that affair is better cleared up, and your difpofition to confider young *Wye* if there be room for it.

We have a report here that Mr. *Saurin* is to have the chancellorfhip of St. *Patrick*'s, which as it is ei-ther infeperably annexed to St. *Werburg's*, or will leave St. *Werburg's* not worth Mr. *Synge's* removing to, if it can be feparated from it, I fufpect to be a miftake for the chantorfhip of *Chrift Church*.

I had yefterday a letter from Mrs. *Weft* *, that fhe hears from *London*, that the penfion to be granted her is likely to be only during pleafure ; fhe is very willing to take it fo, rather than have the affair de-layed for any length of time, but would be very glad if it might be obtained, as was at firft propofed, for
a certain

* Widow of the late Chancellor of that name.

a certain term of years; and seems very apprehensive
that upon her death, without a fresh application of
friends, it might drop in the new way; I sent her
word, that a great many pensions on this establishment, granted only during pleasure, were paid as regularly for many years, as if they had been first
granted for a certain-term; and that as the pension
was to be vested in trustees, her death I thought
would make no change if the children were then living, but that I would write to your Excellency in
her behalf, to get the most advantageous grant for
her.

I must before I conclude, beg pardon of your Excellency for giving you the trouble of so long a letter, and am, with the greatest respect and truth,

My Lord, &c.

P. S. I had forgot to mention to your Excellency
that as the Bishop of *Derry*'s patent was not past till
this week, I believe he cannot receive the *Candlemas*
rents of that bishoprick without a letter from the
treasury in *England* on his behalf; I remember I had
such a letter at my coming hither for the *Lammas*
rents of the primacy: as they amount to near 600 *l.*
which is a sum of consequence to his Lordship, I beg
leave to recommend his case to your Excellency for
obtaining this favour for him.   In *England* there is
a clause of course in the patent for the restitution of
temporalities to any Bishop giving him the profits or
rent that became due during the vacancy.

To the Archbishop of Canterbury.

My Lord,   *Dublin, Feb.* 16, 1726.

I HAVE received your Grace's favour of the 7th,
and thank you for your kind promise of sending
me a copy of the prayers for a fast in MS. as soon as
the

the thing is fixed. I do not wonder that we at this diftance are unable to judge whether we are to have peace or war, when thofe at the helm, who know all that paffes, are at a lofs to know which we fhall have. The reafons of the conduct of *Great-Britain* are reprinted here, and have given great fatisfaction to his Majefty's friends: as for others nothing can fatisfy them.

Our late promotions on the bench have been generally well approved of, and the more as two natives of this country have been confidered in them.

His Grace of *Dublin* has been very ill, but feems now to have got over the prefent fhock. I wifh his place may be well filled, whenever it pleafes God to remove him. I am forry to hear your Grace has been out of order this winter, but hope the approaching fpring will entirely fet you up. I thank you for your kind wifhes, and am with the greateft fincerity and refpect,

My Lord, &c.

To the Duke of Newcaftle.

My Lord, *Dublin, Feb.* 18, 1726.

WE were yefterday furprized with the melancholy news that the new * Archbifhop of *Cafhel*, on *Tuefday* morning laft died of an apoplexy at the palace at *Londonderry*. I am very forry we have loft fo learned and worthy a man.

We have been very much teafed with applications on this occafion: the Bifhop of *Kildare*, who is the oldeft Bifhop on the bench here, except the Archbifhop of *Dublin*, would willingly remove thither; I muft

---

* Dr. *William Nicholfon*, author of an *Englifh, Scotch* and *Irifh* Hiftorical Library. He was tranflated from *Carlifle* to *Derry*, and from thence to *Cafhel*, and died the month following.

I muſt do him the juſtice to ſay, he is an hearty *Engliſhman*, and I believe a thorough enemy to the pretender, his only fault is, that he is rather counted a tory here : if he were thought of, the * biſhoprick of *Kildare* and deanery of *Chriſt Church* will come to be diſpoſed of : if he is not thought of, and the archbiſhoprick of *Caſhel* be filled from hence, I ſhould recommend the † Biſhop of *Kilmore* for *Caſhel*, the § Biſhop of *Fernes* for *Kilmore*, and the Biſhop of *Clonfert* for *Fernes* ; and out of conſideration of his brother Sir *Ralph Gore*, Chancellor of the Exchequer, the Dean of *Down* for the biſhoprick of *Clonfert*.

But as we are now but nine *Engliſh* Biſhops on the bench here out of two and twenty ; I muſt inform your Grace that I think it would be for his Majeſty's ſervice to fill *Caſhel* from the bench in *England*, or to ſend one from *England* to the biſhoprick vacant by any tranſlations made here : if the firſt is done I hope nobody will be ſent hither from the bench in *England* for being reſtleſs or good for nothing there, or who is not likely to agree with me, ſince this will certainly weaken the *Engliſh* intereſt here. If the latter method be taken, I hope a divine of ſome character will be ſent hither, ſince the encouragement is not contemptible, *Kildare* and *Chriſt Church* being worth 1600 *l. per ann.* and *Clonfert* worth better than 1200 *l. per ann.*

I hope likewiſe that whatever recommendations go from hence, none but a native of *England* will be thought of for *Caſhel*.

I am, my Lord, &c.

To

* Dr. *Welbore Ellis*.
† Dr. *Timothy Godwin*.
§ Dr. *Joſiah Hort*.

To Lord Carteret.

My Lord,   *Dublin,* Feb. 18, 1726.

WE had yesterday the melancholy news, that the Archbishop of *Cashel* died of an apoplexy on *Tuesday* morning last at *Londonderry.* I am afraid his family will lose about 500 *l.* by his late translation.

Upon this vacancy of the Archbishoprick, the Bishop of *Kildare* has been with me and the other Lords Justices, and desires to be considered as being the oldest bishop on the bench except his Grace of *Dublin :* he is upon all occasions a most hearty *Englishman,* and I believe an enemy to the pretender ; but your Excellency knows he is rather a tory.

The Bishop of *Kilmore* is the next *Englishman,* that may be thought of, and I scarce doubt but he would take *Cashel,* though he is not here to be asked the question.

The Bishop of *Fernes* would either take *Cashel,* if the Bishop of *Kilmore* should be unwilling to remove, or take *Kilmore* if he accepts *Cashel.*

The Bishop of *Clonfert* would be very glad to succeed the Bishop of *Fernes,* though he will hardly gain any thing by the remove ; but as he has the rectory of *Louth* in commendam, which whenever he leaves it, will fall into the vicarage, and not come to the government to dispose of, he would desire to keep that, without having the commendam the present Bishop of *Fernes* enjoys : and in this case there will be a benefice of 290 *l. per ann.* to be given either as a commendam to the new Bishop of *Clonfert,* or as your Excellency shall judge proper.

For the bishoprick of *Clonfert* there are several who would gladly succeed to it. Dean *Daniel,* Dean *Dobbins,* Dean *Crofs,* but as Sir *Ralph Gore* has been
with

with the Lords Juftices to recommend his brother the Dean of *Down* to the bifhoprick that fhall be left vacant upon other tranflations, and anfwers for his brother's behaviour : I think it will be moft advifeable to gratify Sir *Ralph Gore*.

But if the Bifhop of *Kildare* fhould be tranflated to *Cafhel*, I could wifh fome *Englifhman* were to fucceed him ; and if it were one that would be a proper perfon to fucceed to *Dublin* upon a vacancy it would be the lefs invidious, but in that view it ought to be one from the bench in *England*, which it may very well be, fince *Kildare* and *Chrift Church* are a good 1600 *l. per annum*.

Though the Bifhop of *Elphin* is mentioned in our common letter, and probably Mr. *Conolly* may write in his behalf, yet I believe your Excellency will be of my opinion, that it will be too dangerous a ftep to truft him in that poft.

My Lord Chancellor and I have been computing, that if fome perfon be not now brought over from *England* to the bench, there will be thirteen * *Irifh* to nine *Englifh* Bifhops here, which we think will be a dangerous fituation.

Upon the encouragement your Excellency has given me, I take the liberty to acquaint you, that the oldeft friend I have on the bench in *England*, is Dr.

V o l. I.   H   *Smalbroke,*

* *February*, 1770. At this time there are but two archbifhops, natives of *Ireland*, Dr. *Arthur Smith* of *Dublin*, and Dr. *Michael Cox* of *Cafhel.* The fix fuffragan bifhops, are, the honourable and right reverend Dr. *Henry Maxwell*, of *Meath*, Dr. *Jemmet Browne*, of *Cork*, Dr. *Nicholas Synge*, of *Killaloo*, Dr. *James Leflie*, of *Limerick*, Dr. *William Gore*, of *Elphin*, and Dr. *Charles Agar*, of *Cloyne.* There was at one time in the Houfe of Lords of *Ireland*, a majority of native bifhops ; all of whom were gentlemen of good families, of the greateft charity, piety and learning, among which were five, who had been fellows of the univerfity, to wit, Dr. *Howard* of *Elphin*, Dr. *Edward Synge*, of *Clonfert*, Dr. *Clayton*, of *Cork*, Dr. *Whetcombe*, Archbifhop of *Cafhel*, and Dr. *Berkeley*, Bifhop of *Cloyne.*

Smalbroke, Bishop of St. *David's*, and that I should be very glad to see him here; he has heard very ill reports of the air of *Dublin*, and been frighted with paying down 2000 *l.* for buildings on that archbishoprick. But possibly he may not be afraid of *Cashel*, which is most certainly in a good air, and where there is nothing to pay. I shall by this post write to him, to wait on your Excellency to deliver his own sentiments.

I should be satisfied if the Bishop of *Glocester* or *Bangor* were sent hither either on this occasion, or to *Dublin* when it falls, but I have formerly mentioned * two on the bench to your Lordship, whom I should be sorry to see here.

I am, &c.

To the Bishop of London.

My Lord,   *Dublin, Feb.* 11, 1726.

I AM sorry that I have occasion to acquaint your Lordship, that your very good friend the Archbishop of *Cashel*, was on *Tuesday* morning last found dead on the floor in his room at *Londonderry*: we have lost a very worthy man, and I fear his family will lose 500 *l.* by his late translation. The scheme I would recommend if the Archbishoprick of *Cashel* is to be filled up from hence, is the Bishop of *Kilmore* to have *Cashel*, the Bishop of *Fernes* to have *Kilmore*, and the Bishop of *Clonfert* to have *Fernes*, and on account of the worth and interest of his brother Sir *Ralph Gore*, Chancellor of the Exchequer here, the Dean of *Down* to have the bishoprick of *Clonfert*.

But

* The Bishop of *Bristol* was certainly one of the two.

But I muſt own as by the death of Archbiſhop *Nicholſon* there are but nine *Engliſh* Biſhops on the bench here, and by this ſcheme there will be thirteen *Iriſh*, I cannot but think it will be moſt for his Majeſty's ſervice either to ſend one from the bench in *England* to *Caſhel* or *Kilmore*, (which latter is worth about 2000 *l. per ann.*) or elſe to put an *Engliſhman* into *Clonfert*, that the *Engliſh* intereſt may not decreaſe here. Your Lordſhip knows the oldeſt friend I have on the bench is the Biſhop of St. *David*'s, whom I ſhould be glad to ſee here; but I hope if he is not ſent, no perſon will be ſent hither for being reſtleſs and uneaſy there, or good for nothing, or that is not likely to agree with me.

The Biſhop of *Kildare* would gladly go to *Caſhel*, who is the ſenior on the bench, except the Archbiſhop of *Dublin*; he is a hearty *Engliſhman*, and I believe an utter enemy to the pretender, but he is counted a tory here. If he ſhould be tranſlated to *Caſhel*, his biſhoprick and the deanery of *Chriſt Church* are worth an *Engliſhman*'s coming for, being a good 1600 *l. per ann.*

Mr. *Soal*, formerly of *Magdalen* College, and in your Lordſhip's former dioceſe of *Lincoln*, would I do not queſtion willingly take the biſhoprick of *Clonfert*, which is better than 1200 *l. per ann.* or *Kildare* and *Chriſt Church*; your Lordſhip knows him very well, but I ſhould be ſorry to have ſome weak perſon ſent hither.

As I do not know but very preſſing inſtances may be made from hence, to have the Biſhop of * *Elphin* tranſlated to *Caſhel*, I muſt acquaint your Lordſhip that he is an enterprizing man, and I do not doubt but he would ſoon ſet himſelf, if he had

H 2 that

* Dr. *Theophilus Bolton*, a man of great learning, and vaſt abilities.

that ftation, at the head of the *Irifh* intereft here *.
I am,

My Lord, &c.

To Lord Carteret.

My Lord,　　　　　　　　*Dublin, Mar.* 7, 1726.

I HAD this day the honour of two of your Excellency's, one of the 21ft, the other of the
25th of *February* laft.

Since I wrote to your Lordfhip about Mr. *Wye*,
Mr. Prime Serjeant has been with me, in favour of
a brother of his, who has a living of about 100 *l.
per ann.* in my gift, which he would willingly quit
for *Dunleer*, if it be in the gift of the crown. It is
not for the advantage in point of profit that he
would make the exchange, but that he would come
nearer *Drogheda*, where he was born, and where
fome of his relations live; he is an elderly batchelor in very good circumftances, and I hope
has generofity enough to be perfuaded to build a
parfonage houfe at *Dunleer*, if he had that living.
As I know the regard your Excellency has for the
Prime Serjeant, and as I fhould be willing myfelf to
oblige both him and his brother, and as in this
fcheme Mr. *Wye* will have a living with a parfonage houfe upon it, as there is on Mr. *Singleton's* prefent living, I did not difcourage the Prime Serjeant
from writing to your Lordfhip in favour of his brother; and if I fee Mr. *Wye* before I know your farther pleafure, I will tell him I have heard from your
Excellency, that if *Dunleer* is in the gift of the
crown, fome provifion fhall be made for him.

The Crown-follicitor has been ordered to attend
me, to have inftructions from me what enquiries he

is

---

* He did fo when he was afterwards made Archbifhop of
Cafhel, to his great honour, and the benefit of his country.

is to make in the offices, to know whether the crown has a right to *Dunleer* or not : but he has not yet come near me ; I shall endeavour to quicken him, and as soon as we know any thing certain in this affair, we shall acquaint your Lordship with it.

I think his Majesty's grant to Mrs. *West* is very kind, and though it be during pleasure, will probably be continued as long as she lives, or her children can be supposed to want it ; and I fear if it had been for a certain term of years, and had not been vested in proper trustees, it had soon been sold for ready money.

As to a memorial from the Bishop of * *Derry*, I remember I had the quarter due in the vacancy granted me, without a memorial. We shall to-morrow acquaint your Lordship with the vacancy of the living in that diocese, of which I thought we had wrote by the same post as the Bishop.

I am very much obliged to your Lordship for the kind discourse you had with the Bishop of St. *David's*, and find him not so much afraid of *Ireland* as he was before ; when I have sent him some particulars about the archbishoprick of *Dublin*, which he wants to know, I believe he will be very well satisfied about taking *Dublin* if he can, when it falls ; and I shall be very much obliged to your Excellency for your kind concurrence on that occasion.

§ I find your Lordship of different sentiments from what I have about filling *Cashel* ; I should have been very glad if it had fallen at any time when I could have had a personal conference with you on that subject. I rather think the Bishop of *Elphin* should be kept longer in a state of probation ; I am satisfied
                                                        his

---

* Dr. *Henry Downs*, who was translated from *Meath* to this Bishoprick.

§ My Lord Primate's opinion prevailed at this time.

his great friend is Mr. *Conolly*, and that moſt of
thoſe who follicited here for him, were ſet on by
him ; but it is with great ſatisfaction that I find you
think it is not convenient to place him in the ſee of
Dublin ; and indeed I think none but a native of
England ought to be in that ſtation.

I ſhall cheerfully ſhew what countenance I can to
the gentlemen you are pleaſed to name for the Biſhop of *Killala*'s preferments, particularly to Mr.
Saurin, who as being a ſtranger, will moſt want it.
We ſhall to-morrow give the neceſſary orders about
diſpatching their inſtruments. I am,

Your Excellency's, &c.

To Lord Carteret.

My Lord,　　　　　　　*Dublin, Mar.* 11, 1726.

THE occaſion of my troubling your Excellency at this time, is to put you in mind that it
is generally the cuſtom for the Biſhop of *Maath* to
be one of the Privy Council here, which if your
Lordſhip approves of, a warrant might ſoon be ſent
to admit the new Biſhop.

I have lately had ſome diſcourſe with ſome officers
here, who are under great apprehenſions of the difficulty there will be of raiſing in *England* the additional men deſigned for the ſeveral companies here,
after the *Engliſh* levies are made, and the ſummer is
come on ; and they think if care was taken to admit none into the ſervice but proteſtants, who are
the ſons of proteſtants, it might be very eaſy to
raiſe the number wanted in the north of this kingdom, out of perſons very well affected to his Majeſty. As our foot is now reduced to eleven battalions, and there can be no doubt but the emiſſaries
of *Spain* are at work here to diſpoſe the papiſts to
make a diſturbance ; if this method were approved
of,

of, we might foon have our battalions full, to our greater fecurity.

I am, my Lord, &c.

To the Duke of Newcaftle.

My Lord, *Dublin, Mar.* 11, 1726.

I HAVE of late been talking with feveral officers of the army, who are very apprehenfive, that confidering the great levies of men now making in *England,* and that the fummer comes on apace, it will be very difficult to raife the number of men with which our companies are to be augmented, if they are allowed to beat up for volunteers only in *Great Britain :* and they humbly think that if leave were given to raife men in this country, and none to be admitted but fuch as can have good certificates of their being proteftants themfelves, and that their parents were likewife proteftants, it would be eafy in a fhort time to raife the number wanted here, in the north of this kingdom, of men hearty and zealous for his Majefty and his family.

As we have no more than eleven battalions of foot left in this kingdom, it would be of fervice towards keeping things quiet here, to have our companies augmented as foon as may be ; and it would likewife difcourage the papifts from too haftily liftening to the emiffaries of *Spain,* who are no doubt at prefent very bufy amongft them, and giving them hopes of fome difturbance here.

I thought it my duty to tranfmit to your Grace what is fuggefted here, as proper for his Majefty's fervice, but with an entire fubmiffion to better judges.

I am, my Lord, &c.

To

To the Bishop of London.

My Lord,   *Dublin, Mar.* 16, 1726.

I HAVE troubled your Lordship but with one letter about the archbishoprick of *Casbel*, because I supposed that affair would have been soon settled; but as it runs into some length, and we have various reports about it, I shall venture sending this letter, though it may possibly come too late to signify any thing.

All the *English* here think it will be a dangerous step to make the Bishop of *Elphin* Archbishop. As to another scheme wrote from *England*, of sending one from thence either to *Kilmore* or *Fernes*, as it will be one who is not on the bench in *England*, I think he may very well begin with *Clonfert*, which is worth 1500 *l. per ann.* and hardly 100 *l. per ann.* less than *Fernes*, and then three on the bench will be obliged here.

I have by me a letter of your Lordship's, which I shall speedily answer.

I am, &c.

To the same.

My Lord,   *Dublin, Mar.* 18, 1726.

UPON Dr. *Skirret*'s making a jest of my having recommended him to *Killala*, I sent him word that I thought myself discharged from recommending him any more; and I have since given him 100 *l.* to make him amends for his two journies hither; so that I have now done with him.

I do not find we have yet had a new application in form about Mr. *Monroe*'s children; when we have I shall serve them what I can on account of your Lordship's recommendation.

I do

I do not know any thing of the prefent patent here for printing common prayer books : there is one edition in folio here, that is at leaft equal to the beft in *England*. If any fuch application is made as your Lordfhip mentions, I fhall be ready to do any thing that is fair and reafonable for one whom you are pleafed to concern yourfelf for.

We are in great expectation here of what the Commons did laft *Monday* about the Emperor's memorial.

I was in hopes to have heard before this from your Lordfhip, what is doing about the archbifhoprick of *Cafhel*.

I am, &c.

To the Duke of Newcaftle.

My Lord,   *Dublin, Mar.* 30, 1727.

WE have lately received his Majefty's commands about augmenting the eleven battalions here, and have given all the neceffary orders on that occafion, and have the money ready to advance to the recruiting officers.

By the reports we have here, I am afraid Serjeant *Birch* will not come hither, but I hope my Lord Chancellor will fend us one in his room that is thoroughly well affected.

I was in hopes we fhould have known his Majefty's pleafure about the Archbifhoprick of *Cafhel* before this. As there muft have been fome rubs in that affair, I could wifh your Grace had been at leifure to let me know them, and I might poffibly have cleared up any difficulty. I fhould guefs by the flying accounts we have, that the Bifhop of *Kilmore* will be removed to that Archbifhoprick : he is the beft beloved by his Majefty's friends of any that have been mentioned from *England*, as ftanding here in competition for that fee, as well as much fenior to
the

the others, which used to be a consideration of weight in *England* ; and the *English* here think it of great consequence that it should be given to an *Englishman*.

Every thing here is very quiet, except that in spight of all our endeavours, recruits are still going off for *Spain* as well as *France*.

A Bill that is going on in *England* for reversing an outlawry * here, gives very great uneasiness, both as it will affect the possessions of several who have been fair purchasers under the faith of an act of parliament here ; and as it is looked on as a leading case to others of the same nature, which may shake the property of many hundreds in this nation.

I am, &c.

To Lord Carteret.

My Lord,   *Dublin, Mar.* 30, 1727.

I HAD this day the honour of your Excellency's of the 25th ; I am sorry I should be guilty of such a neglect as not to date my letter.

I am now pretty well master of what title the crown has to *Dunleer*, which the Attorney General is persuaded is a very good one. When the Prime Serjeant returns from the circuit, I will talk with him about it, and if his brother is willing to support the title of the crown, as I believe he will, I shall immediately give your Lordship advice of it, in order to receive your commands ; and I shall take care of Mr. *Wye*. When the Attorney General arrives, he will talk with your Lordship about this affair.

Mr. *Gardiner* has the money ordered for the new levies, ready to advance to the officers, and likewise a month's subsistance for *April*, part of which will go for levy money.

We

---

* Supposed to be that of Lord *Clancarty*.

We have signed the proper orders relating to the pay of the four regiments, from *Christmas* to *Lady-day* ; and likewise to place a serjeant, corporal, drummer, and twenty-five private men in each company on the military establishment, from *Lady-day* last.

We have been frequently pressing Mr. *Gardiner* to get the publick accounts ready to be audited as soon as possible ; and he this day told me the remainder of Mr. *Prat*'s accounts, from *Christmas,* 1724, to the time of his being dismissed, are now engrossing ; and that his clerks have almost finished the accounts from thence to *Christmas*, 1725, which he will soon order to be engrossed ; but he thinks that it would save a great deal of trouble, and 300*l.* to the government, if the accounts from *Christmas,* 1725, to *Lady-day*, 1727, were audited at once, and not broke into two audits : but as your Lordship has intimated formerly, you would have them passed from *Christmas*, 1725, to *Lady-day*, 1726, and then from *Lady-day*, 1726, to *Lady-day*, 1727, we shall make no alteration in that method, without knowing your pleasure. My Lord Chief Baron will set about auditing the remainder of Mr. *Prat*'s accounts as soon as the Barons return from their circuits ; and will afterwards make all possible dispatch that the approaching term will allow in auditing the rest of the accounts to *Lady-day* last.

I am glad to find an alteration is made as to the height of the men required in former levies ; since it was thought it would have been pretty difficult to raise the number wanted, if that size had been insisted on.

As the chief reason why a general officer viewed all the recruits as they arrived from *England*, was to see that they answered that standard, your Excellency will be the best judge, whether there will now be any occasion for sending a general officer to *Cork* to view the new levies as they arrive there.

I am

I am forry to hear it reported that Serjeant *Birch* refufes to come hither, but I hope we fhall have another fent us that is thoroughly well affected.

I am, &c.

To the Archbifhop of Canterbury.

My Lord,   *Dublin, Mar.* 1, 1727.

ON *Monday* laft Mr. *Saurin* * came to me with your Grace's letter of the 7th paft; I recommended him to the Bifhop of *Kildare*, who inftalled him on *Thurfday* in the chantorfhip of *Chrift Church*, and is ready to do him what fervice lies in his power. I am glad to hear fo good a character of this gentleman from your Grace, and hope he may be of fervice in this church. I fhall very readily fhew him what favour I can.

I fear, notwithftanding fome accounts from *England* flatter us with the hopes of a peace, we fhall have a war. The Emperor feems by his carriage to be bent on it, and the *Spaniards* have now money to carry it on for fome time. Whenever a war is declared, and a day of fafting fettled in *England*, I fhall expect to be favoured with the form of prayer from your Grace.

What has kept the difpofal of the archbifhoprick of *Cafhel* fo long in fufpence I cannot tell : I hope as fome accounts fuggeft, it will be given to the Bifhop of *Kilmore*, who is very well beloved here, and many years fenior to thofe who are talked of as his competitors. We have loft a very valuable and ufeful perfon in the late Archbifhop of *Cafhel* §.

God

* He was a very worthy *French* refugee.
§ *Nicholfon.*

God preferve his Majefty if he commands abroad, and give him good fuccefs!

I hope your Grace will recover your ftrength as the warm weather comes on, and I heartily wifh you all health and happinefs.   I am,

My Lord, &c.

To the Bifhop of London,

My Lord,   *Dublin, Apr.* 1, 1727.

I HAVE received your Lordfhip's of the 11th paft, by Mr. *Saurin,* and am glad to find he is a gentleman of fo good a character; I have recommended him to the Bifhop of *Kildare,* who is ready to do him any fervice in his power, and has inftalled him laft *Thurfday* in his chantorfhip. I fhall be always ready to fhew him what countenance I can.

I hope the Bifhop of *Kilmore* is to go to *Cafhel,* as our moft authentick accounts run here; there is not one on the bench better beloved by the King's friends here, and he is feveral years fenior to all who are talked of as his competitors. I fhould have been glad to have heard from your Lordfhip pretty early how things were likely to go, but I fuppofe the uncertainty of what was defigned might hinder you from writing.

We a little impatiently expect fome news from *Gibraltar,* though the officers here that have been at that place, give fuch accounts of it, that we are not apprehenfive the *Spaniards* can take it.

I muft defire your Lordfhip's friendfhip to Mr. *Stephens,* in whofe behalf I fome time fince wrote a very preffing Letter to my Lord *Townfhend.*

I am, &c.

To

To Lord Carteret.

My Lord,   *Dublin, Apr.* 1, 1727.

THOUGH we have in common this day put your Excellency in mind of our being without any guard against *Spanish* privateers, yet I cannot help farther suggesting, that there is no doubt but that we have too many here who neither want the disposition nor opportunity to give an account of our nakedness to *Spain*, and that it may be a temptation to the enemy, if it be only for the disgrace of the thing, to come and insult us in the very harbour of *Dublin*.

I am, &c.

To the Bishop of London.

My Lord,   *Dublin, Apr.* 25, 1727.

AS I have heard nothing from your Lordship since mine of the first instant, and as we have not yet had any orders about the archbishoprick of *Cashel*, I cannot help writing a line or two more on that subject, though it may possibly come too late.

It is reported here that our Speaker has wrote that the House of Commons will be very much disobliged if the Bishop of *Elphin* has not *Cashel*. I am on the contrary assured, that among the whigs of that house, setting aside the Speaker's creatures and dependants, there is hardly one who will not be better pleased to have the Bishop of *Kilmore* made Archbishop than the Bishop of *Elphin*.

I must likewise inform you, that I have discoursed with every *Englishman* of consequence in this town, whether clergy or laity, and can assure you that there is not one who is not of opinion that the giving the
                                                        arch-

archbifhoprick to Bifhop *Bolton* will be a very great blow to the *Englifh* intereft in this kingdom. I would beg of your Lordfhip if the affair be not over, to reprefent this to the miniftry.

I fhall likewife write a letter to the Duke of *New-caftle*, to defire the miniftry to confider who is the proper perfon to recommend to bifhopricks here, an *Irifh* Speaker, or an *Englifh* Primate *. I fhall trouble your Grace no farther at prefent, and am,

My Lord, &c.

To Lord Carteret.

My Lord,   *Dublin*, *Apr.* 27, 1727.

SINCE the Prime Serjeant † is returned from the circuit, he has been looking over the title of the crown to the living of *Dunleer* and the other parifhes that are, or are fuppofed to be united to it; and is defirous to have a prefentation to them for his brother *John Singleton*. As we are not well able to fettle whether they are rectories or vicarages, or which are one which the other, he thinks it will be fafeft if your Excellency pleafes to direct that Mr. *John Singleton* be prefented to the parifhes of *Dunleer*, *Capoche*, *Difert*, *Moylare*, *Drumcarre*, and *Monafterboys*, and againft the patent is drawn, we will take care to give every parifh its proper title of rectory or vicarage.

I begin now to be preffed by the clerk prefented by Mr. *Tenifon*, who has this day brought his prefenta-

---

* Bifhop *Bolton* was at this time fet afide, and Dr. *Godwin*, Bifhop of *Kilmore* appointed; but afterwards the neceffity of affairs required, as the Primate thought, that Bifhop *Bolton* fhould be appointed, and it was accordingly done; but the government had reafon afterwards to repent of what they then did.

† *Singleton.*

fentation ; and, would willingly have a prefentation from the crown to oppofe to theirs, as foon as may be. I have ftill very good reafon to believe the title to all to be in the crown, or at leaft this turn, if there has been a valid union ; and if not, all are certainly in the crown, except *Dunleer*. I am,

My Lord, &c.

To the Duke of Newcaftle.

My Lord,   *Dublin, Apr.* 29, 1727.

THE bearer colonel *Cavallier* * defired I would favour him with a letter to introduce him to your Grace ; if there had been occafion to raife any new regiments, he would have been glad to have ferved his Majefty at this juncture in the new levies. As there has been lately a promotion of general officers, and fome of his juniors have been made brigadiers, he comes over to *England* in hopes that it was purely his being out of the way that made him be forgotten. The figure he made, and the faithfulnefs and the courage with which he ferved the crown in the laft war, are the occafion of my recommending him to your Grace's favour and protection in this affair, though it be fo much out of my fphere. I am,

Your Grace's, &c.

To

* *N. B.* This is that colonel *Cavallier* who made fo great a figure in the *Cevennes,* againft the powerful armies of *France ;* he was in fome refpects the *Paoli* of thofe days.

To *Lord* Townſhend.

My Lord,   *Dublin, May* 9, 1727.

WE were for two or three poſts here under a very great concern upon the news we received of the dangerous ſtate of health Sir *Robert Walpole* was in : his death will at any time be a very great loſs, but we could not but eſteem it a more than or-dinary ſtroke, if it had happened at this critical con-juncture. As our repeated accounts from *England* now give us aſſurance that he is out of all danger, I can-not omit congratulating your Lordſhip on the happy occaſion of his recovery, which muſt be a great ſa-tisfaction to you, both on account of the private re-lation and friendſhip between you *, and your Lord-ſhip's concern for the publick intereſt.

I am, &c.

To *Lord* Carteret.

My Lord,   *Dublin, May* 9, 1727.

WE had this morning advice that Mr. *Forbes* is dead : he was Vicar of *Dunboyne* cum *Kilbride*, and miniſter of *Ballymagleſſan*, both in the diocefe of *Meath :* the former is reputed to be worth 150 or 160 *l. per ann.* and is undoubtedly in the gift of the crown : the latter is worth about 60 *l. per ann.* and is ſuppoſed to be in the gift of the crown, but is claimed by the Biſhop of *Meath*, as being in his patronage. As we do not meet till to-

Vo l. I.   I   morrow,

---

* Theſe two friends and brothers-in-law unhappily differed af-terwards. Lord *Townſhend* retired into the country, and was the greateſt improver of Land ever known in *Norfolk ;* he introduced the cultivation of turnips.

morrow, I was willing to give your Excellency the earlieſt advice I could of this vacancy.

The Biſhop of * *Meath* has been with me to deſire I would recommend Dr. *Philip Whittingham* for the vicarage of *Dunboyne* cum *Kilbride* : if he is preferred to it, he muſt quit the pariſh of *Moyliſker* in *Weſt Meath*, worth from 80 to 100 *l. per ann.* which is likewiſe in the gift of the crown, to which the Biſhop would willingly recommend Mr. *Hugh Vaughan*, whom we have formerly recommended to your Excellency for ſome ſmall living.

I know Dr. *Whittingham* to be a very worthy man, who has a wife and ſeveral children ; and Mr. *Vaughan* is one of a good character. The Chancellor of the Exchequer and Dr. *Coghill* have been with me likewiſe to recommend Mr. *Rogers*, Fellow of the College, to the living of *Ballymagleſſan* ; † (he is one of a very fair character) if that living be in the gift of the crown.

This evening Mr. Dean *Winter* has been with me, to apply for Mr. *Horner* to ſucceed to the living of *Dunboyne*, and himſelf to ſucceed to the living of *Clayne*, which Mr. *Horner* now has. *Dunboyne* is better than *Clayne*, and beſide there is a powerful popiſh gentleman in *Clayne* pariſh, that gives Mr. *Horner* a great deal of trouble, and whom the Dean will be better able to deal with, as he is a native, and one of a good eſtate.

As for the Dean and Mr. *Horner*, your Excellency knows them both ſo well, that I need ſay nothing of them. I am,

My Lord, &c.

To

---

* Dr. *Ralph Lambert*.

† My Lord Primate provided for this gentleman afterwards with one of his own livings : he was eſteemed much.

To the same.

My Lord,   *Dublin, May* 13, 1727.

I HAD the honour of your Excellency's of the 6th, and we have likewife had your order about Mr. *Singleton*'s prefentation.   I have been for near three months preffing the proper officers to get the papers out of the Rolls office, that will fhew whether Mr. *Tenifon* has any title to *Dunleer*, or whether it is in the crown : but partly with the affizes intervening and partly the natural lazinefs of people here, I have not yet compaffed it ; but on *Wednefday* next am promifed this affair fhall come before the Attorney-General in form, and if he reports the patronage to be in the crown, we fhall prefent Mr. *Singleton* to it. I fhall take care of Mr. *Wye* on this occafion, according to my promife.

We have fpared no preffing to get Mr. *Pratt*'s affairs ended, and hope in a little time to fell his eftate. There fhall be nothing wanting on our parts to finifh his matters, and to have Mr. *Gardiner*'s * account paffed to *Lady-day* laft, before your Excellency's arrival here.

Your Lordfhip will by this poft receive an account of what recruits are arrived here already ; and we fhall ftill fend frefh accounts every fortnight according to your order.

I am, &c.

I 2   *To*

* Mr. *Gardiner* fucceeded Mr. *Pratt* ; the firft named perhaps the beft ; the laft the worft Deputy Vice-Treafurer that ever was in *Ireland.*

To the Duke of Newcastle,

My Lord,   Dublin, May 20, 1727.

I HAVE so long forborn troubling your Grace about the archbishoprick of *Casbel*, in expectation of our speedily receiving his Majesty's commands about it ; but as no orders are yet come, and the reports we have here about what is intended are various, and his Majesty's speedy going abroad must occasion some determination in that affair very soon, your Grace will excuse my giving you this trouble to renew my recommendations of Dr. *Godwin*, Bishop of *Kilmore*, to the archbishoprick of *Casbel*, and of Dr. *Hort*, Bishop of *Fernes*, to the bishopricks of *Kilmore* and *Ardagh*.

The present Bishop of *Kilmore* has been some years longer on the bench than any that have been talked of for the archbishoprick ; and is, I may safely say, the best beloved by his Majesty's friends here, of any *English* Bishop : the Bishop of *Fernes* is senior to the Bishop of *Elphin*.

If it be designed I should have that weight with the Bishops as to dispose them to unite in his Majesty's service here, I think my recommendation ought to be regarded on this occasion ; and I can assure your Grace, it is not any particular friendship to the Bishop of *Kilmore*, but a regard to his worth, and to the most likely method of keeping up a good understanding among his Majesty's friends on the bench, that makes me so hearty in recommending him. I hope I may depend on your Grace's friendship to support me in this affair, and shall always remain,

My Lord, &c.

To

To the same.

My Lord,   *Dublin, May,* 23, 1727.

I Should sooner have acknowledged the receipt of your Grace's recommendation of the 11th inst. but that upon speaking to my Lord Chancellor about the * Lady *Tyrconnel's* affair, he told me he had lately increased the number of delegates in her cause, and that he would immediately acquaint your Grace with it.   As the affair lay wholly in my Chancellor's power, and was over before your Grace's writing, I had not an opportunity of shewing my readiness to comply with your recommendations on this occasion, but when I have, I shall always shew that

I am, &c.

To the Archbishop of Canterbury.

My Lord,   *Dublin, May* 23, 1727.

I Had the honour of your Grace's of the 25th past ; and am of your opinion that it would have been better to have held a fast at the beginning of the sessions : but I suppose the ministry might fear that such a step would have been interpreted a sure prognostick of a war, and might have given a shock to publick credit.   I am sorry that the blame of this omission is unjustly thrown on your Grace.

I find by the King's speech, it is still uncertain whether we shall have peace or war ; if the latter, I depend on your goodness to send me the form of prayer for the fast.

We

* Relict of the Duke of *Tyrconnel,* who succeeded Lord *Clarendon* as Lord Lieutenant of *Ireland* in the reign of *James* II. Her Grace was a sister to *Sarah,* Dutchess of *Marlborough.*

We have yet no orders about *Cashel*, and I am forry that my Lord Lieutenant * fhould infift fo much for one, who is much a junior, and as dangerous an *Irifhman* as any on the bench.

I have heard your Grace has been out of order of late, but at the fame time I had the fatisfaction to be informed that you was pretty well again. I heartily wifh your Grace all health and happinefs, and am,

My Lord, &c.

To Lord Carteret.

My Lord,   *Dublin, May* 30, 1727.

LAST *Saturday* we fent your Excellency a memorial relating to the living of *Cabirconglifb* in the diocefe of *Cafhel,* fallen to the crown by the vacancy of the archbifhoprick. Mr. *Hugh Vaughan,* whom your Excellency named to Mr. *Samfon*'s living in *Cork,* if it had been in the gift of the crown, has been with me this evening to defire me to recommend him for this living, and will to-morrow deliver in a memorial on that fubject, which we fhall tranfmit to your Lordfhip ; but as he hears the former memorialift is gone for *England* to folicit for it, he was defirous another poft might not be loft.

I underftand we fhall have a third memorial from Mr. *Gregory,* who has been curate there for fome years, which we fhall likewife fend your Excellency.

* *N. B.* The Lord Lieutenant did not then carry his point againft the Primate, though he had the affiftance of the Speaker to back his recommendation ; Bifhop *Bolton* was a high tory, and a great friend of Dean *Swift*'s, and was undoubtedly a man of abilities ; more need not be faid, as his true character may be eafily drawn from thefe letters.

cy.   I hear the the living is worth from 160 to 200 l. *per ann.*

I am, &c.

To Lord Carteret.

My Lord,   *Dublin, June* 4, 1727.

YESTERDAY we had advice that Mr. Juftice * *Parnell* was dead at his houfe in the country.   Mr. Prime Serjeant, the Attorney and Sollicitor-General, have made no application about fucceeding to his place :   but I hear they have not made very pofitive declarations againft accepting it.   Mr. *Dixon,* who has a very good character both for his abilities and for his affection to his Majefty, has made fome application to be recommended ;   and the Lords Juftices are difpofed to recommend him,   if thofe above-mentioned are not for removing ;   which, I find, as the feffion of parliament is coming on, it is rather wifhed they may not defire.   But I find we all think, as term is over, and confidering the prefent circumftances,   it may be better to keep that place open for fome time.

My Lord Chancellor will write more fully on this fubject to your Excellency.   I am,

My Lord, &c.

To the Duke of Newcaftle.

My Lord,   *Dublin, June* 6, 1727.

I AM fenfible of the trouble I have lately given your Grace with repeated letters relating to the archbifhoprick of *Cafbel,* at a time you was over much preffed with bufinefs of much greater confequence

* He was brother to the Rev. Dr. *Parnell* the celebrated poet.

quence to the publick ; and I do not wonder that
your Lordſhip could not find leiſure to return any
anſwer : but by his Majeſty's letters we received yeſterday relating to that affair, I find I was not forgot ;
I moſt humbly thank your Grace for ſupporting my
recommendations on this occaſion, which I can aſſure you had no other intention than his Majeſty's
ſervice, and the ſtrengthening the *Engliſh* intereſt
here.

I am, &c.

To the Biſhop of London.

My Lord,   *Dublin, June* 8, 1727.

I HAVE been applied to by Mr. *Amy* of *Cam-
berwell,* who has the honour of being known to
your Lordſhip, to recommend his nephew Mr. *Amy,*
of the Church of *Windſor,* to your Lordſhip for a
ſmall prebend of St. *Paul's* : I remember your Lordſhip had occaſion to enquire into his character when
I was in *England,* and ſeemed well diſpoſed to have
done ſomewhat for him in the King's Chapel on a
fair occaſion ; but that view is at an end, by his having a little living given him in the neighbourhood
of *Windſor* by that Church ; but ſtill as he has a
needy mother and ſiſter to ſupport, he ſtands in need
of ſome farther help, which if it ſuits with your
Lordſhip's conveniency, I would recommend him
for.   I am,

My Lord, &c.

To Lord Carteret.

My Lord,   *Dublin, June* 10, 1727.

I HAVE juſt now received your Excellency's of
the 6th, and hope you will pleaſe to remember
Mr.

Mr. *Vaughan* on some other occasion, since your Lordship was at this time pre-engaged in favour of Mr. *Massey.*

I am glad to hear his Majesty is probably landed in *Holland* after an easy passage.

The accounts had been some time ago passed to *Lady-day* was twelve-month, had they not been stopped for a letter that is expected from *England*, at the application of Mr. * *Edgecomb*, not to bring on Mr. *Pratt's* balance on the new account, which must be done according to the methods of auditing accounts here, if no such order comes : but Mr. *Gardiner* assures me the account to *Lady-day* last is preparing as fast as it can, so that no time shall be lost by the aforesaid delay : and I hope the account will be passed to *Lady-day* last before your Excellency's arrival here. There shall no endeavours be wanting on my part to compass it. Mr. *Pratt's* estate is now selling, but the sale goes on but slowly that I can find.

On *Monday* I set out on my provincial visitation, and shall be absent from *Dublin* near five weeks, but as we have a peace now, I shall hardly be wanted for that time.

I am, &c.

To the Duke of Newcastle.

My Lord,   *Dublin, June* 10, 1727.

I AM so very sensible that in the great hurry of business there has been in *England*, my recommendations have not been forgot, that I have already returned your Grace my hearty thanks, as I do again
by

---

* One of the Vice Treasurers of *Ireland*, afterwards created Lord *Edgecomb.*

by this, for your kind support of me in the disposition of *Cashel*.

I have a great value and friendship for the * Bishop of *Salisbury*, and in part know the services he has done the government both formerly and of late, and I am very well acquainted with Dr. *Hoadley* his brother, and know his affection to his Majesty, and that he has spirit to help to keep up the *English* interest here; so that I am very well satisfied with his promotion to the bishoprick of *Fernes*; and I have the more reason to be so, because in my first letter on the vacancy of the archbishoprick, I hinted that I thought it would be for his Majesty's service here, after some translations to fill up the last bishoprick from *England*, since the *English* grew the less number on the bench here.

Next *Monday* I intend to set out on the visitation of my province, which will take me up near five weeks time. I am glad the certainty of a peace gives me an opportunity of quitting *Dublin* to look after my province this summer, which otherwise I should have been unwilling to do, if the war had gone on.

I hope before this the news of his Majesty's landing in *Holland* is arrived at *London*. I am,

Your Grace's, &c.

To Lord Carteret.

My Lord,   *Dublin, June 29,* 1727.

I MOST heartily condole with your Excellency upon the sudden and unexpected death of his late Majesty: I was engaged in the visitation of my province when the melancholy news overtook me, and had some thoughts of going on, since his Majesty would

* Dr. *Hoadley*, afterwards Bishop of *Winchester*.

would be proclaimed, and all the ufual orders given before I could poffibly reach *Dublin*, but upon finding the other Lords Juftices were uneafy at my abfence, I returned hither laft night.

Every body is extremely pleafed with his Majefty's happy and quiet acceffion to the throne, and with his moft gracious declaration in council ; *and they do not doubt but his Majefty will purfue thofe wife meafures which will make him as great as his father, and his people as eafy as they were under him.*

As a new parliament muft be called here, and a feffion come on as foon as poffible, I muft take the liberty to reprefent to your Excellency how much it would be for his Majefty's fervice, by giving them courage to exert themfelves, and a weight with others, if my Lord Chancellor and Lord Chief Baron had new patents fpeedily for their places, as likewife the other judges ; I mention only the two firft in particular, becaufe the prefent doubtful tenure they have of their places muft be a great weakening to the *Englifh* intereft, and of ill confequence in the elections, and at the feffion of parliament.

There is another thing I cannot but fuggeft to your Excellency, though I am under no fear of the experiment being made, that any thing which looks like * bringing the tories into power here, muft caufe the utmoft uneafinefs in this kingdom, by raifing the fpirits of the papifts of this country, and exafperating the whigs, who your Lordfhip knows, are vaftly fuperior among the gentlemen of eftates here.

I find Mr. *Broderick* has declared he will ftand for Speaker againft Mr. *Conolly,* and ufes his utmoft efforts to fecure as many as he can among the new members. The whole kingdom is in the utmoft ferment

* This was no bad admonition to Lord *Carteret,* who appeared to have been much inclined to favour them.

ment about the coming elections ; but I hope this will have no worfe confequences than are ufual on fuch occafions.

I can fafely appeal to your Excellency for my having to the beft of my power ferved his late Majefty, and fupported the *Englifh* intereft here ; and I fhall always ferve his prefent Majefty as faithfully ; but to be able to do it with the good effect I defire, I hope I fhall be as well fupported as I have been : your Excellency knows I have nothing to afk ; and I believe Princes have feldom over many that are difpofed to ferve them as faithfully on fo eafy terms.

It would put a good fpirit into the King's friends here, and particularly the *Englifh*, if they knew by your Excellency's means what they had to depend on. I beg your Lordfhip's pardon for the freedom and length of this letter, and am,

My Lord, &c.

To the Archbifhop of Canterbury.

My Lord,   *Dublin, June* 30, 1727.

I Heartily condole with your Grace upon the unexpected death of his late * Majefty, and at the fame time congratulate you on the happy and peaceable acceffion of his prefent Majefty to the crown.

I was engaged in the vifitation of my province when the news overtook me, and found myfelf obliged to return to *Dublin*, by the importunity of my friends here, though I had not got through half my work. This my abfence has occafioned my not writing fooner to your Grace.

The

---

* Gserge I. who died almoft fuddenly at *Ofnabrug*, the palace of his brother the Bifhop of that diftrict, in his way to *Hanover*, by eating a melon.

The signing of the preliminaries before the late King was taken from us, has I hope procured us that peace, which I fear we should have been otherwise very uncertain of till next summer.

Every thing here is as quiet as in *England*, excepting the heats attending the election of a new parliament, which must come on immediately with us, as the former parliament is diffolved by the King's death, and the funds will expire at *Christmas* next. His Majesty's most gracious declaration in council has given univerfal fatisfaction here.

But your Grace will eafily fee there is great room for people's hopes and fears, till things are a little better fettled, and it is feen what miniftry is to be in *England*, and who are to keep or lofe their places here.

Your Grace knows I have nothing to lofe, but I may be made more or lefs capable of ferving his Majefty, of doing good in the Church, and of fupporting the *English* intereft, which labours under great difadvantages in this country, according as I have more or lefs countenance from *England*. I have in particular done my endeavours here to ferve his late Majefty with the greateft faithfulnefs, and fhall ferve our prefent Sovereign with the fame fidelity; but the fervices I can do will be much leffened, if I am not fupported in my ftation; and as I am fatisfied your Grace will come in for a great fhare of power under the King, I muft beg the favour of you to give me your fupport here upon proper occafions.

It would certainly be of great fervice againft our approaching parliament, if my Lord Chancellor and my Lord Chief Baron had their places fpeedily confirmed by new patents; and till that is done they can neither have courage, nor a proper weight. For matters abroad we have his Majefty's declaration, but what meafures are likely to be purfued at home

are

fo varioufly wrote over hither, that the King's beft friends know not how to act. If your Grace fhall think it any ways proper, I fhould be glad to know a little of what we are to depend upon.

I am fenfible I have very much trefpaffed on your Grace's time and patience, but the great kindnefs I have formerly met with from your Lordfhip, encourages me to give you this trouble.

I am, My Lord, &c.

To Lord Townfhend.

My Lord,   *Dublin, July* 1, 1727.

I WAS engaged in the triennial vifitation of my province, when the melancholy news of the King's death overtook me, and the importunity of my friends here brought me back to *Dublin* before I had half finifhed my vifitation.

I moft heartily condole with your Lordfhip upon this great and unexpected lofs, and at the fame time congratulate your Lordfhip on the quiet and peaceable acceffion of his prefent Majefty to the throne of his father.

We have no other buftle among us than what arifes from the warm canvafs going on in all parts about the election of members for the enfuing parliament.

His Majefty's moft gracious declaration in council has given great fatisfaction here.

I am fenfible of the great hurry your Lordfhip muft be in at this juncture, and fhould not have interrupted your more weighty affairs, if I had not thought myfelf obliged to take the firft opportunity to thank your Lordfhip for all favours, and particularly for the fupport I have found from your Lordfhip to enable me the better to ferve his Majefty in this country ; and I defire the continuance of

the

the fame from your Lordfhip on all proper occafions.

I am, &c.

To the Duke of Newcaftle.

My Lord,   *Dublin, July* 1, 1727.

I MOST heartily condole with your Grace upon
the unexpected lofs of his late Majefty, and at
the fame time congratulate you on the peaceable acceffion of his prefent Majefty to the crown.

I was engaged in the vifitation of my province
when this news overtook me, and returned to *Dublin*
but laft *Wednefday.*

Every thing here is very quiet, and all are very
well pleafed with his Majefty's moft gracious declaration in council.

It is very happy that the preliminaries were figned
before this fatal ftroke, fince otherwife it feems very
probable the Emperor would have taken till next
fpring to confider whether it were better for him to
have peace or war.

I take this opportunity to thank your Grace for
the fupport you have given me fince my coming hither, and to defire the continuance of your favour
on all proper occafions.

I am, &c.

To the Bifhop of London.

My Lord,   *Dublin, July* 4, 1727.

I Yefterday received your Lordfhip's of the 29th
paft, and moft heartily condole with you on the
unexpected death of his late Majefty: the news
overtook me in the middle of the vifitation of my
pro-

province, and the importunity of friends has brought me back to *Dublin*.

I am glad to hear things are likely to go in the ftate pretty near as they were, and hardly think they will mend by changing in the Church; however, I remember when I was in *England*, it was thought other perfons would come into play in the Church upon the change which has now happened.

I have been particularly concerned for Mr. *Stephens*'s ill luck on this occafion, and will follow your Lordfhip's advice to try what my old friends can or will undertake for him.

The prieft your Lordfhip mentions has been feveral times with me, and I do not find any of my brethren object to his fincerity; but moft of the priefts here are fo ignorant, and there is fo much hazard in trufting them in our church, that it is very hard to put them in any way here of getting their bread. If *O Hara* could be put into fome little bufinefs in the *Weft Indies*, I believe it would be better for him; but I have not yet talked with him whether he is willing to go thither, nor fhall I, till I know whether your Lordfhip would be willing to fend him.

By the change that your Lordfhip thinks will happen in the church affairs, I fhall be greatly at a lofs for your friendfhip; but hope ftill for your affiftance as it fhall lye in your way, and fhall on all occafions hope for the continuance of your good advice, as often as I find reafon to have recourfe to it.

It is very likely Dr. *L—l* will look out for fome other way to pufh, as things now ftand.

I am, &c.

To

To the Archbishop of Canterbury.

My Lord,   *Dublin, July* 6, 1727.

AS Dr. *Baldwin,* Provoſt of the College here, goes now for *London,* to wait upon his Majeſty with an addreſs, and to know his pleaſure about their chancellorſhip, which he had whilſt he was Prince, I have given him this my letter, to introduce him to your protection as there may be occaſion. He is a very worthy gentleman, a man of learning, and extremely well affected to his Majeſty and his family, and ſhewed himſelf to be ſo in the latter end of the Queen's time, when he was Vice-Provoſt.

There has lately been an election of a fellow in the College which has occaſioned a quarrel there, in which he has been very much miſrepreſented and abuſed: and he has been threatened with their preferring a petition to the King, and having the power given him by the ſtatutes reduced. The power he has is indeed beyond any thing any Head of a College has in *Oxford,* but is all little enough to keep the college here from being a ſeminary of * jacobitiſm; through the ſtrength of a faction in the College againſt him.

I would beg leave of your Grace, that he may have the liberty to lay his caſe before you, as there may be occaſion, and that you would give him your protection as far as he wants it, and your Grace ſhall think it reaſonable.

                    I am, my Lord, &c.

VOL. I.   K   To

---

* His Grace muſt be very much miſtaken, or to ſpeak in the ſofteſt terms, he was groſly impoſed upon by ſome ignorant malicious people, as the fellows of the univerſity of *Dublin,* have been as remarkable for charity, piety, religion, learning and loyalty, as any other College in *Europe,* ſince the reign of Queen *Elizabeth.*

To the Archbishop of Canterbury.

My Lord,   *Dublin, July* 8, 1727.

I HAVE had the honour of your Grace's, with the King's speech inclosed, which is truly gracious and condescending, and gives the utmost satisfaction to his Majesty's subjects here; and we do not doubt but his Majesty speaks his sincere sentiments and intentions.

I thank your Grace for the favour you intend me of sending the prayers as soon as possible, when that affair is once settled; and I think your Lordship is very much in the right on that occasion, to implore the divine blessing on his Majesty's endeavours for a happy and lasting peace.

I am sorry to hear your Grace is obliged to keep close at *Lambeth* during the present hurry, and pray God to give you better health for the good of the Church and service of his Majesty. We have since seen the address of both Lords and Commons to the King, and are all pleased to find them so hearty and loyal. The last day of *June* I wrote to your Grace to desire your friendship and support in my station upon this turn, which I again request. I likewise recommended my Lord Chancellor and Lord Chief Baron to have their commissions renewed speedily, and must desire your Grace to speak to my Lord Lieutenant and the ministry to this purpose, as an opportunity offers; they have both discharged their offices with great diligence and abilities, and very much to the satisfaction of the people here; and have both heartily concurred with me in the council and elsewhere, in whatever might promote the *English* interest here.

I have no apprehensions but that my Lord Lieutenant and the ministry desire to continue them in their

places,

places, but it would give them more courage and more weight in our prefent circumftances, if they were prefently confirmed in their employments.

I am, my Lord, &c.

To the Duke of Newcaftle.

My Lord, *Dublin, July* 8, 1727.

AS by his late Majefty's demife all commiffions here expire of courfe, within fix months, I take the liberty to put your Grace in mind that I think it would be for his Majefty's fervice, as we are in a ferment over the whole nation about elections, that the commiffions of confequence which are defigned to be renewed, were renewed with all convenient expedition.

And in particular I think it would be of fervice in the prefent juncture, if my Lord Chancellor and Lord Chief Baron had fpeedily new grants of their places. They have both attended their courts with the greateft diligence, and have given an unufual difpatch to the bufinefs of their courts, to the general fatisfaction of the country, on account of their abilities and impartiality. They have always moft heartily joined with me in whatever might be for his Majefty's fervice, and the fupport of the *Englifh* intereft here ; and the fpeedy renewing of their commiffions would enable them to act with more courage and with greater weight than they can do whilft others may imagine their places are doubtful. My Lord Lieutenant knows their behaviour, and the character they have gained here fo well, that I do not doubt but his Excellency is for their continuing here ; and indeed a change in their places would very much weaken the government now the feffion of a new parliament is fo near.

K 2 I take

sure it muſt have been very much owing to your kind representations of my ſervices.

And I am ſenſible of your goodneſs in acquainting his preſent Majeſty, that the ſupporting of me here will be for his intereſt; and I deſire the continuance of your good offices with the King.

I am glad we are not likely to have any alterations in *Ireland*, and that the commiſſions here will be renewed immediately upon the renewal of thoſe in *England*.

We are obliged to your Lordſhip for the early care you took of us *Engliſh* here; and every body here is ſenſible of what advantage it will be to his Majeſty's ſervice that we have had a Governor of your Excellency's abilities long enough amongſt us to know as much of this country as any native.

While the ſame meaſures are purſued as were in the laſt reign, we ſhall be all eaſy here; and it muſt be left to his Majeſty to judge what perſons are moſt proper to be employed in his ſervice. The aſſurances your Lordſhip gives me in theſe affairs are a great ſatisfaction to me.

I hear there is a clauſe in an *Engliſh* bill, which ſpeaks of the chancellorſhip of the Univerſity here as moſt certainly vacant by the King's acceſſion to the crown, but here it is thought at the moſt to be only dubious. We are giving what diſpatch we can to the bills that are to be ſent over to *England*, in order to have a new parliament, and hope we ſhall ſend ſuch as will be approved there, and will meet with little oppoſition here.

I am, &c.

To

To the same.

My Lord,   *Dublin, July 20, 1727.*

I HAVE had the honour of your Excellency's of the 13th, and before the receipt of this your Lordfhip will receive the two lifts of officers which are of importance in our prefent ftate, and with all poffible fpeed an account of all other patents for places.

We have been in fuch a hurry with getting the bills ready to be fent to *England*, that I have not had time to draw up a fhort account of the Bifhop of *Cloyne*'s cafe for your information, but will do it by the firft opportunity. My Lord Chancellor has written fo fully about the bills we have fent, that I have little to add.

The whole council were fatisfied it was our duty to tranfmit a money bill, but we think if your Excellency is here early enough it will be better to make no ufe of it ; as to the corn and tillage bill, the great damage to this kingdom by landlords tying up their tenants from ploughing, the throwing fo many families out of work that might be employed by tillage, and the terrible fcarcity next to a famine that a great part of the kingdom now labours under by the corn not yielding well laft year, and to which we are liable upon any the leaft accident in our harveft, make us all very defirous of having it paft ; and as it is only five acres out of an hundred that are to be tilled, and that every farmer has till *Michaelmas* come two years to lay out his fchemes of ploughing, we hope it will not be counted any hardfhip to force them to plough fo fmall a proportion of their land.

The want of fuch a provifion as is made in the bill about mending bridges, has often occafioned 50 or 100 *l.* expence to the county, where 5 or 10 *l.* would have done at firft.

The

The indemnifying bill fpeaks for itfelf.

As to the bill requiring fome years converfion in papifts before they practife the law, your Lordfhip knows the bad cafe we are in here with new converts practifing, and the dangerous confequence it may have in length of time ; your Lordfhip has likewife feen, that nothing can be moved about papifts or converts in either houfe but what is at laft fo clogged as to come to nothing ; which made us willing to fend over a bill to this one point ; if there are political reafons on the other fide of the water for dropping it, the crown is under no difficulty, becaufe we have fent bills enough without it ; but I believe if it is returned, it will certainly pafs here.

I hear this day, that the addrefs yefterday prefented by fome Roman Catholicks, occafions great heats and divifions among thofe of that religion here.

I am, &c.

To the Archbifhop of Canterbury.

My Lord, *Dublin, Aug.* 10, 1727.

I HAVE had the honour of your Grace's of the 12th and 19th paft. I believe the behaviour of the parliament to the King, in relation to the civil lift, and the King's moft gracious fpeech at the end of the feffions, have univerfally pleafed all honeft men.

I am forry to hear your Grace complain fo much of your infirmities, and hope you may find benefit by the *Tunbridge* waters; and I heartily wifh your Grace may have ftrength to ferve the Church and our country for many years yet to come; and I defire your Grace's protection on all proper occafions.

His Majefty has been gracioufly pleafed to renew his grants to all in place here, except to Mr. *Medlicott,*
one

one of the commiſſioners of the revenue, in whoſe place he has put my Lord *Pembroke*'s ſecond * ſon, whom we expect here very ſpeedily.

The changes made in places in England, *are ſuch as I believe give no uneaſineſs, except to the particular friends of thoſe turned out, ſince thoſe are all left in who will have the direction of affairs.*

I am very much afraid by your Grace's account and the hurry they ſeem to be in about court, that we ſhall ſcarce have a day of prayer and thankſgiving, as has been propoſed by your Grace.

I thank your Lordſhip for your kind reception of Dr. *Baldwin*, and your intention to ſupport him, if there be occaſion.

I find my Lord Lieutenant is likely to come hither later in the year than we could wiſh, for the eaſy diſpatch of buſineſs in the parliament.

We have had a greater run of hot weather together, than there has been ſince I came to this country.   I am,

Your Grace's, &c.

To Lord Carteret.

My Lord,   *Dublin, Aug.* 24, 1727.

WE have been in great expectation of Mr. *Stern*'s † return with the bills, and his Majeſty's orders for iſſuing the writs for a new parliament, but hear nothing of him or his motions by the mail that came in this day and brought the letters of *Saturday* laſt.

I am ſorry to hear two of our bills are loſt on the other ſide, and particularly the corn bill, which is very much wanted here.

It

* Honourable Mr. *Herbert.*
† Clerk of the parliament.

It is thought here that elections will generally go well.

The Bishop of *Fernes* * and his family are arrived here to day, after being at sea four days.

I have here sent your Lordship enough of the Bishop of *Cloyne*'s case to make it understood what he desires, with a copy of the private bill his predecessor obtained in *England*, relating to the lands of *Donagh-more*. If I had more large materials your Excellency should have had a more distinct account of his case.

I shall leave it to your Excellency what change you will think proper to make in the list of privy-councellors here ; your Excellency knows as well as any body, who of the present list are enemies to *England*, and oppose the King's business on all occasions.

I shall submit it to your Excellency whether it may be proper for the strengthening of the *English* interest here, to have the present Archbishop of *Cashel* inserted in the new list.

I am sorry to hear your Lordship has had a fit of the gout so early in life.

I am, &c.

The CASE of
The present Bishop of † CLOYNE,
On which he applies for Relief.

BY an act passed the second session 1° reg. *Annæ* c. 21. the forfeited estates in this kingdom, unsold or undisposed of, were vested in the Queen, her heirs and successors ; and the money arising from them to be brought into the Exchequer in *Ireland*, and

* Dr. *Hoadley* ; he was afterwards Archbishop of *Dublin*, and succeeded Dr. *Boulter* in the primacy.
† Dr. *Henry Maule*.

and there to be kept apart from her Majesty's other revenues, to be applied as the parliament of *England* shall direct.

By an act 2° & 3° reg. *Annæ* c. 10. the money remaining in the treasury of *England* from the sale of forfeited estates here, Lord *Bophin*'s 25000 *l.* and other rents, arrears, &c. were to go towards paying a year's interest on the debentures. Since which, no other disposal has been made by the parliament of *England* of these forfeitures, except in the late Bishop of *Cloyne*'s bill : the state of which is this :

The late Bishop of *Cloyne* understanding that the lands and manor of *Donaghmore* had once belonged to the see of *Cloyne*, had probably by some agent bid 4020 *l.* for the said lands, and paid down 1340 *l.* as one third of the purchase money. After which he applied to the parliament of *England*, and obtained an act of parliament there, by which the other two thirds of the purchase money were remitted. The lands and the manor of *Donaghmore* were for ever united to the see of *Cloyne*.

But in order to reimburse him the 1340 *l.* he had advanced, he was to be repaid that sum out of the undisposed forfeitures here. And because that fund might prove deficient, his executors, &c. were to keep the estate of *Donaghmore* upon his death, &c. till the whole 1340 *l.* or what part of it remained unpaid, with interest from the time of his death, was answered out of the rents of the lands of *Donaghmore*.

The part of that private act relating to this, I have sent a copy of.

Now it seems some of these undisposed estates, and some money from arrears, &c. are still in the hands of the commissioners of the revenue here.

Whether the late Bishop of *Cloyne* applied to the commissioners to be paid the 1340 *l.* I cannot learn ; but the whole sum remains unpaid, and in virtue of

the

the act laft mentioned, the late Bifhop's executors keep the lands of *Donaghmore* from the prefent Bifhop.

And his application to the government is, that purfuant to the act of parliament, the 1340 *l.* may be paid out of the undifpofed forfeited eftates.

By what I have heard the commiffioners here fay, thofe eftates are indebted to the revenue here for the recovery of them near 900 *l.* and fome body has been made receiver of thofe rents at a falary of near half or a third part of the rents. But a thorough knowledge of the ftate of thofe forfeited eftates can fcarce be had till your Excellency in perfon makes thofe enquiries, which we cannot fo well pufh on.

To Lord Carteret.

My Lord,   *Dublin, Aug.* 26, 1727.

EARLY this morning died the Lord Chief Juftice *Whitfhed,* very much lamented for his great abilities and zeal for the fervice of the publick.

I muft take this occafion to prefs your Excellency that his place may be filled from *England**. I can affure your Lordfhip we have by experience found the want of two *Englifh* Judges in the privy council, fince the removal of my Lord Chancellor to his prefent poft ; and I am confident where there is the leaft fhew of an affair between *England* and *Ireland,* or where there is need of impartiality between any contending parties, that may be before the council, we fhall be in the laft diftrefs, if this vacancy be not filled from *England :* I do not fpeak this that I want to have the place filled immediately, fince I rather think it will be of fervice to have it kept uncertain who

---

* An *Englifhman* (Mr. *Reynolds)* was fent, as is requefted in this letter.

who fhall fucceed till the approaching feffions of parliament is pretty well over.

But I would prevent any furprife by an early application from hence for the prefent vacancy, or for a removal from the King's bench, as was done before.

I am, &c.

To the Duke of Newcaftle.

My Lord,   Dublin, Aug. 26, 1727.

THIS morning died my Lord Chief Juftice *Whitfhed*, by which the place of Lord Chief Juftice in the Common Pleas is become vacant.

I muft beg leave on this occafion to acquaint your Grace that it is of the utmoft confequence to have this vacancy filled from *England*.

We have found by experience fince the Lord Chief Baron has been the only *Englifhman* among the three chief Judges, that things have gone very heavy in the privy council here.

When any thing is tranfacting in council that can be thought to be for the advantage of *England*, or where any perfons of confideration here may be offended, the beft we can hope for from a native of this place is, that he will ftay away from council inftead of promoting the King's fervice by his prefence and debating.

I muft likewife take the liberty to caution againft fuffering the prefent Lord * Chief Juftice of the King's Bench to remove to the Common Pleas, which was the game played laft time, with an intent to keep off a perfon from *England*, and played with fuccefs. There will be no difficulty in finding a lawyer of worth in *England* to come over to the Com-

* *Rogerfon*, formerly Recorder of *Dublin*.

Pleas. There was a great deal to be said why the Lord Chief Justice *Whitshed*, who had been worn out in the King's service in the King's Bench should be considered and made easy in a place of less trouble than the post he then held : but this is an application from one in good health, and who has not so much as sat in the King's Bench as yet ; and as he pleads the late precedent, we all think it is the more necessary not to make a second precedent ; which if repeated, will almost rob the crown of the disposal of the most easy place among the Judges in this kingdom. I mention this in particular against the removal of Lord Chief Justice *Rogerson* to the Common Pleas, but must still continue of opinion that it is most for his Majesty's service that the place should be filled from *England*.

I am, &c.

To the same.

My Lord, *Dublin, Sept.* 18, 1727.

YESTERDAY Dr. *Travers*, minister of the round Church (alias St. *Andrews*) died. That parish is by act of parliament to be divided into two parishes, and the gift of it is in seven trustees, of which the Archbishop of *Dublin* is one, and has as is said, a negative on the rest. But beside this the Dr. had the chancellorship of *Christ Church*, which is in your Excellency's gift ; some tell me the chancellorship is worth 80 *l. per ann.* others at least 100 *l.* I shall mention the several persons that have applied to me to be recommended to your Lordship for this promotion, in the order they applied.

Dr. *St. Paul* was the first, who says that your Excellency was pleased to promise to do somewhat for him, and that the chancellorship has no cure of souls,

souls, and is very convenient for his following his school here.

The next that applied was Mr. *Manley* *, in behalf of his son Mr. *Holt* ; he appears for the round Church, and if he succeeds there Mr. *Manley* will be satisfied. But as Mr. *Doogat* the Archbishop's nephew likewise appears, and it is supposed the Archbishop will exert his negative and agree to no other presentation but. that of his nephew, if that should be the case, and there is no prospect of Mr. *Holt*'s succeeding to the living, Mr. *Manley* would be very thankful if his son might succeed to the chancellorship of *Christ Church*.

This morning Mr. *Synge* was with me, and represented that in the last removal your Excellency favoured him with, he bettered himself but 30 *l. per annum*, and that in tythes instead of a rate on houses, and he is desirous to succeed to the chancellorship.

. As your Lordship knows all the candidates and their characters, I only lay their pretensions before you.

My Lord *Santry* has been with me to desire I would acquaint your Lordship that it is his request that his nephew Mr. *Keating*, who is one of the clerks assistant of the House of Lords, might be put on a level with the other clerk assistant: I know his nephew is diligent in his present business, and if what he desires is not to the detriment of another, which I shall endeavour to enquire, I would join in his request to your Excellency.

I believe several of our elections will be over this week, and it is thought they will generally go well. I am,

My Lord, &c.

VOL. I.   L   *To*

---

* Deputy Postmaster General of *Ireland*, whose daughter was married to the Rev. Mr. *Holt*.

To the same.

My Lord,   *Dublin, Sept.* 23, 1727.

I HAD yesterday the honour of your Excellency's of the 14th, and am glad to hear that it is intended that the Lord Chief Justice's place shall be filled from *England*, and should hope people here will be satisfied with the puny Judge's place being filled from this country, but hope neither will be done till the session of parliament is over.

We generally think the session will be easy, though I find there are some very busy in giving out that a land-tax is designed, with what views it is easy to guess.

The Archbishop of *Cashel* * is not yet come, but we suppose he is now at *Holybead*, and will be here to-morrow.

§ I think the reasons for dropping our two bills are not very strong. We shall do whatever lies in our power to have every thing ready against the opening of the parliament.

I have lately received a letter from Mrs. *West*, complaining of the coldness of Mr *Mitchel* to her, on the account as she says, that she paid the *Irish* creditors preferably to what was due to him from Mr. *West*, on account of some bargain about stocks ; and as she fears that Mr. *Mitchel* for this reason may sollicit her affair but coolly, she desires I would put your Excellency in mind of being so kind to her as to get her pension renewed.

I have formerly transmitted her memorial to your Lordship, and should be sorry if she should suffer

for

---

* Dr. *Thomas Godwin.*

§ The corn bill was passed afterwards in another session, and so was the other, if it was the popery bill, as it seems to be.

for having paid the *Irish* creditors preferably to others, since it was what myself and the rest of the *English* here all advised, for the credit of our nation, and to prevent applications to have her pension when granted, stopped, to pay them.   I very much fear that without the pension being renewed, Mrs. *West* and her daughter will be wholly destitute at the death of old Mr. *West*.   I am,

My Lord, &c.

To Lord Townshend.

My Lord,   *Dublin, Sept.* 18, 1727.

HAVING lately had an account from *England*, that Dr. *Burton* *, Canon of *Christ Church*, has been out of order, I beg leave to put your Lordship in mind of your promises in favour of Mr. *Stephens*, that he should succeed to the first vacancy in that Church.   He is the only friend in *England* I shall trouble your Lordship about, and your supporting his pretensions to that canonry, whenever it falls, will always be esteemed the greatest obligation laid on me.

I am, my Lord, &c.

To Lord Carteret.

My Lord,   *Dublin, Oct.* 3, 1727.

I HAD this day the honour of your Excellency's of the 28th past.   Dr. *St. Paul* was with me this morning, and I told him your Lordship did not intend to dispose of the chancellorship till your arrival here.

L 2   I am

* Dr. *Burton* had been tutor to the Primate, when he was entered of *Christ Church* in *Oxford*.

I am very forry that things have fo fallen out as to detain your Lordfhip fo long in *England*, that I fear there will hardly be time to fettle the operations of the parliament in the beft manner before they meet.

We are pretty much alarmed here at an article in the *Englifh* news, that *Alan Brodrick*, fon to the late Lord Chancellor of *Ireland*, is made one of the Commiffioners of the Cuftoms; and we are apprehenfive it may give too much fpirit to the *Brodricks* here, and be made ufe of by them to engage others to obftruct the King's bufinefs in parliament. I am,

My Lord, &c.

To the Duke of Newcaftle.

My Lord,   *Dublin,* Oct. 3, 1727.

LOOKING over the *Englifh* news this day, we find this article, that *Alan Brodrick*, fon to the late Lord Chancellor of *Ireland*, is made one of the Commiffioners of the Cuftoms.   As the whole oppofition the King's affairs met with laft feffion in the Houfe of Commons, came from the *Brodricks*, we are fomewhat apprehenfive that any thing which looks as if that family was in favour in *England*, may give them fpirit, and engage others to join with them in perplexing matters the approaching feffions of parliament.   I am,

Your Grace's, &c.

Te

To the Bishop of London.

My Lord,   *Dublin, Jan.* 11, 1727.

I AM sensible it is a great while since I last wrote to your Lordship, but it has not been owing to my having a less desire of the continuance of your Lordship's friendship, but for want of matter to write about ; your Lordship is in the busy scene of life, and I in a kingdom where little happens worth communicating to any abroad : and I must own as nothing but a disturbance can make room for affairs of consequence passing here, I most heartily wish we may still continue of as little concern to others as we are at present.

The difficulties that might have been apprehended in our session are pretty well over ; the accounts are adjusted, and the usual supply voted, and a bill ordered to be brought in accordingly. We had an attempt made in our House to call for the accounts of the nation, which as it was new here, might have occasioned a quarrel with the House of Commons, and probably was intended so to do, but it was over-ruled by about 28 to 11.

We are going on with some bills to mend the state of our Church, by getting more glebes, Churches, and Chapels of Ease, that we may in time have Churches and resident ministers to answer our wants, for at present many of our people go off to the papists or presbyterians, for want of Churches to repair to.

Here is such a jealousy of increasing the wealth of the Church, that what success our bills will have with the Commons is uncertain.

I hope for your Lordship's support of them in the council when they come there, against which time I shall send you a proper account of them.

I must

I muft again recommend Mr. *Stephens* to your Lordfhip's protection, as to the promife made him of a canonry of *Chrift Church*.

I find the peace is ftill uncertain, though we hope for the beft.

The Bifhop of *Cloyne* will I believe apply for a bill in *England*, relating to his bifhoprick, of which I fhall give your Lordfhip a larger account another time.

I heartily wifh your Lordfhip many happy new years, and am,

My Lord, &c.

To the Archbifhop of Canterbury.

My Lord, *Dublin, Jan.* 13, 1727.

IT is a great while fince I had the honour of a letter from your Grace, which I have not anfwered fooner, becaufe I had nothing new to write from hence ; what little this country now affords is, that our feffion goes on very quietly, and the ufual fupplies are voted, and a bill going on accordingly.

I find by my Lord Lieutenant the miniftry are not defirous that a convocation fhould fit here ; nor do I defire it, except they had fome ufeful bufinefs to do, and I was thoroughly certain they would confine themfelves to that.

I have had no great occafion or leifure to enquire into the nature of our convocation here, but as it is made up of the clergy of four provinces, I find fome of our bench queftion whether they have ever been fettled in fuch a regular method of being called, as to make a truly legal affembly.

I am glad to find things have gone fo very well in England *fince his Majefty's acceffion, and that the late King's friends (who moft certainly are fo to his prefent Majefty) have no caufe of complaint.*

My

My Lord Lieutenant has made no change in any place here.

We were some time ago more certain of a speedy peace here by all accounts than we seem to be at present, but I hope all will end well.

I most heartily wish your Grace many happy new years, and am very much obliged to your Lordship for your readiness to assist me on occasion with your interest : I am sure the steady attachment of your Grace to his Majesty's family and person will always make you have a weight at court.

I believe the Bishop of *Cloyne* will have occasion to apply for a bill in *England*, relating to an incumbrance on his bishoprick ; when it is certain that he must apply I shall trouble your Grace with the particulars of his case.

I am, my Lord, &c.

To the Duke of Newcastle.

My Lord,   *Dublin, Jan.* 16, 1727.

IT is now a great while since I did myself the honour to write to your Grace ; the great hurry of business your Lordship must have been engaged in, and the peaceable state we have been in here, without any particular accidents that required writing about, have been the occasion of so long a silence.

The difficulties that were in part apprehended in the sessions of parliament are now pretty well over : the publick accounts have been stated to the satisfaction of the Commons, and the usual money bill will be ready for the council next *Monday.* As the accounts have been now audited by the Commissioners of Accounts to *Lady-day* last, and will whilst the *English* have any power here, be regularly audited every year, it will not be so easy to embroil a session

as

as it was the laſt time the parliament ſat, when *Prat*'s accounts were in ſuch confuſion, for want of being regularly audited for ſome years.

I hope it has not contributed a little towards things paſſing eaſy here, that ſince the government has been pretty much in Engliſh *hands, things have gone with greater impartiality, and every body of conſequence has been treated with more regard than they have been formerly.*

My Lord Chancellor and Lord Chief Baron have been very diligent in the affair of the accounts ; and it has not been without great preſſing that we could get the ſeveral officers to have the accounts ready to be audited before the parliament met : and I muſt do them both the juſtice to ſay, that they give great content in their reſpective courts.

Our new Lord Chief Juſtice * landed on *Saturday*, was ſworn into his place yeſterday, and was this day ſworn of the privy council ; I hear that good character of him, that I do not queſtion but by his abilities and integrity he will be a great ſtrengthening of the *Engliſh* intereſt.

Your Grace will be ſo good as to excuſe my again recommending Mr. *Stephens* to your protection for the promiſe formerly made me, that he ſhould have the next canonry of *Chriſt Church* that happened to be void.   I am,

My Lord, &c.

To the Archbiſhop of Canterbury.

My Lord,   *Dublin, Feb.* 13, 1727.

AS we are ſending over ſome bills to *England*, which are of great conſequence to religion in this country, and in the ſupporting of which at

council

* *Reynolds.*

council I muſt beg your Lordſhip's aſſiſtance, I give you this trouble to let you know what is our caſe, and what are our views in them.

There are probably in this kingdom five papiſts at leaſt to one proteſtant : we have incumbents and curates to the number of about 800, whilſt there are near 3000 popiſh prieſts of all ſorts here. A great part of our clergy have no parſonage houſes, nor glebes to build them on : we have many pariſhes eight and ten, twelve and fourteen miles long, with it may be only one Church in them, and that often at one end of the pariſh : we have few market towns that ſupply convenient food for the neighbourhood, nor farmers that can ſupply the common neceſſaries of life, which may be had at moſt farmers in *England* ; ſo that all agree no clergyman in the country can live without a moderate glebe in his hands : and as there can be no hopes of getting ground of the papiſts without more Churches or Chapels, and more reſident clergymen, we have been framing two bills, one for explaining and amending an act for the better maintenance of curates in the Church of *Ireland*, 6° *Georgii*. By that act a Biſhop was enabled to cauſe one or two Chapels of Eaſe to be erected in any pariſh where a number of Proteſtants lived ſix miles from the Church, and that was underſtood to mean ſix country miles, which are at leaſt nine meaſured miles, and in many places twelve : we have reduced that diſtance to five meaſured miles, the incumbents and patrons conſent we have omitted, as what we fear will render the bill uſeleſs : the conſents we have made neceſſary are ſuch proteſtant inhabitants as may want a Chapel excluſive of thoſe of the Mother-church, or on the other ſide of it, as they muſt contribute towards building it : at the inſtance of the clergy we have likewiſe excluded ſuch as live within two miles of a neighbouring Church :
the

the Bishop has the same power of appointing a salary for these new curates as that act allowed.

We have likewise there provided for the building of Chapels of Ease in cities and towns corporate.

The other is an act to explain an act for the better enabling of the clergy having the cure of souls to reside on their respective benefices, &c. 8° *Georg.* c. 12. There is by the old act a power of giving land under 40 acres for a glebe, at half the improved rent or more ; but as most of the estates here are under settlements, it has little effect : and there are now three or four gentlemen that would grant 15 or 20 acres for glebes if they were at liberty. This act therefore is to empower those under settlements to give a glebe at the full improved rent, to be settled by a jury, on condition of building and improving.

Beside the benefit of distress for arrears of rent, the bishop is impowered to sequester the whole living upon complaint to pay such arrears. And that the successor may not have an unreasonable arrear come upon him, the Bishop is obliged to enquire at every annual visitation which we hold here, whether the rent is paid, and to sequester and see it paid. The same power of giving a glebe is extended to perpetual curacies in livings appropriate or impropriate.

Having endeavoured to provide glebes, we oblige all future incumbents having convenient glebes to build. All are allowed three-fourths of what they lay out, but we see nothing but force will make them build.

As there are several schools of whose endowments I am trustee, that have some no house, others inconvenient little ones, without land near them, the same encouragement is given to them to build as to the clergy, and they are impowered to exchange

some

fome land for a convenient demefne, under proper in-
fpection.

We have likewife fent over a bill about the recovering of tythes and other ecclefiaftical dues, under
40 s.   We had the *Englifh* act before us, but have
altered fome things to pleafe the Commons, who
have twice thrown out a bill of the fame nature;
oblations and *obventions* are omitted to pleafe them.
We have likewife excluded clergymen from being
the Juftices before whom fuch caufes may be tried,
that they might not play the game into one another's
hands; for in many places here one fourth or fifth
of the refident juftices are clergymen, for want of
refident gentlemen.

The bill is exceedingly neceffary here, fince the
recovery of little dues cofts more than they are
worth, and the juftices will not help.   People ftand
contempt and excommunication, and the taking up
cofts too much, and befide moft of them muft be
abfolutely ruined if taken up.

There is likewife another bill coming which has
been in force feven years already, by which the incumbent that has been a wrong clerk is accountable
for the profits received, after fuch allowances made
for ferving the cure.   The laity in both houfes are
very eager for it, and the *Englifh* Bifhops are for
it, there having been formerly very extraordinary
things done here by Bifhops, in putting clerks in
poffeffion that fcarce had the fhadow of a title *.
I am,

Your Grace's, &c.

*T*o

---

* This and the two following letters were copied and fent to
the Bifhop of *London* alfo.

To the same.

My Lord,   *Dublin, Feb.* 17, 1727.

I Lately troubled your Grace with an account of three bills we are sending from hence; I shall now trouble you with an account of two or three more, in the passing of which in *England* I must desire your Grace's assistance.

The first relates to the more easy recovery of tythes and other ecclesiastical dues of small value. The value settled in the bill is not exceeding 40 *s.* We had the *English* act before us, but have altered some things in it, partly because of the different case we are in from those in *England*, and partly to please the Commons, who have twice thrown out a bill of the same nature. In the first place, instead of small tythes in the *English* act, we have substituted tythes under 40*s. per ann.* The occasion of this change is, that in a great part of this kingdom the bulk of the farmers have but four, six, eight or ten acres, and a farmer of twenty acres is a great farmer, which makes it very troublesome and expensive to recover tythes either in a spiritual court or in the exchequer.

The usual way of suing for tythes here is in the spiritual courts; and for the small portion most people are to pay here, it will not often be worth while to go into the exchequer. Now when one of these sorry wretches is put into the spiritual court, he usually incurs contempt for non-appearance, and afterwards falls under the sentence of excommunication, which he does not regard; if a clergyman should then be at the expence of taking out a writ *de excommunicato capiendo*, and take the defendant up, the costs of the suit and tythes recovered, would absolutely beggar the poor wretch; so that
these

these caufes are feldom carried through : but when the fellow is found not to be frighted with excommunication, (which confidering the number of papifts and diffenters here, is moft generally the cafe) it is dropped.

There is indeed an *Englifh* ftatute 27° *Hen.* 8. c. 20. an act for tythes to be paid throughout this realm, which was plainly intended to affect *Ireland* as much as *England*, by which two juftices of the peace, upon non-appearance in the fpiritual court, might oblige the defendant to appear and to give fecurity to abide the fentence of the court ; but as *Ireland* though at firft mentioned, is not afterwards repeated, the judges and juftices here feem to be of opinion that the juftices cannot act here in virtue of that ftatute ; and the juftices will not affift the fpiritual courts, and the Commons will not hear of an act for the juftices to help the ecclefiaftical judge, fo that this act about recovering tythes, &c. would be of great fervice to the clergy here.

The words *oblations* and *obventions* have been omitted as having been formerly objected againft by the Commons. And to remove any jealoufy that the clergy might try all thefe caufes before one another, we have excluded the clergy from acting as juftices in the execution of this act ; which is the more reafonable here, becaufe in many counties one fourth or fifth part of the refiding juftices are of the clergy ; fince otherwife many tracts of lands of ten or fifteen miles every way would have no refident juftice.

We fhall likewife fend over an act to impower Archbifhops, &c. to part with the advowfon of benefices under 30 *l. per ann.* or more. My brethren the bifhops confented to this bill before it was offered. And that your Grace may the better underftand the expediency of this bill, it will be proper to inform you, that in many parts of this kingdom, by means of impropriations, there are vicarages or curacies
worth

worth but 5, 10 *l.* &c. *per ann.* that in several places the Bishops let the same person enjoy three or four on to seven or eight of these, which possibly all together make but 60, 80 or 100 *l. per ann.* or little more: and there is it may be but one or two Churches on all the denominations, which is the name we give these parishes: that the patronage of the greatest part of these is either in the Crown or the Bishops; that there might be difficulties raised as to the Crown parting with its right, but we think there can be no objection to suffer Bishops to part with their right for the good of the Church, and procuring additional clergymen; and we have the more reason to try what effect this temptation of the sole patronage to a lay benefactor may have, since the act of King *Charles* I. by which any one who restored tythes to the Church was to have a turn with the old patron in proportion to the value of tythes given, in respect of the old income of the Church, has had very little effect. We have in the same bill encouraged people to build and endow Chapels of Ease by giving them and their heirs the nomination to such Chapels.

Your Grace will see that in this act we had before us the act passed in *England* 1ˢᵗ *Georg.* I. only that we have no fund to help such benefactors as there is in *England*; and as there are trustees of the first fruits here for buying glebes or tythes for small livings, we have in this act made them the repositories of the authentick value of small livings, and of all augmentations in virtue of this act, that there may be some to see that the grants are such as they ought to be for value and validity.

In this kingdom the clergy paid the 20th, not the 10th to the Crown, as in *England*, and first fruits; but the 20ths were given off by Queen *Anne,* and the first fruits are the only fund the trustees have, which *communibus annis,* rises no higher than from 3 to 400 *l. per ann.* deducting charges, without a power to receive

ceive any benefactions. I hope it may please God in time to dispose the parliament to permit these trustees to receive benefactions for so good purposes; since what we are now doing in our Church bills seems to be very well liked; though when I first came hither, the laity would not have heard with patience the least proposal of what we are now attempting.

The clause in this bill by which the patron of a Chapel of Ease may nominate, if the Chapel be not actually filled then, though the nomination be then lapsed to the Bishop or Crown, is taken from the *English* bill. There was this day added to the said bill a clause to impower Bishops, &c. to encourage their tenants by a proper lease to enclose and preserve copse wood, which will be of service to all parties.

I must beg your Grace's assistance in the council, that our good designs may not be there sunk and prevented.

I am, my Lord, &c.

To the same.

My Lord, *Dublin, Feb.* 24, 1727.

I HAVE troubled your Grace with two long letters already, and must beg leave to trouble you with a third, about some other bills we are sending over, in getting which returned hither I must beg your Grace's assistance at the council.

As many of the parishes here are very large and intermixed with other parishes, and others of too little income to subsist by themselves, and little enough for extent to be united to some other parish or part of a parish, there was an act passed in the 14° and 15° of King *Charles* the second, by which parishes might be divided or united for conveniency's sake, with proper consents and the approbation of the

the chief governor and the council. As that act was expired, a new act was paſſed 2° *Georgii*, for the real union and diviſion of pariſhes, in which was a proviſo, that no union made in virtue of the former act of King *Charles* the ſecond ſhould be capable of being diſſolved, nor any part of ſuch union be united to any other pariſh, unleſs the pariſh Church of ſuch united pariſh does lye three country miles from ſome part of ſuch pariſh, &c.

Now as three country miles are often five or ſix meaſured miles ; and as ſeveral of thoſe unions were made without regard to the conveniency of the people, but purely to make a rich benefice ; as we are now endeavouring to make it poſſible to have the worſhip of God celebrated in all parts of this kingdom, we find it neceſſary to repeal this clauſe, and to lay ſuch pariſhes open to a diviſion as well as other old pariſhes.

There is another clauſe added to that bill, which relates to the removing of the ſite of Churches. By the act 2° *Georgii*, for the real union and diviſion of pariſhes, it is enacted that the ſite of an inconvenient Church may be changed for one more convenient with the conſent of the patron, &c.

Now with us many Churches ſtand at the end of a long pariſh, or on the wrong ſide of a bog or river, in reſpect of the greateſt part of the pariſhioners, or at leaſt proteſtants ; ſo that it would be very convenient to change ſuch ſituation of the Church ; but where the King is patron, as his conſent is to be had, the expence of having a letter from *England* to give his Majeſty's conſent under the broad ſeal here to ſuch a change, and paſſing a patent for it, is ſo great, as to diſcourage theſe removals : and I can aſſure your Grace 10 *l.* is harder to be raiſed here upon a country pariſh than 100*l.* is in *England* upon a pariſh of the ſame extent, and our gentry part with money on ſuch occaſions as unwillingly as the peaſantry.

It

It is therefore provided in the same bill, that the chief governor, &c. may consent for the King where the King is patron ; and as the King's patronage cannot be hurt by such a change of the site of a Church, but the parish will probably prove of better value ; and as the taking off of this expence may occasion the building several more convenient Churches, we hope the bill will be returned to us : And I can assure your Grace there are instances in two or three acts already where the chief governor, &c. is impowered to consent for the King.

These two clauses make up an act, entitled, an act, for repealing a clause in an act for the real union and division of parishes ; and to enable the chief governor, &c. to consent for the crown, &c.

There is part of another bill which will go over, that is of great consequence to this kingdom ; the title of the act is, I think, an act to prevent frauds, &c. in buying corn, &c. and to encourage tillage.

It is the latter part of this bill about tillage that is of great moment here. The bill does not encourage tillage by allowing any premium to the exporters of corn, but barely obliges every person occupying 100 acres or more (meadows, parks, bogs, &c. excepted) to till five acres out of every 100 ; and so in proportion for every greater quantity of land they occupy. And to make the law have some force, it sets the tenant at liberty to do this, notwithstanding any clause in his lease to the contrary. We have taken care to provide in the bill, that the tenant shall not be able to burn-beat any ground in virtue of this act ; and since he is tied up from that, and from ploughing meadows, &c. the people skilled in husbandry say, he cannot hurt the land though he should go round the 100 acres in 20 years.

I find my Lord *Trevor* objected to a bill we sent from council, that this was a breaking of private contracts, and invading property : but I think that nothing, fince the leffor receives no damage by it, and the publick is very much benefitted ; and this is no more than what is done every feffion in *England*, where rivers are made navigable or commons inclo-fed ; and in many road bills.

I fhall now acquaint your Grace with the great want we are in of this bill : our prefent tillage falls very fhort of anfwering the demands of this nation, which occafions our importing corn from *England* and other places ; and whilft our poor have bread to eat, we do not complain of this ; but by tilling fo little, if our crop fails, or yields indifferently, our poor have not money to buy bread. This was the cafe in 1725, and laft year, and without a prodigious crop, will be more fo this year. When I went my vifitation laft year, barley in fome inland places, fold for 6 s. a bufhel, to make the bread of ; and oat-meal (which is the bread of the north) fold for twice or thrice the ufual price : and we met all the roads full of whole families that had left their homes to beg abroad, fince their neighbours had nothing to relieve them with. And as the winter fubfiftance of the poor is chiefly potatoes, this fcarcity drove the poor to begin with their potatoes before they were full grown, fo that they have loft half the benefit of them, and have fpent their ftock about two months fooner than ufual ; and oatmeal is at this diftance from harveft, in many parts of this kingdom three times the cuftomary price ; fo that this fummer muft be more fatal to us than the laft ; when I fear many hundreds perifhed by famine.

Now the occafion of this evil is, that many per-fons have hired large tracts of land, on to 3 or 4000 acres, and have ftocked them with cattle, and have no other inhabitants on their land than fo many cotti-ers as are neceffary to look after their fheep and black cattle ; fo that in fome of the fineft counties, in ma-ny places there is neither houfe nor corn field to be
feen

feen in 10 or 15 miles travelling: and daily in some counties, many gentlemen (as their leafes fall into their hands) tye up their tenants from tillage: and this is one of the main caufes why fo many venture to go into foreign fervice at the hazard of their lives, if taken, becaufe they can get no land to till at home. And if fome ftop be not put to this evil, we muft daily decreafe in the numbers of our people.

But we hope if this tillage bill takes place, to keep our youth at home, to employ our poor, and not be in danger of a famine among the poor upon any little mifcarriage in our harveft. And I hope thefe are things of greater confequence than the breaking through a leafe, fo far as concerns ploughing five acres in an hundred.

I fhall trouble your Grace no more at prefent, but am,

My Lord, &c.

To the Duke of Newcaftle.

My Lord, *Dublin, Mar.* 7, 1727.

AS we are now very nigh got through our feveral bills at the council, I fhall beg leave to give your Grace an account of fome few of them, in the returning of which from the council of *England*, I would beg your Grace's affiftance.

We have in this kingdom but about 600 incumbents, and I fear 3000 popifh priefts, and the bulk of our clergy have neither parfonage-houfes nor glebes: and yet till we can get more Churches or Chapels and more refident clergymen, inftead of getting ground of the papifts, we muft lofe to them, as in fact we do in many places, the defcendants of many of *Cromwell's* officers and foldiers here being gone off to popery.

M 2 To

To remedy this evil, we have fent over a bill for the better maintenance of curates, by which Bifhops are enabled with the confent of the proteftant parifhioners, to have one or more Chapels built in large parifhes, and to oblige the incumbent to pay for ferving them.

By another bill to enable the clergy to refide, we have empowered perfons under fettlements, and all Bifhops and other ecclefiaftical perfons, to grant a glebe where wanted, not exceeding 40 acres at the full improved rent ; and oblige all future incumbents that have a convenient glebe, and a living not lefs than 150 *l. per ann.* to build a parfonage-houfe ; of which expence they are to be reimburfed three fourths by their fucceffor, the next to be reimburfed two, and the following incumbent one fourth.

There is a third bill to encourage benefactors to increafe our poor livings, (many of which have fo fmall an income, that in fome parts of the kingdom, the fame perfon enjoys four, five, and fometimes on to eight or nine of them, and yet has not 100 *l. per ann.*) by enabling Archbifhops, Bifhops, and other ecclefiaftical perfons to part with the advowfon of livings under 30 *l. per ann.* to fuch benefactor as will endow fuch fmall living with 30 *l. per ann.* or more ; and by giving the patronage of a Chapel to any one who fhall build a Chapel and endow it with 30 *l. per ann.* or more. In this act we had before us, one to the fame purpofe paft in *England* in the firft year of his late Majefty.

In a bill to repeal a claufe in a former bill, about the real union and divifion of parifhes, there is a claufe that the chief governor may, where the King is patron, confent for the King, to the removing the fite of a Church to a more convenient place in the parifh. Our parifhes here are exceeding poor, and the addition of 16 or 20 *l.* in the fees, prevents building a Church in a convenient part of the parifh, where the old Church ftands it may be at one end of a very

large

large parish; and we hope as the King's patronage cannot be hurt, but rather improved by such a change, that this clause will be granted us.

As these are in some sort Church bills, I have not troubled your Grace with a very particular account of them, but have sent a more large account of them to the Bishop of *London*, who will be able to inform your Grace more fully of their nature and design, as well as of the following bills, if your Grace desires it.

There is another bill gone over, part of which is for the encouragement of tillage; it is to the same purpose as one that went from the council to *England* at his Majesty's happy accession. It gives no premium to the exporter of corn, but obliges every person occupying 100 acres or more, to plough five for every 100 acres he possesses, excepting meadows and other pasture lands; and as the landlords in some parts here tye up their tenants from ploughing, it releases the tenant from such articles as far as five acres in 100; but that the landlord may be no sufferer, the tenant is not at liberty to burn-beat the land. For want of tillage our young fellows have no employment at home, and go into foreign service; and upon any accident in our harvest, we are in danger of a famine.

Since I came here in the year 1725, there was almost a famine among the poor; last year the dearness of corn was such, that thousands of families quitted their habitations to seek bread elsewhere, and many hundreds perished; this year the poor had consumed their potatoes, which is their winter subsistance, near two months sooner than ordinary, and are already through the dearness of corn, in that want, that in some places they begin already to quit their habitations. I hope we shall meet with so much compassion at the council, as to let us have this bill returned, that the inconveniencies we are at present fo frequently expofed to, may be gradually removed.

There is another bill gone over, to regulate the admiffion of barrifters, attornies, fix-clerks, follicitors, fub-fheriffs, deputy officers, &c. which is of the laft confequence to this kingdom.

The practice of the law, from the top to the bottom, is at prefent moftly in the hands of new converts, who give no farther fecurity on this account, than producing a certificate of their having received the facrament in the Church of *England* or *Ireland*, which feveral of them who were papifts at *London*, obtain on the road hither, and demand to be admitted barrifter in virtue of it, at their arrival ; and feveral of them have popifh wives and mafs faid in their houfes, and breed up their children papifts. Things are at prefent fo bad with us, that if about fix fhould be removed from the bar to the bench here, there will not be a barrifter of note left that is not a convert.

To put fome ftop to this evil, this bill endeavours to obtain fome farther fecurity of the fincerity of thefe converts : 1. by obliging all that come to the bar hereafter, or practife as attornies or follicitors, &c. or act as fub-fheriffs, fheriffs clerks,, or deputy officers in the courts, to make a declaration againft popery, and take the oath of abjuration before they are admitted or practice : 2. that every convert fhall have been fo five years before his admiffion, or fo practifing or acting : 3. that he breed up all his children under 14. as well thofe born before his converfion, as thofe after, in the proteftant religion : and 4. that whoever fails in any of thefe points, fhall incur the penalties and difabilities to which thofe relapfing from the proteftant religion to popery are liable.

Every body here is fenfible of the terrible effects of this growing evil, and both Lords and Commons are moft eagerly defirous of this bill.

We

We have likewife by this bill inflicted the fame penalties on every convert or proteftant who fhall breed up any child a papift.   But if the latter part be thought too fevere, or have too ftrong a party againft it, I hope, however that what relates to lawyers, attornies, follicitors, fub-fheriffs, &c. will be granted us, or the proteftant intereft muft fuffer extremely here.

I fhould flatter myfelf, that as in this bill we have not meddled with the papifts, but only with perfons profeffing themfelves proteftants, the foreign minifters cannot with any reafon or decency make any application to his Majefty againft this bill.

We have this week had before us a bill, in which the value of feveral goods that pay cuftom, that were before unfettled, is fixed.   By a letter that we fhall fend with it from the council, I hope it will appear that we have acted with a due fenfe of onr duty to his Majefty ; and I can affure your Grace that the altering a rate fent up by the Commons, was done with that gentlenefs and tendernefs, that fome very warm men of that houfe, have thanked my Lord Chancellor and myfelf for the tendernefs we fhewed on that occafion to the fubject, and have affured us they do not queftion the Commons readily acquiefcing in what is done.

As I muft have tired your Grace by this time, I fhall conclude with fubfcribing myfelf,

My Lord, &c.

To the Bifhop of London.

My Lord,   *Dublin, Mar.* 7, 1727.

AFTER the great trouble I have already given your Lordfhip about our bills, I muft defire your farther affiftance at the council about one bill more.

It

It is an act for regulating the admission of barristers, attornies, six-clerks, &c. As the laws stand already these several persons ought to be protestants, but they give no further security of their being so, than that, if they are born of popish parents, they must produce a certificate of their having received the sacrament in the Church of *England* or *Ireland*; and must educate their children under 14 years of age at their conversion in the protestant religion. But as the law stands at present, a man may the day after his real or pretended conversion, be admitted a barrister, attorney, &c. and practise as a sollicitor, or be a deputy officer or sub-sheriff, &c. and we have had several who were papists, and on the road from *London* hither have taken the sacrament and obtained a certificate, and at their arrival here have been admitted to the bar. They likewise pretend that the children born after their conversion are not included in that clause about educating their children protestants, because they were not under 14 at the time of their conversion; so that many of these converts have a popish wife who has mass said in the family, and the children are brought up papists.

Now this grievance is the greater here, because the business of the law from top to bottom is almost in the hands of these converts; when eight or ten protestants are set aside, the rest of the bar are all converts; much the greatest part of attornies, sollicitors, deputy officers, sub-sheriffs, sheriffs clerks, are new converts; and the old protestants are every day more and more working out of the business of the law, which must end in our ruin.

This makes us attempt to remedy this evil by this bill, for the success of which both Lords and Commons are equally sollicitous. In this bill the farther securities we require of all these people are: 1. that for the future, all taking to the law shall make the declarations, and take and subscribe to the oath required

quired in the act to prevent the farther growth of
popery, 2⁹ *Annæ* reg. the declaration is against several of the errors of popery; the oath is that of abjuration: 2. that nobody shall be admitted a barrifter, &c. till five years after his conversion, and continuing in the Church of *Ireland*: 3. that they
breed up the *post nati* as well as the *ante nati* under
14, protestants: 4. that he who offends in any of
these points shall fall under the disabilities, &c. to
which one relapsing from the protestant to the popish
religion is subject.

This is what we tried originally to push at, but
were forced to take in all converts educating their
children papists, and subject them to the like incapa-
cities, and likewise protestants so offending: the occasion of this latter clause is, that the sons of some
converts breed their children papists, and reckon
they do not incur the penalties appointed for converts educating their children papists, because say
they, our fathers were indeed converts, but we are
original protestants.

I find there are great hopes here among the papists,
that the bringing in all converts makes such a
strength against the bill, that it will be sunk in *England*. If there be any danger of that, or what relates to all converts be thought too severe, I would
beg we may have so much returned to us of the bill
as relates to all in any branch of the law; for we
must be undone here if that profession gets into the
hands of converts, where it is almost already got,
and where it every day gets more and more.

I have referred his Grace of *Newcastle*, to whom I
have wrote about some of our bills, to your Lordship,
to be more fully informed than I could inform his
Lordship in the compass of a letter: the bills he is
most likely to enquire after are, the clause about the
chief governor consenting for the King to the change
of the site of a Church, the tillage bill, and the bill
about

about lawyers, but your Lordſhip will be ſo good as
beſide talking to him on thoſe, to inform him of
any of the others he wants to underſtand more dif-
tinctly.

I ſhall trouble your Lordſhip no more at preſent,
but ſubſcribe myſelf,

My Lord, &c.

To the Archbiſhop of Canterbury.

My Lord,   *Dublin, Apr.* 2, 1728.

I HAVE received the honour of your Grace's of
the 19th paſt, and am very glad to have it under
your Lordſhip's hand that you are out of danger,
and daily recovering ſtrength, and pray God to raiſe
you up again for the good of the Church.

I am very much obliged to you for the care you
took of our Church bills, under ſo great weakneſs,
by recommending the care of them to ſo able a perſon and ſo good a friend of the Church as my Lord
Privy Seal *. I find moſt of them are gone through
the committee of council, and hope as my Lord
was fully inſtructed in our wants, that he has ſtruck
out an alteration made by the Attorney-general in
our bill for the reſidence of clergymen, which if
it has ſtood, will defeat the chief intention of the
bill.

Our bench have been very buſy with their friends
in the Houſe of Commons, to paſs our bills when
returned, which if they do, we may hope by degrees to ſee ſomewhat of the face of religion in this
country.

I have been enquiring about the value of Mr.
Horner's living, and believe it to be about 160 *l.*
per ann. I believe he has been under great difficulties,
                                                                as

* *Thomas* Lord *Trevor.*

as he was very bare of money when he firſt took it, and was kept out of part of the tythes of the firſt year, and has had but ſlow payments of the tythes of the ſecond harveſt, ſince it is generally counted good payment if a clergyman gets half his tythes paid him the *Candlemas* after they were due. His uneaſineſs is not owing to his temper, but to very great rudeneſſes he has met with from a popiſh gentleman of a good eſtate in his pariſh, whoſe tenants moſt of the pariſhioners are, as they are likewiſe papiſts. And I do not find he has given any other offence than preaching againſt popery, and talking with ſome of his pariſhioners to bring them over to our Church. As Mr. *Horner* is one who has a ſenſe of his duty, I hope he may be of ſervice here, and after ſome time he may be removed to ſomewhat better.

I am glad the affair of a prolocutor, and the meeting of a convocation are gone off ſo eaſily, and hope things will daily come to a better temper in *England.*

Colonel *Valon*, who came hither with the Marquiſs of * *Montandre*, has been with me, and brought me an account of the kind care you had taken of our Church bills, and of the fair way of recovery your Grace was in, before I had the honour of your laſt.

I ſhall trouble your Grace no more at preſent, but conclude with my beſt wiſhes for your health and happineſs, and ſubſcribe myſelf,

My Lord, &c.

To

---

* **Maſter of the Ordnance in *Ireland*.**

To the *Bishop of* London.

My Lord,   *Dublin, Apr*, 13, 1728.

I MOST heartily thank your Lordship for the trouble you have been at, and the care you have taken about our Church bills; I am very well satisfied with the words *or Churches* being kept in, and the reasons you give for it; and in the main have very little fear of any Bishops giving away the estates of their fees to augment livings, though by that clause they are impowered to do it.

I could heartily wish the powers desired for persons under settlements to grant 40 acres for a glebe had been granted us. * Another time we must try for 20 acres, without which we cannot compass parsonage-houses here. But about this I shall trouble your Lordship no more at present.

Our curates bill has passed the Commons, and there appears a disposition in them to pass our other Church bills; though one of them, *viz.* the tythe bill, has had a petition preferred against it by the quakers, who are to be heard by council against it on *Tuesday* next. I think their petition will do the bill no hurt; since it was resented by the Commons as a shameful piece of ingratitude to the Bishops, without whom their bill about their affirmation could not have passed.

Another sessions, if it please God that I live, I shall endeavour after your Lordship's advice, to make the affair of our Church bills more easy to your Lordship.

My Lord Lieutenant hopes our parliament will have done time enough for him to set out for *England* about the 9th of next month. We shall do our part
in

* A bill did pass afterwards.

in the Houfe of Lords to let him be at liberty by that time. On *Monday* will be the warmeft day this feffion in the Houfe of Commons about the privilege bill, which meets with fo great oppofition there, that the fuccefs is doubtful.

I am, my Lord, &c.

To the Archbifhop of Canterbury.

My Lord,   *Dublin, Apr.* 18, 1728.

I HAVE had with me Sir *Thomas Taylour*, a very worthy gentleman of this country, to defire I would write to fome of my friends in the Houfe of Lords in *England* to attend a caufe he had depending there, in which *John Cahill* and *William Donellan* are appellants, and Sir *Thomas* defendant.

I find they trump up againft him a leafe made in the year 1680, which they never made any claim upon till 1720, after he by laying out above 1000 *l.* on the eftate had raifed the rent about 100 *l. per ann.* If fuch old leafes are once allowed (confidering how eafy it is to get people here to fwear to any thing) the proteftant poffeffors here will have but precarious eftates where they have been fair purchafers, and have laid out great fums in improving eftates.

But the merits of the caufe your Lordfhip will beft know from what is proved at the bar. The only favour I defire is that you would be pleafed to attend at the hearing of the caufe, which will very much oblige,

Your Grace's, &c.

To

To the Duke of Newcastle.

My Lord,   *Dublin, Apr,* 25, 1728.

THOUGH your Grace in the great hurry of bufinefs has not found leifure to honour me with a letter, yet by the fuccefs of our bills in the council, I find your Lordfhip has not forgot the requeft I made to you about them. I have great hopes they will prove of great fervice here to ftrengthen the proteftant intereft, and will prove ufeful both in Church and ftate.

As I was known to be a hearty follicitor for them, their being returned us has given me fome additional weight here, which I need not tell your Grace, with whatever elfe lies in my power, fhall always be employed for his Majefty's fervice here.

To-morrow the fate of the privilege bill, which has already paft the Commons, will be determined in our Houfe ; and I think it will be there carried to the great benefit of this kingdom.

I am, my Lord, &c.

To the fame.

My Lord,   *Dublin, Apr.* 30, 1728.

ON *Friday* laft came on the debate in our Houfe, about the privilege bill, which was carried 25 againft 19 : there was one proxy among the 25, and feven among the 19. Several of our Lords who are very much in debt, and value themfelves upon paying nobody, were from the firft very much againft the bill ; but the great oppofition made on this occafion, was formed and managed by the * Bifhop of *Elphin,*

---

* Dr. *Bolton.*

Elphin, who put himfelf at the head of thofe Lords, and drew in fome others, with a view of making himfelf confiderable by being at the head of a party of lay Lords againft the bench of Bifhops.   All the lay Lords that oppofe the government in whatever they can, joined againft the bill.   There was no Bifhop againft it but the Bifhop of *Elphin*, and of *Waterford*, for whom he was proxy.   The Lord *Middleton* was the firft who fpoke againft the bill, and that very prolixly and to little purpofe : he was very well anfwered by the Archbifhop of * *Tuam*.   After this the Bifhop of *Elphin* made a fpeech with very falfe reafonings, and fome inflaming paffages againft *England :* though in the clofe of his fpeech, he was rather as circumftances now ftand, for the paffing the bill : he has very much loft himfelf with both fides by his fhuffling fpeech on this occafion.   As his fpeech did no hurt to the bill, we let the debate drop without anfwering him.

I hope it will not be thought proper, when a vacancy happens of an Archbifhoprick, to reward one with it who has endeavoured to form a confpiracy of lay Lords againft the Bifhops here, who are the perfons on whom the government muft depend for doing the publick bufinefs.

We fhall probably conclude our feffions next *Monday*, when more truly ufeful bills will have paffed, than have paffed for many feffions put together.

I muft again thank your Grace for your kind care of our bills at the council.

I am, my Lord, &c.

To

* Dr. *Synge*.

To *Lord* Townfhend.

My Lord,   *Dublin, May* 9, 1728.

IT is with great pleafure that I hear from all hands, that I may now congratulate your Lordfhip upon your recovery from a long and dangerous illnefs, and I heartily wifh you may continue many years in a ftate of health for the fervice of his Majefty and your country.

On *Monday* our feffion ended, which has gone on with more quiet and unanimity than ufual ; and in which more ufeful * bills have paffed than for many feffions together before. And I hope both gentry and clergy will ufe thofe powers now given them gradually to plant religion and civility in this country.

I muft on this occafion own the great obligations I lie under to your Lordfhip, and the reft of the privy council, for the regard fhewn to my accounts and recommendations of feveral of our bills.

The chief oppofition that was made here to any of our bills, was to the privilege bill, and the greateft ftand againft it was in the Houfe of Lords. Several of our Lords that are embarraffed in their circumftances, might naturally be fuppofed to be againft it : but the greatnefs of the oppofition was owing to the management of the Bifhop of *Elphin*, who put himfelf at the head of thofe Lords and others who conftantly oppofe the government bufinefs here, and by mifreprefentations drew in fome other Lords of no ill intentions to engage their word and honour to each other to throw out the bill. His view no doubt was to make himfelf confiderable enough by being at the head of this ftrength to be bought off. One part of the pufh he now made was to get all the lay Lords here

---

* His Grace was the framer of moft, if not of all thefe bills.

here to confederate againſt the Biſhops, who muſt always be depended upon for doing the King's buſineſs. But as he has miſcarried in his attempt, and has offended all ſides, ſo as to be in no danger of appearing again at the head of ſo many Lords as he did now, I hope his behaviour will be remembered, when he or his friends puſh for the archbiſhoprick of *Dublin* for him.

As your Lordſhip was ſo good as to promiſe me before I left *England* that Mr. *Stephens* ſhould have the next canonry of *Chriſt Church*, and as Dr. *Burton* cannot probably hold out long, I muſt again recommend Mr. *Stephens* to your Lordſhip's protection and favour on that occaſion ; and your ſupport of his pretenſions will be eſteemed the greateſt obligation by,

My Lord, &c.

To the Duke of Newcaſtle.

My Lord,   *Dublin, May* 25, 1728.

I HAD the honour of your Grace's of the 7th inſt. I am ſenſible of the great hurry you was in during the ſeſſions of parliament, and am the more obliged to your Lordſhip for the great care you was pleaſed, in the midſt of ſo much buſineſs of greater conſequence, to take of our bills, and can aſſure your Grace the returning of all our publick bills was very gratefully taken here. I am ſatisfied we have in ſome of them laid a very good foundation for gradually ſtrengthening the proteſtant intereſt here, and civilizing this country.

The great diſtreſs the poor are in, through a great part of this country, has raiſed a reſolution in many of the gentry to put the tillage bill in execution, which I hope will in a few years prevent our ſuffering little less than a famine almost every other year.

I am very glad to hear that any accounts I sent of our bills were of service to the Attorney-General when he had them under confideration; and make my humbleft acknowledgments for the regard fhewn by your Grace and the other minifters, to what I fuggefted on that occafion.

I am very much obliged to your Grace for your favourably reprefenting my endeavours to ferve his Majefty.

As at the latter end of the feffions a fcheme was formed by a Bifhop to raife a party that might on occafion oppofe the fervice of his Majefty in the Houfe of Lords, I thought it my duty to acquaint your Grace with it at the firft appearance. But I hope we fhall eafily defeat any future attempts of the fame nature.

As my Lord Lieutenant did his part towards procuring a quiet feffion of parliament here, fo I muft do that juftice to the reft of the *Englifh* in power here, to fay that we were not in the leaft wanting in our feveral ftations to promote the fame good end.

As the want of filver grows every day greater here, to the great prejudice of our manufactures, and the retail trade, I fhall in a little time draw up a memorial on that fubject, containing the true caufes of our diftrefs and the proper remedies, which I fhould be glad to have communicated to the * Chancellor of the Exchequer, if he can find leifure to have it confidered. I am,

My Lord, &c.

To

* Sir *Robert Walpole.*

To the fame.

My Lord,   *Dublin, May* 31, 1728.

MR. *Manley*, our Poft-mafter here, having occafion to go to *England* to follicit a continuance of his penfion of 200 *l. per ann.* which dropt by the death of his late Majefty; I was willing to give him what affiftance I could, by recommending him to your Grace for your kind help. He is one who has behaved himfelf well in his poft, and is well affected to his Majefty, and has always diftinguifhed himfelf by his zeal for the illuftrious Houfe of *Hanover*, in the worft times. The pleas he has for having his penfion continued he will inform your Grace of; but your affiftance of him on this occafion will be counted an obligation by,

My Lord, &c.

To Lord Carteret.

My Lord,   *Dublin, June* 6, 1728.

IT was with great fatisfaction I heard that your Excellency was fafely arrived at *London*. I was in hopes we fhould this day have anfwered your Excellency's two letters relating to the *Cæfar*, but as we differed among ourfelves, and likewife the council (whom we fummoned upon this occafion) differed about the fenfe of your Lordfhip's laft letter, whether we were left at liberty to let that fhip go free, if we thought proper, confidering all circumftances, it will be another poft before we can acquaint your Lordfhip with what we have done. Some here applied the King's approbation (mentioned in your letter) to your having put the *Cæfar* under quarantine; and other of us thought his Majefty approved of the

N 2   direc-

directions you was pleafed to give us in yours of the 25th paft, *viz.* to act as we thought proper. I am,

My Lord, &c.

To the fame.

My Lord,   *Dublin, June* 20, 1728.

I HAVE had the honour of your Excellency's of the 13th inftant.

We have fince examined more ftrictly into the cafe of the fhip *Cæfar*, and find fhe has nothing on board befide corn, which is not reckoned very liable to take or keep infection; however what we have at laft agreed on, is to difcharge her at the end of forty days from her firft being under the care of Captain *Rowley.* We fhall be very careful never to depart from the general rules without very good reafon, and the utmoft caution.

We yefterday received Mr. *Twell's* refignation, and elected Mr. *Ellis* chaplain to the hofpital, purfuant to your Lordfhip's recommendation. There was fome little grumbling in favour of Mr. *Hawkins* the reader, but in the end all matters were accommodated.

Since your Lordfhip left us, Dr. *Coghill* has made fome alterations in the paper about the Delegates, which my Lord Chancellor is fatisfied with, and which we fhall, when fully fettled, tranfmit to your Excellency. I thank your Lordfhip for having the affair of the coin in your thoughts, to talk with the miniftry about it when you fee a proper opportunity.

Lord Juftice *Conolly* has been pretty much out of order ever fince the 10th of this month, and ftill continues weak and low-fpirited. As Mr. *Medlicott* is now arrived, he defigns to retire to Mr. *Pearfon's* for fome time, to try to recover himfelf.

We

We fhall on *Saturday* have a council to fwear in
the Lords *Anglefea*, *Shannon*, and *Forbes* *.

I am, My Lord, &c.

To the Duke of Newcaftle,

My Lord,   *Dublin, June* 25, 1728.

IN mine of the 25th paft, I acquainted your
Grace that I hoped in a little time to fend you a
memorial relating to the want we are in of filver,
with the true caufe of our diftrefs, and the proper
remedies to be applied to this evil, which I defired
to be communicated to Sir *Robert Walpole*.

I have here fent it with an account of the prefent
value of our coins ; and the favour I have to defire
of Sir *Robert Walpole* is to look it over, and fee
whether the fcheme there propofed is rational, and
what he will intercede with his Majefty to grant us,
if we apply for it from the council here.

We had this affair before the council, upon a letter from my Lord Lieutenant in the year 1726, and
had made all our calculations of the value intended
for gold and filver coins in a new proclamation upon
the fcheme here propofed ; and had almoft finifhed
the affair, but the apprehenfions of a war and the intereft of the bankers here with fome of the council,
hung up the affair then, and it has flept ever fince.
But as the want of filver every day increafes upon us,
and loudly calls for fome relief, I have fent over this
memorial, that the miniftry may be apprized of what
we would pufh at here, and if the fcheme, which I
take to be rational, and in refpect of *England*, un-
exceptionable, be approved of by Sir *Robert Walpole*, I have no doubt but the Lord Chancellor and

myfelf

In order to facilitate this matter as much as I could on the other fide of the water, I drew up a paper on this fubject, of about two fheets, which I fent to the Duke of *Newcaftle*, to be communicated to the Chancellor of the Exchequer, whofe approbation this alteration of our coin muft have, before it can be paffed.   It is wholly on the fhort fcheme I gave in to your Lordfhip, but as it is for the ufe of perfons who know nothing of our coins, it is worked out into a greater length.   I fhall by the next mail fend your Excellency a copy of it, fuch as it is.

If we have fenfe enough here to come into this alteration of our coin, and your Excellency can get it approved of in *England*, I am fure it will fet our coin on fo reafonable a footing, and be of that advantage to this nation, that your government will be always remembered in this country with efteem *.

As foon as we take any ftep in this affair, I fhall fend your Excellency word.   Mr. *Conolly* is retired for fome time into the country for his health, where I hear he grows better.   I believe his indifpofition will prevent my vifiting my diocefe this fummer; but as his abfence will rob the bankers of one to whom they formerly applied, and on whom they could make fome impreffions, I believe we fhall get the eafier through this bufinefs for his being out of the way.

I am, &c.

To

---

* My Lord Primate himfelf was the firft and moft fteady promoter of this fcheme.

To the same.

My Lord,   *Dublin, July* 15, 1728,

I HAVE by this mail fent your Excellency a copy of the paper I lately fent the Duke of *Newcaftle*, relating to our want of filver. And as this contains a full and diftinct account of the ftate of our coin, and the occafions and remedies of our want of filver, I think we may be the fhorter in the letter from the council to your Lordfhip. If poffible we will bring on this affair before the Judges go their circuits.

Your Lordfhip was pleafed to give fome hopes of giving an enfign's place to my Lord * Mayor's fon, if it fuits with your Lordfhip's conveniency, my Lord Chancellor and myfelf fhould be glad if the prefent vacancy were beftowed on him.

I am, &c.

To the Duke of Newcaftle.

My Lord,   *Dublin, July* 16, 1728.

IN my laft I fent to your Grace a memorial re- lating to our want of filver in this nation, which I defired might be communicated to Sir *Robert Walpole.* Soon after the *Englifh* prints informed us that Sir *Robert* was gone for a fortnight into the country. As his abfence when my letter arrived muft have occafioned my paper being laid afide for a while, I trouble your Grace with this to defire it may not be forgotten at his return.

Our want of filver here is fuch, that it is common to give fix-pence for the change of a moidore, and

to

* Sir *Nathaniel Whitwell.*

to take a guinea or piftole for part of the change. And I know fome in *Dublin*, who have occafion to pay workmen every *Saturday* night, that are obliged to pay four-pence for every twenty fhillings in filver they procure.

We have hundreds of families (all proteftants) removing out of the north to *America*; and the leaft obftruction in the linen-manufacture, by which the north fubfifts, muft occafion greater numbers following, and the want of filver increafing, will prove a terrible blow to that manufacture, as there will not be money to pay the poor for their fmall parcels of yarn.

Since I drew up that memorial I have a certain account that the middle price of filver bullion in *England* * for ten years laft paft, has been 5*s*. 5*d*. *Englifh* per ounce, which makes me defirous (for the more certain procuring of fome foreign filver here) to put our filver at the rate of 5*s*. 4½*d*. *Englifh* per ounce, which is indeed one halfpenny higher than the price propofed in that paper, but is ftill one halfpenny under the middle price of filver bullion in *England*,

If filver grows more fcarce with us, our rents muft certainly fall, not only to our prejudice who live here, but to the damage of the noblemen and gentlemen of *England*, who have eftates here, and of thofe others who fpend their rents in *England*.

I fhould be glad to know Sir *Robert Walpole*'s opinion as foon as he has leifure: and hope we fhall be gratified in an affair of fo much confequence to us, and of no damage to *England*.

I am, &c.

To

* The bankers had told his Grace fo, but it appears afterwards in thefe letters that they had impofed upon him.

To the *Bishop of* London.

My Lord,   *Dublin, Aug.* 20, 1728.

IT is now a great while since I had the favour of one from your Lordship; I hope it has not been any continuance of the illness that hung about you in the spring that has occasioned so long a silence. I should have been glad to have heard from one so likely to know, whether peace or war be more probable, about which we at this distance are still uncertain. I hear there is a great noise about a sermon preached by the Bishop of *Glocester*, but have not yet seen it. I should be sorry to find that he had given any just occasion of offence.

I have lately heard from Mr. *Sparke*, whom your Lordship was pleased to recommend as an interim schoolmaster at *Chigwell*. He complains of unjust and hard usage from the governors there, and tells me that he and they shall soon appear before your Lordship: I do not reckon that I know what the case is, as I have my account only from one side, nor do I farther recommend him to your Lordship than to be protected from oppression, if that be his case.

We have had a rumour here that the Duke of *Newcastle* is dead, I hope there is nothing in the report.

The ill state of health of Lord Justice *Conolly* has confined me to *Dublin* the whole summer, though he is better than he has been.

I am, &c.

To

To *Lord* Cartéret.

My Lord,   *Dublin, Sept.* 3, 1728.

BY the mails that came in laft night, we had advice of *Thomas Clements*'s death, and I have had two or three gentlemen with me to day to defire my recommendation in favour of his brother *Nathaniel Clements*, to fucceed him as agent to the penfioners. I have not feen either of my brethren fince this news came, but was however willing to give your Excellency advice of this application.

       I am, my Lord, &c.

To *Sir* Robert Walpole.

Sir,   *Dublin, Sept.* 14, 1728.

I SOME time ago troubled his Grace of *Newcaftle* with a memorial relating to our want of filver in this kingdom, with the caufes and cures of this want, which I defired might be communicated to you for your confideration : that if you approved of the fcheme as reafonable and not prejudicial to *England*, we might fet the affair going in council in order to make a regular application to his Majefty, for leave to publifh a proclamation here.

I was wilfing, Sir, to know your fentiments, whether we might hope for his Majefty's compliance with our requeft, before my Lord Chancellor and I make any pufh in council for an application to his Majefty, fince we have the whole intereft of the bankers, which is very great here, againft reducing the value of gold ; and we are unwilling to go through a violent conteft here to carry a point,

except

except we had hopes our application would not afterwards be rejected in *England*.

The bankers here own that by the different proportion of gold to silver here, from what it bears in *England*, they get 2 *per cent.* in remittances to *England*, and the popular argument they use against this reduction is, that as things now stand, all gentlemen enjoying estates, pensions, or places, who draw off their money to *England*, lose 2 *per cent.* of what they draw off to the benefit of this kingdom.

In the year 1726, upon a letter from my Lord Lieutenant, we had made a great progress in this affair ; and had in a committee of council, settled the designed value of foreign gold upon the bottom proposed in the memorial Mr. *Delafaye* has delivered you from the Duke of *Newcastle* ; and we had the several species of foreign silver assayed, and had settled their intended value upon the bottom of 5 *s.* 4 *d. per* ounce sterling, but the talk of a war, with the interest of the bankers, put a stop to our proceedings at that time.   But, as the want of silver is since increased upon us, so that in many places of this kingdom 8 *d.* is a common premium for changing a moidore, and 4 *d.* for procuring 20 shillings in silver is what is paid in *Dublin*, if some remedy be not applied speedily, our manufactures must be ruined.

I have given several people of fashion here hopes, that as we desire nothing but putting gold and *English* silver on the same bottom as they stand on in *England*, I could obtain this favour on the other side of the water.   If I succeed in this application, it will give me some weight here, which I am sure shall always be employed in the service of his Majesty.

This makes me a most earnest suitor in behalf of this kingdom, whose manufactures must daily decay,

cay, and rents fink, unlefs the favour of altering
the prefent currency of gold and filver be granted
us ; whilft the whole profit of the prefent inequality
of gold and filver, will reft in the bankers hands.

All the encouragement I at prefent want, is an
affurance that if we go on with this affair in council, and that if we apply in form from hence to his
Majefty, we may hope to have our requeft granted.

In the memorial I mention putting foreign filver
at 5 s. 4 d. *Englifh per* ounce fterling. but as I am
fince informed that the middle price of filver bullion for ten years paft has been 5 s. 5 d. *Englifh per*
ounce at *London*, I fhould rather defire to put foreign filver at 5 s. 4½ d. *Englifh per* ounce here, and
have accordingly ordered a calculation to be made:
but for that I am not fo earneft as for the reft of the
fcheme, without which we are gradually undoing
here.

The occafion of my giving you this trouble is
that the Duke of *Newcaftle* has for fome time been
out of town, and that though I find my memorial
has been delivered to you, I cannot learn that my
letters were communicated to you, to acquaint you
with what I defired.

I hope, Sir, you will be fo good as to favour me
with an anfwer at your leifure.

I am, &c.

To Lord Carteret.

My Lord, *Dublin, Sept.* 17, 1728.

THE Lord Mayor has been with me, and defired I would tranfmit the inclofed to your Excellency: he told me it was in behalf of his fon, that
you would be pleafed to beftow on him the Lieutenant's place he was formerly mentioned for by my
Lord

Lord Chancellor and myfelf. I muft again take this opportunity of recommending him to your Lordfhip's favour, if you are not otherwife engaged. I am,

My Lord, &c.

To the Archbifhop of Canterbury.

My Lord,   *Dublin, Oct. 1, 1728.*

ON *Sunday* I had the favour of your Grace's of the 22d paft, with the occafional offices revifed and publifhed by authority. I thank your Grace for your kindnefs in fending them fo early, and fhall endeavour to have them ordered here againft *November 5.*

I hope your vifitation, and the fpending of fome time at *Tunbridge*, may have confirmed your health, and recovered your ftrength, which I moft heartily wifh for the publick good.

Our accounts from *England* give us great hopes of a peace or a truce.

I muft again thank your Grace for the fervice you did our Church bills in *England* laft winter. As I find the lawyers are againft a tenant in tail granting a glebe, we muft e'en acquiefce.

I am, &c.

To the Duke of Newcaftle.

My Lord,   *Dublin, Oct. 14, 1728.*

THIS day had the honour of your Grace's of the 3d. inftant, and fhould have moft cheerfully obeyed his Majefty's commands relating to the Duke *de Ripperda* *, but as the Duke left *Cork* feveral days ago,

---

* There did not in the prefent century appear a more extraordinary man than this Duke *de Ripperda*; he was born and bred

ago, and by the accounts in the *English* prints, is landed in the weft of *England*, there is no room for any thing more in this affair, than keeping his Majefty's orders a fecret.

I am, &c.

To the Archbifhop of Canterbury.

My Lord, *Dublin, Nov. 9*, 1728.

I AM very much obliged to your Grace for fending me the occafional fervices amended, and the account of an alteration relating to that for the 5th of *November*, which was forgotten in the firft account. I have fince looked the feveral alterations over, and think they are very right, and in a great meafure neceffary: I was unwilling to publifh them here till fome Bifhops came to town, that I might have their approbation; but fhall take care to have them publifhed by authority, before the 30th of *January*.

I am glad to hear your Grace has perfectly recovered the weaknefs occafioned by your laft fit of ficknefs, and moft heartily wifh you all health and happinefs.

We are under great trouble here about a frenzy that has taken hold of very great numbers, to leave

this

bred a merchant in *Holland*; had great abilities; was by the States General fent Ambaffador to *Spain*; turned Roman Catholic; was created a Baron, then a Duke and Grandee, by his moft Catholic Majefty; became a principal Favourite and Minifter of State; had an illicit correfpondence with the miniftry in *England*; was taken into cuftody, and imprifoned; made an efcape, by the means of a fair *Caftillian* woman, to *England*, where he was protected; after fome refidence there, he went to *Muly Abdalla*, Emperor of *Fez* and *Morocco*, turned Mahometan, was circumcifed and made Bafhaw and Prime Minifter to that Prince. See his Memoirs from 1715 to 1736, which have been tranflated into moft *European* languages.

this country for the *West Indies* ; and we are endeavouring to learn what may be the reasons of it, and the proper remedies ; which as soon as we are able, we shall lay before the government in *England*. I am,

My Lord, &c.

To the Duke of Newcastle.

My Lord,   *Dublin, Nov.* 23, 1728.

I A M very sorry I am obliged to give your Grace so melancholy an account of the state of this kingdom, as I shall in this letter, but I thought it my duty to let his Majesty know our present condition in the north.   For we have had three bad harvests together there, which has made oatmeal, which is their great subsistance, much dearer than ordinary, and as our farmers here are very poor, and obliged as soon as they have their corn, to sell it for ready money to pay their rents, it is more in the power of those who have a little money to engross corn here, and make advantage of its scarceness, than in *England.*

We have had for several years some agents from the colonies in *America,* and several masters of ships that have gone about the country, and deluded the people with stories of great plenty and estates to be had for going for in those parts of the world : and they have been the better able to seduce people, by reason of the necessities of the poor of late.

The people that go from hence make great complaints of the oppressions they suffer here, not from the government, but from their fellow subjects of one kind or another, as well as of the dearness of provision, and say these oppressions are one reason of their going.

V o L. I.   O   But

But whatever occasions their going, it is certain that above 4200 men, women, and children have been shipped off from hence for the *West Indies* within three years, and of these above 3100 this last summer. Of these possibly one in ten may be a man of substance, and may do well enough abroad, but the case of the rest is deplorable, the rest either hire themselves to those of substance for their passage, or contract with the masters of ships for four years servitude when they come thither, or if they make a shift to pay for their passage, will be under a necessity of selling themselves for servants for four years for their subsistance when they come there.

The whole north is in a ferment at present, and people every day engaging one another to go next year to the *West Indies.* The humour has spread like a contagious distemper, and the people will hardly hear any body that tries to cure them of their madness. The worst is that it affects only protestants, and reigns chiefly in the north, which is the seat of our linen manufacture.

This unsettled state puts almost a stop to trade, and the more so as several who were in good credit before have taken up parcels of goods on trust and disposed of them, and are gone off with the money, so that there is no trade there but for ready money.

We have had it under our consideration how to put some stop to this growing evil: we think by some old laws we can hinder money being carried abroad, and stop all but merchants, that have not a license, from going out of the kingdom.

By this post we have sent my Lord Lieutenant the representation of the gentlemen of the north, and the opinion of our lawyers what can be done by law to hinder people going abroad; but these are matters we shall do nothing in without directions from his Majesty. But whatever can be done by law,

law, I fear it may be dangerous forcibly to hinder a number of needy people from quitting us.

There is one method that can do no hurt, and we hope may do good, which is keeping corn at a reasonable price till next harvest, that so dearness of bread may drive none from us. And to compass this we are subscribing for a sum of money to buy corn where it can be had the cheapest, and to sell it to loss in the north, to keep the markets down there; and I believe we shall have good success in our subscription.

But I fear except leave be given to prohibit by proclamation the exportation of corn from hence, we shall fail even in this project.

I was just willing to give your Grace an account of our present difficulties, and fear I shall have occasion to trouble you more on this subject.

I am, &c.

To Lord Carteret.

My Lord,   *Dublin, Nov.* 28, 1728.

MR. *Caffell* has been often with me to press me to put your Excellency in mind of his memorial: your Lordship knows his case and pretensions very well; and his great concern is for a provision for his wife, if she survives him.

All I shall add is, that if somewhat is not soon done in his affair, it is unlikely he will live to see it.

I could not well refuse him putting your Excellency again in mind of his request. I am,

My Lord, &c.

O 2

To the Duke of Newcastle.

My Lord,   *Dublin, Dec.* 3, 1728.

I HAVE by the mail that came this day from
England, received letters from two of my brothers in law, Mr. *Savage* * and Mr. *Merrett* §, both
merchants in *London*, and very well affected to his
Majesty, to defire me to trouble your Grace in behalf of Mr. *William Ball*, a merchant at *Alicant*.

I find by them that Mr. *Barker*, late conful of
Alicant, is dead, and they are defirous Mr. *Ball*,
who has been a merchant at *Alicant* about eight
years, may fucceed to that employment. I am confident they would not trouble me to write to your
Grace on this occafion, except they knew Mr. *Ball*
to be every way qualified for that poft.

If your Grace is not otherwife engaged already
your favouring Mr. *Ball* in his affair, would be
efteemed a great obligation by,

                    My Lord, &c.

To the Archbifhop of Canterbury.

My Lord,   *Dublin, Dec.* 3, 1728.

I HAVE had the favour of your Grace's of the
21ft paft, and am very much obliged to you for
fending us the occafional offices as altered, for you
guefled right, that we ufe the fame offices here with
the alterations neceffary for this country ; and I hope
to have thefe offices fettled here before the 30th
of *January*.

                                      We

* A Director of the Bank of *England*.
§ Whofe only daughter married my Lord *Cunningham*, of the
kingdom of *Ireland*.

We are endeavouring here by a fubfcription, to provide againft one reafon given here for people leaving us, which is the dearnefs of provifion, by having three bad harvefts together; and we have confulted the miniftry, to know what other meafures that are in our power, may be proper to be taken.

The keeping of people here by force, will I fear, have bad confequences, the numbers that are infected with this humour, being very great; but the putting fome difficulties in people's way, and obliging fraudulent debtors to pay their creditors, may probably do fome good.

I am very forry for the terrible calamity that has befallen thofe of *Copenhagen*, and heartily wifh them a good collection in *England*, but a collection here will turn to little if any account. We had fince I came hither, a collection for the proteftant Churches in *Lithuania*, about which I fpoke to feveral bifhops at parliament, and afterwards wrote a circular letter to my fuffragans, and to every clergyman in my diocefe, to promote the collection, and yet there was not gathered 300 *l.* in the kingdom, and of that about 100 *l.* came out of my diocefe. But at prefent with the defertion of our people in the north, and the want of corn there, little can be expected from even thence, where proteftants are moft numerous; and *Munfter* and *Connaught* are moftly papifts, and his Grace of *Dublin* is againft all collections for foreigners in his province of *Leinfter*.

I thought proper juft to acquaint your Grace with what may probably be the fuccefs of a collection here, if his Majefty fhould pleafe to order one.

I wifh your Grace all health and happinefs, and am,

My Lord, &c.

To

To Sir Robert Walpole.

SIR,   *Dublin, Dec.* 4, 1728.

MR. *Nuttal*, the Sollicitor to the Commissioners of the Revenue here, has so misbehaved
himself, that he is as I hear, dismissed his office.
The place I understand is in the disposal of the
Commissioners in *England*, which occasions my giving you this trouble, to recommend for his employment one Mr. *Richard Morgan* *, who is my
agent here: he is well affected to his Majesty, and
has been brought up an attorney, and is very diligent and understanding in business, and has the character of a very honest man; I am sure I have always found him to be so.

I am sensible, Sir, I am going out of my immediate province, in meddling in this affair, but I
hope, from your goodness, Sir, whatever you please
to do in it, you will at least excuse this trouble
from,

Sir, your humble servant,

To Lord Carteret.

My Lord,   *Dublin, Dec.* 14, 1728.

I HAD yesterday the honour of your Excellency's
of the 3d. instant, and am glad to find the consideration of the proclamation about corn is likely
to come on in a cabinet council so soon. We had
this day a great many gentlemen with us at the castle, complaining of the accounts of the exportation
of corn in several parts, and the great distress we
are

* This gentleman was also agent to Dr. *Hoadly*, when Archbishop of *Dublin*, as also when Primate.

are likely to be under, except a speedy stop be put to it; and we could scarce pacify them though we assured them your Lordship had acquainted the King with that affair, and that his Majesty had ordered a cabinet council to consider it, and that we did not question receiving his Majesty's commands in a post or two.

The want of such a proclamation is at least made use of as a pretence by the gentlemen of the north, for not coming into the subscription we mentioned in our letter, without which I fear some thousands will perish before next harvest.

I am glad your Lordship is so kind as to think of the affair of our coin. If we had an enlivening letter from your Excellency, I hope we might make some advance here towards an application to the King from the council: but as our brother *Conolly* is pretty much in with the bankers, and they think they shall lose 2 *per cent.* in their remittances, if gold should be reduced, he now talks that at this unhappy juncture in the north, he is afraid that it would be unseasonable: so that I fear if it were to be moved in council, he would encourage several underhand to oppose it. On the contrary, I think in this very juncture, the getting or keeping of silver, as it would promote the little retail business, would be of service to us: and if we had any hint after it has been considered in a cabinet council, that upon application, our desire to have our money altered, would be granted, I believe, with a word from your Lordship to help us, my Lord Chancellor and I could secure the point in council.

I have nothing farther to add to my memorial on that subject, but that upon considering that in the scheme formerly proposed, foreign silver is set at the lowest price it is ever sold for in *England,* and that our people are afraid, if the *Mexico* piece of eight were set at 5 *s. Irish,* we should go too high: I have

thought

thought of a middle way, which is setting the *Mexico* piece of 17 *pwts.* 4 *grs.* at 5 *s. Irish*, on which supposition foreign silver would go at 5 *s.* 9 *d.* 3 *qrs. Irish per* ounce : whereas in the old scheme the *Mexico* piece is but 17 *pwts.* bare, and on that supposition silver will go at 5 *s.* 9 *d. Irish per* ounce, so that the difference will not be quite one halfpenny *per* ounce, and yet that advance will make it more worth while to keep silver here : and this can be done because the full weight of the *Mexico* piece is 17 *pwts.* 12 *grs.*

I shall by the next post send your Excellency a calculation of the foreign silver coins upon this new supposition.

I am, &c.

To the Duke of Newcastle.

My Lord,   *Dublin, Dec.* 17, 1728.

L AST *Friday* I had the honour of your Grace's of the 5th instant, and thank you for laying our melancholy state before his Majesty : I hope we shall speedily know his Royal pleasure about a proclamation, prohibiting the exportation of corn from hence. On *Saturday* we had a great number of the principal gentry here, who pressed somewhat rudely for such a proclamation, and were hardly satisfied with our assuring them the affair was already laid before his Majesty, and that we expected his Majesty's pleasure by one of the next mails. It is certain we had a very bad crop of corn last year, and that commissions are come to buy up great quantities here, so that it is to be feared we shall before spring suffer extremely by its dearness. But I do not doubt, but we shall receive his Majesty's commands in that affair before this comes to your Grace's hands. As we hope in due time to know what he

pleases

pleafes to order relating to the people going to the *Weft Indies*; the infatuation ftill fpreads, and the dearnefs of provifions muft needs increafe it, if not prevented.

I am greatly obliged to his Majefty for the good opinion he is pleafed to entertain of my zeal for his fervice, and hope I fhall never give him reafon to alter it. I am,

My Lord, &c.

To the Bifhop of London.

My Lord,   *Dublin, Dec.* 21, 1728.

*W*E are very much rejoiced here at the arrival of Prince Frederick * at St. James's, as I find by the accounts from England all friends to the government are there.* As I am confined here by being in the government, and by my Lord Juftice *Conolly's* weaknefs, I muft defire the favour of your Lordfhip when you next wait upon his Royal Highnefs to prefent my moft humble duty to him, and to affure him that nothing but my being detained here by his Majefty's fervice fhould hinder me from having the honour of waiting on him, and paying him my moft dutiful refpects in perfon on fo happy an occafion.

This cold weather has pretty much pinched his Grace of *Dublin*, not that he is apprehended to be in any immediate danger, but as reports may be fpread in *England* that he is dead, and pufhes made for naming a fucceffor to him, I beg the favour of you to wait on the miniftry, and defire they would not fix on a fucceffor upon any rumours of his death.

---

* Prince of *Wales*, eldeft fon of *George* II. His Grace had fome fhare in teaching his Highnefs *Englifh*, when he was a Chaplain at *Hanover*.

death. It is a matter of great confequence to his Majefty's fervice, and the *Englifh* intereft here, and I hope that no native will be thought of for the place, nor an *Englifbman* be fixed upon too haftily. I am,

My Lord, &c.

To Lord Carteret.

My Lord,   *Dublin, Jan.* 4, 1728.

I Underftand by his Grace of *Canterbury* there were fome fmall changes made in the occafional offices of the Church in *England*, which he was fo kind as to fend me. As the 30th of *January* is now coming on, I have thoughts of having the like alterations made here, as likewife ordering the office of the King's inauguration-day to be ufed here, but I thought it improper to fpeak to the Lords Juftices or the privy council about it, till I had your Excellency's approbation of the defign. I heartily wifh your Lordfhip many happy new years.

I am, &c.

To the fame.

My Lord,   *Dublin, Jan.* 15, 1728.

THE Rev. Mr. *John Quarterman* died here yefterday, by whofe death the union of *Burn-church*, confifting of *Burn-church*, alias *Kiltranine* vicarage or parifh, *Dunfort* vicarage, *Kilfaragh* whole rectory, and the monaftery or rectory of *Gerpoint*, with all its members and dependencies in the diocefe of *Offory*, is become vacant, and in the gift of your Excellency.

As

As your Lordſhip was pleaſed to promiſe me the diſpoſal of the firſt living I deſired, upon my relinquiſhing a living in the dioceſe of *Clogher*, to Dr. *Delany*, I make it my requeſt to your Lordſhip, that you would be pleaſed to order the ſaid union to be given to the Rev. Mr. *John Richardſon*, on whom I did intend to have beſtowed the living I then relinquiſhed.   I am,

Your Excellency's, &c.

To Lord Townſhend.

My Lord,   *Dublin, Jan.* 16, 1728.

THE age and frequent returns of illneſs the Archbiſhop of *Dublin* has laboured under the greateſt part of this winter (though I do not apprehend that he is in any immediate danger of dying) have made me think it proper to write a few lines to your Lordſhip about a ſucceſſor to him, if he ſhould fall, that there may be no ſurpriſe.

It is certain that it is of the laſt conſequence to the King's ſervice that he be an *Engliſhman*; whether it will be thought beſt to ſend one from the Biſhops bench in *England*, or to remove one from the bench here to that poſt, I ſubmit to your Lordſhip's wiſdom: if the former be thought of, the perſon I ſhould be moſt deſirous to ſee here, as being one of the oldeſt friends I have on the bench there, that would be willing to come, is the Biſhop of St. *David's*, of whoſe behaviour your Lordſhip muſt have ſome knowledge, as he has been in the houſe about five years: if the latter be judged beſt, I think the Biſhop of *Fernes* is the moſt proper that can be thought of here; he behaved himſelf very well laſt ſeſſions of parliament here; he is one of courage, and very hearty for the *Engliſh* intereſt, and is a good ſpeaker; and I am ſatisfied he is one

that

that would concur with me in promoting his Majesty's service; he is very well liked of here for an *Englishman*.

But I muft beg to fpeak freely that I hope nobody will be fent hither, becaufe he is troublefome or uneafy elfewhere. It is of great confequence that there be a good agreement between the Primate and the Archbifhop of *Dublin*; and one in that poft who would fet up himfelf againft the Primate, would be fure of being careffed, flattered, and followed by the *Irifh* intereft here.

I cannot on this occafion omit my thanks to your Lordfhip for your fupporting me here ever fince I came, as you gave me hopes you would, and I hope the good effects of it have appeared. And I think the *Englifh* intereft is at prefent on that good footing, headed by my Lord Chancellor and myfelf, that the continuance of the fame fupport, promifes a pretty quiet ftate of things for the future.

I fhould hardly have given your Lordfhip this trouble before-hand, if we had not reports from time to time that endeavours are ufing to fecure this poft either for fome dangerous perfon here, or not very promifing on the other fide *.

I am, &c.

To Lord Carteret.

My Lord,   *Dublin, Jan.* 25, 1728.

ON the 23d inftant I had the honour of your Excellency's of the 11th, which I this day communicated to the Lords Juftices, and upon advifing with Lord Chief Juftice *Rogerfon*, who happened to be at the caftle, and the Prime Serjeant

with

---

* His Grace feems to place his chief confidence in my Lord *Townfhend*.

with the Attorney and Sollicitor-general, we find it proper to have his Majesty's commands for what alterations are to be made in the occasional offices, as likewise for the late alterations in relation to the Royal family which his Majesty has been pleased lately to order in council in *England*; and we find that in the several proclamations issued on the like occasions, mention is made of our having received his Majesty's commands.

I shall look over the alterations made in the occasional offices in *England*, and likewise see what alterations may be necessary to be made in the occasional office for the 23d of *October*, which is not observed in *England*, and transmit them to your Excellency by the next post, together with a copy of the letter your Excellency was pleased to send us, relating to the alterations made in the prayers for the Royal Family at his Majesty's accession; that so your Lordship may see what form was then used to signify his Majesty's pleasure to us; and as soon as we receive his Majesty's commands, we shall issue a proclamation accordingly.

I shall by this post write to *England* for the form of prayer appointed for the inauguration-day, to see whether there is any thing in it that need be changed here; and shall after perusing it, acquaint your Excellency whether it will require any change, or be proper as it stands in *England*, that we may accordingly receive his Majesty's commands.

I am, My Lord, &c.

To the same.

My Lord,   *Dublin, Jan.* 28, 1728.

IN mine of *Saturday* last I promised your Excellency by this post, on account of what alterations would be proper to be made in the several occasional offices,

offices, purſuant to what has been done in *England*, and I had accordingly drawn them up.

But as your Lordſhip hinted in yours that it ſhould be done in the beſt manner which you thought I knew, I went on at the ſame time with an enquiry at the council and the ſecretaries office, into what method was purſued when thoſe forms of prayer were laſt altered, which was in the year 1715 : and by the books in the ſecretary's office I found things then took a longer train than any body was able to inform me of, which I ſhall communicate to the other Lords Juſtices to-morrow, that we may purſue the ſame method again, and when things are ſettled with them, ſhall ſend your Lordſhip an account of it.

As the time is too ſhort to make any ſuch alteration againſt the 30th of *January* now approaching, there will be time enough to have that affair purſued in the way formerly obſerved, before the 29th of *May*, and care ſhall be taken accordingly.

But the alterations his Majeſty has been pleaſed to order lately in relation to the Royal Family, can be enforced here as ſoon as your Excellency pleaſes to ſend us his Majeſty's commands about them.

And I have here ſent your Excellency an extract of your letter of the 16th of *June* 1727, in which you ſent us his Majeſty's firſt commands on that ſubject, in purſuance of which we then iſſued a proclamation, as we ſhall now, ſo ſoon as we receive the like orders.

I am, my Lord, &c.

To the ſame.

My Lord,   *Dublin, Feb.* 1, 1728.

I HUMBLY thank your Excellency for your kind order to have Mr. *Richardſon* preſented to the union of *Burn-church* ; but as there is ſome reaſon

fon to apprehend that the Crown and the Bifhop *
of *Offory* prefent alternately to that union, and that
this is the Bifhop's turn, the laft turn having been
filled by the Crown, we have ordered enquiry to be
made in the feveral offices, to learn how that affair
ftands, before we make a prefentation, which we
fear can be of no effect ; as foon as we can learn any
thing certain in this bufinefs, I fhall acquaint your
Lordfhip with it.

I am, &c.

To the fame.

My Lord,   *Dublin, Feb.* 13, 1728.

I HAVE lately received a letter from Mr. *Ratcliff*,
in which he acquaints me that he has made application to your Excellency for the new profefforfhip
in the oriental tongues, and defires me to give your
Lordfhip a character of him.   As I do not know
how thofe profefforfhips are to be beftowed, whether
on thofe who are actually of the College, or indifferently on any who are qualified for them, I cannot
tell what to fay on this occafion : but I muft do him
the juftice to acquaint your Excellency that I have
heard him fpoken of as one that underftands the oriental tongues the beft of any body in this country.

I am, my Lord, &c.

To the Archbifhop of Canterbury.

My Lord,   *Dublin, Feb.* 13, 1728.

I AM glad to hear your Grace is mended, and
ftill likely to mend in your health, which I heartily wifh a continuance of.

We

* Sir *Thomas Vefey,* Bart.

We are endeavouring by a * fubfcription to raife money and buy corn, to fupply the neceffities of the north, and have hitherto kept the markets there from rifing unreafonably, and hope to do fo till next harveft. We think this will put fome ftop to the great defertion we have been threatened with there : and fo far as they may be concerned in it, I hope the landlords will do their part by remitting fome arrears or making fome abatement of their rents. As bad as things have been here, I am fatisfied the bulk of thefe adventurers worft themfelves by removing to *America*, and hope the frenzy will gradually abate.

I have lately received a letter from your Grace relating to one Mr. *Carol*, a convert, which I had anfwered fooner, but that I ftaid till I had an opportunity of talking with my Lord Chief Baron about his cafe, who tells me he has an extraordinary bad character, whatever his religion may be, that he has been convicted of endeavouring to fuborn witneffes, and that a profecution has been ordered againft him in the Exchequer for making a rafure in a record; fo that he thinks *Carol* will hardly venture into this kingdom.

I fhall always be ready to fupport any real proteftant here who fuffers from the malice of the papifts, fo far as lies in my power, and ftill the more upon your Grace's recommendation; but I fubmit it to your Grace whether there be a poffibility of
fhewing

---

* There is no doubt but his Grace contributed largely to this fubfcription; but what he did in the year 1739-40, in the great froft, almoft exceeds belief; there was not a poor diftreffed perfon in the great city of *Dublin* who applied, that was not daily relieved to the full, and chiefly by his bounty: the Houfe of Commons took this fo well, that they voted him very juftly their thanks on this very remarkable inftance of his goodnefs. The fums he then expended muft have been very great indeed, yet when he hath been complimented on this and frequent other occafions of the like fort, his ufual anfwer was, that he fhould die fhamefully rich.

fhewing any countenance to one who has fo bad a character. I am,

My Lord, &c.

To the Duke of Newcaftle.

My Lord, *'Dublin, Feb.* 18, 1728.

THE occafion of my troubling your Grace at prefent, is that it is generally talked here, that the affair of the new profefforfhips is juft fettling, and the profeffors going to be named. I find that bufi‐nefs has been wholly managed with Dr. *Coghill,* without acquainting my Lord Chancellor or me with what has been doing *. Dr. *Coghill* has indeed had fome difcourfe with me about what lectures it might be proper to oblige the profeffors to read, and under what penalties; but we have neither of us been let into the fecret who are defigned for the new profef‐fors. I could therefore wifh that before the perfons are fettled, we might be acquainted who they are to be, that your Grace may be informed whether they are fuch as the King's friends here wifh were put in.

I cannot omit mentioning on this occafion, that we the Lords Juftices here were fomewhat furprized that Dr. *Coghill* was rather employed than the Lords Juftices, to acquaint the College that it would be agreeable to the court, if the † Prince of *Wales* were to be elected Chancellor of this Univerfity. I hope you will excufe this trouble. I am,

Your Grace's, &c.

---

* It is to be feared that Lord *Carteret* played the Primate, a flippery trick in this cafe as well as in fome others; he fays him‐felf in one of his letters to Dean *Swift,* when people afk me how I governed *Ireland,* I fay that I pleafed Dr. *Swift.*

† His Royal Highnefs was accordingly elected.

To the same.

My Lord,   *Dublin, Feb.* 20, 1728.

I TROUBLED your Grace but laſt poſt with ſomewhat relating to the College here. But as I have ſince learned ſomewhat more of what is tranſacting there, I think myſelf obliged to give you ſome farther informations.

As it may happen that the * Vice-Chancellor may be ſick at the time of the commencement, when degrees are to be given, of which they have two in a year, one juſt before *Lent,* the other at the time of the *Cambridge* commencement, it was the cuſtom for the Vice-Chancellor to name a Pro-Vice-Chancellor, to officiate in caſe of the Vice-Chancellor's ſickneſs or abſence ; but upon the laſt who was named Pro-Vice-Chancellor coming to be ſworn before Lord Chancellor *Middleton,* it appeared the ſtatutes did not give any power to the Vice-Chancellor to name a deputy, upon which there has been no ſuch deputy here for ſome years.

I am informed that to prevent any accident of that nature, it has been propoſed to have an additional ſtatute or clauſe to the charter, made by the King, to give ſuch a power to the Vice-Chancellor, which I think is reaſonable. But I am informed likewiſe, that this affair is taking another turn in *England,* and that they are for appointing three Vice-Chancellors, with equal power, *viz.* the Biſhop of *Clogher,* the preſent Vice-Chancellor ; the Biſhop of † *Raphoe,* who never comes to town but in parliament time ;
                                                    and

---

* Dr. *Sterne,* Biſhop of *Clogher.*
† Dr. *Nicholas Forſter,* was a ſenior Fellow of the Univerſity of *Dublin,* afterwards Biſhop of *Killaloe,* from whence he was tranſlated to *Raphoe.*

and Dr. *Coghill*, one of the reprefentatives for the Univerfity in parliament, and always in town.

What feems pretty much aimed at in this affair, is to give Dr. *Coghill* a greater weight and authority in the College than he has already. And as he is the perfon with whom the affair of the profefforfhips has been fettled, as well as who are to be profeffors, I think his weight is already pretty great.

He is a perfon of abilities, and of a fair character, but as determined a fupporter of the *Irifh* againft the *Englifh* intereft here, as any body, though with more prudence than many others, and therefore I hope it will be confidered whether it be fo proper to give him fo much authority as feems now putting into his hands by thefe fchemes.

There is one thing I muft fuggeft on this occafion, which is, that as the Chancellor, Vice-Chancellor, and Archbifhop of *Dublin* are the prefent Vifitors of the College, it is poffible one thing defigned by making three Vice-Chancellors (who probably may all three become Vifitors) may be the rendering ufelefs the power of the Archbifhop of *Dublin* in a vifitation of the College, if he fhould ever be an *Englifh-man*.

I cannot help faying I think it would have been for the King's fervice here, if what has been lately tranfacting in relation to the Profeffors, and what is now doing, had been concerted with fome of the *Englifh* here, and not wholly with the natives, and that after a fecret manner, that the College might have thought it their intereft to have fome dependance on the *Englifh*.

And here I cannot help fuggefting, whether if any alteration is made in the charter with relation to the Vice-Chancellor's power, it may not be proper at the fame time to add to the prefent Vifitors, the Lord Primate and the Lord Chancellor of *Ireland*, for the time being; whom his Majefty fhall pleafe from

time

time to time to place in eminent ftations here; but hitherto all thefe College affairs have been kept a fecret from my Lord Chancellor and me.

I hope your Grace will have the goodnefs to excufe the trouble of this long letter.

I am, &c.

To Lord Carteret.

My Lord,   *Dublin, Mar.* 8, 1728.

I THANK your Excellency for your kind order to prefent Mr. *Richardfon* to the union of *Burnchurch*; but before we could actually pafs his patent for it, I procured a copy of the act of union from the Regifter of *Offory*, that in the council-office being burnt; upon perufal of which the Attorney-general fays, there is no doubt but that the Crown and Bifhop of * *Offory* are to prefent alternately to that union, and that as the Crown prefented the laft turn, the Bifhop is to prefent this turn; fo that it is to no purpofe to take any farther ftep in that affair.

We have had feveral tumults in *Cork, Waterford, Limerick,* and other places in the fouth, on pretence that corn was exported thence to *England*; though if we may believe the merchants here, little has been attempted to be exported of late, but to the north of *Ireland*; and by all accounts there is great plenty in thofe parts, and corn at a very reafonable price.

We have wrote to the feveral magiftrates in thofe parts to be diligent in preferving the peace, and have ordered the officers of the army to affift the civil magiftrates on occafion, wherever we have been applied to for it.

We

* Sir *Thomas Vefey*, Bart. fon of Dr. *John Vefey*, Archbifhop of *Tuam*, and Vice-Chancellor of the Univerfity of *Dublin*, and three times one of the Lords Juftices of *Ireland*.

We have by this post sent your Excellency the memorial delivered to us by the dissenting ministers here, from the letters of their friends in the north: we objected against two heads of it, as we have acquainted your Excellency; but there is another part relating to the grievances about tythes, which is very far from being true.   I do not doubt but some persons in the north may have been oppressed by the farmers of tythes.   But I have at every visitation I have held had as great complaints from the clergy of the hardships put upon them by the people, in coming at their just dues, as the people can make of being any ways oppressed by the clergy or their tythe farmers, and I believe with as much reason. As to the expensiveness of the spiritual courts which they complain of, that will be very much avoided by the act passed last sessions for the more easy recovery of tythes of small value.   And indeed the gentlemen have ever since I came hither, been putting it into the heads of their tenants, that it was not their rents, but the paying of the tythes that made them find it hard to live on their farms.   And it is easy to see that this was a notion that would readily take with *Scotch* presbyterians.

We shall in time make some farther remarks on that memorial.   I am,

My Lord, &c.

To the Duke of Newcastle.

My Lord,   *Dublin, Mar.* 13, 1728.

AS we are in a very bad way here, I think myself obliged to give your Grace some account of it.

The scarcity and dearness of provision still increases in the north; many have eaten the oats they should have sowed their land with; and except the
land-

andlords will have the good fenfe to furnifh them
with feed, a great deal of land will lye wafte this
year.

There has been fet on foot a fubfcription here in
Dublin, to buy corn from *Munfter*, where it has
been very cheap, to fend it to the north, in order to
keep the markets down ; but though we have
bought about 3000 *l.* worth of oats, oatmeal, and
potatoes there, yet firft by the continuance of eafter-
ly winds for three weeks, and fince by the infurrec-
tions of the mob in thofe parts, not one boat load is
yet arrived in the north ; which is a great increafe to
their diftrefs.

There have been tumults at *Limerick*, *Cork*, *Waterford*, *Clonmel*, and other places, to prevent the
corn we have bought from going to the north.
Thofe at *Limerick* and *Cork* have been the worft,
where they have broken open ware-houfes and cel-
lars, and fet what price they pleafed on provifions ;
but I hope we fhall hardly hear of any more riots,
having given the neceffary orders both to the civil
and military officers in thofe parts to take care to
prevent or fupprefs all riots. There is no doubt but
the buying of corn there has raifed their markets ;
but ftill as we are affured from thence, there is great
plenty in the country ; and provifions are in fome
places as cheap again as in the north ; but where
deareft, at leaft one third part cheaper. There is
one reflection thefe poor wretches have not made,
that by their riots the country are deterred from
bringing them in provifions, which will make things
dearer in thofe places than the exportation they are
fo angry at.

We have given orders to the feveral magiftrates
and the judges of affize to have the rioters profecuted
and feverely punifhed.

The humour of going to *America* ftill continues,
and the fcarcity of provifions certainly makes many
quit

quit us : there are now feven fhips at *Belfaft* that are carrying off about 1000 paffengers thither ; and if we knew how to ftop them, as moft of them can neither get victuals nor work at home, it would be cruel to do it.

We have fent for 2400 quarters of rye from *Co-ningfbery*; when they arrive which will probably be about the middle of *May*, we hope the price of things will fall confiderably in the north, and we fuppofe they will mend pretty much when our fup-plies arrive from *Munfter*.

The diffenting minifters here have lately delivered in a memorial reprefenting the grievances their bre-thren have affigned as the caufes in their apprehen-fion of the great defertion in the north : as one of thofe caufes relates to the ecclefiaftical courts here, and as it is generally reported here that the *Irifh* gen-tlemen at *London* are for throwing the whole occafion of this defertion on the feverity of tythes, I have by this poft written to the Bifhop of *London* a very long letter on that fubject, and have defired him to wait on the miniftry and difcourfe with them on that head.

I fhall get a copy of this memorial and fend your Grace my thoughts on fome other parts of it. I am,

My Lord, &c.

To the Bifhop of London.

My Lord,   *Dublin, Mar.* 13, 1728.

AS we have had reports here that the *Irifh* gen-tlemen in *London* would have the great bur-then of tythes thought one of the chief grievances that occafion fuch numbers of the people of the north going to *America*, I have for fome time defign-ed to write to your Lordfhip on that fubject.

But

But a memorial lately delivered in here by the dif‑
fenting minifters of this place, containing the caufes
of this defertion, as reprefented to them by the let‑
ters of their brethren in the north, (which memorial
we have lately fent over to my Lord Lieutenant,)
mentioning the oppreffion of the ecclefiaftical courts
about tythes as one of their greateft grievances; I
found myfelf under a neceffity of troubling your
Lordfhip to difcourfe with the miniftry about it.

The gentlemen of this country have ever fince I
came hither been talking to others, and perfuading
their tenants who complained of the exceffivenefs of
their rents, that it was not the paying too much rent,
but too much tythe that impoverifhed them: and
the notion foon took among Scotch prefbyterians, as
a great part of the proteftants in the north are, who
it may eafily be fuppofed do not pay tythes with
great chearfulnefs.   And indeed I make no doubt but
the landlords in England might with great eafe raife
a cry amongft their tenants of the great oppreffion
they lie under by paying tythes.

What the gentlemen want to be at is that they
may go on raifing their rents, and that the clergy
fhould ftill receive their old payments for their tythe.
But, as things have happened otherwife, and they are
very angry with the clergy, without confidering that
it could not happen otherwife than it has, fince if a
clergyman faw a farm raifed in its rent e. g. from 10
to 20 l. per ann. he might be fure his tythe was cer‑
tainly worth double what he formerly took for it.
Not that I believe the clergy have made a proportion‑
able advancement in their compofition for their
tythes, to what the gentlemen have made in their
rents.   And yet it is upon this rife of the value of
tythes that they would perfuade the people to throw
their diftrefs.

In a conference I had with the diffenting minifters
here fome weeks ago, they mentioned the raifing the
                                                value

value of tythes beyond what had been formerly paid, as a proof that the people were oppreffed in the article of tythes. To which I told them, that the raising the value of tythes did not prove any oppreffion, except it were proved that the value was greater than they were really worth ; and that even then the farmer had his remedy by letting the clergy take it in kind.

And there is the lefs in this argument, becaufe the fact is, that about the years 1694 and 1695, the lands here were almoft wafte and unfettled, and the clergy in the laft diftrefs for tenants for their tythes, when great numbers of them were glad to lett their tythes at a very low value, and that during incumbency, for few would take them on other terms ; and as the country has fince fettled and improved, as thofe incumbents have dropt off, the tythe of thofe parifhes has been confiderably advanced without the leaft oppreffion, but I believe your Lordfhip will think not without fome grumbling. The fame no doubt has happened where there have been carelefs or needy incumbents, and others of a different character that have fucceeded them.

I need not mention to your Lordfhip what I have been forced to talk to feveral here, that if a landlord takes too great a portion of the profits of a farm for his fhare by way of rent, (as the tythe will light on the tenants fhare) the tenant will be impoverifhed : but then it is not the tythe but the increafed rent that undoes the farmer. And indeed in this country, where I fear the tenant hardly ever has more than one third of the profits he makes of his farm for his fhare, and too often but a fourth or perhaps a fifth part, as the tenant's fhare is charged with the tythe, his cafe is no doubt hard, but it is plain from what fide the hardfhip arifes.

Nor need I take notice to your Lordfhip of what I have been forced to talk very fully here, that if
the

the land were freed from payment of tythe, the tenant would not be the better for it, but the landlord, who would in that cafe raife his rent accordingly, and would probably receive 15 or 20 s. for additional rent, where the clergyman now receives 10 s. for tythe ; and that it would be the fame in proportion if the tythes were fixed to fome modus below their real value, which I am apprehenfive the gentlemen may attempt to do by a bill next feffions.

As for the complaints of the oppreffions in the ecclefiaftical courts, your Lordfhip knows the dilatorinefs and expenfivenefs of fuits there. And yet till within feven or eight years all fuits for tythes, &c. were there ; fince that time by degrees the clergy have fued in cafes of confequence in the Exchequer ; but for dues of fmall value, they ftill are fued for there. But in the main no body fues in thofe courts that can by fair means get any thing near his due ; fince, when the clergy have put perfons into thofe courts the defendants either give them all the delay and trouble they can, or elfe ftand under contempt for never appearing; and let things go to the laft extremity, and ftand excommunicated, and poffibly when a writ *de excommunicato capiendo* is taken out, and they find they have 7 or 8 *l.* to pay, they run away : for the greateft part of the occupiers of the land here are fo poor, that an extraordinary ftroke of 8 or 10 *l.* falling on them, is certain ruin to them.

I can affure your Lordfhip that at every vifitation I have held here, which is annually, the clergy have made as great complaints of the hardfhips put upon them by the people in getting in their tythes, efpecially their fmall dues, as the people can of any oppreffion from the clergy. And to my knowledge many of them have chofe rather to lofe their fmall dues, than to be at a certain great expence in getting
them,

them, and at an uncertainty whether the farmer would not at laft run away without paying any thing. And I can affirm to your Lordfhip that the laiety here are as troublefome and vexatious as they can be in *England*, and from time to time fight a caufe of no great value through the Bifhop's court, then through the Archbifhop's, and thence to the Delegates, where the clergy fue for what is moft evidently their due.

I would not be underftood by this to deny that any clergyman or farmer of tythes ever did a hard thing by the people, but that there is not frequent occafion of complaint againft them.

However laft feffions we paffed a bill here for the more eafy recovery of fmall tythes, &c. which I believe will remove this caufe of complaint, fince I believe very few will fpend fome pounds to recover that in a fpiritual court, which may be recovered for fome fhillings in another way.

Upon occafion of the conference I had fome weeks ago with the diffenting minifters here, I have enquired of feveral of the clergy, that are underftanding and fair men, who have affured me, that as far as their knowledge reaches, they believe that generally the farmers do not pay more than two thirds of the real value of their tythes.

Another thing they complain of in their memorial is, the trouble that has been given them about their marriages and their fchool-mafters. As to this I told them, that for fome time they had not been molefted about their marriages, and that as to their fchool-mafters I was fure they had met with very little trouble on that head, fince I had never heard any fuch grievance fo much as mentioned till I faw it in their memorial.

Another matter complained of is the facramental teft, in relation to which I told them, the laws were the fame in *England*.

A1

As for other grievances they mention, such as raising the rents unreasonably, the oppression of Justices of the Peace, seneschals, and other officers in the country, as they are no ways of an ecclesiastical nature, I shall not trouble your Lordship with an account of them; but must desire your Lordship to talk with the ministry on the subject I have now wrote about, and endeavour to prevent their being prepossessed with any unjust opinion of the clergy, or being disposed, if any attempt should be made from hence, to suffer us to be stript of our just rights *.

I am, &c.

To Sir Robert Walpole.

SIR,   *Dublin, Mar.* 31, 1729.

THE dissenting ministers of this place having applied to me to recommend their case and that of their brethren to your kind patronage, I have made bold to trouble you with this letter by Mr. *Craghead*, one of their number, and their sollicitor on this occasion. They inform me that his late Majesty was graciously pleased to give out of his privy purse to the ministers of the north 400 *l. per ann.* and the like sum to those of the south, to be distributed to those ministers who had no share of the † 1200 *l.* on the establishment here ; and that his present Majesty has graciously continued this allowance

ance

---

* His Grace does not shew in this letter any partiality to the dissenters, with which he used to be charged by the few tory enemies he had; and he had no others:——The truth is, that he was naturally a very moderate and impartial man, but very steady in the pursuit of those measures he thought just and right, and for the service of the cause he was engaged to support.

† It does not appear from the manuscript whether it is 120 or 1200 *l.*

ance to them: that by his late Majefty's death they apprehend they loft two years, what they hoped to have otherwife received. They are fenfible there is nothing due to them, nor do they make any fuch claim: but as the calamities of this kingdom are at prefent very great, and by the defertion of many of their people to *America*, and the poverty of the greateft part of the reft, their contributions, particularly in the north, are very much fallen off, it would be a great inftance of his Majefty's goodnefs, if he would confider their prefent diftrefs.

Sir, it is certain they are under very great difficulties at prefent, on the accounts they mention; and I am affured from good hands, that feveral of them who have had 50 *l. per ann.* from their flock do not receive 15 *l.* It is but doing them juftice to affirm, that they are very well affected to his Majefty and his Royal Family, and by the beft enquiries I could make, do their endeavours to keep their congregations from deferting the country; not more than one or two of the younger minifters having any ways encouraged the humour now prevailing here. And his Majefty's goodnefs in giving them fome extraordinary relief on this occafion of their prefent great diftrefs, would undoubtedly make them more active to retain their people here.

I cannot help mentioning on this occafion that what with fcarcenefs of corn in the north, and the lofs of all credit there, by the numbers that go or talk of going to *America*, and with the difturbances in the fouth, this kingdom is at prefent in a deplorable condition. But I hope we fhall be able to keep every thing pretty quiet, and that if it pleafe God to fend us a good harveft, things will gradually mend.

I am, &c.

To

To *Lord* Carteret.

My Lord,   *Dublin, Apr.* 10, 1729.

I HAD this day the honour of your Excellency's of the 5th inftant, and have fince talked with my Lord Chancellor about altering the value of our coin, which we fhall endeavour to give all poffible expedition to.

But we are both of opinion that nothing can be moved in the council about it, till the return of the Judges; for the bankers here are all againft it, for a plain reafon which they themfelves told me, which is that they get 2 *per cent.* in the exchange by the prefent inequality of gold and filver, and your Lordfhip knows what ftrength they have in the council.

We are very much obliged to his Majefty for his kind difpofition to this country; and I am fure we ought not to be infenfible that the favourable reprefentations your Excellency has been pleafed to make of our attachment to his Royal Family, have very much contributed to this.

I fhall take a proper opportunity of talking with the Lords Juftices of a copper coinage, and as foon as I know their fentiments, I will write to your Excellency on that fubject.

I am, &c.

To *the fame.*

My Lord,   *Dublin, Apr.* 24, 1729.

AS we find we have two new privy counfellors made here, we cannot forbear putting your Excellency in mind of my Lord *Cavan.* * We both

applied

* This muft be a joint letter from the Lords Juftices *Boulter* and *Wyndham.*

applied to your Lordſhip when you was here, that he might be made a privy counſellor, and you were pleaſed to promiſe us, that you would recommend him to his Majeſty the firſt opportunity, to be made a member of that right honourable board.   By what has happened we apprehend your Excellency may have forgotten him ; and we beg leave again to re-commend him to be made a privy counſellor, as being one of a very antient noble family here, and firmly attached to his Majeſty, and who on all occaſions, has been of great ſervice to the government in the Houſe of Lords ; and we doubt not but he would be equally ſerviceable in the council.   We are,

My Lord, &c.

To the ſame.

My Lord,   *Dublin, Apr.* 26, 1729.

I THOUGHT your Excellency might be plea-ſed to hear by the firſt opportunity, that on *Thurſday* laſt we communicated your Lordſhip's let-ter, and the other papers tranſmitted with it, relating to the coin, to the privy council, and that we then appointed a committee to take the affair into conſide-ration ; ſince which the committee met laſt night, and reduced the value of gold to what it goes for in *England* ; and this night they ſettled the value of foreign ſilver agreeably to the paper your Excellency ſent over, in which the piece of eight of 17 *pwts.* 4 *grs.* is valued at 5 *s. Iriſh.*   As Mr. *Conolly* went out of town yeſterday and does not return till *Tueſday*, we cannot have a council till *Wedneſday*, when I hope we ſhall finiſh this affair.

Several attended to oppoſe the reducing of the va-lue of gold, but were able to ſay little in the com-

mittee,

mittee, and will be lefs able to ftand a debate in the council.

I am, my Lord, &c.

To the fame.

My Lord,   *Dublin, May* 1, 1729.

SINCE I wrote laft to your Excellency, the committee have drawn up and delivered in their report to the council, relating to the coins here current, which council was held yefterday ; but as a petition was then given in by feveral merchants and others, againft lowering the gold, defiring to be heard on that fubject, we thought proper to order them to be heard by themfelves, not by council, next *Monday*, when I hope we fhall one way or another conclude that affair.

The bankers have beftirred themfelves to the utmoft on this occafion, and appear to have that influence over the traders and others of this place, that thofe who are moft fatisfied that what the council are doing, is for the benefit of this nation, dare not publickly own their fentiments. They are fetting about petitions againft this reduction, and playing the whole game of *Wood's* half-pence.

I rather think we fhall carry the affair in the council, and when our letter to your Excellency on this fubject is once gone over I believe they will gradually cool.

At prefent hardly any are capable of hearing reafon, but if they fhould come to temper, fo that there are any hopes that arguments may work upon them, I would willingly know your Excellency's pleafure, whether you would give leave to have the memorial prefented to your Lordfhip printed. Among other things they are pleafed to give out, one is, that the

memorial

memorial was written by Mr. *Conduit*, and is defigned to ruin this nation.

As the bankers have behaved themfelves with great
infolence to the government on this occafion, and are
vifibly facrificing the good of the publick to their
private advantage, and plainly appear to have a
greater power than it is proper they fhould have,
when this affair is a little blown over, I have a propofal to make to your Excellency which has been fuggefted to me by fome in trade, and which I rather
think may be of fervice to the nation, and will confiderably take down the infolence of the bankers.

I am, &c.

To the Duke of Newcaftle.

My Lord,   *Dublin, May* 8, 1729.

A S the Archbifhop of *Dublin* has been out of
order for four or five days, and is now apprehended to be in very great danger, I think it proper
to acquaint your Grace with it, that there may be no
furprife in difpofing of a place of fo great confequence, upon any report of his death from other
hands.   By the next poft I fhall inform your Grace
what is the event of his ficknefs.

I am, &c.

N. B. The fame intelligence was likewife fent to
Lord *Carteret*.

To Lord Carteret.

My Lord,   *Dublin, May* 9, 1729.

U P O N occafion of the vacancy here by the
death of the Archbifhop of *Dublin*, I beg
leave to mention to your Excellency, that if his Majefty

V o l. I.   Q

jesty should fill that see from *England*, I would desire your Lordship to use your interest for the Bishop of St. *David*'s, whom I formerly mentioned to you; but if from hence, I think the Bishop of *Fernes* the most proper person.

I am, &c.

To Lord Townshend.

My Lord,   *Dublin, May 9,* 1729.

YESTERDAY in the evening died his Grace the Archbishop of *Dublin*. As in *January* last I troubled your Lordship with a letter about filling this archbishoprick, whenever it should happen to be vacant, and declared my opinion that for the support of the *English* interest here, it was absolutely necessary that it should be bestowed on a native of *England*, I shall not now repeat what I then wrote : but shall just renew my recommendations at that time, that if his Majesty is pleased to send one from the bench of *England*, the Bishop of St. *David*'s is my oldest friend there : if he is pleased to fill it from hence, the Bishop of *Fernes* is the most proper person.

The filling this place with an able man is of great consequence to his Majesty's service here, and I therefore hope nobody will be thought of in *England* to be sent hither, because he is troublesome or good for nothing there.

I must beg leave on this occasion to recommend to your Lordship's protection Mr. *Stephens*, that he may have a specifick performance of the promise made me of bestowing on him the next canonry vacant at *Christ Church*. I am,

My Lord, &c.

To

To the Duke of Newcastle.

My Lord,   *Dublin, May* 9, 1729.

YESTERDAY in the evening died the Arch-bishop of *Dublin*, after a few days indisposition. I have formerly written of the consequence of filling this post well, and for the support of the *English* interest here, it is necessary it should be an *Englishman*. If it be filled from the bench in *England*, the oldest friend I have there is the Bishop of St. *David's*: if from the bench here, the Bishop of * *Fernes* is I think much the most proper person.   I am,
Your Grace's, &c.

To Lord Carteret.

My Lord,   *Dublin, May* 13, 1729.

I AM sorry I can give your Excellency no better an account of the success of our endeavouring to mend the state of our coin here.   However I think myself obliged to acquaint you with what has passed on this occasion.

Upon the receipt of your Excellency's letter, and the papers transmitted with it, we ordered a council to meet, and communicated your Lordship's letter and the papers to them.   As the affair had been fully considered in the year 1726, and there was no alteration proposed to be made to what the committee of council had then agreed upon, except raising the foreign silver from 5*s*. 4*d*. to 5*s*. 4½*d*. *English* per ounce, I would fain have had a committee withdraw immediately and make us a report, that we might
Q 2   before

* Dr. *Hoadley* succeeded Dr. *King* in the Archbishoprick of *Dublin*.

before we parted have done the bufinefs, and tranfmitted it to your Excellency, before it made any
noife ; but this was oppofed as being too precipitate,
and what might perhaps be called a job-work ; fo the
matter was referred to a committee in the common
way, who on *Friday* was fortnight went through the
gold coins, and the next day the filver ; and if Mr.
Conolly had not gone out of town then we could have
finifhed the affair on *Monday* following ; but he not
returning till *Tuefday* night, we could not have a
council till *Wednefday*, againft which time, the merchants at the inftigation of the bankers and other remitters and their dependants, had a petition ready
againft the fcheme. The y pretended not to be ready to fpeak then, and we gave them till *Monday* to
prepare, I muft own againft my advice.

When we met on *Monday* was fe'nnight to hear
them, we had a petition from the Lord Mayor and
common-council of *Dublin*, the grand-jury of the
county and of the city of *Dublin*, and from the
city of *Cork*, againft what the council were doing.
The merchants who appeared were perfons all concerned in remittances, and one * *Bindon*, a broken
merchant of *Limerick*. I and fome of the council
anfwered what they faid, but in the end they pretended they were not quite ready ; and fo they were
indulged to be heard again as laft *Monday*, and to
offer what they thought proper.

When we met laft *Monday* we had a petition from
the merchants of *Londonderry* to the fame purpofe
with the others ; and the merchants offered a fcheme,
the fubftance of which was, raifing the *Englifh* fhilling to 13½*d*. and finding fome fault with the proportions

---

* *David Bindon*, Efq; a very eminent merchant, of exceeding
good family, of great knowledge in trade, fuffered much in the
South Sea Scheme, in 1720, and was a member of parliament in
the reign of *George* II.

portions of the feveral pieces of gold and filver in our fcheme ; in which if there are any errors, they will beft be corrected by the mafter of the mint in *England*.

On this occafion as there was a great affembly in the council-chamber, in a fpeech I made, I endeavoured to fhew the neceffity of doing what we propofed ; the pernicioufnefs of raifing *Englifh* filver, what the nation loft by our prefent inequality of gold and filver, who were the gainers by it, and anfwered their objections ; and defired all to remember who had hindered the removing of our prefent evil, if the ferment that had been raifed among the people fhould make it advifeable not to proceed any farther in the affair.

When the petitioners retired, the prevailing opinion in the council was, that though the thing propofed by the committee was moft certainly for the advantage of the kingdom, yet confidering the prefent clamour and uneafinefs of the people againft it, it was moft prudent to let the affair reft.

For the better underftanding of this I muft acquaint your Lordfhip that they have univerfally poffeffed the people that the fcheme is an *Englifh* project, formed in *England*, and carried on by my Lord Chancellor, myfelf, and other *Englifh* here, with a defign to drain this kingdom of their gold, as they are already drained of their filver.

As I found this had been induftrioufly fpread among the people, in my * fpeech on *Monday*, I gave them an account what applications had been made to your

* My Lord Primate was faid upon great provocation from *Eaton Stannard*, Efq; Recorder of *Dublin*, to have been a little off his guard at this time, and for this once to have fpoken fome hafty words ; but the Recorder fuffered for his temerity all his life time afterwards, the government would never make him a Judge, though he was a good lawyer and an honeft man ; it appears indeed in *Swift*'s letters, that he had been chofen Recorder by his intereft.

your Excellency on this fubject when you was here the firft time, what had been done in it in the year 1726, in council and out of it, and fhewed that at prefent *England* got 2½ *per cent.* in all goods they bought here, which advantage they would lofe by this reduction, fo that the fcheme could not come from thence.

I am forry his Majefty's gracious intentions and your Excellency's kind endeavour to fave this nation from a certain, though flow ruin, fhould meet with no better a return here ; but I hope thofe things have been faid on this occafion, that with an increafe of our fufferings here, will by degrees, open the eyes of men of fenfe, and that a time may come, when petitions will be offered in behalf of the reduction propofed.

I am, &c.

To the Duke of Newcaftle.

My Lord,   *Dublin, May* 17, 1729.

I HAVE already troubled your Grace with two letters on the occafion of the death of the Archbifhop of *Dublin*, with an account who I think may be moft proper to fill that fee, and to fucceed the Bifhop of *Fernes* if he fhould be promoted to *Dublin.* If the Bifhop of *Clonfert* fhould fucceed to *Fernes*, I think either Dean *Alcock*, or *Effex Edgworth* Chancellor of *Ardagh*, will be very proper to fucceed to the bifhoprick of *Clonfert.*

By our laft mail from *England* we learn that Dr. *Stratford*, Canon of *Chrift Church*, is dead ; and I muft upon this intelligence beg the favour of your Grace to fupport the intereft of Mr. *Stephens*, for whom before I left *England*, I had a promife of the next vacancy in that church : which I did not infift on upon the former vacancy, but let it go in favour of

Dr.

Dr. *Gibert*, but I hope Mr. *Stephens* will not meet with a fecond difappointment ; and your Grace's favour to him in the prefent vacancy, will be efteemed a very great obligation by him who is,

My Lord, &c.

To Lord Carteret.

My Lord,   *Dublin, May* 17, 1729.

I HAVE lately troubled your Excellency with two or three letters in particular, as well as our common letters, on occafion of the archbifhoprick of *Dublin* being vacant.   I have only this to mention farther to your Lordfhip, that if things end in a vacancy of a bifhoprick here, which Dean *Gore* is not willing to take, I fhould willingly recommend to your favour either Dean *Alcock*, or *Effex Edgworth* Chancellor of *Ardagh*, to fucceed.   I am,

Your Excellency's, &c.

To the fame.

My Lord,   *Dublin, May* 20, 1729.

I HAVE received the honour of your Excellency's of the 13th inft. and I hope you have received mine of the fame date, giving an account of what has paffed in council in relation to the coin.

Your Lordfhip might juftly fuppofe after the applications made to you on that head, that the regulation propofed in relation to the gold would have paffed to the univerfal fatisfaction of the kingdom, as it is undoubtedly for its benefit.   But your Excellency rightly obferves, that you are acquainted with the humour of the people here, and fo are lefs furprifed at the oppofition given to it : and indeed
except

except what oppofition was owing to the bankers, all the reft turned upon their being unwilling to be ferved by *Englishmen*, and it was not any argument againft the thing that weighed with thofe who made loud clamours againft it, but its being propofed and fupported by *Engl.fhmen* ; and this was the popular argument to prove there was fomewhat amifs in it.

We have proceeded with as much prudence and caution in this affair as we could. And we chofe to hear the merchants fpeak to the fubject, rather than barely receive their memorial, that we might have an opportunity of undeceiving the people by what we could fay againft them in publick, whereas the people could have known nothing of what paffed in a debate in the council.

As the memorial was fent to your Excellency I thought it would be wrong to print it without your leave ; but I have no thoughts of printing that or any thing elfe on the fubject, till the people are grown cool, and my Lord Chancellor thinks it advifable ; and then it fhall be fuch a one as he approves of, but we will carefully avoid doing any thing in this matter that may enflame the nation.

What has been hinted to me, as a thing that would oblige the bankers to keep more cafh by them than they do, and would probably by degrees bring the merchants to keep their own cafh is, if the officers of the revenue were ftrictly enjoined to take only cafh, and not bankers notes for payments in the revenue, the greateft part of which are at prefent made in bankers notes : befides it would have another great advantage, which is, that as things now ftand, if any run fhould happen upon the bankers, the government has not one penny of money to go on with ; but in the other cafe, they would have fome money at command. But I do not fpeak of this as a thing any ways proper to be done at prefent ; fince I fear in our prefent diftrefs, if the government

were

were to refuſe taking the notes of bankers, it would cauſe an immediate run upon them ; which as our circumſtances now ſtand, would put a ſtop to all trade and payments amongſt us : but I mention it as a thing worth your Excellency's conſideration, when we have the happineſs of your preſence with us.

As every thing is very quiet here, and we hope likely to continue ſo, I cannot apprehend that there is any neceſſity of your Lordſhip's coming hither before *September* ; whenever I can learn that there is occaſion for it, I will not fail giving your Excellency advice of it.

Since we ſent to your Lordſhip Mr. *Eſpin*'s and Mr. *Vaughan*'s memorials, I have learned that Mr. *Eſpin* has already about 200 *l. per ann.* in the church, and as much temporal eſtate ; whereas Mr. *Vaughan* has nothing but a curacy, ſo that the vicarage given to him, will be beſtowed on one who very much wants it.

I am, &c.

To the ſame.

My Lord,   *Dublin, June 5,* 1729.

I HAVE the honour of your Excellency's of the 29th paſt, and thank your Lordſhip for your kindneſs to the Biſhop of St. *David*'s, in the affair of the archbiſhoprick of *Dublin*, with which he acquainted me with great acknowledgments of the obligations you had laid on him.

I am ſorry that affair is likely to be kept long in ſuſpenſe, ſince I think it would rather be for his Majeſty's ſervice, that the new Archbiſhop whomſoever his Majeſty pleaſes to pitch upon, were well ſettled in his ſtation before the parliament meets.

Several here ſeem ſenſible of the folly of the clamour raiſed againſt regulating our coin, but all that
is

is left to be done at prefent, is ftaying till the greatnefs of the evil makes them importunate for a remedy.

I am glad your Excellency approves of the perfons I mentioned as proper to fill fome vacancy, if there fhould be any removes here.

I am, my Lord, &c.

To the Duke of Newcaftle.

My Lord,   *Dublin, June* 10, 1729.

I Have lately troubled your Grace with two or three letters on occafion of the death of the Archbifhop of *Dublin,* with my opinion whom I thought moft proper to fucceed to that fee, according as his Majefty fhould pleafe to pitch upon one on the bench in *England* or here.

I am fenfible his Majefty was in fuch a hurry, as he was juft then going abroad, when the firft advice of his Grace's death came, that it could not be expected that affair fhould be fettled before his departure: but I am forry to hear that it is generally talked at *London,* that the archbifhoprick is not likely to be difpofed of till his Majefty's return.

As our parliament will probably meet in *September,* or the beginning of *October,* I cannot but think it would be for his Majefty's fervice here if a fucceffor were fettled in the archbifhoprick time enough for him to form fome acquaintance and intereft here before the parliament is opened, and to let the difappointments of fome who are feeking for that ftation, be a little digefted before that time; for I very much fear, that notwithftanding all precautions, we are in danger of having a troublefome feffion, as the debts of the nation are very much increafed within a few years.

I thought

I thought it my duty to his Majefty humbly to make this reprefentation. I am,

My Lord, &c.

To the Bifhop of London.

My Lord, *Dublin, June* 12, 1729.

I Have been favoured with your Lordfhip's of the 3d inftant.

I am glad that thofe who make an unjuft clamour about tythes here, have had more modefty than to think they could perfuade people on your fide of the water to believe that to be one of the caufes of proteftants going hence to *America.*

I thank your Lordfhip for defigning to attend when the caufe Mr. *Horan* is concerned in comes before the Lords ; it is a caufe of fome confequence to this country.

There had been formerly fome objection made to Mr. *Stephens* being Canon of *Chrift Church*, on account of there being a want of perfons to bear office there : but I hoped it had been removed by his offering to be treafurer, and finding one to act under him, for whofe honefty he would be fecurity. I believe half the treafurers there have tranfacted their bufinefs by one of their fervants, (and poffibly the Bifhop of *Oxford* did fo) without being fecurity for them.

I cannot but think I am hardly ufed in this affair, to have a ftop put to a promife made me fome years ago and fince renewed, to gratify the oppofition made by my fucceffor, who neither has done, nor is capable (if I may fay fo without vanity) of doing that fervice to the crown which I have done here and at *Oxford.*

I thank

I thank your Lordſhip for the ſervice you have done Mr. *Stephens* in this affair, and recommend him to your farther protection.

Your Lordſhip I dare ſay, does not doubt of my friendſhip to the Biſhop of St. *David*'s, and I am thoroughly ſatisfied of his being a good church-man, and as faſt a friend to that branch of our conſtitution as any man. And I did not ſet up a rival againſt him, but your Lordſhip knows in all recommendations on theſe occaſions I have thought it prudent to mention two perſons ; ſince if one ſhould prove leſs acceptable, I am not preſent to recommend a ſecond. And I have reaſon to believe that great intereſt has been formed for the Biſhop of *Fernes* on the other ſide of the water two years ago, and ſince often renewed there for the poſt now vacant. For this reaſon I thought proper to name him with the Biſhop of St. *David*'s ; ſince it is very much for his Majeſty's ſervice that there ſhould be a good underſtanding between the new archbiſhop and myſelf ; as I am ſure there will be, whether his Majeſty pitches upon the Biſhop of St. *David*'s or the Biſhop of *Fernes* ; and as to the latter, I can aſſure your Lordſhip he has given here no occaſion to be thought no friend to the Church, and is allowed by every body to be a good ſpeaker in the Houſe of Lords, and conſequently will be ſo in the council : and I muſt inform your Lordſhip that is of no ſmall conſequence to the ſupport of his Majeſty's ſervice and the *Engliſh* intereſt here.

I am very ſorry to find the choice is likely to be put off for ſo long a time, ſince it is of moment to our affairs here, that the new Archbiſhop ſhould be ſettled and have time to look about him, if poſſible, before our parliament meets, which will be the latter end of *September* or beginning of *October*. But there is one thing I muſt beg of your Lordſhip to guard againſt, that under a notion of not offending the friends of either

either of the prefent candidates, a new perfon may not be clapt upon us.

I can eafily fee and no one here doubts, but there is fuch a perfon in view, who will neither be acceptable here, nor of fervice to the *Englifh* intereft. I hope, after what I have written in many letters before, I need not again urge the neceffity of the fee not being filled with a native of this country.

I am forry peace and war continue ftill fo uncertain : and fear the *Spaniards* are trifling with us, fo as to lofe the time of action for this year, which if they fhould do it will light heavy on the miniftry. I am,

My Lord, &c.

To Sir Robert Walpole.

S i r,   *Dublin, June* 14, 1729.

THE repeated accounts we have here that the archbifhoprick of *Dublin* is not likely to be difpofed of till his Majefty's return, are the occafion of my giving you this trouble.

If things are not already fixed otherwife, I would beg leave to reprefent that I think it would be for his Majefty's fervice here to have that affair fettled as foon as it conveniently can. The feffion of our parliament will come on in *September* or *October* ; and I could wifh that thofe here who may be difpleafed that they are not confidered on this occafion, or that the poft is beftowed on an *Englifhman*, may have time to cool before the meeting of the parliament.

If his Majefty fhall pleafe to fend us an Archbifhop from *England*, it would be of fervice to the King's affairs here that he fhould be fettled and form fome acquaintance, and begin to have weight againft the feffion. Or if his Majefty fhall pleafe to fill that
ftation

ftation with one from the bench here, I think it would be beft to have the confequent removes over by that time.

I have fo often before the vacancy happened, wrote of the neceffity of filling the place with an *Englifhman*, that I hope I need not make any new reprefentation on that head.

It is likewife of fome confequence that the perfon pitched upon be one whom I may depend upon for there being a good agreement betwixt him and me, which I am fure will be the cafe, if either the Bifhop of St. *David's* or the Bifhop of *Fernes* be the perfon.

And I fhould be very forry if the effect of this delay fhould be the bringing on the ftage fome other candidate, which is what is by many here apprehended to be in fome meafure aimed at, by deferring this matter for fo long a time.

Whether any fuch thing be defigned you are beft able to judge, and I beg leave to recommend it to you to prevent any fuch ufe being made of it.

I am, &c.

To the Archbifhop of Canterbury.

My Lord,   *Dublin*, *July* 3, 1729.

SINCE I had the honour of your Grace's relating to Mr. *Bury* of *Finglafs*; Mr. Baron *Pocklington* has given me a very good character of him; and Sir *Ralph Gore*, a perfon of diftinction here, has introduced him to me, and confirmed what Mr. Baron had faid of him. I fhall upon your Grace's recommendation have a regard to him, and endeavour on a proper occafion to help him to fomewhat in the Church.

I am, my Lord, &c.

To

To Sir Robert Walpole.

SIR,   *Dublin, July* 8, 1729.

AS I troubled you with a letter not long ago, relating to the Archbifhoprick of *Dublin*, I fhould not fo foon have given you a new trouble, but that we are informed, that great endeavours are ufed and much art to bring into play on this occafion, fome new perfon on this fide of the water. I can affure you, fo far as I may be fuppofed capable of judging, there is nobody on the bench here fo able to do his Majefty fervice in this country, nor I think of thofe who would willingly take the archbifhoprick, any fo acceptable to the well affected of this kingdom, nor can I depend fo firmly on being affifted in all publick affairs by any one here, ◼︎ the Bifhop of *Fernes*. I beg leave to lay thefe things plainly before you, and to defire your help, that fome other perfon here may not be worked in, who may be of little or no fervice, (and perhaps differvice) where all poffible help is little enough.

                                         I am, &c.

To the fame.

SIR,   *Dublin, Aug.* 12, 1729.

I Had fooner anfwered the letter you honoured me with of the 19th paft, but that I received it when I was upon my vifitation, from which I am lately returned.

I am very much obliged to you for the kind opinion you are pleafed to exprefs of my endeavours to fupport the King's intereft here, and I can affure you they fhall never be wanting. And I am fenfible how much I am

                                         indebted

indebted to you for the perfonal regard you are pleafed to honour me with.

I am glad to hear the affair of the archbifhoprick continues in fo good a way ; I could heartily wifh that the two Bifhops in *England* who oppofe one another in this bufinefs, could be brought to agree, they are both my very good friends, as are the Bifhops of St. *David*'s and *Fernes,* and I hope the competition betwixt them, will not make way for fome third perfon to be let into the archbifhoprick that may be lefs acceptable, and with whom I cannot promife myfelf to have the fame good correfpondence as with either of them.

I fhould have been glad that this affair had been fettled before my Lord Lieutenant's arrival here ; but am very eafy, as you give me hopes the delay will be of no prejudice.

I beg leave to take this opportunity to thank you for the fupport you have given me on this and all other occafions fince my coming hither.

I am, Sir, &c.

To Lord Carteret.

My Lord,   *Dublin, Aug.* 12, 1729.

UPON my return from my vifitation I had the pleafure of receiving one of Lady * *Difert*'s favours, for which I beg leave to trouble your Excellency to make my compliments, with my moft fincere congratulations to the bride and bridegroom, for in that light they appear yet to me at this diftance : as it is a marriage which has the approbation of your Excellency and my Lady *Carteret,* I queftion not but

* One of the daughters of Lord *Carteret,* who was married to the Earl of *Difert,* a *Scotch* nobleman.

but it will prove happy, which are my moſt hearty wiſhes.

We begin now to look with ſome pleaſure at the near proſpect of ſeeing your Lordſhip amongſt us, and I doubt not but your preſence will by degrees remove thoſe difficulties we at preſent apprehend in the next ſeſſion of parliament.

This city is not ſo free from tumults as it ought to be, and as we hoped the proclamation publiſhed ſome time ago would have made it ; but if it be poſſible to awaken the magiſtrates out of their preſent lethargy, we ſhall endeavour to have all things quiet here againſt your Lordſhip's arrival. I am,

My Lord, &c.

To the Biſhop of London.

My Lord,   Dublin, Aug. 28, 1729.

IN my laſt to your Lordſhip I could not help expreſſing myſelf with ſome reſentment that the oppoſition made by my ſucceſſor againſt Mr. Stephens, ſhould have met with ſuch ſucceſs ; but I was then ſenſible how much I was obliged to your Lordſhip for preventing the canonry of Chriſt Church from being actually given away to another. I ſtill retain the ſame ſenſe of my obligations to your Lordſhip, and as you are beſt able to judge of what can or cannot be done for my friend Mr. Stephens, I again recommend him to your Lordſhip's protection, and leave it entirely to your Lordſhip's goodneſs and prudence to manage that vacancy ſo that he may be put into poſſeſſion of ſomewhat reaſonable before that is given away.

We are ſtill here under an uncertainty who is to be Archbiſhop of Dublin, and I take it for granted ſhall continue ſo till his Majeſty's return. Your Lordſhip knows the Biſhops of St. David's and Fernes are both old acquaintance and friends of mine, and as I

V o l. I.   R   have

have wrote to your Lordſhip, ſo have I wrote to the miniſtry, that I ſhall be eaſy on whomſoever of them the choice ſhall fall ſince I have no doubt of agreeing very well with either of them, but it will be otherwiſe if ſome third perſon ſhould be put into that poſt: and I am the more concerned that it ſhould not be another becauſe it is generally underſtood here that I am a friend to both of them; but it will be clear that if another be made Archbiſhop, my recommendation has been of no ſignificancy, which opinion, I am ſure, muſt have an ill effect on the bench here. I muſt therefore beg of your Lordſhip, who are upon the ſpot, if poſſible, to hinder ſuch a diſgrace from happening to me.

I can aſſure your Lordſhip that if one has *Dublin*, and the other be made ſure of *Caſhel*, *Derry*, or *Kilmore*, the firſt that falls, I believe the perſon who has this promiſe kept to him, will rather be a gainer as to providing for a family.

We have a fine crop of corn on the ground, and have had above three weeks very fine weather to get it in, and though we have now ſome wet, yet if it pleaſe God not to continue it for a long time, it will for the moſt part be got in very well.

I hope in a little time all the doubts written to us from *London* about the peace will be cleared up. I am,

My Lord, &c.

To the Duke of Newcaſtle.

My Lord,   *Dublin, Sept.* 9, 1729.

I HAVE ſo often troubled your Grace on Mr. *Stephens*'s account, that if I could avoid it I would not give you the additional trouble of this letter. Your Grace knows I had the promiſe of the next canonry of *Chriſt Church* for him: and that there has
been

been one vacant for some time by the death of Dr. *Stratford*, and that it was not filled before his Majesty went abroad, that Mr. *Stephens* might be provided with somewhat else in the King's gift, before that was given away: your Grace has frequently renewed the promise of securing an equivalent for Mr. *Stephens*, if he should fail of the canonry of *Christ Church* promised him. I must therefore again recommend him to your Grace's protection, and intreat that the present vacancy at *Christ Church* may not be filled up till Mr. *Stephens* is actually provided for. This favour, if your Grace will please to obtain it for him, will be some security for his being taken care of, but if the vacant canonry be given away first, he will only rest upon a general promise, and be rather in a worse case than he has been in for some years past.

Your Grace's kind support of his pretensions on this occasion, will be esteemed the greatest obligation by,

My Lord, &c.

To Sir Robert Walpole.

SIR,　　　　　　　　　　　　　*Dublin, Sept.* 9, 1729.

AS I have made bold to trouble you in affairs of greater consequence, I hope you will excuse this trouble in a matter of less importance, but in which my friendship for the person concerned makes me very solicitous.

Before I left *England* I obtained a promise of the next canonry of *Christ Church* for Mr. *Stephens*, of *Malden* in *Surrey*, and have since been frequently promised that he should have that or an equivalent.

When a canonry fell there by the death of Dr. *Stratford*, a little before his Majesty went abroad, I renewed my application for Mr. *Stephens*, but found

R 2　　　　　　　　　　　　　　　　that

that upon some objections made to Mr. *Stephens* on account of the misfortune of his eyes, it was rather designed to give that canonry to Dr. *Knipe*, and to give some other equivalent to Mr. *Stephens*; but the better to secure the performance to Mr. *Stephens*, it was thought proper to keep that canonry open till he was actually provided for.

Now as his Majesty is upon his return, and it is probable Dr. *Knipe* will be very desirous to be put in possession of the canonry intended for him, the favour I have to ask of you, Sir, is that Dr. *Knipe* may not be made Canon, till Mr. *Stephens*, who had a prior promise of that preferment, is otherwise provided for. This I hope will be some real security for his being speedily taken care of, but if the present vacancy be once filled up, and instead of a canonry Mr. *Stephens* has only a promise of some other preferment, from what has happened to him already in this affair, I am afraid his future expectations may be very uncertain.

As he always supported the character of an ingenious man and a good scholar at the University, and was thoroughly well affected to the succession in his Majesty's family in the worst times, and has been an old and intimate acquaintance of mine almost from my first admission at *Oxford*, I most earnestly recommend him and his interest in this affair to your favour and protection.

I am, &c.

To the Bishop of London,

My Lord,   *Dublin, Sept.* 13, 1729.

UPON the receipt of your Lordship's of the 4th instant, I immediately wrote to the Duke of *Newcastle*, Sir *Robert Walpole*, and the Speaker, according to your advice. I have this day received
another

another from your Lordſhip on the ſame ſubjeçt, and I am very much obliged to you for your kindneſs on this occaſion to Mr. *Stephens*, and beg the continuance of your good offices for him, that the canonry may not be açtually filled till he is provided for : and hope by your kind aſſiſtance he may get ſomewhat on this occaſion.

I am ſorry to hear my Lord *Townſhend* has declared he will have no concern in Church matters.

I cannot learn whether any thing is yet fixed about the archbiſhoprick of *Dublin*, and hope after all it will go either to the Biſhop of St. *David*'s or Biſhop of *Fernes*; and think if the former ſhould fail now, it may be worth his while to have an eye to ſome other biſhoprick that may fall here; and I cannot but think either *Caſhel*, *Derry*, or *Kilmore* would be rather more beneficial for his family than *Dublin*.

I am ſorry my conduçt in this affair has been diſagreeable to your Lordſhip, whom I ſhould be very unwilling to offend; and I believe if the Biſhop of St. *David*'s knew the true ſtate of affairs here, he would excuſe the part I have açted ſince the death of the late Archbiſhop.

I am glad to find the quarrel with *Pruſſia* is blown over, and that the King is ſo ſoon expeçted in *London*.

My * Lord Lieutenant landed here this day, and will I believe open the parliament *Tueſday* come ſe'nnight, when I heartily wiſh we may have an eaſy ſeſſion. I am,

My Lord, &c.

To

* *John*, Lord *Carteret*, the third time of his being here, which was a great advantage to this kingdom, as it made him well acquainted with all the affairs thereof.

To the fame.

My Lord,   *Dublin, Oct.* 7, 1729.

AS the feffion of our parliament is begun, we are thinking of fome neceffary bills; and as moft of our clergy have neither houfe nor glebe, we are for trying to help them to fome. We attempted laft feffion to have a bill to impower a tenant in tail, to make a grant of 40 acres, at the full improved value for a glebe, which was difapproved in *England.* We would now attempt to impower fuch tenant to grant a glebe of 20, or rather than fail, of 10 acres, on the fame conditions as before. But we would firft willingly know what would be allowed of in *England.* We think 10 acres cannot be thought any great damage to the remainder man; and without fuch an help, as moft of our eftates are under fettlements, there is fcarce any coming at glebes.

We were told my Lord *Trevor* very much oppofed our laft bill, I fhould be obliged to your Lordfhip, if you would talk the matter over with him, and any others your Lordfhip fhall judge proper, and let me know what fuccefs may be hoped for, if we fend over fuch a bill.

I am, &c.

To the Duke of Newcaftle.

My Lord,   *Dublin, Oct.* 23, 1729.

I HAVE had the honour of your Grace's of the 14th inftant, and am too fenfible of the hurry of bufinefs in *England* to expect a regular correfpondence from your Grace's ftation. I have the beft proofs of my not being neglected by your Lordfhip and

and others in the miniftry by my having been hitherto fupported here.

As the feffion of our parliament is now opened,
I think his Majefty does very right in not filling
the archbifhoprick of *Dublin* till our parliament
rifes, and fhall fay nothing farther on that fubject at
prefent, than that I hope it will at laft be filled with
an *Englifhman*.

Your Grace has no doubt had an account of Mr.
Conolly's illnefs, and quitting the chair, and Sir *Ralph
Gore* being chofen in his room. It is likely Mr. *Co-
nolly* will not live many days.

The feffion has opened very well, and moft of the
members feem difpofed and promife to provide fome
fund to pay intereft for about 200,000 *l.* of our debts,
till we are able to pay them. And indeed without
fuch a provifion, the wheels of the government will
be fo clogged here, that in cafe of any accident, we
fhall hardly be able to fend a regiment abroad, if
called for. But at the fame time there is a very bad
fpirit, I fear, artfully fpread among all degrees of
men amongft us, and the utmoft grumbling againft
England, as getting all our money from us either by
trade or otherwife.

And this fpirit has been heightened by a * book
lately publifhed here about the abfentees, who according to the calculation of that author, draw
from us about † 62,000 *l. per. ann.* It is certain
the fum of his calculations are wrong, fince according to them, about 440,000 *l. per. ann.* would
be paid by us as as our ballance of trade, &c. which
if true, would in about three years have left us without money.

And

* Wrote by *Thomas Prior*, Efq;

† Suppofed to be paid to penfioners on the eftablifhment of
Ireland.

And I believe among less intelligent persons, they are for taxing the abfentees 4 *s.* in the pound ; but I am satisfied the men of sense in either house are too wise to make an attempt of that nature, which they know could only exasperate *England,* without ever having such a bill returned to us.

We are no doubt in a miserable condition, by having had three or four bad harvests together, and if God had not blessed us with a plentiful crop this harvest, we had been ruined for some years, but I hope we shall pick up by degrees.

But there is an evil spirit here, that instead of owning whence our calamities really came, would throw all upon *England.*

The absentees spending their money there, the restraints upon our wool and woollen manufactures, the encrease of the establishment pensions, though we tell them his present Majefty has granted none, and our regiments being at *Gibraltar,* though we tell them the common defence of *England* and *Ireland* required it, are the great topicks of complaint. On *Tuefday* they went into a committee on the state of the nation, where these heads were opened with some others, and on *Monday* they are to sit again. Whether they will, as some propofe, draw up a memorial to be presented to his Majefty, setting forth their misery to no purpofe ; or whether they will, as the wifest amongft them are disposed, content themselves to redrefs such evils as they can, is hard to judge. I rather hope things will end the latter way, after the warm men have been permitted to discharge their fire.

God be thanked the government is not concerned in these heats, nor the administration fallen on. And I may venture to say there has not been any such impartial administration here since the revolution, as has been for the five years last past, that the government has been in *English* hands.

If

If I can judge any thing in the matter, there is a neceſſity of continuing to ſupport the *Engliſh* intereſt here, or what things may in time come to, I ſhall leave to others to think.

There is no doubt but Mr. *Conolly's* illneſs and impoſſibility of ever acting again, has made things worſe than uſual, as it muſt be ſome time before the ſeveral clans that united under him, can ſettle under a new director. *But ſteadineſs in* England, *will, I doubt not, by degrees ſettle us again here.*

I am very glad to find my endeavours here are accepted by his Majeſty, and favourably thought of by the miniſtry. I ſhall continue to promote his Majeſty's ſervice here to the utmoſt of my power. I cannot tell but the rights of the clergy may be attacked this ſeſſion : if we cannot make a ſtand here, as I hope we ſhall, I muſt in the behalf of all my brethren, implore his Majeſty's protection on the other ſide of the water.

The Biſhop of *London* has acquainted me how things have paſſed in relation to Mr. *Stephens*, and I am very much obliged to your Grace for being ſo kind as to promiſe to take him under your protection. I muſt beg leave to acquaint your Grace he begins to advance towards 60, ſo that he cannot afford to be long poſtponed.   I am,

Your Grace's, &c.

To the Biſhop of London.

My Lord,   *Dublin, Oct.* 29, 1729.

THE bearer Mr. *John Fulton*, Maſter of Arts, of *Trinity* College in *Dublin*, is deſirous to go to the *Weſt Indies*, where he has ſome relations ; and has applied to me to be recommended to your Lordſhip to be ordained and ſent thither. Beſides the teſtimonials he has to produce to your Lordſhip, I have

I have enquired about the character he bears in the College, and am affured he hath behaved himfelf very well there, and fupports a good character.

If your Lordfhip can difpofe of him to *America*, fo as to have fome employment there, it will be an addition to the favour to give him what difpatch your Lordfhip can, as he does not abound in money.   And your Lordfhip's kind affiftance of him, as far as your Lordfhip fhall find him to deferve it, will be efteemed an obligation, by

My Lord, &c.

To the Duke of Newcaftle.

My Lord,   *Dublin, Oct.* 30, 1729.

I AM very forry I muft acquaint your Grace that the ill fpirit I mentioned in my laft ftill increafes, or at leaft feems to intimidate thofe who are better difpofed in the Houfe of Commons.

The privy council was attacked on *Saturday* laft about the overdrawing of the concordatum for the two laft years ; but the Committee then broke up without any conclufion, by its being carried that the chairman fhould leave the chair.   On *Monday* they feemed to have dropped the farther purfuit of that affair ; but on *Tuefday* it was, through non-attendance of fome, and ill-concerted meafures of thofe prefent, carried without withdrawing, that the over-drawings of the concordatum would be of ill confequence to the kingdom.

To-morrow it is expected that there will be a report to the houfe from the committee, when we are promifed that the houfe will difagree with the committee.   If gentlemen will attend and unite in their meafures it may eafily be done ; but hitherto there has been very little agreement, nor any well concerted management in that houfe.   There is no doubt
but

but Mr. *Conolly*'s illnefs has been one occafion of this disjointednefs, and it will require time to bring the feveral clans which united in him to center in another.

After his death being expected for feveral days, Mr. *Conolly* died this morning about one o'clock. He has left behind him a very great fortune, fome talk of 17,000 *l. per ann.*

As his death makes a vacancy among the commiffioners of the revenue, my Lord Chancellor and I have been talking with my Lord Lieutenant on that fubject, and we all agree it will be for his Majefty's fervice that a native fucceed him : and as Sir *Ralph Gore,* the new fpeaker, does not care to quit the poft of Chancellor of the Exchequer, which he is already poffeffed of, and which by an addition made to the place by his late Majefty is worth better than 800 *l. per ann.* and is for life, to be made one of the commiffioners, we join in our opinion that the moft proper perfon here to fucceed Mr. *Conolly* is Dr. *Coghill *,* who is already a perfon of weight, and has done fervice in the parliament ; and we think by this addition will be more capable of ferving his Majefty both in and out of the houfe.

I am, &c.

To the fame.

My Lord,   *Dublin, Nov.* 13, 1729.

IN my laft I gave your Grace an account of a refolution paffed in the committee of accounts, relating to the overdrawings of the concordatum. When the committee came to make their report, it was unanimoufly agreed to have that refolution expunged.

There

* Right Hon. *Marmaduke Coghill* was accordingly appointed.

There were likewife in the fame committee great heats about over-drawing the military contingencies, but without coming to any refolution about it.

As thefe two articles are the only branches of payment that can be charged with any unforefeen expence, or be ufed in cafe of any emergency, upon talking with feveral members of the neceffity of fome fuch fund to have recourfe to on occafion, they were brought to drop their firft heat.

Almoft every day this week has been fpent in the committee of ways and means; about granting the ufual additional duties there has been no difpute, but about providing for the intereft of 200,000 *l.* debt owing by the publick, whether it fhould be in the grand bill of fupply, or in a bill by itfelf; and the laft being agreed on, whether only for two years, or till the debts are paid, it is carried only for two years. The fund for the payment of the intereft is an additional duty upon wines and brandies, and 4 *s.* in the pound upon abfent officers, civil or military; in the latter, all under field officers are excepted, and fuch of both are excufed as fhall obtain his Majefty's fign manual.

The two bills are now drawing up, and I hope in a few days will be before the council here.

The houfe has not yet been in another committee on the ftate of the nation; and there is no gueffing what meafures they will take there. As the warm men have had fuccefs in fome divifions in the houfe, I do not expect any thing of temper when they are in the committee.

When they have done any thing I fhall acquaint your Grace with it. I am,

Your Grace's, &c.

To

To the fame.

My Lord,   *Dublin, Nov.* 22, 1729.

I THIS day had the honour of your Grace's of
the 11th inftant :   Dr. *Coghill's* being made commiffioner in the room of Mr. *Conolly* is very acceptable here ; and I hope he and Sir *Ralph Gore* will by
degrees get together the friends of Mr. *Conolly* and
others well difpofed, to join heartily in his Majefty's
fervice ; but this is more than they will be able to
effect this feffion : however the King's bufinefs is now
over, though it has met with great rubs and delays,
and has been done with an ill grace ; and our two
money bills were fent off on *Thurfday* laft ; the firft
is the ufual tax-bill ; the other is made up of feveral
little taxes, by which it is propofed to pay the intereft of 6 *per cent.* for 200,000 *l.* of our debts, for
two years, and if more is raifed than 12000 *l. per
ann.* to fink part of the principal. It was attempted to
give this fund till the debt was funk, but that was rejected by a majority of five voices.   There was afterwards a motion made that it fhould be inferted in
the bill, that at the end of two years either the principal fhould be repaid or intereft continued ; but
this was oppofed and dropped, though it was declared to be the fenfe of the houfe.   As the act for the
additional duties of the firft bill granted laft feffion,
expires on *Chriftmas* day, and the new duties of the
fecond bill begin from that day, we hope they will
be returned us foon enough to be paffed before that
time.

The committee on the ftate of the nation is ftill
open, but if I may believe fome of the difcontented
members, there will hardly any thing be done there,
except fettling a better proportion betwixt our gold
and filver, than there is at prefent.   And I very
                                                          much

much fear that the weight of the bankers is fo great here, that it may be carried to raife our filver, inftead of lowering our gold; as a guinea paffes here for 23 *s. Irifh*, which is 3 *d.* more than it paffes for in *England*; and a moidore for 3ɔ *s. Irifh*, which is 9 *d.* the bankers and remitters have had the benefit of carrying out all our filver, and bringing back gold for it; and now they want by raifing the *Englifh* fhilling an half-penny, to have the benefit of carrying out all our gold, and bringing back *Englifh* filver. My Lord Chancellor, myfelf, and feveral others, are doing what we can to prevent this mifchief, but are uncertain of the fuccefs.

If the bankers prevail, I fhall fend over a fhort memorial againft what the Commons may addrefs for, if I cannot get either the Houfe of Lords or privy council to join with me *; for fuch a raifing of the filver will undo us here.

I am, &c.

To the fame.

My Lord,   *Dublin, Dec.* 11, 1729.

THE dangerous condition in which the Archbifhop of *Cafhel* now lies, is the occafion of my giving your Grace this trouble, humbly to defire that no meafures may be taken to difpofe of that Archbifhoprick, till I have an opportunity of acquainting your Lordfhip that it is actually vacant. I am,

My Lord, &c.

Tₒ

---

* This refolution was a very fpirited one, and very confiftent with his Grace's ufual courage, and conduct.

To the same.

My Lord,   *Dublin, Dec.* 13, 1729.

THIS morning died Dr. *Godwin,* Archbishop of *Casbel :* I have just time to acquaint your Grace, that this may be a means of compromising the dispute about the archbishoprick of *Dublin,* by removing the Bishop of St. *David's* to *Dublin,* and the Bishop of *Fernes* to *Casbel* * ; but if this be done, I should think it would be better to defer doing it till after the parliament is up. If it be apprehended that it may give too much offence to bestow at the same time the two best posts in the Church, after the primacy, on *Englishmen,* I must say that I think the most proper person to remove to *Casbel,* will be Dr. *Synge,* Archbishop of *Tuam.* I am,
My Lord, &c.

To the Bishop of London.

My Lord,   *Dublin, Dec.* 14, 1729.

YESTERDAY died, after some days illness, the Archbishop of *Casbel* †, very much lamented here. I should at another time have thought this vacancy might have compromised matters as to the archbishoprick of *Dublin,* but in the present uneasy state of the House of Commons, I think it will be too bold a step at one and the same time to give
two

* It appears clearly by this letter, that the Bishop of *London* had no reason for charging my Lord Primate with a partiality to the Bishop of *Fernes,* which it seems his Lordship misapprehending the thing, had done.
† Dr. *Timothy Godwin,* who was translated to the See from *Kilmore* and *Ardagh.*

two *Englishmen* the two beft pofts in the Church, next to the primacy.

The fcheme pitched on with my Lord Lieutenant and Lord Chancellor, confidering the prefent circumftances of the kingdom is, that the Bifhop of *Fernes* * be tranflated to *Dublin*, the Bifhop of *Clonfert* to *Fernes*; and if there be a difpofition in *England* to make Dr. *Clayton* Bifhop here, as we are affured there is, I have nothing to fay againft his being promoted to *Clonfert*. As to the archbifhoprick of *Cafhel*, it is thought proper to remove the Bifhop of *Elphin* to *Cafhel*, the Bifhop of *Killalla* to *Elphin*, and Dr. *Synge* fon to the Archbifhop of *Tuam*, to *Killalla*.

This is a fcheme I fhould not project, if we were not in a troubled ftate here, but circumftances confidered, is what I hope will moft conduce to keep things quiet in this country.

I am, &c.

To the Duke of Newcaftle.

My Lord,   *Dublin, Dec.* 16, 1729.

SINCE I had the honour to write to your Grace about the affairs of parliament, the Commons have voted that the moidore fhall go for 30 *s*. † and feem difpofed to raife all other coins anfwerably to that value.

As their votes are not laws, I do not apprehend any thing they can vote can do us any more mifchief than putting off the neceffary reduction of our gold till another feffion of parliament. Though if others of the council were of my fentiments, as we are undone

without

---

* Dr. *John Hoadly*, tranflated to *Dublin*, and after the death of Dr. *Boulter* to the primacy of *Ireland*.

† His Grace foretold this furprizing event in a former letter.

without a reduction of our gold, we would with his Majefty's leave fet things to rights before their next meeting: and I am fatisfied the good effects of the alterations propofed in council would be fo fenfibly felt before that time, that there would be no grumbling about it when the parliament meets next.

If they go on farther in the money affair, and addrefs his Majefty to do any thing wrong in it, I fhall trouble your Grace with a memorial againft any fuch deftructive meafures.

The Commons and feveral others without doors, are in a great heat about the alterations made by the council in *England* to our leffer money bill. I believe a great many will be for lofing the bill rather than agree to the alterations. They are by all who know what they are, allowed to be for the better, but the point infifted upon is, that no alteration whatfoever fhall be made either in the *Englifh* or *Irifh* council, to a money bill. It is certain the law here is againft thefe warm men, and fo are the precedents: and it is hoped that the majority of the houfe will be fenfible of the bad confequences of rejecting that bill, which will run this nation much deeper in debt, and may end in a diffolution; and that they will take care that the bill paffes; but it cannot be without much heat and oppofition. On *Thurfday* the fate of this bill will be decided.

I yefterday wrote to your Grace about the vacancy on the death of the Archbifhop of *Cafhel.*

I am, &c.

To the same.

My Lord,   Dublin, Dec. 20, 1729.

IN mine of the 16th I gave your Grace an account of the great ferment we were in here
about the alterations made in our little money-bill
by the council in *England*. Yesterday came on the
debate about it in the House of Commons, and after about four hours debate, it was carried in favour
of the bill, by 124 against 62. There have been
other divisions since upon every step of the bill,
with greater inequality; but the first was the great
trial.

To-day the bill was sent up to the Lords, and we
suppose both the money-bills will receive the Royal
assent on *Monday*. As far as I can find, if the debate had come on before there had been time to
talk with the members, the bill had been lost, the
warmth against the alterations was at first so great.
And I am of opinion the bill had not been carried
by so great a majority, if it had not been for fear of
a dissolution of the parliament, as the greatest part
of our commoners are not willing to be at the expence of a new election.

The King's business is now done, of which I am
glad, though I could wish it had been done with a
better grace.

I cannot but look on this as a very good session,
considering the greatest part of the debts of the nation is put in a method of payment, which will certainly be pursued the next session.

Whether now the commons are got right in one
point, and are very much broken among themselves,
they

they may not be brought to think likewife right about the affair of our coin, I cannot yet guefs.

I am, My Lord, &c.

To the Bifhop of London.

My Lord,   *Dublin, Jan.* 2, 1729.

ON the 15th paft I troubled your Lordfhip with an account of the fcheme about the vacant archbifhopricks, that was thought moft advifeable in our prefent turbulent condition. We yefterday received his Majefty's orders in purfuance of thofe applications, except that Dr. *Clayton* is fent to *Killalla,* and that *Clonfert* is referved for fome *Englifhman.*

I cannot but fay we want fome help on the bench here, where at prefent we have but nine *Englifh* Bifhops out of 22. The perfon we are told is not fixed upon, and I fhould be obliged to your Lordfhip if you would endeavour that it may be fome worthy perfon. I do not well know whether Mr. *Saul* would be willing to come hither, if he would, I fhould think him a very proper perfon for our bench. Of the *Englifh* here, the only perfon I know is Dr. *Longworth,* who is alfo known to your Lordfhip, and who has behaved himfelf very well on his living in the north.

I am forry there has been any mifunderftanding betwixt your Lordfhip and me on account of the archbifhoprick of *Dublin;* and fhould have been for compromifing matters in favour of the Bifhop of St. *David's* on the vacancy of *Cafhel,* if your Lordfhip had not affured me he would think of nothing here if he failed of *Dublin,* and we had not been in a very uneafy fituation in the Houfe of Commons. But I hope things will again fettle, fince I defire ftill,

S 2   and

and hope it is a favour you will grant me, that I may trouble you to difcourfe with the miniftry about what I apprehend to be for his Majefty's fervice in the promotions here.

I have read the Bifhop of St. *David*'s book with a great deal of pleafure, and am glad to hear it takes well in *England*.

We fhall very fpeedily fend over fome bills from hence, and among the reft the glebe bill ; the number of acres mentioned in the bill is 20, but rather than fail, we fhould be glad of 10.

We have had a popery bill brought into our houfe, partly for regiftering a number of fecular priefts, and partly more effectually to drive out the regulars from hence ; but it was this day rejected in the houfe. I muft own I think it is better letting them alone, whatever may otherwife be proper, till after the congrefs at * *Soiffons* is over.

We have had a very uneafy feffion here, but I hope, as the peace with *Spain* is fettled, you will have an eafy one in *England*. I heartily wifh your Lordfhip many happy new years, and am,

My Lord, &c.

To the Duke of Newcaftle.

My Lord,   *Dublin,* *Jan.* 3, 1729.

ITHIS day received a letter from Mr. *Delafaye*, by your Grace's order. I am very fenfible of the great hurry your Lordfhip muft be in upon the change made in the other office, and the approach of the feffion of parliament in *England*, where I doubt not things will go eafy, fince a peace is concluded with *Spain*.

I am

* For a general peace among the principal powers of *Europe*.

I am very much obliged to the ministry for the regard that has been shewn to my recommendations in the late promotions on the bench here.   Dr. *Synge* is a very worthy man, but may very well stay till another opportunity.

I am very glad to hear *Clonfert* is designed for an *Englishman*, since there are but nine *English* on the bench, and twelve *Irish*, and it may be very proper to give some more strength to the *English* there.   But I hope the person to be sent from *England* will be a person of some worth, and who is likely to join with us that are here already.

I think there can be no grumbling here if *Clonfert* be bestowed on an *Englishman*, but it may easily be kept open till the season of grumbling is over.

As far as I can find many among the commons that were concerned in voting to keep up the moidore to its present value begin to doubt whether they have done right in it; and the whole affair of our coin seems to rest there.

We shall consider whether it may not be proper to take that affair into consideration in the House of Lords after the recess, and endeavour to rectify the mistake of the commons.

I have formerly acquainted your Grace that the lesser money bill was carried, and passed in due time. I think there can hardly be any squabble in either house now that can much concern his Majesty.   We have a great many bills now before the council from the commons, to which we shall give all possible dispatch.

I beg leave to wish your Lordship many happy years, and am,

My Lord, &c.

To

To the same.

My Lord,   *Dublin, Jan.* 10, 1729.

I HAVE had the honour of your Grace's of the 30th paft, and had before received an account of the promotions on our bench from Mr. *Delafaye*, by your Grace's orders.

I am very glad things have ended fo well in the Houfe of Commons as they have, and fhall not be wanting in my endeavours to promote his Majefty's fervice there and elfewhere to the utmoft of my power. It is not certain that they will attempt any thing farther there about our coin, if they do I fhall trouble your Lordfhip with a memorial on that fubject. I am obliged to your Grace for the regard you are pleafed to exprefs for my reprefentations, and defire they fhould have no farther weight than the reafons with which I fhall upon occafion fupport them, may deferve.

The Bifhop of *Cork* is at prefent very ill, and there have been reports, though falfe, that he was dead. If he fhould die, as any *Englifhman* would rather chufe *Cork* than *Clonfert*, I think Dr. *Synge* *, (if his Majefty pleafes) may have *Clonfert* beftowed on him, where his father the Archbifhop of *Tuam* had rather fee him, on account of its neighbourhood to *Tuam*, than in any other bifhoprick ; and *Cork* may be beftowed on an *Englifhman*.

I was willing juft to mention this, that *Clonfert* may not be given away till it is known whether *Cork* will be vacant or no.

As

---

* *Edward Synge,* eldeft fon of the Archbifhop. His other brother *Nicholas,* was advanced to the fee of *Killaloe* in 1745, by the Earl of *Chefterfield,* then Lord Lieutenant of *Ireland.*

As any thing occurs here, worth your Grace's notice, I fhall not fail to acquaint you with it.

I am, my Lord, &c.

To the Bifhop of London.

My Lord, *Dublin, Jan.* 10, 1729.

I HAVE received your Lordfhip's of the 30th paft, and am forry the Bifhop of St. *David's* has done with all thoughts of *Ireland,* fince he might ftill fare better here than he may do in hafte in *England.*

In mine of the 2d inftant to your Lordfhip, I took notice of *Clonfert* being in our laft promotions referved for an *Englifhman,* and mentioned two for it, if it was not engaged, one in *England,* one here : I find Dean *Crofs* * would be willing to take it, whom your Lordfhip knows.

This week we had a report for two or three days that the Bifhop of *Cork* † was dead ; but by letters from *Cork* that came in yefterday, he was not dead but ftill ill. If he dies, Dr. *Synge* may be gratified with *Clonfert,* where his father the Archbifhop of *Tuam,* on account of its neighbourhood to *Tuam,* had rather fee him than in any other bifhoprick, and *Cork* may be referved for an *Englifhman.* And I am fure

---

* Rector of St. *Mary's, Dublin,* who had been chaplain to the *Englifh* factory in *Turkey.*

† Dr. *Peter Brown,* was educated in the univerfity of *Dublin,* was a Senior Fellow and Provoft. He was promoted to the fees of *Cork* and *Rofs* in the year 1709, and died at *Cork* in *Auguft,* 1735. He was a prelate of great piety, charity and abilities ; a moft eminent preacher ; two volumes of his fermons were publifhed fome time after his death. He alfo wrote other tracts, one of which was againft drinking to the memory of the dead. He was fucceeded by Dr. *Robert Clayton,* from *Killalla,* who was afterwards tranflated to *Clogher.*

fure any *Englishman* would rather chuse *Cork* than *Clonfert*. I only mention this that *Clonfert* may not be disposed of till it is known in *England* whether *Cork* is like to be vacant or no.

I have this week received a letter from Dr. *Jenney*, relating to the deanery of *Clogher*, in which he acquainted me he had written to your Lordship about it.

Dr. *Jenney* is a very worthy man, but as my Lord Lieutenant in his first commission, had the disposal of deaneries here, and that we think it was a little hard to have them taken from him in his second commission, * I do not care to oppose his recommendation on the other side of the water. I am,

My Lord, &c.

To the Duke of Newcastle.

My Lord,   *Dublin, Jan.* 17, 1729.

IN my last to your Grace, I mentioned that the general report here was, that the Bishop of *Cork* was dead or dying. I do not find that report confirmed this week, so that I rather suppose he may be out of danger : as soon as I hear any thing to the contrary, I will acquaint your Grace with it.

We have sent over to *England* a bill to make more effectual an act to encourage the draining and improving of bogs and unprofitable low grounds, &c. which act was passed in the second year of his
late

---

* This was generous in the Primate. But there was some reason for taking away that power, my Lord Lieutenant had given away three out of four deaneries to high tories, who were Gentlemen of learning, great abilities, fortune, and good character; but the Primate wanted to have the sole appointment of all ecclesiastical preferments.

late Majefty. The former act propofed draining bogs, &c. by voluntary undertakers, but as no fuch have fince offered themfelves, this act provides a fund for doing it, which is computed at about 4000*l.* *per ann.* and is likewife defigned for the encouragement of tillage here.

Laft year we found the terrible effects of the want of tillage, by a want of corn little fhort of a famine ; and when we endeavoured to cure this want by buying corn by fubfcription, and fending it to the feveral parts of the north to be fold there at a reafonable price, we found the land carriage of the corn, for want of fome rivers being made navigable, (that it was hoped would have been fo by the act of the fecond of his late Majefty) to come to a much greater fum than there was occafion to abate in the price given for our corn. So that the intention of this act is to prevent our falling into the like calamity again, by a mifcarriage of one or two harvefts here. And this act is what the whole nation with reafon apprehend to be fo much for their common intereft, that I moft humbly intreat it may be fent us back.

I am, my Lord, &c.

To Sir Robert Walpole.

S i r, *Dublin, Jan.* 22, 1729.

I HAVE been applied to by a perfon of weight in this country to write in behalf of Mr *Foulk,* who has lately been removed from the place of Examinator to the Collector in the Port of *Dublin.*

As it is an affair wholly out of my province, I fhall meddle no farther in it than to inform you that upon enquiry into his character, I find from good hands, that he has been in the fervice of the revenue for

for near 29 years, and has for his diligence and honesty, been advanced from some of the meanest posts, by one step after another, to this of Collector in *Dublin*, which is the most considerable post of that nature in this kingdom, and requires a thoroughly able and honest person in it. Having said this, I shall wholly submit it to your pleasure whether you shall think fit to let him continue in this post, in which the commissioners here have lately placed him, or to appoint some other to that employment.

I am, My Lord, &c.

To the same.

S I R, *Dublin, Feb.* 3, 1729.

I BEG your patience whilst I lay before you the case of a particular friend of mine in *England*, Mr. *Stephens*, Vicar of *Malden* in *Surrey*, and desire your kind interposition in his favour.

He was formerly Fellow of *Merton* College in *Oxford*, and was for some years Chaplain to the *English* factory at *Oporto*, where he suffered very much in his eyes. He was always reckoned a good scholar, and a very ingenious man in the University; particularly he was valued for his skill in the classicks, and polite learning: he has always been a person of good morals, and to my knowledge one well affected to the revolution, and to the succession in his Majesty's family in the worst times.

When I was Dean of *Christ Church*, I made application to my Lord *Townshend* and the Duke of *Newcastle*, to have him preferred to a canonry of *Christ-Church*, where he might be of service notwithstanding his bad eyes, by encouraging polite learning among the youth of the College; and I obtained a promise in his favour on the next vacancy by death.

Some

Some time after, when his late Majefty was pleafed to remove me to the primacy here, I renewed my applications to the miniftry for him, and had a promife that he fhould be taken care of the next vacancy by death there, and that he fhould not fuffer by my removing to *Ireland.* Since my coming hither I have frequently put the miniftry in mind of him, and have had repeated affurances that he fhould have the next vacant canonry of *Chrift Church*, or an equivalent. Particularly upon the death of Dr. *Gaftrel*, late Bifhop of *Chefter*, I renewed my applications for him again, but as that happened juft when Dr. *Gilbert* returned from attending his late Majefty at *Hanover*, and it was thought proper to reward him for that fervice with fome immediate preferment, I defifted, upon repeated affurances that he fhould certainly have the next vacancy or an equivalent.

Here things refted till the death of Dr. *Stratford*, when I renewed my applications again, and with the intervention of the Bifhop of *London*, who has been fo kind as to appear for him, it was fettled that Dr. *Knipe* fhould have the canonry then vacant, but that he fhould not be put in poffeffion of it till Mr. *Stephens* had fome equivalent given him. And upon this foot that affair ftood, when Dr. *Knipe* went to *Hanover* with his prefent Majefty, who was pleafed to fend orders from *Hanover* that Dr. *Knipe*'s patent for the canonry then vacant, fhould immediately pafs, which was accordingly done, and Mr. *Stephens* had nothing done for him, as had been before intended.

The requeft I have to make to you is that you would lay the cafe of this deferving, but unhappy clergyman before her Majefty, and favour his pretenfions with your intereft. The misfortune of his eyes has made it fo, that he could not be put in the ufual methods of advancement, by being made Chaplain to the King.

His

His character I anfwer for, his pretenfions I have laid before you ; and I muft add, that as he advances apace towards fixty, there is not much time left to do any thing for him.

My Lord Bifhop of *London* knows him, and all that has been tranfacted in his affair, and I am fure is difpofed to affift him in his application for fome dignity.

He is the only clergyman in *England* I have or fhall recommend to the miniftry for any thing there, and your kind patronage of him in his juft pretenfions to their Majefty's favour, will always be efteemed a very great obligation laid on,

Sir, your humble fervant,

To the Bifhop of London.

My Lord,   *Dublin, Feb.* 3, 1729.

I HAVE received your Lordfhip's of the 15th paft, and thank your Lordfhip for your readinefs to do any fervice to the general ftate of the Church of *Ireland,* and have hopes your Lordfhip will reconfider the affair of promotions here, and will at the leaft for the good of his Majefty's fervice here, be willing to be concerned with me in recommending to vacancies here. Your Lordfhip is too fenfible of the ill effects of throwing the great preferments of the Church into a fcramble, and I fhall be very forry to be under a neceffity of applying to the miniftry by any other hand than your Lordfhip ; and I ftill flatter myfelf the long friendfhip I have had with your Lordfhip, will on farther confideration, prevail with your Lordfhip to re-affume the kind part you have hitherto acted on that occafion.

I fome

I some time ago mentioned to your Lordship that Dean *Cross* had applied here for the bishoprick * of *Clonfert.*   What is settled about that bishoprick I do not know : if it be still at liberty, I have no objection to Dean *Cross* having it ; he is an hearty *Englishman,* and we begin to grow weak on the bench.

I have by this post written a letter to Sir *Robert Walpole* in pursuance of your directions to be laid before her Majesty, relating to Mr. *Stephens's* affair ; and I hope, as your Lordship is so kind as heartily to espouse his interest, that he will at last meet with better success than he has hitherto.

It was with great pleasure I yesterday read your Lordship's of the 27th ult. with an account that our glebe bill was passed as we sent it over, and I thank your Lordship for your kind assistance in that affair.   I am,

My Lord, &c.

To the Duke of Newcastle.

My Lord,   *Dublin, Mar.* 10, 1729.

OUR session advances towards a conclusion, and I hope will last but a short time after the rest of our bills come from *England.*   But there is still a turbulent spirit in too many of the House of Commons : it is rather expected that they will next week take some farther wrong step about our coin, but what it will be we cannot yet learn.   We are generally very thankful here for the favour intended us in taking off the duty on wool and yarn exported from hence to *England* ; I am fully satisfied it is the only
effectual

---

* This see was filled up by Dr. *Arthur Price,* soon after translated to the united bishoprick of *Leighlin* and *Fernes ;* and to the see of *Meath* in 1733.

effectual way to prevent the running of *Irish* wool to *France*.

We have a very strong report that there is an addition likely to be made to the privy council here: as they are already 60, we find it pretty difficult to carry on the King's service there as we could wish, and if the number be increased, it will be still more difficult. I am afraid the weight and power of the privy council is not sufficiently understood in *England*, which makes me beg leave to acquaint your Grace, that the approving or rejecting of the magistrates of all the considerable towns in this kingdom is in the council here; and that as the correcting or rejecting of any bills from either House of Parliament is in them, if they are increased much more, the privy council of *England* may have more trouble from a session of parliament here than they have at present.

I can assure your Grace the *English* interest was much stronger at the board four years ago than it is now. * I must at the least beg the favour that no addition be made to the council here, till my Lord Chancellor and I are acquainted who are designed to be added, and have time to give our sentiments about them; though it will be less invidious to make no addition at all.

I wish there may not be a necessity before many years are over of reducing the number of the present members. I do not write barely my own sense but that of others of his Majesty's faithful servants here. I am,

My Lord, &c.

To

* His Grace was much in the right to desire this of the Duke of *Newcastle*, and had the more reason for it, as Lord *Carteret* had used him but scurvily in the appointment of privy counsellors, without any participation of such nomination with his Lordship.

To the same.

My Lord,   *Dublin, Mar.* 19, 1729.

ON *Monday* laft the Lords fent down to the Commons, the bill for preventing riots in the city of *Dublin* and liberties adjoining, where after a firft reading, the queftion was put for a fecond reading; when after moft furious fpeeches, it was carried by 93 againft 54, that it fhould not be read a fecond time. Though the bill in our prefent circumftances, as we have fuffered very much from riots and tumults laft fummer, and even during the prefent fitting of the parliament, would be of great fervice, if it be not abfolutely neceffary to the keeping of the peace of this city, yet I fhould hardly have troubled your Grace with an account of the mifcarriage of this bill, if the chief argument made ufe of to inflame the Houfe againft the bill had not been fuch as I think myfelf obliged to acquaint the miniftry with, which is its arifing originally in the privy council here : a thing common to many bills from time to time, and to which the council have an unqueftionable right.

It is very common in debates in the Commons to abufe the privy council, but this is the firft time fince my coming hither, that a bill has been in plain defiance of our conftitution, thrown out for rifing in the privy council.

I fhall, as foon as the parliament rifes, give your Grace an account of the right and power of the privy council here, and of the confequence it is of to his Majefty's fervice here, to have their authority fupported ; as likewife of the prefent difpofition of the Houfe of Commons, that the miniftry may take it into their confideration what will be the moft proper method effectually to fupport the privy council.

We

We had yefterday a motion made in the Houfe of Lords by the Earl of *Barrimore,* for a bill to enable his Majefty to re-affume all penfions granted by the crown from *Lady-day* 1702 to *Lady-day* 1727; the confideration of which motion is put off for a fort-night, and will from thence be adjourned till the parliament rifes, by a majority of about five to one. I am,

Your Grace's, &c.

THE END OF THE FIRST VOLUME.

LETTERS

WRITTEN BY

HIS EXCELLENCY

HUGH BOULTER, *D. D.*

Lord PRIMATE of All IRELAND, &c.

TO

Several Ministers of State in England,

AND SOME OTHERS,

CONTAINING,

An Account of the moſt intereſting Tranſactions which paſſed in IRELAND from 1724 to 1738.

VOLUME THE SECOND.

DUBLIN:

Printed for G. FAULKNER and J. WILLIAMS, Bookſellers.

M,DCC,LXX.

LETTERS

LETTERS

WRITTEN BY

His Excellency HUGH BOULTER,

Lord Primate of All *Ireland*.

To the Duke of Dorset.

My Lord,   *Dublin,* *Apr.* 6, 1730.

IT is with great pleasure that I hear from Mr.
 Gardiner, that the money due to Messrs. *Lawman*
and *Hoburg* to *Lady-day* 1730, is actually remitted to
London. I am sorry that affair met with so great delays, but considering the very low estate of our treasury, we have at last made a good handsome recom-
pence for its being put off so long.

I am, my Lord,

Your Grace's most humble, and

Most obedient Servant,

HU. ARMAGH.

* Luke *Gardiner,* Esq; Deputy Vice Treasurer of *Ireland,* and
soon after sworn a Privy Counsellor.

To the Duke of Newcastle.

My Lord,   *Dublin, Apr.* 21, 1730.

HIS * Excellency the Lord Lieutenant embarked yesterday morning for *England:* as the wind has not been very favourable since, we believe he can hardly reach *Park-gate* before this night. There is a misunderstanding between his Excellency and the Bishop of *Clonfert,* whom his Majesty has been pleased to name to the bishoprick of *Fernes,* about a commendam. The Bishop is very thankful to his Majesty for the bishoprick of *Fernes,* and designs to take it, but hopes nothing will be decided against him about the commendam, or any stop put to his having the bishoprick of *Fernes,* till he has an opportunity of laying his case before his Majesty, to whose pleasure about the commendam, he will most chearfully submit. I am,

My Lord, &c.

To Lord Carteret.

My Lord,   *Dublin, Apr.* 25, 1730.

SINCE your Excellency left us, I have done what I could to bring the council to declare their opinion about the reducing of gold; but though much the greater part think it is what ought to be done, yet they are so afraid of the House of Commons, that I have not been able to bring them to say as much.

My brother justices are both against the council giving their opinion in the matter, so that at the

* Lord *Carteret,* afterwards Earl of *Granville* in Right of his Mother.

council

council held to day on that subject, it was to no purpose to press it; it was almost with difficulty that
we got the affair recommitted in order to draw up a
letter to your Excellency with an historical narration
of what has passed in council relating to the coin,
since the year 1711, with particular orders to insert
the resolutions of the committee 1729, relating to
gold and silver coins, that the whole may be laid before his Majesty.

* Sir *Ralph Gore* would fain have the game of last
summer played over again, by hearing the merchants
and receiving petitions, but my † Lord Chancellor
and I are resolved not to permit it.

The committee are to meet on *Monday*, and my
Lord Chancellor has promised to have a council, and
send away those resolutions with a letter by *Tuesday*'s
post.

I find by Sir *Ralph Gore*'s proposal to day, that
the merchants are now as some of them last year
were, for raising foreign silver, though nothing be
done about the gold; but as the whole view of this
is to carry on their present gainful trade of importing
gold and carrying out silver, by the help of foreign
silver, now the trade begins to fail for want of *English*
silver, my Lord Chancellor and I shall take care to
prevent any such application from the council.

I am sorry I can give no better account of this affair, but my endeavours have not been wanting to
make things go better.

I am, &c.

---

* Then one of the Lords Justices, and Speaker of the House
of Commons of Ireland.
† Thomas Lord *Wyndham*, who died some Years after in
England, by whose Death the Title became extinct.

To the same.

My Lord, *Dublin, Apr.* 30, 1730.

I Am sorry to inform your Excellency that the affair of the coin meets with such difficulties in the council, that the letter we shall, I suppose, agree to-morrow to send to your Excellency, will come to just nothing. Those of the House of Commons in the council seem backward to agree to any thing contrary to the vote of their House; but I lay the whole miscarriage at the door of others; * one of which is wrong in his notions about the coin, and the other, † I think, at least as much afraid of the House of Commons as any commoner there. Had the last of these shewn any spirit, all would have gone right, and I believe most of the commoners would have had courage to do what they think is right. But when they see their governors afraid of the House of Commons, how can we expect courage in the members of that House? The Lords in council have courage to do the right thing, but it is to no purpose to push at what two of the Lords Justices will not sign.

I gave your Excellency a hint of this before you left us, and then foreboded what I now am more certain of, the difficulties the government here will lye under, if any accident should happen that requires a little courage.

I think we shall send your Lordship the resolution of the committee of the council about the alterations proposed last summer, without daring so much as to desire your Excellency to lay them before his Majesty.

---

* Sir *Ralph Gore.*   † Lord Chancellor *Wyndham.*

The

The warm men of the House are as noisy about town against the reduction of gold, as they were in the house. But I have had several others of fashion to beg it may be done to save us from ruin.

All the hopes now left us are, that your Excellency will from the resolutions of both Houses, and the papers sent from the council (though without any resolution, or so much as desiring your Excellency to lay them before his Majesty) take occasion to move his Majesty to refer the matter to the officers of the mint, and to order what he shall judge proper upon their report.

Your Excellency knows our distress, and the genuine remedy, and except you have the goodness to represent our case truly to his Majesty, and obtain relief from his goodness, we want either sense or honesty, or courage enough so much as to ask for a cure of our evils from hence.

I am, &c.

To the Duke of * Newcastle.

My Lord, *Dublin, May 2, 1730.*

I Have formerly troubled your Grace with some accounts of the distress we are in here for want of silver, and the proper remedy of this evil, by a reduction of our gold to the value it obtains in *England,* and raising the foreign silver to near the middle price it bears in *England.*

The privy council here have more than once had this affair under consideration, and a committee of council last summer had settled the value they proposed gold and silver should pass for here, if approv-

* *Henry Holles Pelham,* then Secretary of State.

B 3 ed

with this affair, notwithftanding the heats about it, fince our manufactures and retail trade are under the laft diftrefs for want of filver. The loweft price of changing a moidore in moft parts being 8*d.* and often 1*s.* or more.

The refolutions of that committee 1729, are to be feen in a printed vindication of the alterations intended to be made by the council in the value of the coins current in this kingdom, which I underftand was fent your Grace.

Whether foreign filver be raifed or not, as in that fcheme, is not of that great confequence, though the raifing of it will be of fome fervice to us, but the lowering of the gold, as is there propofed, is of the laft confequence to us.

If his Majefty would be gracioufly pleafed to order fuch a proclamation, the bankers who have made all the difturbances and oppofition to this reduction, are the very people that would labour to keep every thing quiet, becaufe any difturbance on fuch a proclamation, will end in a run on themfelves.

And the certainty of our having filver, and the benefit to our trade by it will fo foon appear, that I am fure before another feffion of parliament, the face of affairs will be fo altered, that every honeft man in or out of the Houfe of Commons, will be thankful for the change.

If I did not think this an affair of the laft importance to the welfare of this kingdom, and confequently to his Majefty's fervice here, I fhould be for holding my peace (as is the behaviour of fome other of his Majefty's fervants here) and let the nation labour under its prefent diftrefs, till they come to a better mind*. I am,

Your Grace's, &c.

* In this letter his Grace fhews great ability, refolution, and honefty.

To

* *To the Bifhop of* London.

My Lord, *Dublin, May* 5, 1730.

IN purfuance of the laft letter I was favoured with by your Lordfhip, I defired my brethren on the bench not to fend over any more miffionaries for the *Weft Indies* from hence, till we heard from your Lordfhip that a fupply was wanting. Some time before the receipt of that letter, one or two had been very well recommended to me for that fervice, but I fhall not now trouble your Lordfhip about them, till farther advice.

The great numbers of papifts in this kingdom, and the obftinacy with which they adhere to their own religion, occafions our trying what may be done with their children to bring them over to our church ; and the good fuccefs the corporation eftablifhed in *Scotland* for the inftruction of the ignorant and barbarous part of that nation has met with, encourages us to hope if we were incorporated for that purpofe here, that we might likewife have fome fuccefs in our attempts to teach the children of the papifts the *Englifh* tongue, and the principles of the Chriftian religion † ; and feveral gentlemen here have promifed fubfcriptions for maintaining fchools for that purpofe, if we were once formed into a corporate body. This has fet the principal nobility, gentry, and clergy here on prefenting an addrefs to his Majefty to erect

* This letter was copied and fent likewife to the Archbifhop of *Canterbury.*
+ Dr *Maul* Bifhop of *Cloyne,* afterwards Bifhop of *Meath,* being a gentleman of good family and fortune, expended a great part of his eftate, to eftablifh this foundation, which is now fupported by Parliament, and voluntary contributions. His Grace the Lord Primate had alfo great merit in promoting this charity, of the Proteftant charter fchools in *Ireland.*

fuch

such persons as he pleases into a corporation here
for that purpose, which we have sent over by the
Lord Lieutenant, to be laid before his Majesty : the
copy of this address I have here sent your Lordship,
in which you will in some measure see the melancholy state of religion in this kingdom. And I do
in my own name and that of the rest of my brethren,
beg the favour of your Lordship to give it your
countenance. I can assure you the papists are here
so numerous that it highly concerns us in point of
interest, as well as out of concern for the salvation
of those poor creatures, who are our fellow subjects,
to try all possible means to bring them and theirs over
to the knowledge of the true religion.

And one of the most likely methods we can
think of is, if possible, instructing and converting
the young generation ; for instead of converting those
that are adult, we are daily losing many of our meaner people who go off to popery.

I am sure your Lordship will be glad of any opportunity of advancing the glory of God, and promoting his service and worship among those who at
present are strangers to it.

I thank your Lordship for your second pastoral
letter, I hope it will do great service to religion in
England ; and we hope it may be of service to us
here, though irreligion does not shew itself so bare-
faced amongst us ; I have therefore encouraged its
printing here. I am,

My Lord, &c.

To

To the Duke of Newcastle.

My Lord,   *Dublin, May* 7, 1730.

THE number of papifts in this kingdom is fo great, that it is of the utmoft confequence to the proteftant intereft here to bring them over by all Chriftian methods to the Church of *Ireland.* In order to do this, we are labouring to increafe the number of Churches and of parfonage houfes, for the benefit of refident incumbents; and have paffed fome acts the three laft feffions, to come at glebes for the clergy to live on, the greateft part of the livings here having neither houfe nor land belonging to them.

But the ignorance and obftinacy of the adult papifts is fuch, that there is not much hope of converting them. But we have hopes if we could erect a number of fchools to teach their children the *Englifh* tongue, and the principles of the Chriftian religion, that we could do fome good among the generation that is growing up. And as we find this defign has been carried on with good fuccefs in *Scotland,* under the conduct of a corporation erected in that country by his late Majefty, we hope we may have the fame fuccefs under a like corporation in this kingdom: and great numbers of nobility and gentry have expreffed a willingnefs to come into fubfcriptions for that end, if there were a corporation eftablifhed here to take on them the management of fchools for inftructing the popifh youth.

This has been the occafion that the principal nobility, gentry, and clergy here have joined in an addrefs to his Majefty, to erect fuch a corporation here, in fuch manner as his Majefty fhall judge proper, which we defired the Lord Lieutenant to lay before his Majefty. A copy of this addrefs I have herewith
fent

fent your Grace, by which you will fee the bad ftate the proteftant religion is in here.

And I make it my requeft to your Grace in my own name, and that of my brethren the Bifhops, that you would be pleafed to give your countenance to our addrefs, that we may obtain the charter * we defire.

I am, my Lord, &c.

To Lord Carteret.

My Lord,   *Dublin, May* 20, 1730.

I Have received the honour of your Excellency's of the 14th inft. and thank your Excellency for your great kindnefs to this nation in obtaining of his Majefty that the papers tranfmitted by the privy council be referred to the officers of the mint, in order to lay a foundation for fuch orders as may put a ftop to the prefent calamity we lye under. And I muft renew my requeft to your Excellency that you would complete our deliverance, which I find thofe here who know well enough the method of compaf-fing it have not the courage to attempt, without fome orders from *England.*

Upon the leaft encouragement from your Excellen-cy, I think I could bring the privy council to join in an application to his Majefty for the coining of 15,000 *l.* in copper at the mint, fince in private con-verfation, the moft † timorous of them own to me, that they do not think the refolution of Lords and Commons inconfiftent with one another.

I moft gratefully acknowledge your kindnefs in thofe favourable reprefentations your Lordfhip has

* It was granted.
‡ He certainly means Chancellor *Wyndham,* if not Sir *Ralph Gore* alfo.

                                                    been

been pleafed to make of my conduct for the fervice of his Majefty, and I fhall continue to endeavour not to give any juft caufe of complaint againft me. I am,

My Lord, &c.

To the fame.

My Lord, Dublin, May 28, 1730.

BY fome letters which have been fhewn me here, I find his Majefty and your Excellency have been very much folicited in behalf of Mr. * *Daniel Kimberly*, but that your Excellency was of the fame opinion as we were of here, that the crime was fo common in this country, as well as fo heinous in it-felf, that there was no room for mercy.

We have had a great deal of trouble here in this affair, by giving way to Sir *Ralph Gore's* defire to reprieve him from *Wednefday* to *Saturday* laft week : upon which Mr. *Kimberly* got an opinion from an ob-fcure lawyer, that by his being reprieved, the fheriff could not lawfully execute him, till there was a new rule of court made about him, the day being lapfed on which he ought to have been executed by the firft order of court. The fheriff was at a ftand upon this, but advifed with Mr. + Juftice *Bernard* and fome other lawyers, who affured him the reprieve did not cancel

---

* *Daniel Kimberly* was an Attorney, and fome Way aiding and affifting in the Marriage of Mr. *Brad. Mead* with Mifs *Reading*, who was an Heirefs in Right of her Mother, which Marriage, by Act of Parliament, was contrary to Law, without Confent of Parents, or Guardians; upon which Warrants were iffued againft Mr. *Mead* and Mr. *Kimberly* who made their Efcape; the firft to *Holland*, and the other to *London*, where he was taken, brought to *Ireland*, was tried, found guilty, and executed.

+ A Judge of the Common Pleas, a very eminent Lawyer, and Perfon of large Fortune, having purchafed a great Part of the Earl of *Cloncarty's* Eftate.

the

the order, but only fufpended it for fo many days. On *Saturday* laft we had the Judges, the Prime Serjeant, Sollicitor, and Mr. Serjeant *Bowes* * to confult with, who were all of the opinion that the fheriff could execute him on the day to which he was reprieved. But fome of them faying they had not thoroughly ftudied the point, we thought fit to reprieve him till yefterday, and fent to the Prime Serjeant, Attorney, Sollicitor, and Mr. *Bowes*, to have their opinion in writing on this fubject, which they gave in on *Tuefday*, agreeing that he might be executed at the expiration of the reprieve, without any new order. Upon this, fince the prerogative was deeply concerned, that the granting of a reprieve for a few days fhould not be carried to reprieve a malefactor till next term, and fince fuch a precedent muft probably have raifed fcruples in every fheriff in *Ireland*, whether after any reprieve they could without a new order from the Judge execute a criminal, we thought fit to give no farther reprieve, and he was executed yefterday.

I muft own I was very much furprized at this difficulty being raifed here, having not heard the leaft hint of any fuch thing in *England*; but I think the affair is now fo fettled, that for fome time at leaft no attempt of this nature is likely to be made on the prerogative here.

I thought it my duty to give your Excellency this fhort account of an affair, that has given us more trouble than I think it need have done.

Sir *Ralph Gore* went into the country laft *Monday* morning.   I am,

My Lord, &c.

* Afterwards Lord Chancellor of *Ireland*, and was created a Peer of that Realm. The Title is extinct, his Lordfhip having no Iffue.

To

To *Sir* Robert Walpole.

SIR,   *Dublin, Jan.* 4, 1730.

THE gentleman that waits upon you with this, is Mr. * *Dobbs,* one of the members of our Houfe of Commons, where he on all occafions endeavours to promote his Majefty's fervice.

He is a perfon of good fenfe, and has for fome time applied his thoughts to the improvement of the trade of *Great Britain* and *Ireland,* and to the making our colonies in *America* of more advantage than they have hitherto been † : and has written his thoughts on thefe fubjects, which he is defirous to offer to your confideration.

As he has not the honour to be known to you, he applied to me to open a way for his waiting on you.

I need fay nothing of what his thoughts are on thofe fubjects, fince he will be better able to explain them, and you are more capable of judging of them than I can be.

I prefume no farther than to recommend him for an audience at leifure, and to do afterwards in the affair as you fhall think moft proper.

          I am, &c.

To *Lord* Carteret.

My Lord,   *Dublin, June* 6, 1730.

YOUR Excellency by the laft mail will receive two applications about fome livings vacant by the death of Mr. *Martin* ; one from Mr. *Gardiner,* in

---

* *Arthur Dobbs,* Efq; Author of the North-Weft Paffage to *India.*

† He was afterwards made Governor of *North Carolina.*

           behalf

behalf of his nephew ; the other from another gentle-man for the vicarages of *Erk* and *Claragb.*

I have been able to meet with nobody that can give a diftinct account of what livings Mr. *Martin* had, and whether the living Mr. *Gardiner* applies for is either the living of *Erk* or *Claragb* ; if it be, he ap-plies for it by fome other name.

I need fay nothing in favour of Mr. *Gardiner*'s peti-tion, fince I am fure he wants no recommendation to your Lordfhip's favour.

I have fince received a letter from the Bifhop of *Offory*, in favour of Mr. *John Read*, to whom he has lately given the Church of St. *Mary* in *Kilkenny*, which he fays is a moft laborious cure, and not worth above 60 *l. per ann.* and he defires that your Excellency would be pleafed to give Mr. *Read* the rectory of *Claragb*, not worth above 30 *l. per ann.* which is con-tiguous to St. *Mary*'s, and has no Church, but the parifhioners conftantly refort to St. *Mary*'s. *Claragb*, his Lordfhip fays, has often been given to the Minifter of St. *Mary*'s, to help him out ; and this he affures me is the true cafe of thefe parifhes.

I thought proper to fend your Excellency this re-prefentation of the Bifhop of *Offory*, that we may know your Excellency's pleafure.

I am informed the prefent Bifhop of *Clonfert* had the provoftfhip of *Galway* worth about 150 *l. per ann.* which I do not find is held in commendam by his Lordfhip, or difpofed of to any body elfe. I fhould be obliged to your Excellency if you would be plea-fed to beftow it on Mr. *John Richardfon*, Minifter of *Belturbet*, whom I defigned to have named to the College for the living of *Derivoilan* in the diocefe of *Clogher*, but quitted my recommendation that Dr. *Delany* might have it, which accordingly he had. I am,

My Lord, &c.

To

To the fame.

My Lord,   *Dublin, June* 11, 1730.

I Have had the honour of your Excellency's of the 4th inft. and am glad to find our conduct relating to *Kimberly* is approved by your Lordſhip.

I hope as applications on this occaſion were diſcouraged on your ſide of the water, ſo they will always be, or there muſt be a dangerous obſtruction of juſtice here.

I thank your Lordſhip for putting the affair of our coin in ſo hopeful a way, and ſhall be very well pleaſed to receive his Majeſty's commands on that ſubject.

I was ready to have granted Dr. *Delany* * the faculty your Excellency deſired, but upon conſulting with the learned, he thought his buſineſs might be done without one. I am,

       My Lord, &c.

To the Duke of Newcaſtle.

My Lord,   *Dublin, June* 24, 1730.

I Am ſorry I am to acquaint your Grace that my Lord Chief Baron *Dalton* died yeſterday, after a ſhort confinement.

His Majeſty had not a ſervant here of greater abilities or courage, nor that ſerved him with more zeal and fidelity. He has been directly worn down in the diligent attendance on his buſineſs ; and I rather believe has worſted his circumſtances by coming hither.

---

* Dr. *Delany* in the latter part of the Primate's time, made as much court to him as ever he had done before to Dean *Swift*,

I have this day joined with my Lord Chancellor in a letter to your Lordſhip, repreſenting who we think is the fitteſt perſon to ſucceed him, if his place be filled from this ſide of the water. But I moſt humbly repreſent, that it will, we both think, be of ſervice to his Majeſty here, if an able perſon be ſent us from *England* for that employment. And I do not queſtion but ſome may be found there of the profeſſion of great ſkill in the law, and proper to ſtand a debate in the privy council, who will not think much of coming to *Ireland* for 12 or 1300 *l. per ann.*

But all this is moſt humbly ſubmitted to his Majeſty's pleaſure. I am,

My Lord, &c.

To Sir Robert Walpole.

SIR,   *Dublin, June* 24, 1730.

YESTERDAY died here, after a ſhort indiſpoſition, Lord Chief Baron *Dalton*; he has rather been declining in his health for ſome time, and has been directly worn down by his great attention to buſineſs.

His Majeſty had not a ſervant here that ſerved him with greater abilities, diligence, and zeal, than he did. I believe his family has rather ſuffered by his coming hither.

My Lord Chancellor and myſelf have by this poſt acquainted my Lord Lieutenant and the Duke of *Newcaſtle*, what removes we judge moſt proper for his Majeſty's ſervice on this occaſion, if the place be filled from hence.

But by what has been already done for three ſucceſſions in that poſt, we think it is moſt likely to be filled from *England*. And we cannot but think that it will be of great ſervice to have a worthy perſon

ſent

fent over.   The Lord Chief Baron is one of the council here, where a good man will be very useful.

I believe there may be some at the bar in *England*
of great worth, that may think it worth while to come
hither for 12 or 1300 *l. per ann.*

I hope, Sir, you will excuse my giving you this
trouble, since it is a matter of great concern to his
Majesty's service here.

I am, &c.

To the *Duke* of Dorset.

My Lord,   *Dublin, June* 27, 1730.

WE yesterday received the agreeable news we
have been long in expectation of here, that his
Majesty had been pleased to declare your Grace our
Lord Lieutenant.   I can assure you, my Lord, that
those who are best affected to his Majesty, are very
well pleased with it.

I should have taken the liberty from the little acquaintance I have had the honour to have with your
Grace, and the character you have always borne, to
write on any occasion freely to your Grace what I
apprehended might be for his Majesty's service.

But it is a great pleasure to me, that I have received the Duke of *Newcastle*'s assurances, that I may
write at all times to you without any reserve, and that
I may depend on having (as he is pleased to express it)
your Grace's having the same regard for me, and
treating me with the same confidence and distinction
that I have constantly met with from the ministry ever
since my coming hither.

I most heartily wish your Grace's government may
prove easy and successful, and do assure your Lordship
nothing shall be wanting on my part to contribute to
its being so.

C 2   Sir

Sir *Ralph Gore* is this evening returned from the north, and on *Monday* I set out on the visitation of my province, which will take me up about five weeks: but any commands your Grace shall honour me with, directed to *Dublin*, will be forwarded to me. I am,

> My Lord, &c.

To *the Duke of* Newcastle.

My Lord,   *Dublin, June* 27, 1730.

I Have been honoured with your Grace's of the 20th inst. I am very glad to hear that the alteration which has been made in the government here, has been by the advice of your Grace and the other ministers, and that there is so perfect an union between the ministry and the Duke of *Dorset* and Lord * *Wilmington*; and doubt not but this conjunction will very much contribute to his Majesty's service, and defeat the efforts of the discontented.

I did indeed hope from the good character of the Duke of *Dorset*, that I might write to him what I thought might be for his Majesty's service. But it is with great pleasure that I receive those encouragements from your Grace to write to him with the same freedom and openness, that your Lordship has permitted me to use to yourself. And I desire to meet with no greater regard or confidence from him, than I have met with from the ministers ever since they were pleased to send me hither. And I take this opportunity to return my most humble thanks to your Grace and the other ministers for all the favour and countenance I have now for some years constantly re-

* *Spencer Compton*, Speaker of the *British* House of Commons, afterwards Earl of *Wilmington*.

ceived

ceived from them: and fhall always endeavour to make that return which I am fure will be moft acceptable to them, the promoting of his Majefty's fervice to the utmoft of my power.

I thank your Grace for giving me leave to do myfelf the honour of troubling you on occafion with a letter, and for affuring me of the continuance of your friendfhip and protection.

As my Lord Lieutenant is a ftranger to the affair of our coin, I beg leave to defire that his Majefty's orders, if he fhall pleafe to fend us any, may not be tranfmitted hither till my return from my triennial vifitation, on which I fet out next *Monday*, and fhall not return till about the 5th of *Auguft*. For I believe that the Lords Juftices will not care to do any thing in the affair till we are all together : and I am fatisfied it will be of great fervice, that whatever fhall be ordered may be immediately executed, without allowing time to the bankers and remitters here to fow any uneafinefs in the minds of the people about that affair. I am,

My Lord, &c.

To Lord Carteret.

My Lord, *Dublin, June* 28, 1730.

WE this day received the honour of your Lordfhip's of the 23d. As I am to fet out tomorrow on my vifitation, I fhall mifs of the opportunity of joining with my brethren in thofe juft acknowledgments they will no doubt make of the many fervices you have done this kingdom during your adminiftration ; and it is with great pleafure I find the zeal any of us have under your Lordfhip's conduct, fhewn for his Majefty's fervice, is approved by

your

your Lordſhip, and that we have had the happineſs to ſatisfy you that we had a ſincere regard for your Lordſhip.

I thank your Lordſhip for retaining ſo great a concern for *Ireland*; and am glad this kingdom has a friend, who will on all occaſions be able to ſerve it.

I heartily wiſh your Lordſhip all health and proſperity, and if you ſhould at any time honour me with any commands here, I ſhall receive them with the greateſt pleaſure and ſatisfaction. I am,

My Lord, &c.

To the Duke of Newcaſtle.

My Lord,   *Dublin, Aug.* 6, 1730.

I Had the honour of your Grace's letter about Mr. *Creſſet* when I was upon my viſitation, from which I returned laſt *Tueſday.* I have enquired ſince and find Mr. *Creſſet*'s inſtruments were paſſed in my abſence. He has been with me ſince my arrival at *Dublin*, and I acquainted him with the recommendations your Grace had given of him, and my readineſs to ſhew him any favour on your account.

The Lord Biſhop of *Oſſory* died to-day, and we ſhall in our letter to my Lord Lieutenant, mention ſuch as may be proper to be promoted to that ſee: but I muſt beg leave to inform your Grace that I think it will be very much for his Majeſty's ſervice to fill that ſee with a worthy perſon from *England**. I am,

My Lord, &c.

* It was done accordingly, and Dr. *Teniſon* was appointed.

To

To the Duke of Dorset.

My Lord,   *Dublin, Aug.* 7, 1730.

I Had the honour of your Grace's upon my vifitation, which kept me from *Dublin* till *Tuefday* laft.

I am very much obliged to your Grace for the encouragement you give me to write to you with the
utmoft freedom, and I affure you, my Lord, I fhall
never offer you any advice but what I think will be
for his Majefty's fervice, and your Grace's honour.

Since my return the Bifhop of *Offory* is dead, and
we have this day joined in a letter to your Grace,
mentioning the moft proper perfons here to be promoted to that fee. But I muft beg leave to affure
you Grace that I think it is of great importance to
the *Englifh* intereft, and confequently to his Majefty's
fervice here, that fome worthy perfon fhould be fent
us from *England* to fill this vacancy. If any perfon
here fhould be thought of, I take the promotion moft
for the King's fervice here, will be the making Dr.
Baldwin Bifhop, and Dr. *Gilbert* * Provoft in his room,
         I am, &c.

To the fame.

My Lord,   *Dublin, Aug.* 22, 1730.

I Have the honour of your Grace's on the 15th inft.
I am glad to hear of the promotion of Dr. *Edward Tenifon* to the bifhoprick of *Offory*, and thank
your Grace for the news. He is an old acquaintance

* Revd. Dr. *Claudius Gilbert*, a Gentleman of great learning
and abilities, who purchafed a large and fine Collection of Books
at different Times, which he bequeathed to the Univerfity of
Dublin, of which he was one of the Fellows.
      C 4   of

of mine, and I have always known him to be heartily attached to his Majesty's family: and I remember his often speaking of the countenance your Lordship was pleased to give him. I make no doubt but he will behave himself here, so as to make himself agreeable to his Majesty's friends. I am,

My Lord, &c.

To the same.

My Lord, *Dublin, Sept.* 3, 1730.

THE deanery of *Duach* or *Kilmacduach*, I know not which they call it, is now vacant by the death of Dr. *Northcote*, worth about 120 or 140 *l. per ann.*

I should be very much obliged to your Grace if you would be pleased to bestow it on Mr. *John Richardson*, Rector of *Belturbet*; he is a worthy person and well affected to his Majesty, and was many years ago concerned in a design to translate the Bible and Common Prayer into *Irish*, in order the better to bring about the conversion of the natives; but he met at that time with great opposition, not to say oppression here, instead of either thanks or assistance; and suffered the loss of several hundred pounds expended in printing the Common Prayer-book, and other necessary charges he was at in that undertaking.

I should be very glad, I could contribute somewhat to make him a little easy in his circumstances, and procure him by your Grace's favour, some dignity in the Church.

I am, my Lord, &c.

To

To the Duke of Dorſet.

My Lord,   *Dublin, Oct.* 1, 1730.

I Have had the honour of your Grace's of the 19th paſt, and moſt humbly thank your Lordſhip for your kind intention to beſtow the deanery of *Duach* on Mr. *Richardſon,* upon your receiving the uſual notification of the vacancy from the Lords Juſtices. Mr. *Richardſon* has ſince delivered a memorial on that occaſion, which we have tranſmitted to your Grace with our recommendation.

I am ſenſible how much I am obliged to your Grace for the readineſs you have ſhewn in this affair to comply with my requeſt.

I am, &c.

To the Duke of Newcaſtle.

My Lord,   *Dublin, Oct.* 14, 1730.

ON *Friday* laſt Lieutenant Colonel *Hennecy* brought me your Grace's of the 26th paſt ; I told him as we were ſeveral mails behind-hand, by the packet-boats being all on this ſide, I had not received the letter your Grace referred to, but that upon the recommendations your Lordſhip gave of him, I ſhould afford him all the protection I could ; and I directed him to call upon me after the arrival of the next packets.

As he acquainted me with the buſineſs he came about, I took occaſion to found the Lords Juſtices the next day on the ſubject of his errand, and found there would be a neceſſity of laying before them what commands I received from your Grace, to be able to do any thing in the affair.

And

And as the mails arrived yesterday morning, by which I received the honour of your Grace's other letter of the 26th past, with the other papers you was pleased to send me, I have since discoursed with the other Lords Justices on the subject, and find they apprehend there will be greater difficulties in this affair than at first offered.

If we encourage the *French* officers to set about raising their recruits, upon assurances that we will take no notice of it, they will be liable to great molestations, since every Justice can take examinations against them and commit them, nor can we release them, but by due course of law, or by granting them a pardon. And whether they may not be the more busy in disturbing those levies, if they find them rather countenanced by the government, we cannot answer.

What has happened to several of them formerly when they were raising recruits here in a clandestine way (though as we knew his Majesty's intentions, we slighted, and as far as we well could discouraged complaints on that head) your Grace very well knows from the several applications made to your Lordship from the *French* Embassador. And what spirit may by artful men be raised among his Majesty's subjects when they hear some hundred recruits are raising in this kingdom for *France*, and how it may set magistrates every where on distressing the officers employed in this service, no one can tell.

To what excesses of heat people are capable of running here, when they once take a thing right or wrong into their heads, the ferments raised here about * *Wood*'s half-pence is too plain demonstration.

And.

* See the Drapier's Letters on this occasion, wrote by the Rev. Dr. *Swift.*

And I must beg leave to hint to your Grace that all recruits raised here for France *or* Spain, *are generally considered as persons, that may some time or other pay a visit to this country as enemies.* That all who are lifted here in those services, hope and wish to do so, there is no doubt.

There is without controversy a power in his Majesty to grant leave to any persons to *levy men here under his sign manual,* by an act passed 8°. *Georg.* 1. c. 9. and by the same act the government here can grant such a licence under their hands ; but I find that without his Majesty's express orders for it, nobody here dares venture to grant a licence to the *French* officers to raise the intended recruits, since no one can answer what heats that may possibly occasion at present as well as at the next meeting of parliament.

I should be very glad if I knew how to manage this affair to his Majesty's satisfaction, and am very much obliged to his Majesty for having so good an opinion of me as your Grace is pleased to assure me in your letter.

I am sure it will be always my greatest ambition to promote his Majesty's service. But I am sorry I cannot give a more promising account of the success of this affair, since I perceive nothing can be done in it till his Majesty is pleased directly to signify his pleasure. However effectual care shall be taken that none of the officers who are come hither, suffer on this account.

Lieutenant Colonel *Hennecy* called on me this morning, and I directed him and his officers to appear as little as may be in publick, and to wait till we are further instructed in his Majesty's pleasure, since at present there were some difficulties in the way.

I have communicated your Grace's letter to none but the Lords Justices, to whom I found it necessary

so to do, and shall take all the care I can, that no
other person knows any thing of it. But I find by
some of the prints published here this day, that
some * accounts are come from *England* that a number of recruits for the *Irish* regiments in the *French*
service is to be raised here by his Majesty's leave,
and that the *French* officers employed in that service
are arrived here.

I am, &c.

To the Duke of Dorset.

My Lord,   *Dublin, Oct.* 15, 1730.

I Had the honour of your Grace's of the 29th past,
at the same time that I received one from the
Duke of *Newcastle* ; which I have communicated to
my brethren, without whom nothing could be done
in that affair ; and as there appeared great difficulties in the management of that business, I have sent
an account of them to the Duke of *Newcastle,* that we
may receive his Majesty's commands.

I am sure I shall on this and all other occasions
with the utmost zeal and diligence, promote his Majesty's service. I am,

My Lord, &c.

To the same.

My Lord,   *Dublin, Nov.* 17, 1730.

I Did not receive the honour of your Grace's of the
20th past, till the 8th instant, and I deferred an-
swering it since, in hopes I might bring things to
bear to your Grace's satisfaction. But though I have

* See *Swift's* Works, vol. 9.

taken

taken what pains I could in the matter, and have defired my brethren to concur with what your Lordfhip propofes, by drawing up the directing claufe of the warrant agreeably to what has been fettled to be the meaning of his Majefty's letters, yet I have not been able as yet to prevail with them.

They feem chiefly to infift on its being wrong to fign a warrant purfuant to letters in which part is not agreeable to act of parliament, and are apprehenfive, that as thofe letters of courfe are before the Houfe of Commons every feffion, it may furnifh a handle for raifing fome heats there.

And on the other fide, they make a difficulty of explaining the fenfe of his Majefty's letters in the directing claufe of the warrant, though it is putting no other fenfe on the King's letters, than what is fettled with your Grace, as we fuppofe with the knowledge of the reft of the miniftry.

I have on this occafion given them fuch hints as I thought I might, that I heard if the letters were returned, we fhould receive new ones, that would put the affair of excufing thefe penfions from the tax out of all difpute as to the whole fums: and that I was fatisfied the penfions were in favour of fuch perfons, as that they would not be funk by their being returned to *England*.

But I have hitherto had no fuccefs; I fhall make another effort, and if nothing can be done, I think it will be more advifeable to have the letters called back to *England*, than to lie unexecuted here.

I am forry to find the affair of the *Irifh* recruits makes fuch a noife in *England*, fince I hardly doubt but near the fame number, as there is a difpofition to allow of this year, have been clandeftinely raifed here annually for fome years paft. There is a great ferment here on the fame account.

This kingdom is very much obliged to your Grace for your kind intentions to endeavour, on all proper
occafions,

occasions, to leffen any weight that may be laid on us. And I shall not be wanting in acquainting the gentlemen of this nation, how much we are indebted to your Lordship for this your good difposition in our favour.

I am, your Grace's, &c.

To the fame.

My Lord, *Dublin, Dec.* 5, 1730.

I Yefterday received the honour of your Grace's of the 28th paft, and fhall do what I can to get warrants figned upon *Lawman*'s and *Hoburg*'s lettets, that the miniftry may not have any new trouble about them.

And we this day have referred the confideration of that affair to the Prime-ferjeant, Attorney and Sollicitor-general : and I likewife gave them the two draughts your Grace fent me, to fee whether they might not either follow them, or from thence take fome hint of fomewhat that they thought would do.

I told them as from myfelf what your Grace fuggefted about the acts of 1727 and 1729, and that *the late act* could not refer to the firft, but only to the laft ; fo that our lawyers have now the whole affair before them.

I fhall do what I can to difpatch this affair to your Lordfhip's mind, but find I cannot anfwer for the event. I am,

My Lord, &c.

To

To the same.

My Lord,   *Dublin, Dec.* 8, 1730.

I Yefterday received the honour of your Grace's of the firft inft. and it is with great pleafure I find by your Lordfhip's that the *French* officers will foon be recalled from hence : fince that affair of the recruits makes a great noife here, and as far as I underftand, a much greater at *London.* They have met with no rudenefs here, and I believe will meet with none at their going off. They fhould be treated more civilly than they have been, if I had not found myfelf clamoured at here, and fallen upon in the papers of *England,* for a civility I did not fhew them : and if there fhould be any apprehenfions of their being infulted, we fhall take what care we can to prevent it. I am,

My Lord, &c.

To the same.

My Lord,   *Dublin, Dec.* 26, 1730.

I Hope we fhall put the defired end to the affair of Mr. *Dawfon* and *Hobury,* by figning the ufual order, upon his Majefty's letters in their favour, as foon as Sir *Ralph Gore* comes to town, who is gone into the country for the holidays, the Prime-ferjeant, Attorney and Sollicitor-general having agreed in a favourable report ; but they think the fureft way to prevent any canvaffing of that affair in parliament will be to have their agent make no difficulty of letting the taxes be deducted till *Chriftmas* 1729, fince which time there is no doubt but they are legally excufed cuſed from the 4 *s.* in the pound on their * penſions. And this I think is what agrees with your Grace's ſentiments in this affair. When we have ſigned their warrants, I ſhall make it my buſineſs to help them to ſome money, as ſoon as our treaſury can furniſh any.

Colonel *Hennecy* called on me two or three days ago, and acquainted me that he and the officers with him had orders to leave this kingdom; and that as ſoon as two or three of them who were gone to ſee their friends in the country were returned (which would be in eight or ten days) they would embark for *England.*

I muſt do the Colonel the juſtice to acquaint your Grace that I have not heard any complaint of his or the other officers behaviour whilſt they have been here †.

I am, my Lord, &c.

To the Duke of Newcaſtle.

My Lord,   *Dublin, Dec.* 31, 1730.

LAST week Colonel *Hennecy* called upon me to acquaint me that he had received orders to quit this kingdom, with the other officers who followed him, and that he hoped if he ſtaid a few days, till he could call ſome of the officers to *Dublin* that were then in the country viſiting their friends, to take them

---

* This Tax dropped at the Expiration of the Act, but was again renewed by Parliament in 1757. See a moſt excellent Pamphlet, entitled, a Liſt of the Abſentees of *Ireland,* and an Eſtimate of the yearly value of their Eſtates and Incomes, ſpent abroad, two Editions of which were printed in 1767, and 1769.

† Sir *Robert Walpole,* the moſt frank and ingenuous man in the world confeſſed, (which few miniſters are apt to do) that he had been wrong in this meaſure, and immediately adviſed the recalling of the officers; convinced perhaps more by the reaſons in the letter, Pag. 25, than by all the clamours of the *Craftſman,* &c.

over

over with him, it would not be taken ill, which I told him I thought it could not. He has fince been with me to acquaint me that he fhall go off with the yacht which is expected to fail every day for *England*.

As he defires I would give your Grace an account of his behaviour here, he waits upon his Lordfhip with this letter, to inform you that he has behaved himfelf with great prudence during his ftay here, and has kept himfelf and his officers from appearing in any publick places, or giving any offence ; and has from time to time called upon me to know whether I had any orders to give him, that he might punctually obferve them ; and he has readily complied with any directions I thought it might be proper to give him.

I am glad this affair is at laft happily concluded, after having been the occafion of fo great a noife here, and of a much greater in *England*.

I am, my Lord, &c.

To the Duke of Dorfet.

My Lord,   *Dublin, Jan.* 9, 1730.

AS probably an affair that has lately happened here may make a greater figure in the *Englifh* papers than it juftly deferves, I think it my duty to give your Grace an account of it.

On *Tuefday* laft juft before midnight Sir *Robert Echlin* called upon me, to tell me that there was a fellow came to the horfe guards here, giving an account that a *French* officer had fent him over with a horfe to *Bullock*, a place about five miles from hence, where he endeavoured to perfuade him to go over to *France* with him, offering him money, which he refufed, that there were four or five *French* officers there, and about 60 men lifted in the pretender's fervice, who lay there to go on board a sloop for *France*. I was very much surprized at Sir *Robert's* chusing to come to me about such an affair at such a time of night.   But as I have been but ill used both in the prints here and in *England* about the *French* recruits, I thought I could not refuse taking notice of his information; and the rather because Colonel *Hennecy* had assured me that none of the officers who came with him had raised any recruits here.

Accordingly I directed Sir *Robert* to have the fellow carried before the Lord Mayor to be examined upon oath, and I sent by him a letter to the Lord Mayor, acquainting him what Sir *Robert* had told me, and desiring him to examine the informant on oath, and according as the examinations came out, to send to the Town Major and acquaint him with the case. Upon examination, the substance of what Sir *Robert* had told me came out, only that there was nothing sworn about the Pretender, and that there were but about 40 men.   Upon taking those examinations the Lord Mayor sent them to the Town Major, who immediately waited upon the * General, who ordered 50 foot and four dragoons to march to *Bullock*, and either seize or disperse those people. When they came there on *Wednesday*, they found there had been about forty men listed for abroad, and four or five *French* officers with them, but that they went on board a sloop about eleven o'clock the night before.

I am, my Lord, &c.

* *Thomas Pearce*, General, and Commander in Chief of the Forces in *Ireland*.

To

To the same.

My Lord,   *Dublin, Jan.* 12, 1730.

I Have juft now received the honour of your Grace's of the 7th inft.   We expect Sir *Ralph Gore* in town on *Saturday*, and fhall I believe the firft opportunity afterwards, fign the warrants for *Lawman* and *Hoburg*, fince as we have a favourable opinion from the lawyers, Sir *Ralph* cannot well make any difficulty about it; and my Lord Chancellor now makes none.

I mentioned the affair of the taxes before *Chriftmas* 1729, at the defire of others, fince I thought your Grace had fpoken very plain in that affair.   As foon as the warrants are difpatched I fhall make it my bufinefs to get them fome money as faft as our treafury can fupply it, confiftently with the fervices abfolutely neceffary.

I believe Colonel *Hennecy* and the other officers went off in the yacht to day, fince he told me they were to go in it.

There is a clergyman, a man of worth, one Mr. *Horner*, a native of *Switzerland*, recommended hither by his Grace of *Canterbury*, to whom Lord *Carteret* gave the rectory of *Clane*, in the diocefe of *Kildare*; he has been very ill treated, and is made very uneafy there by a popifh gentleman, to whom the greateft part of that parifh belongs; and as he is a ftranger, is but ill fupported by the neighbouring proteftants: he has had his ftack of fuel fired in the night, and I think part of his houfe burnt down by it, and is daily threatened to be ferved fo again.   I have now an opportunity of removing him to a proteftant neighbourhood in my diocefe, where I hope he will be very ufeful, if your Grace will be pleafed to beftow the recto-

D 2   ry

ry of *Clane* upon his refigning it, on Mr. *Hofkins*, that I may be able to provide for a clergyman who lies on my hands, by giving him the living that Mr. *Hofkins* now enjoys; which I fhall acknowledge a great favour.

I am, &c.

To the fame.

My Lord,   *Dublin, Jan.* 26, 1730.

ON the 12th inftant I did myfelf the honour to acquaint your Grace that I believed the firft opportunity after Sir *Ralph Gore*'s arrival in town, we fhould fign the warrants for *Lawman* and *Hoberg*, fince as we have a favourable opinion from the lawyers in that affair, Sir *Ralph Gore* could not well make any difficulty about it; and my Lord Chancellor then declared, he made none, as we had the opinion of the lawyers to juftify us. But fince then, my Lord Chancellor is pleafed to declare, he is of different fentiments in that affair; and Sir *Ralph Gore* joins with him. We are to have another conference on that fubject; and have as good as agreed to fend a letter to your Excellency, to let you know what canvafs that affair may poflibly go through in the Houfe of Commons; but that as we have the opinion of the lawyers in the point, if your Grace after our reprefenting what may happen in the Houfe of Commons, fhall direct us to fign thofe warrants, we fhall do it. This was our fenfe, when laft together; but after the unexpected turns this affair has taken, I will not anfwer what may be our fenfe to-morrow.

I am, my Lord, &c.

To

To the same.

My Lord,　　　　　　　　*Dublin, Feb. 6, 1730.*

I Have had the honour of your Grace's of the 23d
　paſt, and am very well pleaſed with your approbation of my conduct upon Sir *Robert Echlin*'s information.

I am very much obliged to your Grace for coming
into the ſcheme about the rectory of *Clane*, and will
take care to have the reſignation ready againſt you
are pleaſed to give orders for beſtowing that rectory
on Mr. *Hoſkins*, upon Mr. *Horner*'s giving in his reſignation of it.

We have troubled you, my Lord, with a letter relating to Meſſrs. *Lawman* and *Hoburg*'s affair ; and I
ſhall, according to your Grace orders, forward that
affair immediately, and get as large a payment on
thoſe warrants, as our treaſury can admit of.

　　　　　　　　· I am, my Lord, &c.

To Mrs. Wall,

MADAM,　　　　　　　　*Feb.* 13, 1730.

I Have received yours of the 9th of *January* and the
　1ſt inſt. but the laſt came not to hand till *Thurſday* laſt.　I am very ſorry to hear of the death of my
couſin *Tomes.*　I have gradually broken the matter to
her ſon, and hope he will behave himſelf under this
loſs like a good Chriſtian.　I am ſorry to find you
are ſo much dejected, as you appear to be by both
letters ; and hope you will get over *March* better than
you expect.　I am very glad to hear your ſon goes on
well with his ſtudies ; and the beſt thing he can do,
is to purſue his learning at the Univerſity for three

　　　　　　　D 3　　　　　　　　　　　or

or four years more, without thinking of any ramble, either here or any where elfe.   My fpoufe and I give our fervice to you and your family.   Pray my fervice to my coufin *Tomes,* and let him know I am very much concerned for his great lofs.

I am, Madam, &c.

To the Duke of Dorfet.

My Lord,   *Dublin, Feb.* 20, 1730.

ON the 8th inft. Mr. *Brandreth* * brought me the honour of your Grace's of the 10th paft.   We have fince difpatched his inftruments agreeably to your Grace's directions.   I found he did not want a faculty to hold the two preferments, elfe I was ready to have granted one, as I fhall be to give him my favour and protection on all occafions.   He feems to be a fenfible gentleman, and very well behaved; and I doubt not but he will give general fatisfaction here.

I am, my Lord, &c.

To the fame.

My Lord,   *Dublin, Feb.* 27, 1730.

I Have the honour of your Grace's of the 20th, and return my thanks for the directions you intend to fend about the living of *Clane.*

We are very well pleafed with the two new letters of his Majefty relating to Meffrs. *Lawman* and *Hoburg,* and hope to fatisfy your Grace upon your arrival here, that it will be of fome fervice to your Grace's adminiftration here, that they did not pafs in the old form.   I fhall endeavour to get a very hand-

---

* Mr. *Brandreth* had been tutor to Lord *Middlefex,* his Grace's eldeft fon.

fome

some payment upon them : but it could be larger, if your Grace thinks we may stay till after *Lady-day* for it, that it may not appear in the account to be laid before the Commons next session of parliament. I should be glad to receive your Grace's directions in this point as soon as may be. I am,

Your Grace's, &c.

To the Duke of Newcastle.

My Lord,   *Dublin, Mar.* 1, 1730.

THE affair of the *French* recruits is blown over without any thing farther than uncertain rumours here of some letter from somebody to encourage the officers in their levies.

But as there are two or three persons likely to be tried the approaching assize in the country, I thought proper to write to your Grace, to know what his Majesty will please to have done, if they should happen to be convicted. I rather fancy it will happen, as it has happened on most of the like occasions, that the evidence on which they have been committed will fall short at the trial, so that they may be acquitted. But for fear of the worst, I should be glad to know what is to be done, if it should prove otherwise. For I find on account of the noise that has been made in *England* and here about that affair, the Lords Justices will not interpose without his Majesty's commands.

If I am not much mistaken, when Mr. * *West* Mr. † *Connolly* and myself were in the government

---

* Lord High Chancellor, and one of the Lords Justices of *Ireland.*

† *William Conolly,* another of the Lord Justices, Speaker of the House of Commons, and a Commissioner of his Majesty's Revenue in *Ireland.*

D 4

in

in his late Majefty's reign, his Majefty was pleafed to order us not to permit any to be executed for lifting in foreign fervice, till we knew the King's pleafure.

The officers who are fuppofed to have enlifted them are got off. I am,

My Lord, &c.

To the Duke of Dorfet.

My Lord,   *Dublin, Mar.* 23, 1730.

I Have had the honour of your Grace's of the 13th inftant : and I have fince fpoke to Mr. *Gardiner* to provide money for a good handfome payment upon Meffrs. *Lawman* and *Hoburg*'s penfion ; and intend to-morrow to get an order to him for it as foon as may be after *Lady-day*. Money is very low in our treafury, but we will ftrain as far as poffible.

To the Duke of Dorfet.

My Lord,   *Dublin, Apr.* 21, 1731.

THE terrible diftrefs we are under in this nation, upon account of the difproportionate value of our gold and filver coins, to what they bear in *England*, and the want of filver confequent upon it, is what your Grace has probably heard of, and what I fhall take the liberty to write more to your Lordfhip about, if I am encouraged by your Grace to do it.

But befide the want of filver, the ordinary people here are under the laft diftrefs for want of copper money : of this I met with complaints laft year at every place in the vifitation of my province ; and it is what is every day complained of in this town. Tradefmen that retail, and poor people are forced to

pay

pay for getting their little filver changed into copper, and are forced to take raps or counterfeit half-pence, of little more than a quarter of the value of an *Englifh* half-penny, which has encouraged feveral fuch coiners, and muft end in the great lofs of the poor, whenever they pafs no longer ; and the farther that time is put off, the greater the lofs will be.

As we have long laboured under this calamity, the Houfe of Lords towards the clofe of the laft feffions, applied to the then Lord Lieutenant, to defire his Majefty to let us have 15,000 *l.* coined in farthings and half-pence, of the fame finenefs as the *Englifh* copper money, at the rate of 26 *d.* the pound of copper, as we then thought that 24 *d.* were coined in *England* out of a pound of copper, the *Englifh* had 24 *d.* upon the bottom of two fhillings *Englifh* going for 26 *d.* here, and that what profit arofe from this coinage might go to the ufe of the publick here.

I was the perfon that moved for this addrefs, and added the latter part, upon an affurance I had from my Lord *Carteret* that his Majefty had promifed to grant us as much, if we defired it.

There was likewife a refolution paffed in the Houfe of Commons, probably on occafion of this addrefs of the Houfe of Lords, that it would be for the benefit of the nation to have a mint erected here, without any mention of any copper, filver, or gold coinage.

What my Lord *Carteret* did at his return to *England* in this affair, I know not, as he never fent us any letter about it.

And thus things have refted, till fome time ago, when my Lord * *Forbes* made application to me, that confidering the deplorable condition the poor were in for want of copper money, it would be of the greateft fervice to get fome ; and that by fome difcourfe he had had with Mr. *Conduit*, Warden of the Mint, he

* Son of the Earl of *Granard.*

fancied

fancied we might buy a quantity from the mint, for
this nation, and that he and many others would readily
advance a fum of money, if I thought proper, and
would join in it. I told him how fenfible I was of
the great diftrefs the poor were in here for want of
copper, and that I would join in any fuch undertaking.
He then promifed to write to Mr. *Conduit* on this fubject, to know whether we might be private purchafers,
or muft apply to his majefty for leave to have fome
copper coined, fince we wanted copper in another
proportion to the *Englifh* fhilling than what it bears
in *England*. He fometime after received an anfwer
from Mr. *Conduit*, that nothing could be done for us
without his Majefty's leave, and fent an eftimate of
the coinage as in *England*, and as would be proper
for us, * a copy of which I have here fent your Grace,
with what he apprehended would be the gain upon it.

Upon Lord *Forbes*'s communicating this to me
I talked with my brethren the Lords Juftices on
the fubject, who concurred with me in opinion, that
fuch a copper coinage was both exceedingly ufeful
and neceffary, and that it would be of fervice to have
it as foon as poffible, confidering our prefent diftrefs,
fince though the parliament fhould come into proper
meafures about it, it could not be brought to bear in
lefs than nine or twelve months, but in this way it
could be brought to bear in three months.

We have fince founded fome of the council about
this affair, who concur with our fentiments, and we
had in part refolved upon having a council, in order
to apply to your Grace about this affair, but we have
fince confidered that we would not directly apply to
your Grace with the weight of the council, till we
had previoufly acquainted your Grace with the matter, and in part knew how you were difpofed; and
befides, if it were once known that fuch an application was made to your Grace, it would give fome
obftruction to the circulation of raps, which though

it

it muft happen at laft, we would not have happen
without a remedy of better money following as foon
after as may be.

In Mr. *Conduit*'s fcheme we find that only 23*d. halfp.*
are coined out of a pound weight of copper, fo that
to keep our copper money as near in intrinfic value
to the *Englifh* copper as may be, we propofe coining
only 25*d. halfp.* out of a pound weight of copper.

If your Grace gives us leave to apply, we think
of applying only for 50 tuns, which will make
11,900*l. Irifh,* but we have no doubt but we fhall be
preffed to apply for more foon ; nor do I think that
lefs than 150 or 200 tuns will anfwer the occafion ;
but we are willing to be petitioned for more when the
goodnefs of thefe and the want of more is feen by
every body.

Mr. *Conduit* tells us about 1000*l.* will fet the affair
a going, which we fhall raife here, without defiring
any intereft or other profit by it. We propofe paying the money advanced into Mr. *Gardiner*'s hands,
and to make the firft payment and let him receive the
copper money as it is fent hither, and difpofe of it;
and with the produce anfwer any fubfequent payments, till the whole is difpofed of. So your Grace
or the parliament may have a Crown officer to examine
about the gains, if you fhall think proper.

As to the gains, Mr. *Conduit* does not allow for de-
duċtions which muft be made, which will ftrike off
above half the profit he computes ; as your Grace
will fee by the fcheme +, No. II. inclofed. Indeed,
if the exchange fhould prove but 10 *per cent.* which
it poffibly may prove very foon, the profit will be on
Mr. *Conduit*'s quantity 202*l.* greater, and on ours 101*l.*

The refolution of the Lords relating to a copper
coinage, and that of the Commons about a mint,
were twice confidered in council, whilft my Lord
Carteret was Lord Lieutenant, and it was the opinion
of every body that they were no ways inconfiftent,
since

since it might be for the good of the nation to have a mint, but as it would be long before that could be established and brought to work, it might at the same time be very proper to afford a more speedy remedy to our present sufferings, which was what the Lords proposed.

I think it my duty at the same time that I acquaint you what was and still is, as far as I can learn, the sense of the privy council, to acquaint your Grace likewise, that by what I have been told, the view of some warm men in the House of Commons in moving that resolution about a mint, was, that as they are very zealous for a mint here, they were against coining even copper at the tower, left it should mark out a way for coining gold and silver for us, if there were occasion, and it should appear by a plain experiment with how much greater expedition, ease, and cheapness we might have any money coined at the Tower, than it can be coined here.

I have now informed your Grace of our present wants of copper money, and the readiest remedy for this evil, and likewise what are the views of those who possibly intended to hinder the address of the House of Lords being complied with, for an immediate coinage of copper : and your Grace will be the best judge whether you ought to encourage our immediate application for the coinage of 50 tuns of copper at the Tower, or will leave that affair to take what turn may happen to be given it in parliament.

And here I must inform your Grace that some of the most understanding men of the Commons tell me their opinion is, that their House will be able when they sit, to agree upon no present remedy for our evil.

As your Grace designs to honour us with your company in a few months, if it be thought proper to do any thing in this affair, there is no time to be lost. And if your Grace pleases to send for Mr. *Conduit*, he

can

can beſt inform you in what time a good quantity of copper money can be coined for our uſe.

As your Grace will ſee I have wrote with the utmoſt confidence in your Grace, I hope my letter will be kept a ſecret.

I am, my Lord, &c.

* NUMBER I.

Mr. CONDUIT's *Scheme.*

Formerly the mint gave 18*d.* a pound for all the copper they coined; but the *Engliſh* Copper Company having contracted to furniſh the mint with 100 tuns of copper at 13 $\frac{1}{4}$ *d.* a pound, they find themſelves loſers by it, and declare they will furniſh no more under 15*d.* a pound.

The reaſon why more is given than the market price is, that they muſt deliver it in bars of the exact ſize of the ſpecies to be coined, and take back and work over again what is amiſs, which is uſually $\frac{2}{3}$ of the whole.

A pound avoirdupoiz of copper is coined into 23 $\frac{1}{2}$ *d.* in *England*, which is - - - - - - - - - - -	0	1	11$\frac{1}{2}$
If the pound of copper coſt 0 1 1$\frac{1}{4}$			
And the coinage - - - 0 0 4$\frac{3}{4}$			
	0	1	6
Remains gain on the coinage	0	0	5$\frac{1}{2}$

It is offered to coin at the mint in *England*, copper for *Ireland*, 26 *d.* in the pound avoirdupoiz $\frac{1}{6}$ farthings, and $\frac{5}{6}$ halfpence, for 5 *d.* a pound, all charges

charges included except 20 *s.* a tun to be given to the Comptroller.

26 *d.* a pound is   –   –   –   0   2   2

So that if the pound of
copper comes   –   –   –   0   1   3
And the coinage   –   –   0   0   5
                                   0   1   8

Remains profit on the coinage   0   0   6

Which on 100 tuns comes to 5,600 *l.* out of which deduct 20 *s.* a tun to be paid to a Comptroller, there remains 5,500 *l.* neat profit.

† NUMBER II.

Observations on the calculation of profit to be made by the coinage of 100 tuns of copper in Mr. Conduct's scheme.

AS we propose coining but 25 ½ *d.* a pound instead of 26 *d.* a pound of copper, there will be a profit of 5 ½ *d.* so that instead of 56 *l.* profit on a tun, deducting a half-penny a pound (which comes to 4 *l.* 13 *s.* 4 *d.* a tun) there will remain but 51 *l.* 6 *s.* 8 *d.* profit on a tun, out of which deduct 20 *s.* a tun to the Comptroller, the remainder is 5033 *l.* 6 *s.* 8 *d.*

Again, as there must 20 *d.* a pound be paid in *England* for copper and coinage, that will amount to 186 *l.* 13 *s.* 4 *d.* a tun to be paid in *England*, this on 100 tuns will amount to 18,666 *l.* 13 *s.* 4 *d.* to which add 100 *l.* the Comptroller's fee, the total to be paid in *England* will amount to 18,766 *l.* 13 *s.* 4 *d.* If we suppose to be paid more in *England* for agency, casks, packing, carriage, and shipping, at the rate of 3

per

per cent. on the above fum, that will amount to better than 561 *l.* to be anfwered there, the total will be 20,254 *l.* 13 *s.* 4 *d.* to be paid there.

As the middle exchange here is 11 *per cent.* the return will coft better than 2123 *l.*

Suppofe then the total gain on 100 tuns to be - - - - -			5033	6	8
Deduct from this agency, &c. - - - 561 0 0					
Charge of remittance 2123 2 0			2684	0	0
Remains ftill of profit			2349	6	8

Out of which, when freight, landing, and other expences here are anfwered, probably the remaining profit may be from 2100 *l.* to - - - 2200 0 0

And as we propofe to begin with but 50 tuns of copper, probably the profit may be from 1050 *l.* to 1100 0 0

To the Duke of Newcaftle.

My Lord,   *Dublin, Apr.* 24, 1731.

ON *Wednefday* I was honoured with your Grace's of the 14th inftant. I wifh our treafury had been in a better condition, but as it is, I have taken care to have a year's penfion paid in to Mrs. *Spence's* agent, which clears her to *Chriftmas* laft inclufive, and a bill is remitted accordingly to-day. It is with a great deal of pleafure that I received your Grace's commands, which have given me a fmall opportunity

of

of ſhewing my readineſs on all occaſions to own the many obligations you have been pleaſed to lay on me.

I am, &c.

To the Biſhop of London.

My Lord, *Dublin, May* 11, 1731.

IT has been a very great ſurpriſe to me this winter to hear of the attacks made on the rights of the clergy by two bills brought into the Houſe of Commons, one relating to tythes, the other to the fines for renewal of Church leaſes.

I find that what always uſed to be of weight in both houſes, that theſe were manifeſt attempts on the undoubted right and property of the clergy, was with too many of no weight at preſent.

I am very glad the ſtorm is blown over for this ſeaſon, and I hope the open declarations their Majeſties were pleaſed to make in favour of the rights of the clergy, may prevent any new attack being haſtily made on them.

If I am not miſinformed, your Lordſhip has been very uſefully employed in publiſhing a ſhort but full vindication of the rights of the clergy as to tythe. To which I have ſeen an anſwer, publiſhed, as the title ſays, by a member of parliament. I think we of the clergy are very much obliged to that author, ſince he ſpeaks pretty plain, that in his opinion the nation ought to pay nothing to the clergy except they pleaſe, and that the fewer the clergy are reduced to, the better for the nation.

The rights of a free people ſeem to be carried a great length by ſome people in *England* in their writings. In ſeveral pamphlets one of their rights has been aſſerted to be, to publiſh what they pleaſe about religion, and another to publiſh the ſame about all affairs of ſtate ; and this author has now ſtarted a third,

third, which is, to be eafed from the burthen of tythes. I wifh the landed gentlemen would reflect, whether the next privilege of a free-born *Englifhman* may not be to be excufed from the burthen of rents, fince the tenants of *England* do almoft as much out-number the landlords, as the laiety do the clergy. I muft own it is with great grief that I fee daily fuch things publifhed, and thofe liberties taken with perfons in power, and fuch a difregard to all the rights and properties of the fubject, as I think muft by degrees end in fome publick difturbance.

As to the clergy in particular, I believe there never has been a time, when there has been lefs reafon to complain of any opprefflions from the fpiritual courts, or difaffection to the conftitution than at prefent; and I cannot but think by what I am informed, that one caufe of thefe attacks made on them, is from thofe who are very uneafy to fee fo great a ftrength on the bench of Bifhops fupporting his Majefty and his miniftry; but of this your Lordfhip is a better judge.

But at the fame time I cannot but believe that if there were fewer pluralities, and more of the clergy difcharged their duty on their livings, it would take off a great deal of that envy and malice which feems to be raifed.

It is very happy for us of the clergy here, that our brethren in *England* are able to ftand their ground; for if you are once borne down, all that may pafs in *England* againft the clergy, will feem to be acts of calmnefs and temper, in refpect of thofe warm attacks that would foon be made on us here.

I moft heartily wifh our brethren in *England* good fuccefs in maintaining their rights, and congratulate their having a perfon fo knowing and prudent as your Lordfhip to affift and conduct them in the defence they are obliged to make of their

VOL. II.   E   property,

property, againſt ſo unjuſt and ſo unreaſonable attempts.

I am, &c.

To the Duke of Newcaſtle.

My Lord,   *Dublin, May* 27, 1731.

I AM very much obliged to your Grace for taking
in ſo good part the late ſmall return made by me
for the many favours received of your Grace ; and
ſhall always ſet the higheſt value on the continuance
of your favour and friendſhip.

I muſt likewiſe deſire your Grace to acquaint the
Dutcheſs of *Newcaſtle* how much I am obliged to
her for the honour of her acknowledgments of my
having befriended Mrs. *Spence*.

I am glad the ſeſſion of parliament is ended ſo well
in *England*, and heartily wiſh ours may ſucceed as
well.

We are very much obliged to your Grace for your
zeal in the promoting of the act for explaining the
naturalization act, in which as you rightly obſerve,
the intereſts of *England* and *Ireland*, and the honour
of his Majeſty's government are highly concerned.
But we are apprehenſive here that three clauſes
which were added to that bill, as ſent up by the
Commons, will do ſome miſchief here.

As to the *Iriſh* yarn bill, which was thrown out in
the Houſe of Lords, I can aſſure your Grace, that I
am fully ſatisfied the part you acted in that affair,
was not out of any diſregard to *Ireland*, but purely
that you thought the rejecting of it at preſent, was
for the ſervice of *England**. But at the ſame time

---

* The Primate ſeems to argue like an *Iriſh* Patriot in this letter,
but in truth he argues like a true friend to both *England* and *Ireland*, whoſe intereſts, as he thought were inſeparable.

I muſt

I muſt beg leave to inform your Grace, that it is my opinion upon converſing with gentlemen of thoſe parts of *Ireland* where moſt wool is run, that the paſſing of that bill would have more effectually prevented the running of wool from hence to *France*, than all the laws beſides, which you in *England* or we in *Ireland* can deviſe, to prevent that clandeſtine trade; ſince it would have made it the general intereſt of the landed gentlemen, and of the poor people, every where to have endeavoured to hinder any wool being carried off from hence to *France*; and I believe the gentry in thoſe parts would have done their utmoſt to prevent it.

But at preſent, as you have done nothing in *England* to ſet us an example of what you would expect from us, unleſs my Lord Lieutenant comes over with inſtructions what it is that is deſired of us, I believe we ſhall be put to it, to find out what method to take to hinder the running of wool. And after we have taken in the former ſeſſions, one ſtep to encourage carrying our yarn to *England* by taking off a duty amounting to 12,000*l. per ann.* which muſt be made good by ſome new duties, and after nothing has been done on the other ſide agreeable to our hopes, not to ſay to the promiſes made us, I wiſh the ſeſſions may prove as eaſy as *all his Majeſty's ſervants here wiſh, and will uſe their utmoſt endeavours to make it.*

I am, &c.

To the Duke of Dorſet.

My Lord,   *Dublin, May* 29, 1731.

SINCE your Grace was ſo good as to ſend orders to have Mr. *Hoſkins* preſented to the rectory of *Clane,* upon Mr. *Horner's* reſigning it, Mr. *Horner* has reſigned that living, and I have collated him to

E 2   a living

a living in my diocefe.   But before any thing farther is done about *Clane*, I would beg the favour of
your Grace to let Mr. *Daniel* of *Killybegs* be prefented
to the rectory of *Clane*, upon Mr. *Hofkins* being prefented to *Killybegs*, which I doubt not obtaining from
the Bifhop of *Rapho*, who is patron of *Killybegs*.

It will be for the conveniency of thofe two clergymen to make that exchange ; and I hope your
Grace will be fo good as to permit it.

I am, &c.

To the fame.

My Lord,   *Dublin, Jan.* 22, 1731.

THE lady that waits upon your Grace with thefe
is relict of Lord *Roche*, as he was commonly
called, whofe anceftor was attainted and loft his title
and a large eftate about the rebellion of 1641. His
late Majefty was pleafed to give him a penfion here
during his life : I think it was 200*l. per ann.* which
I believe was the only fupport of him and his family.   Since his death, his widow being deftitute of
fupport, made application to his prefent Majefty for
a penfion for the maintenance of herfelf ; and as I
underftood by her, my Lord *Carteret* gave her hopes
that his Majefty would grant her requeft ; but as nothing is yet done in it, fhe thought proper to go
over to *England* to folicit in perfon.   I believe fhe
has fome friends there who will affift her with their
intereft, but as your Grace's good will muft be of
the greateft fervice to her, I humbly recommend
her to your Grace to help her to fomewhat that may
be a fubfiftance for her, fince I am fully perfuaded
fhe is at prefent without one.   As for the particulars of her cafe, I refer your Grace to her own relation. I am,

My Lord, &c.

To

To Lord Carteret.

My Lord,   *Dublin, June* 24, 1731.

MR. *Ransfield* has lately brought me the honour of your Lordfhip's of the 26th of *April*, recommending him to my protection here. If your Lordfhip is fo good as to fpeak for him to my *Lord Lieutenant, I fhall be very ready to do him what good offices I can with his Grace, as occafions offer. I am,

My Lord, &c.

To the Duke of Dorfet.

My Lord,   *Dublin, June* 26, 1731.

I Have the honour of your Grace's of the 17th inft. and I fhall be obliged to your Grace if you pleafe by the firft opportunity to fend an order for prefenting Mr. *Daniel* to the rectory of *Clane*, that there may be no fquabble about tythes, as harveft is juft coming on now.

I had to-day fome talk with my Lord Chancellor about the copper coinage, and we are both of opinion that it is now too late to do any thing in that affair till we have the opportunity of difcourfing with your Grace in perfon on that fubject.

As to purchafing in the raps†, we are both of opinion that it will be very wrong to do it; nor have either of us heard any body here fuggeft that fuch a thing would be proper: and we would both beg that there never may be the leaft hint dropt of any fuch intention; fince it may occafion the coining of fome thoufands of pounds more of raps, the lofs

* *Lionel*, Duke of *Dorfet*.   † A bafe fort of half-pence.

E 3   of

of which will be heavy enough on the poor, as things ſtand already.

Sir *Ralph Gore* is in the country at preſent, ſo that I could not have his ſentiments on this ſubject.

I am, &c.

To the ſame.

My Lord,   *Dublin, Aug.* 3, 1731.

I Had deſigned not to have troubled your Grace about an affair of no greater importance than is the ſubject of this letter, till I had the honour of ſeeing your Grace at *Dublin* ; but as your Grace may then be in a great hurry, and I am informed you have already fixed ſeveral of your chaplains, I take the liberty to recommend to your Grace's fa- vour, to be put in that liſt, Dr. *Eſſex Edgworth,* Chancellor of the dioceſe of *Ardagh,* a biſhoprick held by the Biſhop of *Kilmore.* I ſhould not recom- mend him on this occaſion, if did not know him to be every way a moſt worthy clergyman.

I am, &c.

To the Biſhop of London.

My Lord,   *Dublin, Aug.* 12, 1731.

T HE perſon who waits upon you with this, is Dr. *Delany,* miniſter of one of the principal * Churches in this city, and one of our moſt celebra- ted preachers. He has of late employed his thoughts and pen in the vindication of our moſt holy Religion, and has ſome thoughts of printing what he has writ-

* St. *Werburgh's* Pariſh.

ten,

ten †, if it shall be thought to be of service. I knew of no person to whose judgment it was more proper to submit his performances than your Lordship, who have so happily engaged yourself in the controversy; and seem to have the conduct of the defence of our most holy cause against the present most audacious insults of unbelievers. He comes over with a disposition to submit his writings, and the printing of them, to your Lordship's opinion.

I am, &c.

To the Duke of Newcastle.

My Lord,   *Dublin, Dec.* 4, 1731.

I Hope your Grace will have the goodness to excuse my giving you this trouble on account of one of the bills now sent over to be laid before the privy council in *England*, for rendering more effectual an act for the better securing of the government by disarming papists ; since the papists here declare publickly, that they have employed agents on the other side of the water to have the bill sunk there.

That your Grace may the better understand the case, I must beg leave to acquaint you that in the 7th of King *William* an act was passed here, entitled, an act for the better securing the government by disarming papists. The intent of which was not only to take away the arms then in the hands of papists, but constantly to keep them and their successors disarmed ; and it has been the opinion of the Judges from time to time, that the law had forbid all papists at any time to keep or carry arms. But upon a papist being indicted last summer assizes in the county of *Galway* upon that act, for carrying arms, though it was not

† *Revelation examined with Candour* ; the Life of King *David*, and many other Pieces, with a Volume of Sermons.

E 4

disputed

difputed either that he was a papift, or carried arms, yet the jury were pleafed to acquit him. Upon this it has been underftood by the papifts every where, that the faid act only concerned the papifts then living, and the arms they had in their poffeffion at the time that act was paffed; and upon talking with the Judges, we find that act was drawn up fo ill, that there is too much room for fuch an opinion. This occafioned the Houfe of Lords to bring in heads of a bill to render that act more effectual, and this new act is very little more than the old one corrected to what it was originally defigned for; only this being thought more prudent than to bring in a bill, which by its very title fhould have owned the firft act to be grofsly defective.

The power given in the old act to the government to licenfe fuch papifts to bear arms as they thought proper, is here continued, with a power of revoking fuch licenfes, when they fhall think fit, which was forgot in the former act. The chief additions to this new bill are, that no proteftant fervant to a papift fhall have any arms whilft he is in that fervice; for this was one way of eluding the act, whilft it was thought to be in force, to keep a proteftant fervant, who pretended to be the proprietor of all arms found in the houfe of his popifh mafter. That the proof of a perfon being commonly reputed a papift, fhall be fufficient to convict fuch perfon offending againft this act, except he prove himfelf a proteftant, for on fome trials it was found very difficult to prove a man to be a papift, though the whole country knew him to be fo.

And another is, that no papift fhall be on the jury in any trial upon this act.

My

My Lord,

As what has happened has in a manner repealed the act of the 7th of King *William*, so far as relates to the disarming of papists; and as the papists in *Dublin* have upon it put on swords, and those in the country in *Conaught* at least travel publickly with swords and fire-arms, we cannot think ourselves nor the government here safe, unless the act we now send over be passed. The papists by the most modest computation, are about five to one protestant, but others think they cannot be less than seven to one. And what use they have formerly made of their arms in this kingdom, our histories give too melancholy an account of.

And I can assure your Grace, that the papists in the country, before the defects of this act were discovered, were so formidable, that scarce any magistrate durst put any of the laws against regulars, &c. in execution, for fear of being murthered, or having his houses fired in the night. And if our present bill miscarries, they will grow much more formidable and insolent; nor have the papists scrupled, often giving threats against every magistrate that was more active on any occasion than his neighbours.

They had found out several evasions of the act of the seventh of King *William*, which we would willingly have prevented; but as some difficulties arose in drawing up proper clauses for that purpose, and too many in the House of Commons shew a disposition to favour the papists more than is consistent with the protestant interest here; we have omitted all such clauses, and confined ourselves to what was the undoubted intention of that act, and to some new clauses which nobody can well object to, to make it in some measure effectual.

And

And I muſt beg of your Grace to uſe your intereſt with the council, to return us this bill without any ways weakening it ; ſince without this bill his Maĵeſty's government will be in great danger here if any unhappy occaſion abroad ſhould give the papiſts a little more boldneſs than they have at preſent, and the proteſtants will not be ſafe in their perſons.

I am, my Lord, &c.

To the Duke of Dorſet.

My Lord,   *Dublin, Mar.* 20, 1731.

I Have had the honour of your Grace's of the 11th inſtant, and am very much obliged to your Grace for your anſwer to mine of the 21ſt paſt. What my Lord *Carteret* had done with the reſolutions of the Houſe of Lords and Commons, which he took over with him, we had no account of before. But judging it probable they were referred to the Commiſſioners of the Treaſury, we were for ſerving the nation in their preſent extreme want of copper money, by a method that might avoid any enquiry into ſo complicated an affair, as the ſetting the value of the gold and ſilver coins current here, and the conſidering whether it were more proper to have a mint erected here, or to have leave given us to have copper money to ſuch a quantity, coined at the tower ; which method was, by an addreſs from the Lords Juſtices and Privy-council for leave to have fifty tuns of copper coined at the tower, without any relation to any thing done either by the Lords or Commons here. Whereby all that would have been brought before the Treaſury had been, whether his Majeſty would pleaſe to let us have fifty tuns of copper coined at the tower, at ſuch a rate as anſwers to the *Engliſh* copper coinage, and to permit the gain made by it to come to the uſe of the publick.

And

And I can affure your Excellency that I have never heard of any application made by any but the privy-council here to the King on any occafions relating to the coin, till laft feffion. And fo far were the Houfe of Commons from thinking it a point belonging to them, that Mr. *Conolly* acquainted my Lord Chancellor and me that a few years before I came hither there had been a committee appointed by the Houfe of Commons, to confider at what value gold and filver coins ought to pafs here ; but after fome time fpent in it, they dropped making any report to the Houfe of what refolutions they had come to in the commit-tee, as thinking that an affair wholly belonging to his Majefty's prerogative. Nor had they meddled with it laft feffions but that the remitters and merchants of *Cork* thought it more to their advantage to have things continue in their prefent bad ftate, than have them reformed according to the rational fcheme de-figned by the privy council : and they were the per-fons who engaged fome members in that houfe to drive them to the refolutions they came to : and the refolutions of the Houfe of Lords * were defigned only as a ballance againft the hafty refolutions of the other houfe.

After thefe hints, I fhall reft the affair with your Grace. I am,

My Lord, &c.

To the fame.

My Lord,   *Dublin, May* 4. 1732.

AFTER the difficulties and dangers your Grace met with in your firft attempt for *England*, it was a great pleafure to hear to-day, that your fecond voyage proved fo favourable.

* Thofe refolutions were framed by his Grace, and fupported by him in the Houfe of Lords.

By

By the accounts we have from *England* there is no doubt of your Grace's having time to lay before his Majefty what you fhall judge proper for the fervice of this country before he fets out for *Hanover* ; and we are all fatisfied we cannot defire a better follicitor.

I take this opportunity to make my acknowledgments to your Grace for all the favours I received from you here, and defire I may be honoured with the continuance of them.   I am,

My Lord, &c.

To the fame.

My Lord,   *Dublin, May* 11, 1732.

WE have wrote to your Grace by this mail, recommending Mr. *Meredith* for the deanery of *Ardfert.* The deanery is of little value, and is rather defired for the dignity than the profit of it.

Mr. *Agmondefham Vefey* is father-in-law to Mr. *Meredith,* and he came to me with him, and took occafion to affure me of his readinefs to concur in all meafures the government could defire next feffion, which a man of honour could poffibly join in.   I told him I was very fure the government would never defire any thing a man of honour could not comply with, and affured him I would write to your Grace in behalf of his fon.

As your Grace had been mentioning Mr. *Vefey,* as one proper to be gained, I was glad of his applying on this occafion : fince the boon he afks is not great, if he fhould fly off.   But I hope this may open a way to fix him againft another feffion.

He has given the fame affurances to other friends, whom he employed to fpeak to Sir *Ralph Gore* and me.   As this is the ftate of this affair, I muft defire
your

your Grace to be fo good as to recommend Mr. *Meredith* to his Majefty for the faid deanery.   I am,

My Lord, &c.

To the fame.

My Lord,   .   *Dublin, May* 27, 1732.

IT was with very great pleafure I received the account from your Grace, of your family being all arrived at *London* in good health.

I am fenfible the lofs of time your Grace fuffered by your troublefome paffage, muft have hindered your knowing his Majefty's pleafure about fome of our *Irifh* affairs ; but the diftrefs we are in for want of copper money, and the ready concurrence that affair was likely to meet with from the miniftry, make me hope your Grace has found an opportunity of confulting his Majefty about the copper coinage.   I am,

Your Grace's, &c.

A

MEMORIAL

T O

His Grace the DUKE of DORSET.

May it pleafe your Grace,

THE want of copper money is fo great in this kingdom, as to put the more ordinary fort of people, particularly the foldiers, under the greateft difficulties in all their little tranfactions : obliging them to pay for the exchange of filver, and to take

raps

raps that are not of a fourth part of the value of an *Englifh* half-penny. And their neceffities have encouraged feveral wicked people to make counterfeit copper money at this time, which muft end in the great lofs of this nation.

We therefore think it would be of great fervice to his Majefty, and of great advantage to his good fubjects here; if a quantity of good copper money were, as foon as conveniently may be, coined for the ufe of this kingdom. And we defire your Grace will be pleafed to obtain his Majefty's permiffion, that we may have fifty tuns of copper coined at the mint, of the fame finenefs as the *Englifh* half-pence are coined of, part in half-pence, and part in farthings; and that as the *Englifh* fhilling paffes with us for 13 d. and out of a pound of copper is coined at the mint 23½ d. *Englifh*, we may be permitted to coin out of a pound of copper 25½ d. that our copper money may be as near as may be of the fame proportionable value as the copper money of *England*: and that no private perfon may make any advantage of this coinage, we defire that his Majefty may be pleafed to order that after the expence of the copper, coinage, exchange for remittance, carriage, and other neceffary expences, the remaining profit may go to the ufe of the publick here.

It is propofed that this copper money fhould have his Majefty's head on one fide, and the *Irifh* harp and crown on the other. The fum of copper money that will arife out of 50 tuns coined after this propofal, will amount to 11,900 l. *Irifh*. The money that may be neceffary to fet this coinage a going, will be little more than 1000 l. which is propofed to be advanced here without any profit to thofe who advance it.

As our prefent calamity for want of good copper money is very great, and grows every day greater, and as the defign will take up fome time in executing, after his Majefty has gracioufly given us the permiffion

                                                                 we

we defire, we humbly beg your Grace will take the firft opportunity to obtain his Majefty's leave, that we may immediately fet about an affair that will be of fo great fervice to the ordinary people of this kingdom.

The H o u s e of L o r d s, &c.

To the fame.

My Lord,   *Dublin, July* 22, 1732.

I Was in hopes to have given your Grace the trouble of a letter relating to the copper coinage fooner, but it was not before *Thurfday* laft that we could finifh the affair, and fign a letter.   I am forry it is in fo perplexed a manner, with fo much regard to what paffed in the two houfes two feffions ago : but your Grace will fee that in the opinion of the council, our neceffities require fuch a coinage, and that fpeedily.   I firft opened the affair upon receipt of Mr. *Cary's* * letter, in council, on *Wednefday* the 12th inftant, when we appointed a committee to confider the matter and make a report.   My Lord Chancellor feemed to have a little courage then, Sir *Ralph Gore* was not then returned out of the country, laft *Saturday* we received the report from the committee, when my Lord Chancellor expreffed great fears of offending the Houfe of Commons, and the affair was re-committed.   Sir *Ralph Gore* fpoke very plainly that he had laft feffions talked with feveral members about what was defigned, that except Mr. *Stephenfon*, who wanted to have the coinage himfelf, every one approved the defign ; and thought it beft to be done by the council, for fear of any unreafonable addition, if the affair was moved in the Houfe of Commons.   I likewife affured them

---

* Secretary to his Grace the Lord Lieutenant of *Ireland.*

I had

I had promifed fome members to get the thing done, if they would keep it out of the houfe, which was accordingly done. However, my Lord Chancellor infifted on not concluding till the Lord Chief Juftice and Lord Chief Baron returned from the country; and that notice fhould be taken of the refolutions of the Houfe of Lords and Commons two feffions ago. Againft *Wednefday* the 19th the committee had the report ready agreeably to my Lord Chancellor's defire. In the debates we had, every body allowed it was the moft reafonable fcheme as to the goodnefs of the half-pence, and moft advantageous, as the publick was to have the profit : that the neceffities of the nation required a fpeedy remedy, and this was the only one; but as fome few were afraid of offending the Commons, I put them in mind that we were to act for the King's intereft, without regard to the fenfe of either houfe; and that though the Commons, in a fudden heat had come to a refolation, yet as they had fate fince for four or five months, and never meddled with that affair, it was a tacit retractation. Several of the members in town, that ufually are in the oppofition, have been fpoke to, and highly approve of the affair.

I muft beg that we may be favoured with leave to have 50 tuns coined at the mint, of the fame finenefs as the *Englifh* copper coin, at 25¼ d. *per* pound avoirdupoiz, and that the profit may go to the publick here.

We are not fure whether we fhould in our letter defire your Grace to apply to his or her Majefty, but we mean to have it obtained as foon as may be. The want of good change is fo great, that the fooner we may fet about it the better. As 1000 or 1500l. may be wanted to fet the affair a-going, care will be taken to provide it : there is no doubt but we fhall want about 100 tuns more.

About

About letting the old half-pence circulate, I believe there wants no order from *England*, but if your Grace approves it, as it is neceſſary, and is a ſort of condition of the new coinage, we can do it by proper orders to the Vice-Treaſurer.   I am,

My Lord, &c.

To the ſame.

My Lord,   *Dublin, Aug.* 15, 1732.

I Had ſome time ago a memorial tranſmitted me by Mr. *Cary*, that had been laid before your Grace by the Biſhop of *Meath*, relating to the archdeaconry of *Kells* granted to him in commendam, in order to have part of the endowment of it annexed to the biſhoprick in lieu of ſeveral impropriations he is willing to give up, to the ſeveral pariſhes they are in, deſiring to know my ſentiments of the matter.

As I know how poorly thoſe pariſhes are provided for at preſent, I cannot but approve the deſign, as do my brethren the Lords Juſtices.

But to prevent any miſunderſtandings or exceptions, I deſired the Biſhop of *Meath* to deliver in a memorial to the Lords Juſtices, that we might in common conſider the matter, and recommend it jointly to your Grace; but as my brethren have been lately out of town at Sir *Ralph Gore's*, and I am going this week on my viſitation, where I ſhall be abſent for a fortnight, nothing can well be done in it till my return. However I promiſed the Biſhop of *Meath*, that I would in the mean time acquaint your Grace with my approbation of it, and would give it all poſſible diſpatch at my return; with which he was well ſatisfied. And I hope at my return to *Dublin*, we ſhall jointly recommend it to your Grace. He

propofes by your Grace's affiftance to have the affair
fettled by an *Englifh* act of parliament next feffion ;
but it is neceffary he fhould have the archdeaconry
in commendan in the mean time, that it may not
lapfe.　When the affair is fettled in better form, I
fhall trouble your Grace with a more particular account of it.　I am,

My Lord, &c.

To the fame.

My Lord,　　　　　　　　　*Dublin, Sept.* 27, 1732.

THE bearer, Mr. *Horan*, is a gentleman whom
I prefented to your Grace in this kingdom,
when he gave you a memorial of his cafe.

He is the perfon who had a trial here with a de-
fcendant of one of thofe who went to *France* upon the
furrender of *Limerick*, and afterwards followed the
caufe to the Houfe of Lords in *England* ; and was
encouraged by thofe in power here to folicit an application of the 7° and 10 of Queen *Anne*, by a new
act in *England*, fo as to fecure proteftant purchafers
againft the defcendants of thofe who chofe to go
and ferve *France*, rather than ftay in their own
country.

On this occafion he has taken feveral journies to
England, and been at very great expences, and has
certainly been a confiderable lofer, the eftate of which
he had been a purchafer, not making him amends
for his expences.　He therefore hopes that as he has
ftood the expence of a law-fuit here, and an appeal
in *England*, and been at great trouble and expence in
foliciting an affair, the well fettling of which is of
confequence to the proteftant intereft of this kingdom, your Grace would be fo kind as to recommend
him

him to his Majefty's favour for fome place in this kingdom.

Moft of the facts he mentions fince 1724, I know to be true, and I am thoroughly fenfible he muft have been a fufferer in this affair, which I think it is a pity he fhould be, and therefore I recommend him to your Grace's favour.

I am, my Lord, &c.

To the fame.

My Lord,   *Dublin, Oct.* 17, 1732.

I Had owned the honour of your Grace's fooner but that I found by it there were very little hopes of any thing being done in the affair of our copper coinage, till his Majefty's arrival brought the feveral great officers to town. As that is now done, and the hurry of compliments on that occafion is now over, I muft beg of your Grace to forward that affair as much as you can. I hope what is fo reafonable in itfelf, fo neceffary for us, and of no damage to *England*, will meet with no difficulty on your fide of the water.

Your Grace moft juftly thought it could have met with no objections here, efpecially after what you had heard on that fubject from fo many of the principal perfons here. Nor had there been any obftacle here, but for the timoroufnefs of one perfon*.

But as the thing is fo much wanted, and the method propofed for doing it, in itfelf fo reafonable and juft, I make no doubt but when it is once well executed every body will applaud it.

I am, my Lord, &c.

* Lord Chancellor *Wyndham.*

F 2

To the fame.

My Lord,　　　　　　　*Dublin, Oct.* 28, 1732.

SINCE I came to town to fettle, there have been with me my Lord *Mount Alexander* and Lord *Strangford*, to defire I would put your Grace in mind of them, now upon his Majefty's return.

The cafe of the firft your Grace knows is that he has nothing at all to fubfift upon, and is ready on all occafions to attend his Majefty's fervice at the Houfe of Lords. The cafe of the latter is, that there is a penfion granted for the maintenance of my Lord and his mother; but as he is now of age and learning fit for the Univerfity, he would willingly profecute his ftudies at the college here, but without an additional penfion from his Majefty's bounty, he is unable to be at the expence. I am told he is a good fcholar, and foberly difpofed; and I fhould think it is a pity he fhould not be encouraged to go on and improve himfelf.

As this is their cafe, I take the liberty to recommend them to your Grace for your interceffion with his Majefty, that he may be pleafed to grant to each of them fome mark of favour out of his royal bounty *. I am,

　　　　　　　　　　　My Lord, &c.

To the fame.

My Lord,　　　　　　　*Dublin, Nov.* 2, 1732.

SINCE we wrote yefterday to acquaint your Grace with the death of General † *Stern*, my Lord *Cavan* is come to town, and has delivered in his

* The Primate's requeft was granted.

† Governor of the Royal Hofpital, or invalid Soldiers at *Kilmainham* near *Dublin*, and much on the fame Foundation as that of *Chelfea* near *London*.

　　　　　　　　　　　　　memorial

memorial relating to the mafterfhip of the hofpital.
I believe there is no one applies on this occafion, that
has been longer in the fervice than his Lordfhip, and
that more conftantly attended his duty whilft he was
in the army.   Your Grace very well knows he is the
only Lay-Lord that is a man of bufinefs in the Houfe
of Lords, where he is never wanting to ferve the
government : and I fhould hope it will not be thought
amifs to confider one of that houfe, for a poft now
vacant.   And if he has this preferment, he will always be at hand to affift in the Privy-council.   He is
very willing, if this provifion be made for him, to
drop the penfion he at prefent enjoys of 400 *l. per
ann.* which will be an eafe to our eftablifhment, and
that your Grace knows is of fome confequence here.
On thefe confiderations I cannot but heartily recommend him to your Grace, for his Majefty's favour on
this vacancy.

I am, my Lord, &c.

To the fame.

My Lord,   *Dublin, Dec.* 7, 1730.

AS we have not yet had any intimations of his
Majefty's pleafure about the mafterfhip of the
hofpital here, I juft take the liberty to put your Grace
again in mind of my Lord *Cavan*, as I cannot but
think, if the place is difpofed of to any perfon here,
it would be of fervice to his Majefty in the Houfe of
Lords, to beftow it on his Lordfhip.   I am,

My Lord, &c.

F 3   To

To the fame.

My Lord,   *Dublin, Jan.* 11, 1732.

I Had the honour of your Grace's of *Dec.* 28, laft
   Sunday.

I do not queftion but there were good reafons why
my Lord *Cavan* could not be provided for at prefent;
but I hope fome care will be taken of him on another
opportunity. We fhall to morrow have a meeting of
the governors of the hofpital, when we fhall take care
to appoint Colonel * *Bragg* mafter of the hofpital,
whom I heartily wifh joy of this promotion.

My Lord † *Altham* has within this poft or two
written to your Grace to have fomewhat farther done
for him by his Majefty, and I promifed him to write
to your Grace on his behalf. His prefent penfion is
200 *l. per ann.* which I fear is pretty much anticipated by debts he had contracted for his fubfiftance,
before his Majefty was pleafed to grant it him. But
if it be not anticipated, as he has a lady and three
children alive, and one coming every year, it will be
very hard for him to carry the year about with his
prefent penfion. If your Grace could prevail on his
Majefty to make fome addition to what he has at prefent, it would be a very feafonable relief to one who
I am certain·is at prefent reduced to fuch neceffities,
as it is a pity a peer of this kingdom, and who may
poffibly be a peer of *Great Britain*, fhould be reduced to.

I am, &c.

---

  * Suppofed to be the natural Son to the late E. of *D.* and Brother to his G. the D. of *D.* then L. L. of *I———d.*
  † Nephew to *Arthur* Earl of *Anglefea*, and prefumptive Heir to
that Title and Eftate, who died before his Uncle. He was fucceeded in both Titles and Eftate by his Brother *James.*

To

To the same.

My Lord,   *Dublin, Jan.* 25, 1732.

I Am very forry I am obliged to trouble your Grace on an occafion fo melancholy to myfelf.   My wife's breaft has been very bad for fome time, but of late is grown much worfe, which makes me very defirous to carry her over to *England,* to fee whether I can meet with better advice there than here.   But I am fenfible, as I am in the government here, I cannot ftir without his Majefty's leave, whether by his letter, or by fignifying his pleafure to the government here by your Grace, I cannot tell.   I muft therefore beg of your Grace to obtain his Majefty's leave for my coming to *England,* as foon as may be, for I am under apprehenfions, that if my wife is not removed foon, her breaft may be fo bad, that it may be dangerous for her to travel.

I think there will be no difficulty in letting the government ftand as it does, or that an order from his Majefty may be lodged here to grant a commiffion to my Lord Chancellor and Sir *Ralph Gore* to act jointly or feparately, in cafe either of them fhould be taken ill.   I do not fpeak this upon my own account, fince I fhall not reckon myfelf entitled to any falary from the day I leave *Ireland.*   I have communicated this affair to my Lord Chancellor, but no farther; and I can affure your Grace I fhall not ftay needlefsly in *England,* if his Majefty pleafes to give me his gracious leave to take this journey.   And it may happen, that after leave obtained, I may find it impracticable to ftir.

Your kind and fpeedy interpofition with his Majefty on this occafion, will be a very great obligation to,

My Lord, &c.

To the same.

My Lord,   *Dublin, Feb.* 12, 1732.

I Humbly thank your Grace for procuring me his Majefty's leave to come to *England.* I hope by the next mail to receive his Majefty's letter in due form.

If I had been apprehenfive of their wanting a form at the fecretary's office, which I fear has occafioned fome delay in my affair, I fhould at firft have fent them the King's letter, granted to his late Grace of *Dublin,* on a like occafion, but it was not fuggefted to me till late, and I fent it to Mr. *Delafaye* *, this day fe'nnight. But I hope they will have found a form before that comes to hand.

ı As foon as his Majefty's letter comes, I fhall make what hafte I can to *London,* if my fpoufe is able to undertake the journey; when I hope to have the honour to wait on your Grace.

I am, your Grace's, &c.

To the fame.

My Lord,   *Dublin, Feb.* 24, 1730.

Y O U R Grace fo well knew Sir *Ralph Gore,* and the deferved efteem he had, that I need fay nothing of his character, or the lofs the publick will have by his death. For my own particular, it has put me in my prefent circumftances, under the greateft diftrefs.

I thank your Lordfhip for obtaining for me his Majefty's leave to come over to *England,* and his

* One of the Under Secretaries of State.

Majefty's

Majefty's letter to alter the quorum here to make my abfence the lefs inconvenient. When the letter came, Sir *Ralph* was in a very bad way, fo that if the new commiffion had paffed, there was I believe a neceffity of paffing it before his death, which would have made it the more practicable for me to go to *England* though he died ; not that I would have done it, without firft knowing his Majefty's pleafure. But as the government was in danger of being in a cafe unforefeen when that letter was granted, and your Grace enjoining me not to produce that letter except my journey was certain, I did not think myfelf fufficiently authorized to have a new commiffion paffed, and accordingly nothing was done it, and I believe now nothing can be done in virtue of that letter.

As Sir Ralph Gore *is dead, there feems to be an opportunity, without any offence, of putting the General* in as the third perfon in the commiffion†, who I remember your Grace thought was the proper perfon, and that it was inconvenient and even dangerous to let the government keep on too long with the office of the fpeaker.*

My Lord Chancellor and I fhall very foon trouble your grace with our opinion, whom we think it will be moft for his Majefty's fervice to recommend for fpeaker.

As I cannot but wifh that I may be at liberty, if her health will permit it, to carry my wife over to *England*, for advice, *I would humbly offer, that if my Lord* § Shannon *be added to the commiffion of Lords Juftices, and the claufe for enabling* one Lord Juftice to act in the abfence or ficknefs of the others, though my Lord *Shannon* could not be here fo foon, yet, as one of this country would actually be in the commiff-

---

* Of the Army. † Of Lords Juftices.

§ ――――― *Boyle*, Lord Vifcount *Shannon*, general and commander in chief of the forces in *Ireland*, whofe daughter married the Earl of *Middlefex*, eldeft fon to *Lionel* the firft Duke of *Dorfet*.

fion,

fion, and might be expected here in a little time, I might be able to go to *England* in lefs than three weeks, if my wife fhould not by that time be too ill to travel. But if my journey at this time be thought prejudicial to his Majefty's fervice here, I entirely fubmit.

The point is a matter of great moment to the peace of this kingdom, not only during your Grace's adminiftration, but probably under feveral fucceffors to your Grace; and I hope will not therefore be too baftily determined.

I am, my Lord, &c.

To the fame.

My Lord,   *Dublin, March* 6, 1732.

IN the letter from the council to your Grace, notice is taken that no anfwer is come to their former application for the currency of the old copper money for fome time: and it is apprehended that without fome order on that head there may, upon iffuing out the new fpecies, be fuch a ftagnation of the old copper, as may occafion great diftrefs, if not fome difturbance among the meaner people. It was therefore the opinion of the council that his Majefty fhould be defired to give fuch orders as he fhall in his wifdom judge proper in that affair, to prevent a fudden ftop to the currency of the old fpecies. The raps were by all thought to be out of the queftion. And this was fo much the fenfe of the council, that till fomewhat of this nature be done, I am fatisfied my Lord Chancellor will not advance one ftep in this affair.

I have fince talked with the commiffioners on that fubject, whofe opinion is, that as in *England* the collectors are not obliged to receive more than 5 ¼ d. in any one payment in copper, as 6 d. is there the
leaft

leaſt piece of common ſilver money; ſo here, where 6½ d. is our leaſt piece of ſilver coin, they ſhould not be obliged to receive more than 6d. in copper in any one payment; though they may be left at liberty to receive more, if they pleaſe.

But I cannot but think it will be neceſſary to put ſome reſtraint upon that liberty, ſo that they may not e. g. at the moſt take more than one ſhilling in the pound in copper in one payment, to prevent as much as may be, the fraud of collectors.

There is another trouble I muſt give your Grace in this affair: I think the directions your Grace ſent us in your letter, to give what orders were proper in this affair, were ſufficient to authorize us to appoint an agent, or take any other neceſſary ſtep; but my Lord Chancellor is grown ſo much more ſcrupulous ſince the death of Sir *Ralph Gore*, that at firſt he talked of appointing no agent, except ſuch agent would be ſecurity to indemnify him in caſe of any accident or miſmanagement: but I have ſince brought him, upon the advice of my Lord Chief Juſtice *Rogerſon*, to conſent to appoint an agent, and ſet the work a-going, if your Grace will ſignify to us that it is his Majeſty's pleaſure that we ſhould appoint an agent in this affair: I think it would not be amiſs if it were expreſſed *ſuch an agent or agents as we ſhall judge proper either here or in* England.

Mr. *Gardiner* is willing to undertake the agency of this affair, and will anſwer the calls for money out of his own caſh; and as the bankers here ſtand obliged to him for his favour on many occaſions, he hopes to engage ſome of them to get a correſpondent of theirs in *London*, to negociate the contract, and do what elſe is neceſſary there, without being paid for agency. He was even willing to have indemnified my Lord Chancelor, but that I thought was too much.

I ſhould

I fhould be glad if we had his Majefty's pleafure fignified to us to thofe two points, as foon as may be conveniently, becaufe I fear no material ftep will be taken here till that is done.

Mr. *Gardiner* will in the mean time write to a proper perfon in *London* to enquire about the price of copper, and prepare matters there. but till his Majefty's pleafure be fignified, we fhall not be able to advance farther here.

I am very forry your Grace fhould have fo much trouble in an affair that every body allows to be even neceffary for carrying on all fmaller tranfactions here. And if it were in my power, I would fave your Grace this trouble. I am,

My Lord, &c.

To the fame.

My Lord, *Dublin, March* 15, 1732.

WE received the honour of your Grace's letter of the 10th inftant, and write again in the fame manner, that what paffed on this occafion, may as far as in us lie, be a fecret to all perfons here.

In our laft we reprefented to your Grace our thoughts concerning the feveral candidates, and that Mr. *Boyle* appeared to us to have by much the beft perfonal intereft, and fuch as could not without difficulty be oppofed, if he perfifted in his pretenfions. If this was not the cafe of one of the candidates, it might be advifeable to wait for fuch accidents as time may throw in the way, before his Majefty favoured either of them with his recommendation; but as it is a thing hardly to be expected that any number of perfons fhould keep themfelves difengaged for fo long a time as fix months, and as there may not be wanting thofe who may endeavour to perfuade Mr.

Boyle

Boyle that he has not been kindly used by the government's taking no favourable notice of his applications, we are very apprehensive that such delay may give room to the forming some party, which may raise a dangerous opposition to so late a recommendation as your Grace proposes. We should be very unwilling to disoblige either of the candidates, as being persons for whom we have a great regard, but we beg leave to observe, that since such declaration must be made before the election, the effects of any resentment on that account may be worn out the sooner it is made, especially if it be in favour of one, who it is generally thought cannot fail of success. It may be proper to take notice that it is almost a general notion, that if Mr. *Boyle* was once recommended by the government, all other opposition would be at an end.

People have not been wanting to surmise here that Mr. *Boyle*'s standing was only in order to transfer his interest at a proper time to some other. The effect of this has been, that Mr. *Boyle* has by his friends, discountenanced any such suggestion, and many of his friends have declared against any such transfer.

We assure your Grace we continue in the same opinion we were of when your Grace was here as to the filling up the third place in the government, and this seems a favourable opportunity for putting that scheme in execution.

Your Grace must be sensible that 500*l.* a session cannot be a sufficient provision for the expence of a speaker, and therefore he will be apt to expect some other support from the government. Whether the chancellorship of the Exchequer be a post proper for a speaker not otherwise provided for, is a matter we shall not presume to meddle with; but we cannot help taking notice, that from the nature and duties of that office, it may be for his Majesty's service that it should be given to some person of weight, who usually resides here.

We

We fhall ufe our beft intereft and endeavours to keep the friends of the government difengaged till his Majefty's further pleafure is known.

Your Grace will excufe us for being fo particular in an affair wherein his Majefty's fervice, the eafe and honour of your Grace's adminiftration, and the quiet of this kingdom, are highly concerned*.

We are, my Lord, &c.

To Mr. Walter Cary, *Secretary to the Lord Lieutenant.*

S I R,   *Dublin, Apr.* 7, 1730.

I Have received yours of the 24th paft, and hoped to have anfwered it fooner, but that we are ftill ftarting difficulty after difficulty in the matter of the copper coinage, which made me willing to fee them all through if I could, before I give you any farther trouble : and 1 hope we fhall upon the return of the Judges from the circuit, be able to fettle them all. As for money, I had taken care about that, but I find now it is doubted whether any private perfon may advance it with fafety, though he defires to get nothing by doing fo. However in whatever way the money is advanced, there can never be more than about 2000 *l.* paid before hand. I thought all was over when my Lord Lieutenant was pleafed to fignify to us that it was his Majefty's pleafure we fhould

---

* The two principal candidates were Mr. Prime-ferjeant *Singleton,* (afterwards Chief Juftice of the Common Pleas, which he refigned ; and was in a fhort Time after appointed Mafter of the Rolls in the Room of Mr. *Carter* who was deprived of that office) and Mr. *Boyle,* who was created Earl of *Shannon ;* and it was generally thought that the Primate turned the fcale in favour of Mr. *Boyle,* who was chofen fpeaker. Mr. *Boyle* was a ftanch whig, and a fteady friend to the Houfe of *Hanover,* and ever acted in perfect harmony with the Primate.

name

name an agent, but I find myself mistaken. I have begged hard that all may be thought of at once, and as there will be a necessity of a King's letter for keeping on the circulation of the old half-pence, and circulating the new, and as the Commissioners answer to what was referred to them is now come to our hands, I flatter myself we shall draw up the form of a King's letter, that will contain all the powers we *fancy* we want, and set this affair a going at last. I must beg the favour of your assistance to expedite the passing of the King's letter, when we send it over. I shall then trouble you again on this subject. In the mean time I thank you for putting my Lord Lieutenant in mind of Mr. *Warren's* affair ; and I shall by this post thank his Grace for his favour on that occasion. I am,

Sir, your humble servant,

To the Duke of Dorset.

My Lord,   *Dublin, Apr.* 7, 1733.

I Humbly thank your Grace for your favour in giving leave to Mr. *Digby* to resign his place of Porter to the Castle in favour of Mr. *Warren.* But though I was desirous to serve Mr. *Warren,* yet had I known what Mr. *Cary* has informed me of, *viz.* the sollicitations Mr. *Digby* had used not long ago to get into that place, I should have staid for some other opportunity to have served Mr. *Warren.* l am,

Your Grace's, &c.

To the Duke of Newcastle.

My Lord,   *Dublin, May* 3, 1733.

I Hope your Grace will have the goodness to excuse my giving you this trouble. One Mr. *Godly* is chaplain to Brigadier General *Dormer's* regiment on

our

our eftablifhment, and I am difpofed to beftow on him a parfonage in my gift, but as I have feveral of the clergy here on my hands, I muft at the fame time make fome provifion for one to whom I lye under a promife of preferment, his name is *John Richardfon*, Dean of *Kilmacduagh*; fo that the removal of Mr. *Godly* depends upon the Brigadier General being fo good as to permit Mr. *Godly* to refign his chaplainfhip in favour of Mr. *Richardfon*. I am fenfible there is ufually upon thefe occafions a prefent to the Colonel for his confent, but as the chaplain who quits cannot well make any fuch prefent, and the perfon I propofe to fucceed him, is too poor to make it, I muft beg the favour of Mr. *Dormer* to permit the refignation without any prefent. He will have one advantage by the change, that Mr. *Richardfon* is at leaft 25 years older than Mr. *Godly*. As I have not the happinefs to be acquainted with the General, I cannot apply to him myfelf for this favour, but I am affured your Grace's kind follicitation in this affair will obtain what I defire. I therefore make it my requeft to your Grace, that you would intereft yourfelf for me in this exchange, and add this to the many obligations I already lye under. As the living I defign for Mr. *Godly* is already vacant, I fhould be glad the fooner the refignation were agreed to.

I am, &c.

To the Duke of Dorfet.

My Lord,   *Dublin, May* 25, 1733.

AS the fummer is advancing apace, I cannot but beg leave to renew my application to your Grace for obtaining the King's letter relating to our copper coinage; though it will be impoffible to finifh it before the parliament meets, yet as we may eafily have 2 or 3000*l*. worth of copper coin over before

that

that time, I think the fureft way to prevent any wrong votes about that affair, is to let the nation fee what good copper they are to have, and to let it appear by the King's letter, that the publick and not any private perfon is to have the benefit of the coinage. And I am fully perfuaded that the determining this affair by the King's letter, and putting it in part in execution, is the moft likely way to prevent what probably may otherwife be voted, an addrefs to his Majefty for erecting a mint here; and I can affure your Grace feveral members of parliament with whom I have difcourfed, think with me in this affair.

I have by this poft wrote to Sir *Robert Walpole*, to defire his affiftance in difpatching the King's letter.

I have lately received the honour of your Grace's letter recommending Sir *Daniel M'Donald*, to whom I fhall be ready to fhew all proper favour.

I fhall be obliged to your Grace, if you will pleafe when you fee a proper occafion, to remember Mr. *Moland**, one of my family, for a pair of colours.

I am, my Lord, &c.

To Sir Robert Walpole.

SIR, *Dublin, May* 25, 1733.

AFTER his Majefty had been gracioufly pleafed to give us leave to coin what copper we wanted at the Tower, and to iffue his warrant to the mafter of the mint to coin for us, I was in hopes we fhould immediately have fet about a copper coinage, but I find that it is ftill apprehended here, that his Majefty's letter to the government is wanting to authorize us to name an agent for carrying on that coinage, and for circulating it here, and providing for a proper

---

* Mr. *Moland* was his Grace's gentleman, but a man of good family, who had an Eftate left to him fome Time after.

VOL. II, G circulation

circulation of the copper now current here, that has been coined under former patents.

I have sent my Lord Lieutenant, who I hope will apply to you on this occasion, a draught of such a letter as we want, as well drawn up as we could get it done here, though I do not qustion but in point of form it is very deficient, but by it will however appear, what are the things we apprehend we want to receive his Majesty's commands for, and in the Treasury it may easily be put into a right form, and any thing else added, that shall be thought necessary there. As the summer is now advancing, I think it would be of service to have such a letter dispatched soon, that we may have a quantity of the new copper coin over here, before the meeting of parliament, that it may be seen how much better it is than any that has yet been coined, and that by such letter it may appear no private person is to have any benefit by this coinage. And I am the more desirous to have the matter settled and in part executed before the parliament meets, because it will be the most effectual way to prevent any votes about a coinage in the House of Commons, where I think, and I find others that know the House very well, are of the same opinion, they are very likely, if this affair be not first fixed by such a letter, and in part put in execution, to vote an address to his Majesty for erecting a mint here, which though it may appear a very idle project in itself, yet is a very popular thing here.

I must own it would have been better if the whole copper coinage could have been over by this time ; but it is so much wanted and so much enquired after by all people in business here, that it is to be wished it may now be dispatched as soon as may be.

I should have troubled you sooner on this account, but the hurry of affairs in *England*, made me unwilling

willing to interrupt any thing of greater confe-quence.

But I hope you will be able in a little time to find leifure to caft a thought on the wants of this king-dom, and I am fure the diftrefs the trading people here are under for want of copper money is fo great, that we fhall be very much obliged to you if you will be fo kind as to give fome difpatch to the King's let-ter, without which we can make no farther advance in the affair of our copper coinage.

I am, Sir, &c.

To the Duke of Newcaftle.

My Lord,   *Dublin, June* 7, 1733.

I Thank your Grace for the honour of your's of the 19th paft. I am forry I fhould have occafion to apply to your Grace for your kind affiftance, at a time when your Lordfhip cannot well afk Major Ge-neral *Dormer* for the leave I defired, fince I make no doubt of your readinefs to comply with any requeft of mine, that may not happen to be improper.

I am, my Lord, &c.

To the Bifhop of London.

My Lord,   *Dublin, June* 21, 1733.

THE bearer is Mr. *Lafont,* who was educated in this College, where he took his mafter's degree five years ago, and was two years ago admitted *ad eundem* in *Oxford.* I am affured from very good hands, that he is a good fcholar, and one of a fober life and converfation. As he has fome relations at *London* from whom he has fome expectations, he is going to fettle there, and defigns for orders. On

G 2

this

this occasion he desired me to recommend him to your Lordship for your countenance ; which from the good character I have of him, I believe he will very well deserve.

I am, my Lord, &c.

To Sir Robert Walpole.

SIR,   *Dublin, Aug.* 25, 1733.

I Make bold to trouble you in behalf of Mr. *Ambrose Philips,* a gentleman who came over to this kingdom with me, and for whom I have not been able hitherto to make any provision. He is member of parliament for *Armagh,* and very zealously affected to his Majesty. As there is now a Collector's place vacant at *Maryburrow,* in the Queen's county, by the death of the late Collector, I would beg the favour of you to name him for the said collectorship * to his Majesty's Commissioner's here, which will be a great addition to the many favours I have already received from you. I am,

Sir, your humble servant, &c.

To the Bishop of London.

My Lord,   *Dublin, Nov.* 1, 1733.

I Heartily thank your Lordship for the effectual care you have taken of Mr. *Stephens* †, upon the death of Dr. *Burton.* He has in his letters to me expressed

---

* Mr. *Philips* was not provided for on this occasion, but his Grace made him ample amends afterwards, by giving him a considerable place in his own gift, which was that of Judge of the Prerogative Court.

† He was made a Prebendary of *Winchester.*

his

his grateful fenfe of the obligations he lies under to your Lordfhip on this occafion.

I am obliged to your Lordfhip for fending me an account of the amendments defigned in the bill about ecclefiaftical jurifdiction, and I think you was putting things upon a right foot; but I do not wonder that the officers of the fpiritual courts were againft it.

Since the opening of our parliament feveral diffenting minifters are come from the north to folicit the repeal of the teft; they are rather fanguine in their hopes of fuccefs, if the government here lay its whole weight to it. But by the beft information I can get, the fuccefs in the Houfe of Commons will be very doubtful with all the help that can be given them: and if it be brought in, whatever be the event of the bill, it will throw the whole country into very great heats.

Our feffions, as far as it has gone, has been pretty uneafy, though I hope all will end well. I have no doubt but yours will be very warm; nor will the people be fuffered to cool till the new election is over. I hear the fuccefs the applications from without doors had laft feffions will bring on petitions to the Commons about reducing the army, &c. except the prefent ftate of *Europe* prevents it. We here look upon a war as unavoidable, which may poffibly make things more quiet at home.

I am, &c.

To the Duke of Newcaftle.

My Lord,   *Dublin, Dec.* 18, 1733.

AS an affair of great confequence is juft over with us, I mean the pufh for repealing the teft in favour of the Diffenters, I thought it my duty to acquaint your Grace how that affair ftands.

When

When my Lord Lieutenant firſt came hither this time, he let the Diſſenters and others know, that he had inſtructions, if it could be done, to get the teſt repealed; and he has ſince ſpoke to all any ways dependant on the government, as well as to others, whom he could hope to influence, to diſpoſe them to concur with the deſign, and ſo have others done that have the honour to be in his Majeſty's ſervice.

But it was unanimouſly agreed, that it was not proper to bring that affair into either houſe of parliament till the ſupply was ſecured. However as the deſign could not be kept ſecret, and as the Diſſenters ſent up agents from the north to ſolicit the affair among the members of parliament, it ſoon occaſioned a great ferment both in the two houſes and out of them, and brought a greater number of members to town than is uſual. There came likewiſe many of the clergy from the ſeveral parts of the kingdom to oppoſe the deſign; and a pamphlet war was carried on for and againſt repealing the teſt, in which thoſe who wrote for it ſhewed the greateſt temper.

And thus the perſons who came to town to oppoſe it, by degrees heated one another, and viſibly gained ground, and the members of the Houſe of Commons were, by adjourned calls of the Houſe, kept in town.

There were daily reports ſpread, that the bill would be brought in ſuch or ſuch a day; and ſome in the oppoſition gave out, they would move for it, that the point might be decided one way or another: till at length, after much impatience ſhewn on the occaſion, on this day ſe'nnight, a very unuſual, and I think unparliamentary motion was made, that after the next *Friday* the Houſe would neither receive bills nor heads of bills, for repealing any part of the acts to prevent the growth of popery, in one of which the ſacramental teſt is enacted. There was ſome oppoſition made to the ſhortneſs of the time, and the next *Monday* moved for, but the warmth of the

House

House, which was a very full one, against any farther delay, and indeed against any repeal of the test, appeared so great and so general, that it was thought most prudent not to divide about that resolution.

And upon considering what then appeared to be the sense of much the greater part of the House, and what was found to be the disposition of the members by talking with them, it was concluded at a meeting at the Castle on *Wednesday* morning, and another on *Thursday* morning, where some of the agents for the Dissenters were present, to be most for the credit of the government and the peace of the kingdom, not to push for a thing which plainly appeared impracticable: and it was thought a very dangerous step to unite a majority of the House in an opposition to the intentions of the government, since it was not so certain when such an union might be dissolved.

And at a meeting of several members of the House of Commons, who were disposed to repeal the test, it was agreed that in the present state of affairs, it would be wrong to push for a thing that would certainly miscarry.

Whilst this affair has been depending, there have been great heats in the House of Commons, and a more than usual obstruction of publick business; and the House of Lords has had their share in their coming to some resolutions, though not on this subject, which would scarce have been carried or moved at another time. And I am fully of opinion that though the repeal had passed in the Commons, it would have miscarried among the Lords. But I hope now this uneasiness and handle of discontent is over, things will gradually cool, and return to their former course.

I find some of the Dissenters now say, the thing ought to have been tried sooner in the session. But, as I mentioned before, it was the opinion of his Majesty's servants that the supplies ought to be secured before any danger was run of raising heats in the

House:

House: and besides, in the method of our parliament, no bill can be carried by surprize, because though the heads of a bill may be carried on a sudden, yet there is a time for a party to be gathered against it by that time a bill can pass the council here, and be returned from *England*, when it is again to pass through both Houses for their approbation before it can pass into a law.

What has happened here will probably the less surprize your Grace, because the Archbishop of *Dublin* in *London* acquainted the ministry that he thought such a repeal could not pass here: which has been my opinion from the beginning of the session.

What representation the Dissenters here may make of this affair I cannot tell: but I believe their agents from the north had at first met with either such encouragement or such general civil answers, that they had given greater hopes of success to their friends in the country than there was just reason for. And some of them at the meeting at the Castle * last *Thursday*, were for pushing the affair at all adventures, urging that they thought they should not lose the cause very dishonourably, though upon what passed there they seemed to have little hopes of its succeeding, in which I think they looked more at their own honour than his Majesty's service. But this I am sure of, that all present in the service of the crown, were of opinion, that the push ought to be made, where there was no probability of success.

I am, &c.

To

* The Castle meant here is the King's palace in *Dublin*, where in the absence of the Lord Lieutenants the Lords Justices meet, have their levies, and do the publick business.

To the Bishop of London.

My Lord,   *Dublin, Dec.* 20, 1733.

THE affair of repealing the teft is now over with
us: whilft it was carrying on it occafioned very
great heats in the Commons: and your Lordfhip will
eafily guefs that many of the * Clergy were not wanting in their zeal to raife what oppofition they could
againft it.   I am apt to think that there were near
three to two againft it among the Commons; and the
majority was fo clear, that I queftion whether many
who were for it would not have abfented themfelves
or have voted againft it, if it had come to a divifion,
to avoid marking themfelves to no purpofe.   And I
am fully fatisfied that in the Houfe of Lords, there
would have been at leaft two to one againft it.

My Lord Lieutenant was not wanting in his endeavours to difpofe thofe in the fervice of the government, or whom he could any ways influence, to promote the repeal.   But for two days before the day
fixed in the Houfe of Commons for bringing it in, if
at all, there was a meeting at the Caftle of thofe of
diftinction in his Majefty's fervice, and at the fecond
meeting the principal agents for the Diffenters from
the north were prefent, when it was the unanimous
opinion of thofe in his Majefty's fervice, that the repeal could not be carried in the Houfe of Commons,
and that therefore no fuch bill ought to be brought
in, fince a fruitlefs attempt would be to the difhonour
of the government, and would probably bring about
fuch an union among oppofite parties as might not
                                              foon

* Dr. *Synge* Archbifhop of *Tuam,* Dr. *Swift,* Dr. *Tifdell,* and
many other Gentlemen of great Abilities wrote feveral excellent
Pamphlets on this occafion.   Befides, the Miniftry and Clergy of
England were violently againft it.

foon be diffolved. Some of the agents of the Diffen-ters there prefent, feemed fatisfied, but one or two of them were for háving the thing hazárded, infifting it would not be loft by a difhonourable majority. I hear fome among the Diffenters, efpecially among their minifters, are very angry on this occafion.

I am apt to think one reafon of it may be, that when they firft canvaffed among the members, they miftook civil anfwers for promifes, and wrote to their friends in the north with greater hopes of fuccefs than they had reafon for; and now do not care to own that they were miftaken in their calculations. Though befides I am fatisfied they were miftaken in their numbers, becaufe feveral who had promifed them at firft, upon feeing fuch a heat raifed by it, fell off.

Another reafon given by them to feveral for puſh-ing it, when it feemed defperate, was that their friends in *England* inftructed them to puſh it at all adventures.

The heat among the churchmen here will, I think be foon over; but I do not hear of much difpofition to temper among the Diffenters. It is certain their preachers are drawing up a memorial to fend over to their friends in *England* to throw the blame of the mifcarriage on my Lord Lieutenant, though unjuftly, fince he was not wanting in his endeavours to ferve the Diffenters, but really it was not at all practicable, at leaft at this time. But fome of their laity, thofe efpecially of more temper and prudence, are endea-vouring to hinder it, but with what fuccefs is not yet known.

As this is an affair of fome confequence, I thought proper to give your Lordfhip a fhort account of it.
I am,

My Lord, &c.

To the Duke of Newcaftle.

My Lord,   *Dublin, Jan.* 6, 1733.

ON New-year's day died Dr. * *Ellis,* Bifhop of
Meath. As that Bifhop by his ftation, is the
firft Bifhop in *Ireland,* and ufually a privy counfellor,
the perfon thought moft proper to fill that fee by my
Lord Lieutenant, my Lord Chancellor, the Archbifhop of *Dublin* and me, is Dr. † *Price,* the prefent
Bifhop of *Fernes* ; and the perfon moft proper to fucceed him is thought to be Dr. *Synge,* the prefent
Bifhop of *Cloyne* ; they are both firmly attached to his
Majefty, and of great fervice to the Houfe of Lords,
and I think they are both in the *Englifh* intereft : I
would therefore moft humbly recommend them to his
Majefty's favour for the faid tranflations.

As to a fucceffor to the bifhoprick of *Cloyne,* my
Lord Lieutenant looks upon it as fettled in *England*
that Dean § *Bekerley* is to be made Bifhop here the
firft occafion. I have therefore nothing to fay on that
head, but that I wifh the Dean's promotion may anfwer
the expectation of his friends in *England.* I am, .

My Lord, &c.

---

* Dr. *Welbore Ellis,* who had been chaplain to *James Butler* the
laft Duke of *Ormond.* .

† Dr *Price* had been chaplain to Mr. *Conolly,* and Dr. *Synge,*
was a fon of the Archbifhop of *Tuam.*

§ Dr. *George Berkeley,* Dean of *Derry,* author of the Minute
Philofopher, and many other learned Works, among which were
Queries relative to *Ireland,* and other ufeful Papers on that Occa-
fion, publifhed by *George Faulkner.*

To the same.

My Lord,   *Dublin, Feb.* 25, 1733.

AMONG other bills sent over for passing the privy council in *England,* is one for the relief of the creditors of *Ben. Burton* and *Francis Harrison,* &c. which I must beg leave to recommend particularly to your Grace's care, that it may return to us. The several bankers mentioned in the title of the bill, continued the same bank without interruption with great credit; but as appears at last, had drawn off unreasonable dividends, and *Ben. Burton* and *Fr. Harrison* had bought great estates, so that the bank was worth nothing at the time of *Harrison*'s death, but the succeeding banks paid off the former bank with the money of the new creditors, till at last payment was stopped. The equity of the bill is founded on the first bankers having had their debts of the bank paid with the later creditors monies; and an act 8 *Georg.* 1. by which the unsettled estate of any banker is liable at the time of his death to all the bank debts; so that when *Harrison* died his estate was liable to pay all the debts of the bank as well as *Burton*'s, since they were answerable jointly and severally. His estate is since got into the hands of strangers, from whence it could by long and expensive suits be fetched out by the 8 *Georg.* 1. but as this would be very tedious and expensive, and no little creditor could have any benefit that way, this act vests the estates of the several bankers in trustees, who are to determine all claims in a summary way, and to sell as much as will pay the debts of the several banks; but as to *Harrison* they are not to sell more than will answer the debts of the bank at the time of his death; and if by such sale he has paid more than his share of

those

those debts, it is to be made good out of the unfold eftates of the other bankers, or the remaining debts and fecurities belonging to the bank ; fince that is not an affair between the creditors and the bankers, but between the bankers themfelves to adjuft their feveral proportions.

When this bank ftopped payment laft *June*, it had very nigh overturned all our paper credit here, and if this bill mifcarries, it is not doubted but our bankers will all be blown up. And at the fame time, we have fo little fpecie here, probably at the moft not above 500,000 *l.* that without paper credit, our trade cannot be carried on, nor our rents paid.

Your Grace may have feen my name in the votes, as a petitioner for this bill, but there is little more than 200 *l.* owing to me on my own account, and I can affure your Grace that it is not any regard to my own concern in the bank, which is a mere trifle, but a regard to the publick credit of this kingdom, which is in danger of being funk if this bill fhould mifcarry, that occafions my preffing your Grace to get us this bill returned.

I am, &c.

To the fame.

My Lord,   *Dublin, Mar.* 2, 1733.

THE traders in filks and ftuffs here have been with me to defire I would write in behalf of a bill gone from hence to prohibit the wear of *Eaft India* goods in this kingdom. They affure me the filk weavers and others at *London* will folicit for the bill before the privy council, as what will be of advantage both to the *Englifh* and *Irifh* manufacturers.

I do not pretend to be a very good judge in the matter, but muft refer your Grace to what the manufacturers in *England* have undertaken to make out ;

and

and if it is probable the bill may be of service to both nations, I heartily recommend it to your Grace's countenance. I am,

My Lord, &c.

To Sir Robert Walpole.

SIR, *Dublin, Mar.* 28, 1734.

BY the last two mails are come several private letters that talk doubtfully of the success of *Burton's* * bill, and insinuate that there have been letters from great persons in *Ireland* representing that the passing it would be of great detriment to this kingdom.

That the Lord Chief Justice *Rogerson* should have written against that bill is not strange, since whatever is taken from *Harrison's* estate towards paying the debts of the bank is taken from Mr. *Creighton* who married the Lord Chief Justice's daughter; so that the Chief Justice's letter is not from an indifferent hand.

But the truth of our case, and what every man of sense here knows, is, that if this bill miscarries, it must put an end to our paper credit here, by an immediate run upon the bankers or gradual forbearing to lodge money there: and it is certain we have not cash enough in the nation to carry on our common trade or pay our rent or taxes: and I very much question whether if our paper credit fails, it would not be with the utmost difficulty that our army could be subsisted. And as this is the opinion of every body here, the miscarriage of this bill cannot but make a great disturbance in both Houses of Parliament.

It is likewise reported that the bankers bill is likely to be lost. If there is any hardship in it, it was

* For the Relief of the Creditors of *Benjamin Burton*, *Francis Harrison*, *Charles Burton*, and *Daniel Falkiner*, Esqrs, Bankers in *Dublin*, which Bill was passed into a Law.

by

by the confent of the bankers here; and all new in it is, that they cannot fettle any part of their eftate upon a marriage, &c.

There was a claufe offered in the council, that their eftates fhould be difcharged from the debts of the bank within a term of years after the death of a banker, or his giving notice that he was quitting the bufinefs: but it was thought, confidering that if this had been a law at the time of Mr. *Harrifon*'s death, the creditors of the bank would have loft about 40 *per cent.* it was there apprehended that if fuch a claufe paffed, the firft banker that died or gave notice of his defigning to quit the bufinefs, would occafion all the notes of that bank being called for, and that might bring a run on the others, fo it was not thought fafe to venture fuch a claufe.

The banker's bill will pleafe, and yet gives no fuch great fecurity to the creditors more than before; but if it is loft it may do mifchief.

I am, my Lord, &c.

To the Duke of Dorfet.

My Lord,   *Dublin, June* 4, 1734.

MR. Dean *Marfh*, Dean of *Kilmore*, died yefterday morning: his deanery is reckoned worth 300 *l. per ann.* As I have not had an opportunity of talking with the other Lords Juftices about a proper perfon to recommend to your Grace for this deanery, I fhall not mention any till we meet at the caftle next *Friday*, but only defire the favour of your Grace not to engage for any body till we can write about it.

I take this occafion to put your Grace in mind of the kind promife you was pleafed to make me of providing for Mr *Robert Moland* in the army.

I am, my Lord, &c.

To

To the same.

My Lord,   *Dublin, June* 11, 1734.

LAST week we troubled your Grace with a re-commendation of Mr. *White* to the deanery of *Kilmore* upon the requeſt of Mr. Juſtice *Gore.* As nobody elſe applied, we recommended him for the deanery, though Mr. Juſtice would have been very well ſatisfied if ſome other perſon had had the deanery, who might have left ſome other thing to provide for Mr. *White* with. I have ſince had a letter from Mr. *John Richardſon,* Dean of *Kilmacduagh,* that he would be very thankful if I could get him the deanery of *Kilmore,* which is within two or three miles of his pa-riſh of *Belturbet,* for the deanery of *Kilmacduagh.* As this would be a very advantageous change to him, and as he at preſent lies a very heavy burthen upon me, till he has ſomewhat better than the deanery of *Kilmacduagh,* which your Grace was ſo kind as to give him on my recommendation, it would be a very great obligation laid on me, if your Grace would be pleaſed to obtain the deanery of *Kilmore* for Mr. *Rich-ardſon,* and the deanery of *Kilmacduagh* for Mr. *White.*

I am, my Lord, &c.

To the same.

My Lord,   *Dublin, Aug.* 14, 1734.

I Had the honour of your Grace's with an account of your having taken care of Mr. *Moland.* I have lately been to viſit my dioceſe, or I had ſooner re-turned my thanks to your Lordſhip for obtaining his commiſſion, which is ſince arrived here ; and I do not

not queftion but he will behave himfelf well in his poft, if any occafion offers.

I thank your Grace likewife for remembering the Bifhop of *Kildare*, who has fince taken his place in council. As for the deanery of *Kilmore*, if Dr. *Witcomb* has it, or it is any ways difpofed of for his fervice, I fhall not any ways defire to break any fuch fcheme.

I muft beg leave to put your Grace in mind of my Lord *Altham*, that he may have an addition made to his penfion, fince what he has at prefent is too little for him to fubfift upon, though he were a better manager than he is. Your Grace knows he never was wanting to attend the King's fervice at the Houfe of Lords.

The Bifhop of *Derry* continues much in the fame way as formerly, only that he muft be weaker than he was. I hope as to the tranflations that may be proper, whenever it pleafes God to remove him, they continue as your Grace was pleafed to fettle them when you was here; though I find by what is faid here from good hands, there have been fome endeavours ufed to alter them, but I would flatter myfelf, without fuccefs, fince I think it cannot be done without creating a general difcontent on the bench of Bifhops. I am,

My Lord, &c.

† *To the Bifhop of* London.

My Lord,   *Dublin, Sept.* 9, 1734.

MR * *Auchmuty* has every way anfwered the good character your Lordfhip was pleafed to give of him. He has had the misfortune to be ta-

* Had been Chaplain to the army and garrifon at the ifland of *Minorca*.

ken ill, as he was spending some time among his friends in the north. It is possible this climate did not agree so well with him, after having been so long in a much warmer. I find by him Mr. *Shaw*, a * fellow of Queen's, is publishing his travels, which are likely to be curious, and that your Lordship gives the author your countenance on that occasion. I have taken some of Mr. *Shaw*'s receipts, and shall endeavour to dispose of them here, but we are very little given to promote subscriptions here, and especially for what is going on in *England*.

We are here very uneasy about the superiority of the *French* arms, and I can assure your Lordship the papists here are more than ordinarily insolent on that occasion. I have no doubt but the government are doing what is most prudent in the present situation of affairs. I am,

My Lord, &c.

To the Duke of Dorset.

My Lord,   *Dublin, Oct.* 14, 1734.

AS my Lord *Altham* is by the advice of some of his friends in *England* going thither, to solicit an addition to his pension, and as his principal hopes are in your Grace's recommending his case heartily to his Majesty, he desired me to give him a letter to your Lordship on this occasion. Your Grace may remember he was by the House of Lords recommended to his Majesty for some farther provision ; and your Grace knows he has on all occasions constantly attended at the House of Lords to carry on his Majesty's service. He has a wife and several children, and is likely to have more ; and his present pension

---

* He was afterwards King's Professor of Greek in *Oxford*, and a Head of a House there.

of

of 200*l. per ann.* is what, with the beft management muft be a very fcanty maintenance for a nobleman. I would therefore humbly beg of your Grace, that you would recommend his Lordfhip to his Majefty for fome other provifion. It ought not to be forgot, that at the death of my Lord *Anglefea,* he will be a peer of *Great-Britain,* whether he be able to fucceed to his Lordfhip's eftate or not.

I am, &c.

To the fame.

My Lord,   *Dublin, Dec.* 28, 1734.

I Was in hopes your Grace had perfected the affair of removing Enfign *Pepper* in Colonel *Hamilton's* regiment, to Lieutenant's half-pay, and bringing Mr. *Wye* into his room; but I have lately heard from the Colonel, that it is not yet done: I muft therefore renew my moft earneft requeft to your Grace that you would bring that affair about in favour of a fon of a deceafed clergyman of my diocefe, and one who it is believed by thofe who know him, will make a very good and diligent officer in his Majefty's fervice: the doing of which will be efteemed a great favour, by

My Lord, &c.

To the fame.

My Lord,   *Dublin, Jan.* 27, 1734.

INclofed I take the liberty to fend your Grace the memorial of the bearer Lieutenant *Cunningham,* in which he defires on account of his long ftanding in the army, and his conftant zeal for the Houfe of *Hanover,* to be advanced to a Captain's commiffion up-

on

on a proper occasion. I believe what he affirms of his zeal for the present family, and the dangers he ran on that account in Queen *Anne*'s time, to be true; and do make bold to recommend him to your Grace for a better commission, when your Grace shall meet with a convenient opportunity,

> I am, my Lord, &c.

To the same.

My Lord,   *Dublin, Jan.* 14, 1734

THIS morning died the Bishop of *Derry* after five or six days extreme pain and weakness.

As your Grace was pleased to settle it with my Lord Chancellor, the Archbishop of *Dublin*, and me, that in this case the Bishop of *Kilmore* should be tranflated to *Derry*, and the Bishop of *Killalla* to *Kilmore*, the Speaker is come into that recommendation in our publick letter; and the Lord Chancellor and I shall by this post write to Sir *Robert Walpole* to promote those tranflations. And I hope as there can be little more than 200 *l. per ann.* difference between those bishopricks, neither Mrs. *Clayton* nor any other person will be for removing the Bishop of * *Killalla* directly to *Derry*, which considering his years, and how few juniors he has on the bench, must certainly create great uneasiness among the other Bishops.

As to the bishoprick of *Killalla*, we have in our publick letter, named three for it, whom we all think to be well affected to his Majesty. But I cannot but

---

* This was that Dr. *Clayton* who soon afterwards removed to *Cork*, and some time after to *Clogher*, afterwards made such a noise in the world, by his *Essay on Spirit*, and who actually sickened and died upon being informed that he would certainly be attacked in the House of Lords in *Ireland* on account of that book. *London* Edition.

think

think with my Lord Chancellor and the Archbifhop of *Dublin*, that it will be very dangerous to let the majority of natives, who are already twelve on the bench, grow greater : and we cannot but be apprehenfive that as they grow ftronger there, they will grow more untractable. I have therefore by this poft wrote to Sir *Robert Walpole*, and I make it my earneft requeft to your Grace, that fome prudent *Englifh* divine of good character, may be thought of to be fent amongft us; fince we have not any *Englifhman* here at prefent of that age, prudence, and good character, as to avoid a clamour if he were made a Bifhop.

I think I am obliged to tell your Grace that the affair of Dr. *Whitcomb's* * having a royal difpenfation to hold his fellowfhip with the living of *Lowth*, begins to make a great noife here ; and fo far as I can fee, is likely to make a much greater, as hindering the fucceffion in the college, and opening a door to farther difpenfations, when they fay, as the living is probably better than 500 *l. per ann.* he has no occafion for fuch a favour.

I hope your Grace will excufe my taking this liberty to let you know what I take to be for his Majefty's fervice in the prefent juncture.

I am, my Lord, &c.

To Sir Robert Walpole.

S I R,   *Dublin, Jan.* 14, 1734.

EARLY this morning died the Bifhop of *Derry :* his death has been long expected ; fo that when the Lord Lieutenant was here, upon the tranflation of the Bifhop of *Fernes* to *Meath*, and the Bifhop of

---

* College Tutor to Lord *George Sackville*.

Cloyne

Cloyne to *Fernes*, the Lord Chancellor, and the Arch-bishop of *Dublin*, and I agreed with his Grace, that if he would come into those translations, we would very readily join with him in recommending Dr. *Hort*, Bishop of *Kilmore* to be translated to the bishoprick of *Derry*; and Dr. *Clayton*, Bishop of *Killalla* to the bishoprick of *Kilmore* : and we have accordingly this day, with the Speaker, sent such a recommendation. We have had some reports here, that a push is making at *London* to pass by the Bishop of *Kilmore*, and remove the Bishop of *Killalla* directly to *Derry*. As the Bishop of *Killalla* is very young for a Bishop, and has but four juniors on the bench, I am satisfied it will create a great uneasiness, if he should be translated to the best bishoprick in this kingdom. And as there can be but about 200 *l. per ann.* difference in the two bishopricks, I would hope Mrs. * *Clayton*, if she were talked to, would not make a push for a point that may very much distress us here.

As for those we have recommended to succeed to the bishoprick of *Killalla*, I think them all to be well affected to his Majesty's service ; but as there are already twelve of this country on the bench, I must beg leave to represent it as a thing of very great consequence, that the last in the remove should be an *Englishman*, that by degrees we may at least be an equality on the bench, for I fear if the majority increases on the other side, we shall soon find them unmanageable. I could therefore most heartily wish that a prudent person of good character were sought for in *England* to be sent over for the bishoprick of *Killalla* ; as the bishoprick is worth full 1100 *l. per ann.* it is no contemptible thing in this country. But I would at the same time beg that we may not have one sent over who may be a burthen or a disgrace

* A very favourite Lady of the Bed-Chamber to Queen *Caroline*, Consort of *George* II.

to us. You will have the goodnefs to excufe this freedom, which I take to be wholly for his Majefty's fervice. I am,

My Lord, &c.

To the Duke of Dorfet.

My Lord,   *Dublin, Jan.* 31, 1734.

AS by the death of the Lord *Santry* the government of *Londonderry* is become vacant, I cannot but take this occafion to recommend the Earl of *Cavan* to fucceed him.

Your Grace knows very well of what fervice he has been in the Houfe of Lords, and how necefſary he is to carry on his Majefty's fervice there: when he was put by the Mafterfhip of the Hofpital, your Lordfhip feemed difpofed to remember him upon Lord *Santry*'s death; and I think as it was the only government poffeffed by a Lord, it may occafion an uneafinefs among the Lords, if this poft fhould be given to a Commoner.

I find my Lord *Cavan* is willing to quit his prefent penfion of 400 *l. per ann.* from the crown, if he may have this government, and a penfion of 200 *l. per ann.* for his fon Lord *Lambert*, to enable the father to beftow a proper education on him.

I cannot but reprefent it as a thing highly for his Majefty's fervice, that his Lordfhip fhould have this government. I am,

My Lord, &c.

To the fame.

My Lord,   *Dublin, Feb.* 1, 1734.

THE bearer is Mr. *Hanfard*, Secretary to the Charter Society of Proteftant Schools in this kingdom. As there is a much greater fpirit in *Lon-*

H 4

don

don towards promoting any good and pious defign, and they are much abler to do it than we are in this country, we have fent him to *London* to promote fub-fcriptions for carrying on our good defigns, and we are the more encouraged to do fo, becaufe we find the like fociety in *Scotland* have in a few years got about 3000 *l*. in *London* for the like charity in *Scotland*. And we hope as we have the fame eftablifhed church as *England*, and are of the fame blood, we may rea-fonably expect greater affiftance than has been given to the *Scotch* fociety. And befides, we have a parti-cular claim on the noblemen and gentlemen of this country that live in *England*; who we think ought to contribute to any good defign that is carrying on in their country.

We have on this occafion directed our fecretary to wait on your Grace, to receive any commands you fhall pleafe to give him, and in hope of your Lord-fhip's countenance.

The greateft part of our fociety are for applying to his Majefty for his bounty to our corporation, as he was pleafed to give the *Scotch* fociety 2 or 3000 *l. per ann.* but I have differed from them in my fenti-ments as to applying to his Majefty at prefent, and have told them both in private and publick, my rea-fons for it, That as the nation is at prefent very much in debt, I do not know but if his Majefty fhould give us a grant of a handfome annuity, it may occafion fome clamour and uneafinefs in the Houfe of Commons; and befides that I am defirous we fhould by repeated trials, come to fuch a method of educating the chil-dren of poor papifts and others in Chriftian knowledge and honeft labour, as to be able boldly to fay, that we only want a greater fund to be able to make fo ufeful a defign more general. And I hope in two or three years we fhall make thofe experiments, and meet with that good fuccefs, as to pitch upon a fettled me-thod

thod of inftructing and ufefully employing the poor children.

But this whole affair I entirely fubmit to your Grace's better judgment. Your Lordfhip will like-wife be the beft judge whether it may be proper at this time to apply to the * Queen and the reft of the Royal Family for their bounty, or ftay till a farther feafon. And if your Grace fhall judge it proper to apply now, we muft entirely depend on your Grace's directions in what manner it is beft to be done, and on your affiftance in doing it. I am,

My Lord, &c.

To the fame.

My Lord,   *Dublin, Feb.* 20, 1734.

I Have had the honour of your Grace's of *Jan.* 23. and *Feb.* 13. I am obliged to your Lordfhip for your kind information, that there was room for accidents in *England,* in relation to the bifhoprick of *Derry,* which otherwife was likely to go as was defired from hence. But till you knew fomewhat certain, I thought there was no occafion to trouble your Grace with another letter. I hope your Grace will be fo good as to forward the removes in Colonel *Hamilton*'s regiment, as foon as there is a Secretary of War fettled.

I confefs I am very forry to hear that the publick fervice has made it neceffary to give the bifhoprick of *Derry* to Dr. *Rundle* †, becaufe your Grace cannot but

---

* *Caroline.*

† Notwithftanding what my Lord Primate mentions in this place, when he came to be perfonally acquainted with the Bifhop, he entertained the higheft efteem for him, and the good Bifhop was by no means behind his Grace in his affection towards him ·
Dr.

but be fenfible it will give a handle to fome clamour here. But to be fure our affairs muſt give way to the more weighty concerns in *England*. I hope however the new Biſhop will foon come, and fettle amongſt us.

There is a favour I have to afk of your Grace, which is that if, by procuring a refignation, I can make a vacancy in the entire rectories of *Killorglin*, *Knockane*, *Killtallogh*, *Killgarrinlander*, and the rectory of *Currens*, worth about 200 *l. per ann.* in the prefent poſſeſſion of Mr. *Elias Debuts*, in the diocefe of *Ard-fert* and *Aghede*, in the county of *Kerry*, all in the gift of the Crown, your Grace would be pleaſed to order Mr. *George Palmer* to be prefented to the faid rectories. Mr. *Palmer* is a clergyman of a very fair character in my diocefe, and was born in that neigh-bourhood, or he would hardly have the courage to think of removing into *Kerry*. The granting this re-queſt will be efteemed an obligation by him, who is,

My Lord, &c.

Dr. *Rundle*, as Mr. *Pope* fays, *had a heart*; and he fhewed it much to one of my Lord Primate's relations, when his Grace was de-ceafed, and incapable of making him any return: this good man had been moſt abominably abuſed, and my Lord of *London*, the Primate's old friend, had given too much ear to that abufe, fo that it may eafily be imagined, that his Grace was prejudiced againſt the Biſhop of *Derry* at the firſt; but my Lord Chancellor *Talbot*, who was perhaps not only the beſt, but alfo the moſt able and dif-cerning perfon of his time, could never have recommended an im-proper perfon; and it was a pity that my Lord of *London*, who certainly meant well, had not taken the Chancellor's recommen-dation in that light. Dr. *Rundle* would undoubtedly have made as good a Biſhop of *Glouceſter* as he afterwards did a Biſhop of *Derry*, where to his own honour, and to that of thofe who pro-moted him, he obtained the well merited applaufe of all good men.

To

To the fame.

My Lord,   *Dublin, Mar.* 13, 1734.

I Should have been glad if it had been thought moſt conſiſtent with his Majeſty's ſervice to have beſtowed the government of *Derry* on my Lord *Cavan,* becauſe I fear we may have ſome occaſion for his help in the Houſe of Lords, except he is made ſome way eaſy, which I hope from what your Grace is pleaſed to ſay, will not be forgot, if an opportunity offers.

I have had the honour of your Grace's letter of the 20th paſt, and had anſwered it ſooner but that I was willing to make the beſt enquiries I could relating to Dr. *Whitcomb*'s affair, before I wrote to your Lordſhip. And I muſt beg leave to acquaint your Grace, that as far as I can learn, the apprehenſion of his holding the living of *Louth* creates much uneaſineſs, as it at preſent will ſtop a ſucceſſion in the College, and may probably be uſed as a precedent for holding any the greateſt preferment with a fellowſhip for the future ; and if the diſpenſation be granted, is likely to raiſe ſo much clamour, that I cannot but think it moſt adviſeable not to interpoſe his Majeſty's authority in his favour at preſent : and I hope your Grace will have it in your power on ſome other occaſion, to make him amends for this diſappointment.

On *Tueſday* the Viſitors cited the Provoſt, Fellows, &c. to a viſitation of the College, to be held on the 20th inſtant. There have been ſuch difficulties ſtarted from the College, and ſo much liſtened to by their Vice-Chancellor, the * Biſhop of *Clogher,* that I fear the viſitation will not prove ſuch as will anſwer expectation. I have taken all opportunities of deſiring the fellows and their friends to avoid all needleſs

    * Dr. *Stern.*

           diſputes

disputes and oppositions for fear of their falling into the hands of worse Visitors next session of parliament. I hope and wish the best, but things do not promise very well.   I am,

Your Grace's, &c.

To the same.

My Lord,   *Dublin, Mar.* 14, 1734.

SINCE I wrote to your Grace yesterday, I have received a letter from Mr. *Cary*, expressing your Lordship's readiness to present Mr. *George Palmer to* the entire rectories of *Killorglin, Knockane, Killtallogh, Killgarrinlander,* and the rectory of *Currens,* now possessed by Mr. *Elias Debuts,* and in the gift of the Crown, upon Mr. *Debuts* resigning them.   I most humbly thank your Grace for this favour ; and I shall by to-morrow's post write to Mr. *Debuts* to resign them immediately : and if your Lordship please to signify your pleasure to the Lords Justices to present Mr. *George Palmer* to the said rectories, upon such resignation, I believe your Grace's order and the resignation will arrive at *Dublin* near the same time.   I am,

My Lord, &c.

To the Bishop of London.

My Lord,   *Dublin, Mar.* 20, 1734.

I Thank your Lordship for your kind and patient attendance on my Lord *Doneraile's* cause, I am glad things went so unanimously in the House.   Mr. *Horner,* whom your Lordship mentions, is since dead at *London.* I esteemed him a very good man, and had removed him from another diocese into mine.   If he had lived, your Lordship's good opinion of him would

have

have been an addition to what I had before conceived of him.

Though the prints tell us that *France* feems to come into our plan of pacification, I can hardly believe a peace fo near at hand.

I am glad to hear things go fo well in parliament in the main. There is no doubt but the committee of elections will increafe the majority : I hope as your Lordfhip does, that the ftrong oppofition which has been made, will keep people in fome reafonable bounds. It is to us here a melancholy confideration, that there feems to be fo great a difpofition to attack the moft eminent perfons in the Church, and to ftrip them all of their juft rights. *But I think the fame spirit prevails againft all governors alike, and indeed againft every thing that is ferious and orderly.*

I am glad the Diffenters are difpofed to be quiet this feffion; what may be the ftate of affairs another year, God only knows.

I find your Houfe has pretty well got through the affair of the petition of the *Scotch* Lords, only we have not yet heard what is done upon the proteft made in *Scotland.*

If your Lordfhip can find leifure, it will be very obliging if you would now and then fend an account of what paffes.

I am, &c.

To the Duke of Dorfet.

My Lord,   *Dublin, Apr.* 8, 1735.

I Thank your Grace for your orders to prefent Mr. *Palmer* to Mr. *Debuts*'s livings, upon his refignation, which I expect every day from *Limerick.* Your Lordfhip will be fo good as to excufe my putting you in mind again of *Dillon Wye*'s affair.

Mrs.

Mrs. *Humphreys* the housekeeper of the Castle and *Chappel-Izzod* has some time ago delivered in a memorial about rebuilding the gardener's house at *Chappel-Izzod*, which is so ruinous that Sir *Edward Pearce* (in whose time *Carter* the gardener applied either to have it repaired or rebuilt) and Mr. * *Dobbs* have both reported that they thought it not worth while to repair it, because there were those cracks in it, that they could not answer for its standing when repaired.

It is proposed making it a little better than it need have been, if the housekeeper did not design to live in it: but as by her patent she is to have lodgings there as well as in the Castle, it may not be thought amiss to be at a small expence more for her convenience than a meer gardener would have required.

There has been a scheme drawn of the intended building, and a calculation of the expence, which Mr. *Dobbs*'s clerk assures us will not exceed the computation, which we shall speedily transmit to your Grace: for as the expence will amount to 280*l.* we are unwilling to do any thing in it without directions from your Grace. I should not have given you the trouble of this, but that Mrs. *Humphreys* is now in *London*, as well as Mr. *Dobbs*, who has seen the house, and knows the affair, so as to be able to inform your Grace fully of the matter; and Mr. *Humphreys* is afraid Mr. *Dobbs* may leave *London* before our letter can wait upon your Grace, as we shall not meet this week: I submit the whole affair to your Grace's pleasure, and am,

My Lord, &c.

* *Arthur Dobbs*, Esq. who succeeded Sir *Edward Lovet Pearce*, Master of the King's Works, who was the Designer and Architect of that superb Structure the Parliament-House in *Dublin*.

To

To the Duke of Newcaftle.

My Lord, ·   *Dublin, Apr.* 18, 1735·

THE occafion of my troubling your Grace at prefent is, that we have this week learned that there is a bill brought into the Houfe of Commons with a fpecious title, that it is apprehended here may be of great prejudice. The title of the bill is, A bill for fecuring the title of Proteftants, &c.

On this occafion I muft beg leave to obferve to your Grace, that it muft be dangerous to give way to paffing bills originally in *England* relating to private property in *Ireland*, where the intereft of *England* and his Majefty's fervice no ways calls for it, where the legiflature are wholly unacquainted with the laws, and the reafon of enacting them. And it can hardly be fuppofed, that fuch bills are not moved for with fome private views, which the perfons concerned in promoting fuch bills know would be immediately difcovered here, but cannot eafily be gueffed at there.

And the time of bringing in this bill is the more fufpicious, as it muft needs be hurried through now towards the latter end of a feffion, before there is fufficient time, for thofe who are likely to fuffer by it here to know that any thing is going on in parliament, that may affect their property, or having time to make a proper oppofition to it. If this be often practifed it muft needs create great uncertainty in our property here, and give great and juft caufe of uneafinefs without the leaft fervice to the Crown, or benefit to *England* *.

I have fent your Grace inclofed a copy of fome particular remarks, by fome of our ableft lawyers here,

* The Primate fhews himfelf in this letter to be a true friend to *Ireland*, and to the proper diftribution of juftice to all parties.

of the particular inconveniencies that will follow from
it ; but they are what only offer themfelves at firft
view to them, having but juft received a copy of the
bill this week.

I muft beg of your Grace that if this bill be not
dropped in the Houfe of Commons, it may be effectually oppofed in the Houfe of Lords, as it will over-
turn the property of many proteftants here.' I have
heard of one this very afternoon that will be ftripped
of an eftate of 2000 *l. per ann.* if this bill paffes into
a law.

I am, &c.

To the Biſhop of London

My Lord,   *Dublin, May* 20, 1735.

I Am obliged to your Lordfhip for your late letter,
and am glad that the beft pieces againft popery,
written in King *James*'s time, are defigned to be reprinted.   I think it is much better than what was
intended here fome years ago, to reprint all that was
then publifhed.

I fhall very cheerfully promote fubfcriptions here,
into which I think the Bifhops will generally come,
and feveral of the clergy, and fome few of the College.
I think I cannot fail of getting forty or fifty fubfcriptions, but little can be done in it till the parliament
brings people to town in the winter.   We are very
much troubled with popery here, and the book cannot but be very ufeful, but we are not over-much
given to buy or to read books.

I thank your Lordfhip for the affiftance and encouragement you are pleafed to give Mr. *Hanfard,* in getting fubfcriptions for carrying on proteftant working
fchools here : I am fure we can hardly hope to get
any ground of the papifts without them.

I am

I am glad to hear from your Lordſhip that thoſe attackers of all Church eſtabliſhments, are leſs regarded than formerly. I am very ſure if the notions every day printed about liberty, can get much ground among the people of *England*, things will not continue quiet many years.

The *Perſian Traveller* is reprinted here, but I do not hear any great character of the performance, but ſcandal ſells the beſt of any thing with us, as well as in *England*.

We think that if the quarrel between *Spain* and *Portugal* goes on, *England* muſt be drawn in.

I find by yeſterday's mail that your ſeſſion is over: I heartily wiſh you may have the next ſeſſion as eaſy.

I am, my Lord, &c.

To the Duke of Newcaſtle.

My Lord,   *Dublin, Dec.* 2, 1735.

I Humbly thank your Grace for the kind compliments you were pleaſed to make me by my Lord Lieutenant: I am truly ſenſible of your favourable regard at all times to any requeſts or repreſentations I have had occaſion to make from hence, and promiſe myſelf the continuance of your protection and countenance.

It was with a great deal of pleaſure that I heard from his Grace your good diſpoſitions in favour of Mr. *Eſte* *, my chaplain: as the poor Biſhop of † *Oſſory* died here laſt *Saturday*, there is now an opening for him on the bench of Biſhops, and my Lord Lieutenant is ſo kind to him as to recommend him for ſucceſſor

---

* Mr. *Eſte* had been a Student of *Chriſt Church* in *Oxford*, and ſucceeded to the biſhoprick as then recommended.

† Dr. *Edward Tenniſon*, who died in *Dublin Nov.* 29, 1735.

to the late Biſhop.   I moſt heartily concur with the
recommendation, and do aſſure your Grace that Mr.
Eſte is one heartily well affected to his Majeſty and
his family, and who has by his behaviour here gained
a general love and eſteem.   I muſt beg your Lordſhip's kind concurrence and aſſiſtance in this recommendation, which will be owned as a new obligation
laid on,

My Lord, &c.

To the ſame.

My Lord,   *Dublin, Dec.* 27, 1735.

IN the laſt tranſmits of bills we have ſent over one
  entitled, " An act for rendering more effectual an
act to amend and explain an act to encourage the
building of houſes, and making other improvements
on Church lands, and to prevent dilapidations."

As what is enacted in this act, and thoſe referred
to in it, is wholly different from any law in *England*,
I muſt recommend it to your Grace's protection, that
it may not be thrown out by the gentlemen of the
law on your ſide, by reaſon of their not knowing the
neceſſity and uſe of it here.

By the wars in this country in 1641 and 1688,
moſt of the Biſhops palaces and the parſonage-houſes
were deſtroyed ; and as it was found that people were
unable or unwilling to rebuild them, where the whole
expence was to light on the builder, there was an act
paſſed in the 10th of King *William*, to encourage the
rebuilding of houſes, and making other improvements
on Church lands, in which the encouragement was to
divide the expence or loſs equally among three ſuc-
ceſſive incumbents, ſo that the builder or his executors
ſhould recover two thirds of his expences of his next
and immediate ſucceſſor, and that ſucceſſor one third
of

of the original expence of his immediate fucceffor, and fo the affair ftopped.

As this encouragement had not much of the defired effect, and few parfonage-houfes had been then built, farther encouragement was given by a new act paffed the 12th of *George* 1. by which the lofs was divided among four fucceffive incumbents, and the builder or his executors, &c. were to receive three-fourths of the original expence of his immediate fucceffor ; and fuch fucceffor two-fourths of his fucceffor ; and fuch fucceffor one-fourth from his fucceffor ; and there the affair ftopped.

In thus diftributing the expence this bill makes no change, but endeavours the better to fecure to the builder or his fucceffors, fuch money as they were by that act defigned to be reimburfed.   Now by the former act, the builder or other perfon entitled to a payment from the fucceffor, had no remedy but againft his immediate fucceffor, nor could that next fucceffor fue his fucceffor, except he had entirely paid his pre-deceffor ; fo that whenever the fucceffor proved infol-vent, the builder, &c. loft all the money he or his executors were not paid.   By this act the builder, &c. may come upon the fecond fucceffor for what was un-paid by the firft, fo that it do not exceed what the firft fucceffor could have demanded of him, if he had made his entire payment to the builder, &c. and if the fucceffor to the builder had paid more than he was to lofe, he is allowed likewife to fue the fecond fuc-ceffor for what he had paid more than he was to lofe. And becaufe it fometimes happens that an incumbent dies before he has received fo much of the profits of his living as may at all affift him to pay his predecef-for, this act enacts, That no incumbent fhall be deem-ed a next fucceffor for the purpofe of paying to his predeceffors, for any buildings or improvements made in virtue of thofe acts, who was not before his death or removal, entitled to a year's profits of the benefice,

but

but that the first person so entitled, shall for this purpose only, be reckoned the next successor.

There is then a clause to make the act of a piece,
that as it cannot be seen till the end of a year, who
is the next successor as to payments, it allows even in
case of the death of the builder, &c. which was not
allowed before, a year for the payment of half what
was due, and the rest to be paid the year following
in two half yearly payments.

The next clause relates to an omission that may
have been made in the Bishop's certificate settling
what was *bona fide* laid out, of an account of the clear
yearly value of the benefice on which the building or
improvement was made; and allows the time of two
years to rectify such omissions by an additional certificate, containing an account of the clear yearly value
of the benefice.

There is another clause that enacts, that though an
account of the intended building had not been given in
to the Bishop three months before it was actually begun,
yet this omission shall not invalidate any certificate;
and for the future enacts only a fortnight as necessary
to deliver in an account of the intended building.

There is another clause for security's sake, and to
cut off subterfuges for not building; which enacts,
that bishopricks that have usually gone together, shall
be reckoned but as one preferment for the purpose of
settling the two years income, beyond which no person by the 12th of *George* 1. can certify for any building or improvement on Church-lands.

As these several things were settled by the unanimous consent of the Bishops in town before the bill
was brought into the House of Lords, as necessary to
encourage the building on Church-lands, I must beg
of your Grace that the bill may be returned without
any alteration that may defeat the intention of any of
the clauses. I am,

My Lord, &c.

To

To the same.

My Lord,   *Dublin, Jun.* 20, 1735.

IN several parts of this kingdom our parishes are
very large, and run to a great length, with no proportionable breadth, so that we find it would be very
convenient to divide many parishes, and to erect new
parishes out of parts it may be of two or three parishes; and to this purpose we have an act for the
real union and division of parishes. But upon considering that bill it is found, that where a new parish
is formed out of the parts of two or three old parishes,
there can be no presentation to such new parish, till
all those old parishes become void, which may possibly be a course of many years. As this is a great
discouragement to erecting new parishes, how much
soever they may be wanted, we have sent over a bill,
entitled, An act for explaining an act for the real
union and division of parishes: which is wholly designed to enable patrons upon erecting new parishes
of pieces of old parishes, to present upon any one
piece being vacant, and to direct how such incumbent is to be inducted, &c. still saving to the survi-
ving incumbents all the rights they had during their
respective incumbencies. And as no union nor division can be made without the consent of the patrons,
and it has been found that the consent of his Majesty,
either under his sign manual or great seal, where he
is patron, is both troublesome and chargeable to get,
and till a new parish can be presented to, which cannot be till after an union already made takes place,
there is no person to be at that trouble and expence;
by this act the chief governor or governors for the
time being are impowered to consent for his Majesty,
who can be no loser by any such union or division,

I 3   because

becaufe the patronage continues where it was before, after every union or divifion.

As this will be of great fervice in this country, I beg of your Grace that you would get it returned to us. I am,

My Lord, &c.

To the fame.

My Lord, *Dublin, Feb.* 9, 1735.

THE bearer is the Rev. Mr. *Cox* *, one of a very good family here, and of a good character. The occafion of his going to *England* now is, the apprehenfion he is under of the attainder of the late Lord *Clancarty* being reverfed. He is in poffeffion of about 400 *l. per ann.* bought by his father from the Hollow - Sword - Blade Company, who had bought great eftates here of the *Irifh* truftees, which they afterwards fold, and obtained a particular act in *England* to fecure the titles of thofe who purchafed under them ; fo that his title is under the faith of two *Englifh* acts of parliament, the *Irifh* truftee act, and the act obtained by the Hollow-Sword-Blade Company.

But the purchafers under either or both acts are very much alarmed here at the talk of the Lord *Clancarty*'s attainder being reverfed ; fince they do not know how far it may affect their titles, who are thought to poffefs amongft them to the value of 60,000 *l. per ann.* as they have improved their eftates. Nor are they the only people alarmed here, but all that are the purchafers of forfeited eftates, apprehend that if one attainder is reverfed, other forfeiting families may from time to time, obtain the like favour,

---

* The prefent Archbifhop of *Cafbel*, formerly of *Chrift Church, Oxford.*

which

which may affect above half the eftates now enjoyed by proteftants. The Houfe of Commons have made an addrefs on this occafion to his Majefty, and the like about two feffions ago was made by the Houfe of Lords, which they did not repeat now, becaufe his Majefty then gave them a very gracious anfwer, and nothing has been fince done of that nature.

I can affure your Lordfhip any thing of this nature will be a great blow to the proteftant intereft here, and will very much fhake the fecurity proteftants think they now have of the enjoyment of their eftates under his Majefty and his Royal family. As for either the general cafe, or his cafe in particular, Mr. *Cox* will be able fully to inform your Lordfhip ; and I think the affair of the laft importance to the proteftant intereft here, which makes me take the liberty to lay the cafe before you.

I am, &c.

To the Bifhop of London.

My Lord,   *Dublin, Feb.* 9, 1735.

THE bearer is the Rev. Mr. *Cox*, one of a very good family here, and of a fair character. He goes over to *England* to oppofe the reverfing of the Lord *Clancarty*'s attainder, if any fuch thing fhould be attempted this feffion : he is in poffeffion of 400 *l. per ann.* part of the *Clancarty* eftate, which his father bought under the faith of two *Englifh* acts of parliament, the *Irifh* truftee act, and a particular act obtained by the Hollow-Sword-Blade Company, who had bought great eftates here of the truftees, to make good the titles of thofe who purchafed under them. He will be beft able to give your Lordfhip an account of thefe feveral acts. But as not only he, but great numbers of proteftant purchafers, who have improved the *Clancarty* eftate to near 60,000 *l. per ann.* think

I 4   they

they may be affected by such a reversal, I need not tell your Lordship what a ferment the discourse of it has occasioned in those parts where the estate lies. But I must farther add, that as probably two-thirds of the estates of protestants here were popish forfeitures originally, the uneasiness is universal ; since they think if the attainder of any family be reversed now, another family may at another time obtain the same favour, and another at another season, so that no possessor of such forfeited estate can tell how long he or his may continue in the quiet enjoyment of what they have bought under the faith of *English* acts of parliament, and on the improvement of which they have laid out their substance.   The House of Commons here have represented their sense of this matter to his Majesty, as the House of Lords did two or three sessions ago, to which they then received a most gracious answer, which was the reason they did not address now.

As a step of this nature would give great uneasiness to his Majesty's protestant subjects here, I desire your Lordship would, where you shall judge it proper, represent the importance of the case.

I have wrote a letter on this subject to his Grace the Duke of *Newcastle*, and sent it by the same hand.

I am, my Lord, &c.

To the same.

My Lord,   *Dublin, May* 18, 1736.

THE clergy here have been attacked in a violent manner, in relation to tythe of agistment, and associations over a great part of *Ireland* have been entered into against paying it.   We intended to have applied to your Lordship and our other friends in
England

England for proper help on this occasion ; but to our great surprise, we find the clergy of *England*, and the Bishops in particular, in a worse state than we are yet come to. I am sorry they have been so ill supported by those from whom they might so justly expect help, and whose interest it was to have given it them.

But I cannot help thinking that one great occasion of this rancour against the clergy, is the growth of atheism, profaneness, and immorality. God in his good time put a stop to it.

I see very little more to be done by us, than endeavouring to discharge our several duties consistently, and recommending ourselves and the cause of religion, to the divine protection.

I am sorry to hear your Lordship has had so great a share in what abuses have passed on the Bishops. I have, I think, disposed of most of the receipts your Lordship sent me for the subscriptions, and received most of the money : as soon as I can settle those accounts with one or two that have undertaken to dispose of some of the receipts, I will send your Lordship an account of it, with the persons who are to be called on for the second payment, and shall be ready to pay the money received.

I am, my Lord, &c.

P. S. My Lord Lieutenant embarked yesterday for *England.*

To Sir Robert Walpole.

SIR,   *Dublin, May* 25, 1736.

MY Lord Lieutenant takes over with him an application from the government and council here for lowering the gold made current here, by proclamation, and raising the foreign silver.

My

My Lord *Carteret* has formerly talked with you about the diftrefs we were then under for want of filver, and fome fteps were then taken to lay that evil and the remedy before his Majefty ; but the oppofition then made by the bankers, and the change of the Lord Lieutenant, was the occafion of the defign dropping at that time. But as the evil has fince increafed, and has been by fome of the beft underftanding and moft difinterefted perfons fully laid before my Lord Duke of *Dorfet*, he has been fo kind as to join with the privy council here, in a reprefentation of our deplorable cafe for want of filver, and what we apprehend to be the proper remedies for our prefent calamity.

It is certain that filver is fo fcarce with us, that the loweft price ufually paid for 20 s. in filver, is 4 d. premium ; but it is more commonly in the north (which is the feat of our linen manufacture) 6 d. and 7 d. in the pound. And the occafion of this want of filver is, that our feveral fpecies of gold made current here by proclamation, pafs for more filver here than they do in *England*, *e. g.* a guinea paffes here where an *Englifh* fhilling goes for 13 d. at 23 s. *Irifh*, or 21 s. *Englifh* and 3 d.

A moidore, which is worth about 27 s. in *England*, paffes here for 30 s. *Irifh*, or 27 s. *Englifh*, and 9 d. and the reft of our gold is in the main in proportion to the value of the moidore. And whilft this is our cafe, no man in trade will carry a moidore from hence, to inftance in one piece of gold, if he can get filver, when he lofes 9 d. by the moidore as foon as he lands at *Chefter* ; nor will he bring from *Chefter* 27 s. *Englifh*, when he can gain 9 d. by bringing a moidore.

And to exprefs this in greater numbers ; if a merchant brings with him 100 l. from *London* ; if he brings it over in *Englifh* filver, that will be 108 l. 6 s. 8 d. here, which arifes from the fhilling paffing here

for

for 13 *d.* but ftill that is the fame money under another name : if he brings it in guineas, he will put them off at 109 *l.* 10 *s.* 4 *d.* *Irifh,* if in moidores or other *Portugal* gold, he will put it off at 111 *l.* 2 *s.* 2 *d.* So that by bringing over what is only 100 *l.* in *England,* in guineas he will gain 1 *l.* 3 *s.* 8 d. and by bringing it over in moidores, &c. he will gain 2 *l.* 15 *s.* 6 d. and on the contrary by taking over guineas to pay 100 *l.* *Englifh* on the other fide of the water, he will lofe 1 *l.* 3 *s.* 8 *d.* and by taking over moidores, &c. to pay 100 *l.* there, he will lofe 2 *l.* 15 *s.* 6 *d:* And as the merchant in all his importations and exportations will mind his gain, the effect of this is, that no trader will take gold out of his country if he can help it, but filver ; nor moidores, &c. if he can get guineas.

So that in our prefent ftate our filver daily decreafes, and the gold grows upon us. And the diftrefs the want of filver muft occafion to our manufacturers, labourers, fmall retailers, and all the leffer tranfactions of trade and bufinefs, I need not expatiate upon.

But this is not our only calamity, but unfortunately the value of the new fpecies of *Portugal* gold has been fo fettled here, that there is 2 *d.* profit in bringing over a 4 *l.* piece, as we call the larger pieces of *Portugal* gold, rather than two 40 *s.* pieces ; and 2 *d.* profit in bringing our a 40 *s.* piece, rather than two 20 *s.* pieces ; and fo on with refpect of the filver pieces of that fpecies ; befides which, as the leaft want of weight in the foreign pieces of gold, or even their not turning the fcale, carries an abatement of 2 *d.* a piece, there may be a lofs of 2 *d.* on every leffer piece on that account, and confequently fo much greater as the number of fmaller pieces is to make up a greater of the fame value, *e. g.* upon eight, 10 *s.* pieces, there may be a lofs of eight 2 *d.* if the 4 *l.* pieces do not turn the fcale : fo that

it

it is to the profit of the merchant to import the larger
pieces of gold rather than the smaller ; and they have
gone on in using this advantage, till half the money
we have at least is in 4 *l.* pieces, which are of no
service at the market, and in all lesser transactions of
trade ; and the next species with us is the 40 *s.* piece ;
and to be sure above three quarters of our money is
in those two species, and without some remedy we
shall in two or three years have scarce any money
but 4 *l.* pieces.

And there is another inconvenience that follows
from our scarcity of silver, that we suffer from 2 to
2 ½ *per cent.* in the exchange, and are really paid so
much less in the price of what we sell to foreign merchants, and lose so much in paying for what goods
we buy from abroad.

And it is certain that all the noblemen and gentlemen of this country, who live in *England*, lose from
2 to 2 ½ *per cent.* in the remittances of their money
to *England*, which is used as a popular argument
against the proposed reduction, that the absentees
will get so much *per cent.* by it ; whilst they will
not consider that the nation at present loses five times
as much in the export and import of goods, and the
absentees will gain by this reduction of the exchange.

Now the remedy we propose in our representation
to his Majesty, is a very easy and obvious one, that
we may have leave to reduce our gold, to go for as
much *English* silver as it is worth, in proportion to
the guinea going for 21 *s. English* ; and accordingly
we have calculated what we reckon the several
species of gold ought to go for, according to their
weight and fineness, in *Irish* money valuing an *English* shilling at 13 *d. Irish* ; and to get rid as much as
we can of the larger pieces of foreign gold, we have
set the lesser pieces about a penny a piece above their
value in respect of the larger piece above them. And
this

this reduction of the gold is the more reasonable, because gold has in effect reduced itself the 6 *d*. in the pound we propose in our scheme, since 6 *d*. is about the middle price that is paid to get 20 *s*. in silver.

There is no doubt but it would be absolutely right when we are reducing, to reduce the *English* shilling to 12 *d*. which it went for here before the recoining of the silver in King *William*'s time ; but as the shilling is in effect the measure of all payments, and as the *English* shilling has gone so long for 13 *d*. we think that cannot be done without an act of parliament to settle an answerable reduction in the rents and debts.

Our bankers and remitters here continue to make great opposition to this reduction, since our present inequality of gold and silver is an article of great profit to those through whose hands all the money of this nation passes ; and we make no doubt but they will, by their partners and correspondents in *England*, make what opposition they can to the scheme proposed by the council, and we apprehend they may think it worth their while to advance money, if they can find persons to take it among the number thro' whose hands this affair must pass, to obstruct it ; and that many merchants who deal in *Ireland* will join with them, to keep up the advantage they have by the exchange being always from 2 to 2½ *per cent*. against us.

But as we are almost on the brink of ruin, by the present unhappy state of our money, and as by the farther want of silver, and the increase of our larger pieces of gold, our linen manufacture must soon decay, and our inland trade be at a stand ; I most earnestly beg of you to give us your utmost assistance on this occasion to have our gold reduced, and put us in a possibility of carrying on our trade and manufactures, by having a tolerable proportion of silver, without which we must soon be a ruined nation.

I have

I have now explained our reasons and views in the scheme we proposed for reducing gold, but if we have been any ways mistaken in our calculations, those errors will be easily corrected by the abler hands this affair must pass through in *England*.

In relation to the other branch of our scheme, about raising the price of foreign silver, I believe there will be great room for amendment. It was a scheme more come into to gratify the bankers and merchant re-mitters, who clamoured for it, and by what I can learn, they have misinformed us about the price of foreign bullion,which they affirmed to be 5 *s.* 4 ½ *d.* *English per* ounce; whereas I have been since told it has not been above 5 *s.* 3 *d. per* ounce for two years past ; but this will be before those who know how the fact is.

The great thing we want is, the reduction of our gold, which I beg we may obtain leave to do by your powerful intervention.

The importance of the affair to this nation, and your goodness, will I hope, excuse the length of this letter *. I am,

My Lord, &c.

To Lord Anglesea.

My Lord, *Dublin, May* 27, 1736.

THE knowledge your Lordship has of the want of silver in this country for some years, the causes of it, and the attempts made to remedy the evil

---

* This letter in some time produced the desired effect, which was looked upon by the Lord Primate and his friends, as the most useful, and therefore the most important transaction of his life. It is scarce conceiveable, considering the clearness of the case, what a bitter opposition was made by Dean *Swift* and others ; and how

poorly

evil in my Lord *Carteret*'s time, your Lordfhip is fo well acquainted with, that I need not repeat them; all that I need inform your Lordfhip of is, that the evil has gone increafing as it could not but do, but with one unhappy circumftance that was not apprehended when I talked with your Lordfhip on that fubject, which is, that one half of our money here at leaft, is in 4 *l*. pieces, fome think three quarters; but by the beft accounts I think there can be little lefs than three quarters in them and 40 *s*. pieces, fo that the bulk of our money is ufelefs at markets, and for paying all the manufacturers; 4 *d*. is the loweft price that is paid for 20 *s*. filver, and very often 2 *s*. 8 *d*. and 2 *s*. 10 *d*. is given for changing a 4 *l*. piece into all filver.

The occafion of our money running into the larger pieces is, that as the not turning the fcale lofes 2 *d*. in the piece, that lofs is but fingle upon a larger, but is repeated in the number of leffer pieces that make up the fame value, *e. g*. it can be but 2 *d*. on 4 *l*. but it may be 8 *d*. on four 20 *s*. and 16 *d*. on eight 10 *s*. pieces. We have leffened this lofs in our fcheme by propofing to make ufe of the half quarter, and allowing 1 *d*. for that, fo that where the lofs ufed to be 2 *d*. for not turning the fcale, it will be but 1 *d*. for the future.

And befides, our new fpecies of *Portugal* gold has been fo unhappily fettled, that there is 2 *d*. profit by bringing over a 4 *l*. piece, rather than two 40 *s*. pieces, and fo on in that line; fo that if fome remedy be not applied, in two or three years more we fhall fcarce have any fpecies but 40 *s*. pieces.

poorly the Primate was affifted, nay he was even oppofed by fome who ought to have been his fupporters from reafon, from intereft, and from the duty they owed to their country, and to government. *London* edition.

This

This has been so effectually represented to my Lord Lieutenant, that he has joined with the council in a representation to his Majesty of our calamity, and the remedy we desire to be applied to it : which is setting the foreign gold at the proportional value that the guinea has to the shilling in *England*, agreeably to the scheme formerly intended in the council, only that to obviate an inconvenience not observed before, we propose giving about a penny advantage to every lower piece of gold, in respect to the piece immediately above it.

The bankers and remitters have raised the same clamour as formerly against it, and the most popular plea against it is, that this reduction of the gold will fall the exchange at least 2 *per cent.* which will turn to the advantage of the absentees. I have endeavoured to satisfy them that if the absentees get 2 *per cent.* by this reduction, the nation will get 2 *per cent.* in all their exports and imports, which will be four or five times as much as the absentees will gain by this reduction : but all arguments are nothing against the prepossessions of the bankers.

As I know your Lordship's concern for the good of this kingdom, and your sense of our distress and the proper remedy, I thought proper to acquaint your Lordship in what posture this affair stands, that as we have got the matter on the other side of the water, whither I could never get it before, your Lordship may be pleased to solicit our having orders for issuing a proclamation to reduce gold, &c. I am but little solicitous about the raising of foreign silver, and am rather apprehensive of the bankers having misrepresented things to us, in affirming silver bullion sells usually at 5 s. 4 ½ d. *English* ; whereas several tell me it has not for two years past sold for 5 s. 3 d. And if silver bullion is over-rated here, the bankers will in time carry our gold out, and we shall be over-run with foreign silver ; but that will be be a much lefs evil than what we labour under at prefent; but what has been the price of filver bullion in *England* for fome time can eafily be known there. I take the liberty to recommend this affair of our coin to your Lordfhip, as of the utmoft confequence to this kingdom.

I am, my Lord, &c.

To the Duke of Newcaftle.

My Lord,   *Dublin, May* 31, 1736.

HIS Grace the Lord Lieutenant has taken over with him a reprefentation to his Majefty from the government and privy council here, giving an account of the deplorable condition we of this kingdom are in through the want of filver, and the method we apprehend will relieve us; which is, the lowering of gold to pafs here for what it is worth in *England*, at the rate of 21 *s. Englifh*, or 1 *l.* 2 *s.* 9 *d. Irifh*, where a fhilling paffes for 13 *d.* for as gold is over-rated with us at prefent, whoever brings over foreign gold hither, gets 2½ *per cent.* and whoever carries out gold from hence, lofes 2¼ *per cent.* and whilft this is our cafe, we muft every day grow worfe: and indeed by fome particular advantages attending the 4 *l.* pieces of *Portugal* gold, above half our money is run into thofe pieces, and in a little time we fhall hardly have any other money. If we continue in this cafe, our linen manufacture muft decline, and our inland trade every day fink.

It already cofts from 4 *d.* to 8 *d.* or 9 *d.* in the pound to get filver, fo that what we defire to reduce gold to by proclamation, is in reality already done.

I fhall not run through the particulars, becaufe they are fufficiently explained in our memorial; and

VOL. II.   K   the

the remedies. But I muſt beg your Grace to help us to have orders for the proclamation, or we muſt be a ruined people ſoon.   I am,

My Lord, &c.

To the Duke of Dorſet.

My Lord,   *Dublin, June* 1, 1736.

I Thought it my duty to acquaint your Lordſhip that it is ſuppoſed Mr. *Harriſon* the commiſſioner is paſt recovery : how far it may be proper, if he dies, to ſend over ſome *Engliſhman* that underſtands buſineſs, and has ſpirit enough not to be too much over-awed here, I leave to your Grace's conſideration.

I am, my Lord, &c.

To Sir Robert Walpole.

Sir,   *Dublin, June* 4, 1736.

I Take the liberty on occaſion of the death of Mr. *Harriſon,* to repreſent to you the abſolute neceſſity there is, if a ſucceſſor to him be ſent from *England,* to ſend one that has a good ſkill in the affairs of the revenue, and that is a man of application and courage ; the more weight he is of in himſelf the better.

If one be appointed to ſucceed him that fails either in ſkill or diligence, the revenue, which is at preſent rather in a declining condition, will moſt certainly fall ſtill more, and this will draw on a deficiency in the proviſion made for the eſtabliſhment here : and increaſe our debts, which cannot but make every following ſeſſion of parliament more uneaſy.

You

You will be fo good as to forgive the freedom I take.   I am,

Sir, your humble fervant, &c.

To the Duke of Dorfet.

My Lord,   *Dublin, June* 4, 1736.

I Am very glad to hear of your Grace's fafe arrival at *London*, but could have wifhed his Majefty had ftaid a little longer, that the affair of our coin might have been put in fome method before his departure ; but I hope the fame thing may be done under her Majefty.   My Lord *Granard* gives me great hopes from the difcourfe he had with fome of the great men, that if the affair be pufhed it will certainly be granted.   I am afraid the bankers have over-reached us in the value of foreign filver : I fhall trouble your Grace with a particular letter on that fubject before I go on my vifitation, which will be in about ten days.

Mr. Harrifon died yefterday, and the only perfon that has applied to us to fucceed him is Dr. * *Trotter*, whom I think the fitteft man in this kingdom for that poft ; but as I take it for granted fome perfon will be fent from *England* for that employment, I beg your Grace would be pleafed to reprefent the neceffity that the perfon they fend be one well verfed in the bufinefs, and a man of probity, courage, and application : if they fend us a weak or indolent man, the revenue here will certainly fall, and your Lordfhip knows better than any body the trouble a Lord Lieutenant has with a parliament upon the increafe of our debts.

I am, my Lord, &c.

* *Thomas Trotter*, Efq; a Civilian, Vicar-General of the Diocefe of *Dublin*, and a Member of Parliament.

To

To the *Duke* of Dorset.

My Lord,   *Dublin, Jan.* 10, 1736.

BEFORE your Grace left this kingdom, I acquainted your Lordſhip that I feared the bankers
had miſinformed the council about what was the middle price of bullion in *England*, which they affirmed
was 5 s. 4 ½ d. *Engliſh per* ounce ; but I am ſince aſſured that for two or three years paſt, it has hardly
reached 5 s. 2 ½ d. *per* ounce ; and if this be the caſe,
I muſt beg leave to deſire that the reduction of the
gold may go on without any alteration of the preſent
proclamation price of foreign ſilver, or that at the
higheſt it may not be ſet higher than at 5 s. 2 ½ d. *per*
ounce, or 5 s. 3 d. *Engliſh* at moſt.

To ſtate this matter in a tolerable light, I muſt obſerve, that the reaſon of thinking at all of raiſing the
price of foreign ſilver was, that by ſetting it at a price
that might make it worth while to utter it as money
here, we might have ſome of it as it was brought in,
circulate here as money ; whereas whilſt the proclamation price is leſs than the bullion price, it will ſtill
be carried into *England* or *Holland* as a commodity :
and if 5 s. 4 ½ d. were that price, though it was ſome-
times as low as 5 s. 3 d. yet if at other times it ſold
for 5 s. 6 d. there was no fear of our being over-run
by it, for though it might be imported here at 5 s. 4 ½ d.
Engliſh as long as it bore a leſs price at other markets,
yet when the price came to 5 s. 5 d. or more, our
bankers would pick it up, and ſend it where it bore
a better price than that given by proclamation.

But if things are ſo altered that in *England* it ſel-
dom is above 5 s. 2 ½ d. and or at moſt 5 s. 3 d. *Engliſh*
per ounce, there will always be a gain of three half-
pence for carrying it to *England*, and often 2 d. *per*
ounce : the effect of which will be that the bankers
will

will change all our gold when reduced into foreign silver ; for in that cafe by buying up foreign silver at 5 s. 3 d. with gold from hence they will gain 2 l. 7 s. and near 2 d. *per cent.* If they can buy it at 5 s. 2 ¼ d. they will make 3 l. 4 s. *per cent.* profit, and this is gain enough to carry out all our gold, and furnish us with only foreign silver. This evil indeed will not be fo detrimental to our trade and all the leffer tranfactions of life, as our prefent cafe is, but is an inconvenience worth our guarding againft.

Your Grace knows the original intention here was only lowering the gold, but that as fome of their petitions againft that preffed for raifing foreign filver, it was thought it could do no hurt to gratify them in that point, if it was fet at the middle market price in *England* ; but in that the merchants here have deceived us, reprefenting it at 5 s. 4 ½ d. *Englifh*, when it is really but 5 s. 3 d. at higheft.

I have with this fent your Grace two calculations of the feveral pieces of filver mentioned in the memorial fent by the council ; one upon the bottom of an ounce of filver paffing for 5 s. 2 ½ d. *Englifh*, or 5 s. 7 d. 708. *Irifh* ; the other at 5 s. 3 d. *Englifh*, or 5 s. 8 ¼ d. *Irifh.*

In the memorial the *Maximilian, Leopold, Holland, Bear, Crofs, Danifh* and *Lion* dollar, are left at the old proclamation price, becaufe as they are below ftandard, they are more liable to be counterfeited, and therefore the council did not like to give any encouragement to their importation.

If any thing is done about raifing the price of foreign filver. I would hope it may not be fet above 5 s. 3 d *Englifh*, at the higheft ; but I think it would be better if it were left at the prefent proclamation price : but if we are not permitted to reduce our gold, we fhall foon have none but great pieces of gold, which are entirely ufelefs in all leffer commerce.

I am, your Grace's, &c.

K 3

To

To the same.

My Lord,   *Dublin, July* 31, 1736.

I Have been often thinking that Mr. *Gardiner* would be a very useful person in the privy council here, but I questioned whether any in his station had ever been of that body; but as I now understand that Sir * *William Robinson,* who was in the same station, was at the same time a privy councellor, that difficulty is removed: and as we now hardly know when the government is secure of a question, I apprehend it would be for his Majesty's service, if he were made a privy councellor. As Mr. *Tighe* is dead, this would not increase the number of the council, and I think he stands upon a bottom that few others could plead for being admitted to the council. But I submit all to your Grace's better consideration, and am,

My Lord, &c.

To the same.

My Lord,   *Dublin, Aug.* 3, 1736.

I Am very glad to hear from your Grace that our affair of reducing the gold is likely to go on, which I hope will be done very speedily, since Sir *Robert Walpole,* according to the prints, is returned to *London,* and that the affair of the rate foreign silver ought to be set at, will at the same time be taken into consideration. I understand by my wife's † brother, who has been here to see me, that for six or seven

---

* Deputy Vice-Treasurer.
† Mr. *Savage,* an eminent Merchant in *London.*

years

years foreign filver has feldom rifen to 5 s. 3 d. per ounce in *London*.

I muft beg of your Lordfhip to prefs this affair to the utmoft : at the fame time I muft likewife beg of your Grace to give Mr. *Gardiner* leave to go on with the copper coinage, which wants no reference, and only a compliment to be made to her * Majefty for leave to go on with what has been already granted. I can affure your Lordfhip the diftrefs in the north for want of filver and copper, is inconceivable, people for want of better fmall money, taking pieces of copper not worth a half-penny, and promiffory notes on cards for 3 d. or 4 d. that are iffued to the value of fome hundred pounds, by perfons worth nothing, and that will certainly run away when they are called upon to change them.

Sir *Marmaduke Wyvil* † brought me a recommendation from your Grace, on which account I will fhew him all the refpect I can.

Since we wrote to your Lordfhip about the death of Mr. *Vefey*, my Lord *Cavan* has wrote to the Lords Juftices fingly about fucceeding to the Hofpital, and is willing to quit his penfion of 400 l. *per ann.* for it, which will be a faving to the nation. I have nothing new to add to what I formerly wrote to your Grace on the like occafion.

Colonel *Tichbourn* has likewife defired the fame poft, by which the government of *Charlemont* fort would be vacant. I am,

My Lord, &c.

* Queen *Caroline*. Confort of *George* II.
† Deputy Poft-Mafter General in *Ireland*.

To

To the same.

My Lord,   *Dublin, Aug.* 28, 1736.

I Have had the honour of your Grace's of the 15th inftant, and am glad to hear our reprefentation is gone to the Treafury, though at prefent it cannot be hoped it can be very much expedited; but I would beg of your Grace to direct Mr. * *Cary* to forward it as much as may be.

As Mr. *Gardiner* has your Grace's leave to proceed in the affair of the copper, I believe he will make what difpatch he can, for our want of it is very great. As to his being admitted of the privy council, I am glad your Grace thinks the fame of his ufefulnefs there as I do, and I hope your Lordfhip will find a way to let him in, and yet keep the door fhut againft the numbers that have afked for that favour; and in that view I muft acquaint your Grace, that by the deaths of Mr. † *Parry,* Mr. § *Tighe* and Sir ‖ *T. Taylour,* who were always at hand to make a number at the council, we are now hardly able to get a council, efpecially when the Chief Judges are on their circuits, fo that there will be a neceffity of making two or three privy councellors that always live at *Dublin.*

I am fenfible of your Grace's conftant regard to the low circumftances of this kingdom, and do not doubt but what additions are ordered to the powder magazine, were thought neceffary upon advifing with the

---

* Secretary to the Duke of *Dorfet,* then Lord Lieutenant of *Ireland.*
  † Publick Regifter of deeds and wills. He was a *Welfhman.*
  § Right Honourable *Richard Tighe.*
  ‖ Sir *Thomas Taylour,* Bart.

proper

proper officers.   And as for any thoughts of a citadel, the barrack with the regiments quartered there, without any offence or grumbling, is another sort of a citadel than this can ever be reprefented to be.   I hope I fhall manage it fo, as that your Grace may hear no more of that affair.

I am, my Lord, &c.

To the Duke of Newcaftle.

My Lord,   *Dublin, Sep.* 28, 1736.

MR. *Dillon* has brought me the favour of your Grace's.   I am glad to hear he has behaved himfelf fo much to the fatisfaction of all who knew him in *England*; and doubt not but his behaviour here will be anfwerable: and as your Lordfhip is pleafed to recommend him, I fhall moft readily favour him with my good offices on all proper occafions.   I am with the greateft truth and refpect,

My Lord, &c.

To the Duke of Dorfet.

My Lord,   *Dublin, Nov.* 11, 1736.

SINCE I had the honour of your Grace's laft commands, the building of the magazine has not been ftopped for want of money.   But of late one of the arches has fallen in, which they are endeavouring, as I hear, to repair, fo that what was intended to be finifhed againft the winter, will yet take up fome time.

I muft again renew my requeft that the affair of our coin may be forwarded as much as poffible, that it may be over before his Majefty's return, when greater

affairs

affairs will call for the attendance of the miniſtry and council. I underſtand our repreſentation is referred to the officers of the mint, and that they have a co-py of the letter I troubled your Lordſhip with on that ſubjeċt, but that Mr. *Conduit* is doubtful whether they can take any notice of it, becauſe it is not re-ferred to them. I rather think that in their report no particular notice need be taken of it ; but if they will have ſuch regard as they ſhall think proper to what is there ſuggeſted, it is all that can be deſired, ſince it may be taken very ill here, if the report of the officers of the mint, which has uſually been ſent hither with his Majeſty's commands on ſuch occa-ſions, it ſhall appear that a particular member of the council made a different repreſentation from that of the board, though it ſhould be founded on our hav-ing been deceived in our former accounts of the va-lue of ſilver buḷlion.

Every thing here is very quiet, but the Lords Juſ-tices have a troubleſome buſineſs to come on, that of appointing ſheriffs. I am,

My Lord, &c.

To Mr. Walter Cary.

S i r, *Dublin, Nov.* 11, 1736.

I AM very glad to hear our copper coin is at laſt ſet a going, but at the ſame time I find it is likely to proceed ſo ſlowly, that it will drive us to great extremities in the mean time, as the currency of all raps, if not of other true half-pence will be ſtopped by it. To prevent the latter, we have in-deed orders to order the taking the old patent half-pence in the revenue ; which I think will keep them current, and accordingly as ſoon as the new half-pence are upon arriving, we ſhall give orders accord-ingly.

ingly. But ftill, if the copper company could fupply a greater quantity than one tun *per* week, and the mint could coin them, it would be better for us. I fhall write to Mr. *Bowes* about the former, and if the company can perform their part, I muft defire you to prevail on the mint to do theirs. I could heartily wifh that 50 tuns at leaft were coined fome time before the parliament met, if a fecond fifty were not then going on, though I fhould be more glad of the latter: and indeed I am fully fatisfied, that lefs than 150 or 200 tuns will not make things eafy here, and that it is of great confequence to have them with all poffible difpatch.

The Sollicitor-general gave me a copy of a letter from Mr. *Conduit*, relating to our gold and filver coins; on which I would beg leave to make the following remarks.

1. If there be no objection to that part which relates to the reduction of gold, I wifh they would report that clearly.

2. As to my letter, I do not apprehend there is any occafion to take notice of it in their report, and it is only to put them in mind that we in our reprefentation went upon a fuppofition that filver bore fuch a price, which afterwards I learned was greater than it really bore; and indeed in our reprefentation, we mention that we fuppofe filver to bear fuch a rate, but at the mint they could not but know it was the true middle price of it.

3. That though 5 *s*. 4½ *d*. may be the middle price of filver in bars, yet if foreign filver coin has for fome years fold but for 5 *s*. 2 *d*. to 5 *s*. 3 *d*. *per* ounce, that ought to regulate the price intended to be given to the value of foreign coins here, becaufe it is their value, and not that of filver in bars which is to be fettled.

4. That the fettling fuch a price on old pieces of eight, and another on new, will produce confufion here,

here, where the ordinary people will not foon learn the difference betwixt the one and the other.

5. That I am fenfible the value of the *Mexico* piece and the *French* crown in the old proclamations, is lefs than they will fell for as a commodity, that value having been fixed by the advice, as I have reafon to believe, of the bankers, on the bottom of the *Englifh* filver coin, at the rate of 5s. 2d. *Englifh* per ounce, the effect of which has been, that by getting the gold raifed, they are all carried out of the kingdom.

6. As to the weight of the *Mexico, Seville,* and *Pillar* pieces of eight, and of the *Portugal* gold, we have fet them at the weight the generality of thofe had that came amongft us; and as the weight of thofe pieces both of filver and gold is reckoned higher in *England* than we have fixed them at in our proclamations, it is plain we have fet each piece at a higher value than it bears in *England.*

7. In diftinguifhing the *Pillar* and *Peru* pieces of eight, we follow the former proclamations.

8. As to the *Maximilian, Leopold,* &c. dollars, or ducatoons of *Spain,* they may well enough be omitted, if they are fcarce in *England,* for they are all vanifhed from hence.

9. I am fenfible it is a difadvantage to have foreign coins current as money by weight, but abfolute ruin to have them current by tale; and therefore could wifh we had as little of them as may be.

In our cafe, foreign gold is neceffary, but I would gladly prevent foreign filver from being fet at fuch a price as to make it worth our bankers while to exchange our gold for foreign filver, by raifing it, as they have already changed all our filver for gold, by raifing that.

As for the affair of a coinage of filver at the tower, for the ufe of this country, it is what will require mature

mature confideration, and is more than I fhall pretend to fpeak to on fo fhort a warning.

As you know our prefent diftrefs for want of change, I muft beg of you to prefs the reduction of our gold, if poffible, before his Majefty's return, after which it will not be eafy to get the council to attend to *Irifh* affairs: and if our filver is raifed, I beg it may not exceed the middle value of foreign filver coin; but I could heartily wifh the foregn filver were left as it is, and then a fmall pittance of *Englifh* filver money with the copper would anfwer our purpofe.

I am, Sir, &c.

To the Duke of Dorfet.

My Lord, Dublin, Nov. 25, 1736.

WHEN your Grace was in *Ireland*, I delivered your Lordfhip a petition, including her cafe, from the Widow *Feilding* rel ct of * Col. *Feilding*, and fifter to the late Lord *Santry*. I have been fince very much importuned by her and feveral of her friends to remind your Grace of her application. I am fatisfied fhe is in a very poor and miferable condition, and in danger of being arrefted by fome of her creditors. I fhall fay nothing farther on this occafion, but fubmit the whole to your confideration.

I am,

My Lord, &c.

* Governor of the Royal Hofpital near *Dublin* for invalid Soldiers.

To

† *To the Earl of* Granard.

My Lord,   *Dublin, Nov.* 29, 1736.

AS your Lordſhip thoroughly knows the diſtreſs
we are in for want of ſilver, and the advantage
the bankers make of the inequality of our gold and
ſilver ; and as the repreſentation of the council here is
now before the officers of the mint, I muſt beg of
your Lordſhip to follow this affair cloſe with Mr.
Conduit, and get a report from the mint, and afterwards to forward that buſineſs before the committee
of council, that if poſſible, we may receive the neceſſary orders before his Majeſty's return ; after which,
I fear we muſt expect but little diſpatch in any *Iriſh*
affair from the miniſtry, till the ſeſſion of parliament
is over in *England*.

By what I can learn, they have no difficulty at all
at the mint about the reduction of go d, but about
the ſilver they ſeem at a loſs how to take any notice
of a letter I ſent to my Lord Lieutenant on that ſubject, to ſhew that we had over-rated foreign ſilver in
our repreſentation, and rather to wiſh nothing was
done about the ſilver coins ; which letter my Lord
Lieutenant has communicated to them, but it was not
referred to them by the council. As to that, I would
obſerve, that I do not apprehend there is any occaſion
of any notice being taken of that letter in their report
from the mint ; but if that ſuggeſts any hints to them
that may be of uſe, they may make uſe of them as
of any other knowledge they have in that affair : and
there is the more room for it, becauſe in our repreſentation we obſerve, that in our calculations we
reckoned 5 s. 4 ½ d. *Engliſh* as the middle price of
foreign ſilver, but refer ourſelves to the mint as knowing that better than we do.

I find

I find likewife that it is fuggefted on the other fide that $5 s.$ $4\frac{1}{2} d.$ is the middle price of filver in bars, but that of late, becaufe of their being fomewhat bafer than formerly, the price of pieces of eight has been from $5 s.$ $2 d.$ to $5 s.$ $3\frac{1}{2} d.$ per ounce, and that therefore there ought to be a diftinction between old and new pieces of eight, and that the old at leaft may be fet at $5 s.$ $4\frac{1}{4} d.$ per ounce.

To this I obferve, that we fhall not eafily bring the people here to know the old from the new pieces of eight, and that we are not fixing the price of filver in bars, but of foreign filver coin.

They fay they do not find any calculation of the * Leopold, Maximilian, &c. dollars, among any of Sir Ifaac Newton's calculations, and therefore think they are not to be met with in England. On this I obferve, that we have none of them now in Ireland, and if they have none of them in England, they may very fafely be omitted, for we only put them in becaufe they were in former proclamations here, when they were more common.

What your Lordfhip and I both think is, that it were to be wifhed that by degrees the gold and filver current here, was chiefly gold and filver Englifh coin: that if our gold was reduced we might hope to get rid of our prefent inundation of foreign gold ; and that there is a neceffity of not over-valuing foreign filver coins, which will make it worth the bankers while to carry out our gold and over-run us with filver coins from abroad. And the fureft way of preventing that would be by leaving the foreign filver coins at their prefent value here ; but if fomewhat muft be done about them, I hope they will not be fet higher than at the rate of $5 s.$ $2\frac{1}{2} d.$ or $5 s.$ $2\frac{1}{4} d.$ Englifh per ounce, which I hope would not hurt us.

* German Silver Coins.

I fhould

I should not have troubled your Lordship with so
long a letter, but that I know your heart is thoroughly
set on redressing our present deplorable estate; and if
by your Lordship's diligent sollicitation of this affair,
it can be brought to bear whilst the ministry is at
leisure before his Majesty's return, your Lordship will
do one of the greatest pieces of service to this nation.

Our copper coinage is I believe before this, actually begun at the mint; all I could wish about it is,
that it could receive greater dispatch than I fear it is
likely to meet with. I am,

My Lord, &c.

Article relative to the gold, delivered to Lord *Granard*.

WE desired it might be reduced according to the
value of the *English* guinea.

We desired that the lesser species of each sort of
gold might have about half a grain advantage allowed to make it worth while rather to import the lesser
pieces than the greater pieces.

But if it be considered that the least want of full
weight causes a deduction of a grain according to the
present way of allowing for a grain, and half a grain
according to what we proposed in our application to
his Majesty, it is possible a little more should be allowed; since to exemplify in the 4 *l.* piece, though
the 40 *s.* piece be set half a grain lower than half the
weight of the 4 *l.* piece, yet this does little more
than answer the allowance of half a grain for any
want of weight in a 4 *l.* piece, and of two half grains
for the least want of weight in two 4 *s.* pieces; and
so of the other lesser pieces in that and other species.

But at the same time, if too much be allowed for
the small pieces, they will be imported instead of
silver.

Article

Article relative to the filver fpecies, delivered to the fame.

WE have from the reprefentation of the merchants and bankers, and from what was the middle price of foreign filver or bullion at *London*, when we were endeavouring to make application before, defired to fet foreign filver at 5 *s.* 4 *d. per* ounce *Englifh* ; but I have fince learned that foreign filver in *England* fince the year 1728, has feldom been higher than 5 *s.* 2 ½ *d. Englifh per* ounce, and never higher than 5 *s.* 3 *d. Englifh per* ounce.

But if foreign filver be worth at the higheft but 5 *s.* 3 *d. Englifh per* ounce, and we have made our calculations upon 5 *s.* 4 *d.* there will be a profit of 1 *l.* 5 *s.* 4 *d.* &c. decimals in importing 100 *l. Englifh* in foreign filver.

If foreign filver be worth but 5 *s.* 2 ½ *d. Englifh per* ounce, there will be a profit of 2 *l.* 2 decimals *per cent.* by importing it.

And in either cafe it will be worth the bankers while to change our reduced foreign gold into foreign filver fo advanced.

We have indeed referred this matter to the confideration of the mint, who can beft tell what is the middle price of foreign filver at *London.*

I have fince our reprefentation fent to my Lord Lieutenant a full ftate of this matter, defiring that if there are difficulties in this matter of fettling the price of foreign filver, they would drop this part of our application relating to foreign filver, and only order the reduction of foreign gold as defired.

To the Duke of Dorfet.

My Lord,   *Dublin, Dec.* 13, 1736.

WE this day troubled your Grace about a living in the diocefe of *Offory*, vacant by the promotion of Mr. *Tifdall* : it confifts of three denominations, the rectory of *Gaulfkill*, and vicarages of *Dunkit* and *Kilcollum*, worth about 100 *l. per ann.*

Of the three perfons we recommended, I cannot but wifh your Grace would beftow it on Mr. *Samuel Hairy*, who was recommended to your Grace by the Bifhop of *Kilmore* and myfelf, when your Grace was laft in *Ireland* ; he came over from the Diffenters to the Church fome years ago, and has hitherto got nothing but a curacy of 40 *l. per ann.* and that rather precarious. He is one of a good life and converfation, and a moft diligent curate : he is about 60 years old, and has a fon and two daughters on his hands to maintain, and has been obliged to fell a fmall paternal eftate he had for their fupport, fo that his neceffities are very preffing : but I fubmit the whole to your Grace's judgment. I am,

                              My Lord, &c.

To the Duke of Newcaftle.

My Lord,   *Dublin, Dec.* 23, 1736.

I Have had the honour of your Grace's of the 22d paft, but it did not come to hand till laft week ; and we had long before appointed one Mr. *Herbert* Sheriff for *Kerry* ; and as this gentleman was formerly in a preffing manner recommended by Mr. *Herbert* of *England* for that office, but was then put by for reafons that have now ceafed, I doubt not but Mr *Herbert*
                                        will

will be as well fatisfied with his name-fake being made Sheriff, as if Mr. *Markham* had been fo.

Had there been room I fhould have been on this, as I fhall, on all other occafions be, very forward to acknowledge the obligations I lye under to your Lordfhip.

I cannot conclude without preffing your Grace to get the affair of lowering the gold here expedited, for want of which we are in the laft diftrefs in this country.   I am with the greateft truth and refpect,

My Lord, &c.

To the Duke of Dorfet.

My Lord,   *Dublin, Dec.* 29, 1736.

THE bearer is Mr. *Wye,* who has had an affair long depending in the army about removing one Mr. *Pepper* out of the army into the room of one upon half-pay, and putting him into commiffion in Mr. *Pepper's* place, in Col. *Hamilton's* regiment : the particulars of the cafe he will inform your Grace of. The bufinefs had probably been done two years ago, but for the ill ftate of health Sir *William Strickland,* then Secretary of War was in.   As the perfon in half-pay may chance to die, if the affair is ftill depending, which will raife new difficulties, and as Mr. *Wye* has long ago done all on his part, I muft intreat your Grace to bring the affair about as foon as it can conveniently be done, or Mr. *Wye* will be in danger of being ruined.   I am very forry I have been obliged to give your grace fo much trouble in this matter both here and in *England.*   I am,

My Lord, &c.

L 2

To

To the * Earl of Granard.

My Lord,   *Dublin, Jan.* 2, 1736.

I Learn from *London* that the reprefentation of the
council has been fome time before the officers of
the mint, and that as to the reduction of the gold,
they feem to make no difficulty, and I believe they
are not againſt reporting as to the filver, agreeably to
the reprefentation ; but as in a letter I wrote to the
Lord Lieutenant on that fubject, which they have before them, they are at fome lofs what notice they can
take of it, as it has not been referred to them by the
council, I think they need not in their report take any
notice of it, but only attend to what it fuggeſts.

They fay filver bullion is about the price of
5 *s.* 4 ¼ *d.* but pieces of eight about three half-pence
lower. I have wrote to Mr. *Cary* that it would be a
difficulty here to diſtinguiſh between the old and new
pieces of eight ; that we are fettling the price of
foreign money not bullion ; that if we over-rate it,
the bankers will change away our gold for foreign
filver.

My Lord,

I muſt beg of your Lordſhip, as you know the cafe,
and have the intereſt of this nation at heart, which is
in the laſt diſtreſs for want of filver, that you would
follow this affair clofe with Mr. *Conduit,* that if poſſible, it may be done before his † Majeſty's return,

* This Nobleman was an Admiral in the *Engliſh* Fleet, of great
Experience and Bravery ; a Privy Counfellor in *Ireland*; a *Britiſh*
Member of Parliament ; an Embaffador to the Court of *Ruſſia*;
and Governor of the Counties of *Weſtmeath* and *Longford.*
† King *George* II. who frequently made Journies to *Hanover,*
his native Country, as did alfo his Father *George* I.

when

when there will be such a hurry of *English* business, that it will be in vain to hope for any thing till the seſſion of parliament is over.

I am, my Lord, &c.

To the Duke of Dorſet.

My Lord,   *Dublin, Jan.* 8, 1736.

AS Major *Don* in Sir *James Wood's* regiment is lately dead, and there may probably be several removes in the regiment on this occaſion, I ſhall be much obliged to your Grace if you would pleaſe to beſtow a firſt lieutenancy on *Robert Moland*, at preſent a ſecond Lieutenant in the ſaid regiment by your Grace's favour.   I am,

My Lord, &c.

To the Earl of Angleſea.

My Lord,   *Dublin, Jan.* 8, 1736.

I Am very much obliged to your Lordſhip for your kind letter, and the concern you expreſs both for this kingdom in relation to our coin, and for the rights of the clergy.

I am ſorry my letter did not come to your hands till you was in the country, ſince I make no doubt but your Lordſhip's repreſentations would have a good effect both with my Lord Lieutenant and the miniſtry.

I have not been wanting in my endeavours to get our evil remedied, and the memorial of the council is referred to the officers of the mint : and I hear thoſe in power ſeem all convinced that we are in a very bad way, and that our gold ought to be lowered ; but nothing is yet done, and I hear my Lord Lieutenant is too much diſpoſed to make the reduction at twice, which will defeat the cure ; for there will be above 1 *per* cent. to be got by importing gold upon a half

L 3   reduction,

reduction, so that it will help us to no silver, and the bankers are so much masters of the House of Commons, that I apprehend if the affair be not quite over first, they will get some idle votes to prevent any farther reduction.

I shall represent this to my Lord Lieutenant as soon as I have an answer to my last letter to him on that subject.

I have sent your Lordship the resolutions of the House of Commons, in relation to agistment, but there were some other votes ready to have been passed, one particularly to fall on the Barons of the Exchequer on that subject, which though they were stopped by some of the House that were wiser, yet seem to have intimidated that court almost as much as if they had passed. After these votes were over, associations were entered into by most of the Lay-lords and Commoners, to join against agistment; and the like associations were sent down to most counties against the assizes, and signed in most counties, though refused in some. In some places they went so far as to talk of chusing a country treasurer, and supporting any law-suit on that subject against the clergy by a common purse.

I was told by some of sense that went the circuits, that there was a rage stirred up against the clergy, that they thought equalled any thing they had seen against the popish priests, in the most dangerous times they remembered.

I could not forbear telling my Lord Lieutenant on occasion of these associations, that though the rights of the clergy were in particular attacked at present, yet this method was of most dangerous consequence to the government, since by the same method that was now taken to distress the clergy, the execution of any law or act of parliament might be effectually obstructed.

As some that were more prudent than others amongst them, said they would endeavour to settle
things

things another feffion in fome reafonable way, and hoped the clergy would let things reft in the mean time, and as the latter part of the laft refolution feems to promife fomewhat of that nature, the Bifhops thought it moft advifeable to perfuade the clergy to be quiet till next feffions, that it might not be faid things would have been amicably fettled if it had not been for the heat of the clergy. I expect nothing from them, but the clergy have behaved themfelves with a temper that has furprized their enemies. I believe they will bring in a bill next feffions, that will half ruin the clergy here, which there will be no pof-fibility of ftopping here, but I hope the friends to the conftitution in Church and State, will fink fuch bills in the council in *England*.

We generally fuppofe this ferment is encouraged from *England*, as are our great out-cries for a com-mon-wealth. What things will end in God only knows, but I am very much furprized to hear from *England*, that the young noblemen that travel abroad, come back zealous for a common-wealth, as fome of our young noblemen here fhew themfelves to be. I cannot but think by the experiment that has been made formerly, the nobility have very little reafon to hope they fhall keep their ground, if monarchy be once ruined.

I have likewife fent your Lordfhip the covenants Lord * *Piefly* has inferted in the pieces lately made on his father's eftate, which if followed, muft difable the clergy from gathering their dues, or having more, for them than the tenant is pleafed to pay.

There was likewife a paper delivered by Lord *Piefly* among his tenants, which though ftrictly legal, will, confidering the number of tenants concerned, in fmall pieces of ground, very much diftrefs the clergy.

* Eldeft fon to the Earl of *Abercorn* in *Scotland*, and Lord Vifc. *Strabane* in *Ireland*.

L 4

I fhall

I ſhall not be wanting to write to our other friends in *England* to ſupport us there, for here no ſtand can be made.

What has been already done, is but the beginning of what is intended, for ſeveral of them ſpeak out, that the preſent claims of the clergy, even thoſe about the legality of which there is no diſpute, are matter of frequent controverſy, and breed quarrels between the clergy and laity, and which ought to be taken away, and they mention in particular ſmall dues, tythe of flax, and potatoes, the laſt at leaſt to be reduced.

All we deſire is, that we may be upon the bottom of other ſubjects as to our dues, and enjoy the like benefit of the courts of juſtice as others do, for the recovery of our juſt rights.

I muſt beg of your Lordſhip to forgive the length of this letter, and to continue the ſame good friend to the clergy both of *England* and *Ireland* that you have hitherto been.

I am, my Lord, &c.

To Mr. Walter Cary.

Sir,   *Dublin, Jan.* 13, 1736.

YEſterday I received yours of the 4th inſtant, and the intended report, together with nine mails more. I am ſorry to hear you have been ſo much out of order, and are not yet quite well, but I hope as the ſpring advances, your health will improve.

I am glad the affair of our coin is in ſo good a way, and that no time may be loſt, have returned my ob-ſervations on the report and memorandums of Mr. *Conduit*, by which you will ſee I am very well ſatisfi-ed with this report, and deſire little or no change to be made, and what I do I ſubmit to him. I have

likewiſe

likewife returned the report and paper annexed, as his Grace intimated.

I fhall communicate the affair to none but fuch as I can abfolutely truft, and hardly to them. I hope it may be pufhed on as faft as may be, on the return of the report, that the good effects of the reduction may be fenfibly felt before the end of the fummer.

I am forry any accident has happened about the copper coinage ; I fhould be glad if the mint and the company could furnifh us with a greater quantity *per* week than has been hitherto talked of.

My * Lord Chancellor is not yet come, but expected from *Chefter* the firft fair wind.

I heartily return your good wifhes, and many happy new years, and am,

Sir, your humble fervant,

To the Duke of Dorfet.

My Lord,   *Dublin, June* 13, 1736.

I Had not the honour of your grace's of the 1ft inftant till yefterday, when we received the mails together.

I am glad to find the affair of our coin is in fo good a way, and think Mr. *Conduit* has dropt the bufinefs of foreign filver in a very decent manner. And I cannot defire he fhould fpeak more fully of the neceffity of reducing our gold than he has.

As to any difference in their valuation of the gold coin and ours, I am very eafy about it fince though I had ours from the beft hands here, I make no doubt but they of the mint are better fkilled in that matter, and have more frequent opportunities of examining the weight and intrinfic worth of foreign gold coins than any here can have.

* Lord *Wyndham.*

I have

I have drawn some few remarks on the memorandums, at the bottom of the valuation paper, which I have sent to Mr. *Cary*, to be communicated to Mr. *Conduit*, which will make no difficulty in the affair, let him judge as he thinks proper.

My Lord Chancellor is not yet arrived and the wind at present is against him.

I shall endeavour to have the magazine finished as your Grace desires, and hope it may be done without giving your Grace any farther trouble.

I thank your Grace for your kind intentions to Mr. *Henry*.

I thank your Lordship for your kind wishes, and am sure nobody can with greater sincerity and heartiness, wish your Grace many happy new years than,

My Lord, &c.

* To the Bishop of Down.

My Lord,　　　　　　　　　*Dublin, Jan.* 15, 1736.

MR. *Oneal* has called upon me with your Lordship's letter and the certificate of several clergymen. I know not what to say to what they have testified, but I must acquaint your Lordship that for several reasons your brethren on the bench here think, if you have any regard to your character and the notions every body has of the occasions of your original design, you will certainly drop it. And I must assure your Lordship, that I so far concur with them, that I declare to your Lordship, if you go on with it, no part of the blame or clamour shall directly or indirectly lye on me.

I am, my Lord, &c.

* Dr. *Hutchinson*, author of a book on witches, and an almanack.

To

* *To the Bishop of* Rochester.

My Lord,   *Dublin, Jan.* 25, 1736.

I Have had application made to me in behalf of *James Shiell*, at *Westminster* school, lately removed with great credit as I am informed into the fifth form. I am assured he is a very good lad and a good scholar; he wants to get upon the foundation † the approaching election, but fears without some friend appearing for him he may be postponed. His father is proctor of the prerogative court here, of a very fair character, and very desirous his son may have the advantage of being educated under his good discipline. If the lad answers the character I have of him, I heartily desire your favour in his behalf, that he may be brought into the college next election.

I am, my Lord, &c.

To the Bishop of Elphin.

My Lord,   *Dublin, Jan.* 27, 1736.

WE had this day a navigation board, where we were informed your Lordship must by this time be at *Bath*.

As we have dismissed ‡ Mr. *Cassel* from that work, and are making enquiries about a proper person from

* Dr. *Wilcocks*.
† He did get on the foundation, and was afterwards Student of *Christ Church*, and now is an eminent Lawyer, a King's Council, and one of the Commissioners of appeal in *Ireland*. *(February* 1770)
‡ One of the greatest Architects in *Europe*, who designed that noble Edifice of Leinster House, in *Dublin*; the Lying-in-Hospital; the Musick-Hall, and many other superb Structures in *Ireland*. He was born in *Germany*, and made the grand Tour, which gave him the most elegant taste.

England

England that has been concerned in works of the like nature, and is able and willing to undertake the conduct of that affair, I was defired by the board to prevail with your Lordfhip to difcourfe with Mr. *Allen* †, who made the *Bath* river navigable, whether he can recommend a proper perfon for that undertaking, and on what terms fuch perfon or perfons would be willing to come.   Mr. *Lucas*'s brother has had fome difcourfe on that fubject with Mr. *Allen*, but as your Lordfhip has ufually been prefent at thofe boards, you will be better able to talk with Mr. *Allen* ; and the account you fend us will be more fatisfactory.   And as Mr. *Allen* is very underftanding in thofe matters, whatever lights you can get from him, which I find he is not backward to communicate, may be of fervice to us.

Your Lordfhip can conclude nothing with Mr. *Allen*, but only get the beft lights you can : for we are at the fame time making two other enquiries of the fame nature, and intend to employ him whom we apprehend to be moft capable of executing the work, and who will come on the moft reafonable terms.

As I know how much your Lordfhip has the intereft of this kingdom, and in particular the fuccefs of the work at heart, I need not prefs you to undertake the trouble we defire you to be at.

It will be of fervice to us to have an anfwer with all convenient fpeed, that we may be able to determine on fomewhat before the feafon advances too far.

I am,

My Lord, &c.

† This is the celebrated *Ralph Allen*, Efq; of *Pryor-Park*, near *Bath*.

To

To Sir William Chapman.

S I R,   *Dublin, Feb.* 19. 1736.

I Am almoſt aſhamed to write to you ſo long after the receipt of the letter you favoured me with, together with the reſolutions of our correſponding ſociety, in favour of Mr. † *Hanſard.* But I was then in the country, and unfortunately miſlaid your letter, and have but lately found it : the reſolutions I immediately communicated to the ſociety, where, though they were of weight, yet they had not all the ſucceſs I heartily wiſhed they might have had in his favour. For my part I did him all the ſervice I could.

We are very much obliged to you and the other gentlemen of the ſociety for ſo heartily eſpouſing our intereſt ; I am ſure what our charter ſociety are labouring after, is the moſt rational puſh that has been made for eſtabliſhing the proteſtant religion more univerſally in this kingdom, than it has hitherto been. And I hope that through the bleſſing of God, and the aſſiſtance of charitable perſons in *England,* joined with our endeavours here, there will be a ſenſible change made here in a courſe of ſome years.

I am very glad of this opportunity of renewing a correſpondence with ſo worthy a gentleman, whom I had the happineſs to know in *England.*

I muſt beg of you and the other gentlemen who are ſo kind as to correſpond with us in our deſign, to promote as much as in you lies, the contributions of well diſpoſed perſons in *England,* that we may

* Merchant in *London.*
† Was Agent for the Proteſtant Charter Schools in *Ireland,* ſent to *England* to ſollicit Subſcriptions for this moſt religious and uſeful Undertaking, and was very ſucceſsful therein.

make

make our views the more extenfive. And I have no doubt but if we are once able to fet on foot about 20 working fchools, in the feveral diftant parts of the kingdom, and put them into a right method, we fhall meet with fupport and encouragement here from the legiflature.

I am, &c.

* To the Bifhop of Derry.

My Lord, *Dublin, Feb.* 19, 1736.

AT our laft meeting of the charter fociety we had before us the minutes of the laft meeting of our correfponding members in *London,* with an account of their having appointed † Mr. *Cole* a falary of 8o*l. per ann.* for officiating as fecretary, and folliciting for us. There is no doubt that what they did was purfuant to a defire we formerly made to them to chufe fuch a fecretary as they thought proper, and to appoint him what falary they judged reafonable, to be paid out of the monies collected in *England.* However as we had given our fecretary here but 5o*l. per ann.* it occafioned fome heat amongft us. I faid what I could to pacify them, that we were very much obliged to the gentlemen there for their kind affiftance ; that if we had any mifunderftanding with them it would very much obftruct our fubfcriptions there, and that what they had done would oblige them in honour to be the more diligent in raifing contributions for our aid, fince 8o*l.* would make a very large deduction out of 22o*l.* annual fubfcriptions that Mr. *Hanfard* had obtained in *England* before his return, and which we did not find

---

* Dr. *Rundle.*

† Another Agent, for the Proteftant Charter Schools, who refided in *London.*

had

had been yet enlarged : fo that upon the whole I prevented their coming to any rafh refolution, and efpecially upon my promifing to write to your Lord-fhip upon the fubject.

I could heartily wifh they had made the fecretary a lefs appointment, but I much fear it would be a dangerous ftep to defire our correfpondents to make an alteration in what they have done.

And though fome here were of opinion that one commiffioned by us to make collections at *London* would want no other help to obtain large contribu-tions, yet I am fully perfuaded, that without being recommended or introduced by fome gentlemen of weight, and having the way firft prepared for him, fuch a perfon would not fo eafily obtain admiffion, nor meet with the fame encouragement. And be-fides, gentlemen among their acquaintance have thofe frequent opportunities of opening the nature and probable good effects of our defign, that a meer fe-cretary at a fingle audience could not poffibly pro-mife himfelf. As this is the cafe, I think it abfo-lutely neceffary to court the affiftance of thofe gen-tlemen, and to get as many more as are willing to join with them, and think we muft avoid whatever may offend thofe who have already engaged to affift us.

I have told your Lordfhip what others have faid, and what are my fentiments in this affair : your Lordfhip who is on the fpot will beft judge what is moft proper to be done, and will accordingly either wholly conceal what has happened here, or commu-nicate fo much as you think may be without damage to our defign communicated. And you will be fo kind as afterwards to write me fuch a letter on the occafion, as I may lay before the fociety here.

Your

Your Lordſhip knows how ignorant we are here of what paſſes in *London,* that I ſhould be thankful for a little intelligence from thence.

I am, my Lord, &c.

To the London Society.

Gentlemen, *Dublin, Mar.* 8, 1736.

I Have been favoured with your letter relating to the diſputed * election at *Londonderry,* and think you are acting very honourably in endeavouring to ſupport your rights and privileges there, and was in hopes that I might have had intereſt enough in the council to have both elections declared void, that the citizens and Freeholders of *Derry* might have proceeded to another election, when they fully underſtood what was your ſenſe about that affair ; but I found there was ſuch a number of privy councellors come prepoſſeſſed about that election, that there was no room for oppoſing ſo great a torrent. And I rather think your ſureſt way of ſupporting your privileges, will be by due courſe of law, if things ſhould take a wrong turn at another election.

I can aſſure you I have always had a diſpoſition to ſerve you, and maintain your privileges to the utmoſt of my power; and ſhall on all proper occaſions ſhew that I am ſo diſpoſed.

I am, &c.

‡ *To the Archbiſhop of* Canterbury.

My Lord, *Dublin, Mar.* 8, 1736.

THough I am late in my congratulations on your Grace's promotion to the ſee of *Canterbury,* yet I am behind none in my heartineſs and ſincerity. I

* Of Magiſtrates for that City.
‡ Dr. *Potter.*

am

am glad to hear from *England* that your character, learning, and prudence has made all parties well pleafed with your advancement. And I queftion not but your caution and temper will be of great ferviee to the Church, at a time when fhe feems to be fo violently attacked on all fides. I pray God to direct you in that high ftation, and grant that you may long enjoy it to the benefit both of Church and State.

I am, my Lord, &c.

To the Duke of Dorfet.

My Lord,   *Dublin, Mar.* 17, 1736.

I Have lately received a letter from Lord *Cavan,* renewing his application for the government of *Derry* upon the prefent vacancy, with the condition of giving up 400*l. per ann.* of his prefent penfion. Your Grace remembers what then paft, and knows how ferviceable he is in the Houfe of Lords.

How the affair of the Hofpital ftands I do not know, but if Colonel *Tichbourn* be thought of for it, I believe the feveral candidates on the late vacancies might all be made eafy; and I cannot but wifh my Lord *Cavan* were confidered, or we may find the want of him in the feffion of parliament. I am,

My Lord, &c.

To Mr. Walter Cary.

SIR,   *Dublin, Mar.* 26, 1737.

I Received yours of the 8th, and am glad to hear Mr. *Conduit* has delivered in to the Lords of the Treafury his report. Your poftfcript about his relapfe, has fomewhat alarmed me, but I hope the

VOL. II.   M   accqunt

account we have fince had in the prints, that he is recovered, will hold true.

Two tuns of our copper half-pence are arrived here, and four tun more has been fhipped fome time, which we hope fpeedily to receive ; and fince that a tun and half more. As foon as we have received about 2000 pounds worth, which we compute will anfwer the wants of *Dublin*, we fhall iffue a proclamation about their circulating. Dean *Swift* has raifed fome ferment about them here, but people of fenfe are very well fatisfied of the want and goodnefs of them. I muft beg the continuance of your good offices both as to the filver and gold, and to pufh on coining the copper as faft as may be.

We all talk of an exchange of places between the Dukes of *Dorfet* and *Devonfhire*. I hope it is to the fatisfaction of our prefent Lord Lieutenant; but I fear I fhall be a lofer in my intereft at the Caftle by the exchange.

I thank you for your kind compliments, and in return wifh you all health and happinefs, and fhall, as you give me leave, trouble you on occafion, for what may be of fervice to this country. I am,

Sir, your humble fervant, &c.

To the Duke of Dorfet.

My Lord, *Dublin, Apr.* 9, 1737.

I Have the honour of your Grace's of the 2d inftant ; and as his Majefty has thought fit to eafe you of the fatigue of our government, I am glad he has been pleafed to reftore you to your former ftation.

I have heard from others a very good character of the Duke of *Devonfhire*, but it is a great fatisfaction

faction to me to hear it fo fully confirmed by your Grace.

I have not the honour to be perfonally known to our new Lord Lieutenant, and fhall therefore be obliged to your Lordfhip, if you will pleafe to fpeak to him about me as you fhall think proper; and his Grace may depend on my poor affiftance in whatever may promote his Majefty's fervice here, and the true intereft of this kingdom.

We are very much obliged to your Grace that you quit us with an intention ftill to promote our good by your intereft on the other fide of the water: *and I am fure we want from time to time fuch powerful patrons to help and protect us.*

I return your Grace my moft hearty thanks for the many civilities and favours I have met with from you, in the courfe of your government; and fhall always own it as a great addition to them, that you are pleafed to give me leave to continue a correfpondence with your Grace, and to apply to you for your affiftance on proper occafions.

I am, your Grace's, &c.

P. S. I find Mr. *Dillon Wye*'s affair is not yet completed. If, as I fear, it cannot be done before your Grace entirely quits the management of *Irifh* affairs, I fhould be glad your Grace would recommend it to our new Lord Lieutenant, and, if you fhall think proper, recommend him at the fame time to be a gentleman at large to his Grace the Duke of *Devonfhire,* that he may have the better chance to be remembered.

To

To the Lords Juſtices of Ireland.

My Lords,   *Piccadilly, Apr.* 18, 1737.

HIS Majeſty having been graciouſly pleaſed by
letters patent under the great ſeal of *Great
Britain,* dated the 9th inſtant, to appoint me Lord
Lieutenant of his kingdom of *Ireland,* I take this
opportunity to acquaint your Excellencies therewith,
and that there is inſerted in the ſaid letters patent,
a clauſe continuing your Excellencies to be Lords
Juſtices of that kingdom, during my abſence, with
the ſame powers and privileges, as were granted by
letters patent under the great ſeal of *Ireland,* appointing you to be Lords juſtices in the abſence of the
late Lord Lieutenant.

It is a ſenſible pleaſure to me that your Excellencies are continued in the government of *Ireland,*
as during your former adminiſtration, your Excellencies conducted the affairs of that kingdom with
ability and integrity, and with zeal and affection to
his Majeſty's perſon and government : I aſſure myſelf that the honour and intereſt of his Majeſty, and
the welfare and proſperity of his ſubjects, will be
the conſtant care and concern of your Excellencies,
and I ſhall on all occaſions make a faithful repreſentation to his Majeſty of your zeal and regard for
his ſervice.

I deſire to hear frequently from your Excellencies
concerning all matters relating to his Majeſty's ſervice, and that you will order the proper officers
to lay before you, as ſoon as may be, the following
particulars, *viz.*

I. An account of the preſent ſtate of the revenue,
and of the expence of the management thereof,
each diſtinguiſhed under its proper head.

II. The

II. The eftablifhment both civil and military of the expence of his Majefty's government, as it now ftands, with the particular dates, as far as the fame can be collected, of the time when every particular charge was brought upon the eftablifhment.

III. A lift of the officers both civil and military, in his Majefty's fervice, with the dates of their refpective patents, (diftinguifhing thofe that are for life or lives, during good behaviour, and during pleafure) Warrants and Commiffions.

IV. A lift of all the officers upon the eftablifhment of half-pay, with the dates of their commiffions, and an account alfo, as far as the fame can be collected, of their ages and places of refidence.

V. A ftate of his Majefty's regiments of foot, horfe, and dragoons in *Ireland*, with their complements ; a ftate of the cloathing, off-reckonings, effectives, &c. together with a lift of the prefent quarters of the army.

VI. A lift or lifts of the governors and cuftodes rotulorum of the feveral counties of *Ireland*, of the juftices of the peace, deputy lieutenants, and officers of the militia, together with a lift of the independent companies and troops of militia.

All which feveral accounts and lifts I defire your Excellencies will be pleafed to tranfmit to me as foon as conveniently you can.

Having appointed Mr. * *Edward Walpole* to be my chief fecretary, I defire your Excellencies will favour

---

* Second Son of Sir *Robert Walpole* Knight of the Garter, who was many Years firft Minifter of State in *England.* Mr. *Edward Walpole* was afterwards made a Knight of the Bath.

M 3   him

him with your correspondence on all proper occasions.

> I am, my Lords,
>> With great truth,
>>> Your Excellencies,
>>>> Most faithful humble servant,
>>>>> DEVONSHIRE.

To the Duke of Dorset.

My Lord, *Dublin, Apr.* 28, 1737.

I Have the honour of your Grace's of the 25th past, by Mr. *De Ioncourt* ; and since his arrival we have had a linnen board, and have furnished him and his brother with money to go with their workmen to *Dundalk*, where we have fixed this new manufacture *, which I hope will turn to good account to this nation, and deserve our further encouragement. I shall still be ready to give them what further support may be necessary upon your Grace's recommendation, and shall always be proud to receive your Grace's commands.

> I am, my Lord, &c.

To Horace Walpole, *Esq*;

SIR, *Dublin, Apr.* 28. 1737.

MR. *De Ioncourt* has lately brought me the favour of yours of the 4th instant. On account of your former recommendation, I did him what service I could at the linnen board, where we

* This manufactory was established by a voluntary subscription of 30,cool. at *Dundalk*, on the estate of lord viscount *Limerick*, afterwards earl of *Clanbrassille*, and is now a thriving manufacture. *February* 1770.

agreed

agreed with him and his brother on the terms for which they are to carry on the cambrick manufacture; and gave one of the brothers money to go to *France* and bring over fkilful workmen. Before his return we had fixed upon *Dundalk* for the place to fettle that manufacture in, with the approbation of his brother, and fince his return we have advanced money to fend the workmen thither to begin their bufinefs.

And whatever fupport I can give them at the board fhall not be wanting. And I have great hopes this manufacture will turn out well to the great advantage of this kingdom, which muft in the end be to the advantage of *England.* I am,

My Lord, &c.

To the Duke of Devonfhire.

My Lord,   *Dublin, Apr.* 28, 1737.

IT was with great pleafure that I faw your Grace's letter to the Lords Juftices, notifying his Majefty's having appointed you Lord Lieutenant of *Ireland.*

The great character your Grace has from every body, fatisfies me we fhall be happy under your adminiftration, if it be not our own fault.

I have made it my endeavour to ferve his Majefty faithfully here, and fhall always labour to promote his intereft and honour, and the profperity of his fubjects; and am glad that I and the other Lords Juftices have been rightly reprefented to your Grace on that head : and I dare anfwer for them as well as myfelf, that we fhall do our utmoft to make your adminiftration here eafy.

Befide thofe publick letters you are pleafed to encourage us to write, there will be occafions when it may be for the fervice of his Majefty and the good of

M 4   this

this kingdom, that I fhould give your Grace an account of my particular fenfe of affairs, which I hope
you will allow me the liberty to write to your Grace.
I can promife that I will never knowingly miflead
you, and your Grace will always be judge of what I
propofe *.

I am glad your Grace has appointed Mr. *Edward
Walpole* your fecretary, whom, befide the univerfal
good character he fupports, I have had the pleafure
of knowing here †.

I fhall always be very proud of receiving your
Grace's commands, and beg leave to fubfcribe
myfelf,

My Lord, &c.

To the Duke of Dorfet.

My Lord,   *Dublin, May* 7, 1737.

I Heartily thank your Grace for your favourable recommendation of me to the Duke of *Devonfhire.*
I think I may venture to fay he will never find me

---

* His Grace's adminiftration was the happieft, the longeft, and
perhaps the moft ufeful that was ever known in *Ireland,* fince the
Houfe of *Hanover* came to the crown, which was greatly owing to
the confidence he placed (advifed fo to do by his good friend
Sir *Robert Walpole*) in my Lord Primate. My Lord Primate died
in this adminiftration, but had gone through three feffions of parliament, without lofing as it is beft remembered, a fingle government queftion ; but at the fame time this is obferved, be it alfo
recollected, that his Grace of *Devonfhire* did greatly ftrengthen his
own hands, and by that means thofe of the government, by a double alliance in marriage with the powerful family of *Ponfonby,* who
then had great weight, and now are of ftill greater confequence in
that kingdom. This alliance, no doubt, contributed much to
making things go eafy then, as it did afterwards during the fhort
adminiftration of that amiable, moft worthy, and truly noble per-
fonage, the laft Duke of *Devonfhire.*

‡ Mr. *Walpole* being in a very bad ftate of health, came to
Ireland to drink Goats Whey at the mountains of *Moran,* by
which he perfectly recovered.

aiming

aiming at any job-work, and that he may depend on my always promoting his Majesty's service, and the ease of his Grace's administration, to the utmost of my power.

I am likewise obliged to your Lordship for your kindness to Mr. *Dillon Wye*, and hope somewhat may offer to be done in his favour by my Lord Lieutenant.

It is very kind in your Grace, and agreeable to the treatment I have always met with from you to give me leave to apply to you on proper occasions.

I cannot help acquainting your Grace, that we yesterday signed a proclamation for giving currency to the new half-pence, after a most tedious course of delays and difficulties ; from what quarter you may easily guess : *and I hope this affair will very much sink the popularity of Dean* Swift *in this city, where he openly set himself in opposition to what the government was doing.*   I am,

My Lord, &c.

To the Bishop of London.

My Lord,   *Dublin, May* 10, 1737.

I Have been several times asked by some of the subscribers to the poetry tracts, when they would be published, and as I hear nothing about them this *May*, when your Lordship in your last seemed to think they would be published, I must again enquire of you when we may hope for them.

I did intend to have waited on your Lordship and my other friends in *England* this spring, but it was so late before our new Lord Lieutenant was declared, that I must lay aside all thoughts of such a journey this year.

I shall be ready to encourage the buying Mr. *Serce's* book here so far as I can ; but we are less given to buy books here than can be imagined.

We

We have endeavoured during the interval of parliament, to keep our clergy quiet about agiftment, in hopes fome reafonable compofition might have been thought of, but I cannot find that any of the laity have troubled themfelves about it, or are difpofed to come into any thing which we might propofe as reafonable. And I fear if we fhould propofe any thing, it would create the fame ferment as they raifed laft feffions, fo that I am very apprehenfive the parliament may pufh at fome bill which may ftrip the clergy of a great part of their legal dues : and I do not fee any poffibility of making a ftand here ; fo that our whole hope is in the protection of his Majefty, by throwing out any unreafonable bill in the council of *England*. For my part I fhall do what I can to prevent any bill of that nature coming into either houfe, but with what fuccefs I cannot tell.

If we are attacked, we muft beg the hearty affiftance of our friends in *England* ; every body gives us a very good character of our new Lord Lieutenant, fo that I hope we fhall live eafy under his adminiftration. I am,

My Lord, &c.

* *To the Bifhop of* Litchfield.

My Lord, *Dublin, May* 10, 1737.

IT was with great pleafure that I received your Lordfhip's. I am very much obliged to you for your civilities to the Bifhop of *Elphin*, and am fatisfied if he had ftaid longer in town, your Lordfhip would have had more full proofs of his being a perfon of learning.

I am very glad your Lordfhip is willing to throw a vail over any mifunderftandings that have happened

* Dr. *Smallbrooke,* who had been removed from St. *David's.*

betwixt

betwixt us formerly. † I can affure you that I have all along been fo fenfible that in that affair all appearances have been fo much againft me, that I have never had the leaft anger or refentment on account of any warmth you may have expreffed on that occafion, and I fhall be very glad to have a correfpondence renewed between two old friends.

I was in hopes I fhould have had an opportunity of waiting upon you in perfon this fpring at *London*, but the appointing a new Lord Lieutenant was delayed fo long, that I have laid afide all thoughts of that journey at prefent.

I thank your Lordfhip for your excellent charge, and am forry to find that you are infefted with popifh emiffaries in *England* as we are in *Ireland*.

My fpoufe gives her duty to your Lordfhip, and both of us our fervice to your good lady.

I am, &c.

To the Duke of Dorfet.

My Lord,   *Dublin, May* 16, 1737.

I Have been honoured with your Grace's of the 5th inftant, and have written by this poft to the Duke of *Devonfhire* on the two points your Grace directed. I have defired the favour of him to make Mr. *Gardiner* a privy counfellor, and given him the juft character he deferves, and for further information have referred to your Grace. As I could not tell but the King's letter on this occafion might be kept to be brought over by his Grace, I defired it might be fent over as foon as his Grace pleafes, if he complies with my requeft; particularly that he might be

‡ See the Primate's former letters of recommendation, where he always names the Bifhop of St. *David's* firft for the fee of *Dublin*.

of

of fervice if any difpute fhould arife about a proclamation for lowering our gold.

On which fubject I have likewife written to his
Grace, telling him how forward that affair is on the
other fide of the water, and defiring it may be difpatched as foon as he pleafes, that the ruffle which
fuch a reduction muft caufe, whenever it is done,
may be quite over before the feffion of our parliament draws near. I have likewife defired his Grace
that his Majefty's orders on that head may be very
clear and exprefs, that we may not be troubled with
any delays or difficulties here. I have no doubt but
your Grace is fenfible why I defire this, from many
things that have happened under your Grace's adminiftration.

I have referred the Duke of *Devonfhire* to your
Grace to be fully informed how this affair of the
coin ftands, and what has been done in *England* about
it, and where it now refts. If your Grace would be
fo good as to order Mr. *Cary* to give his Lordfhip a
copy of the memorial to his Majefty on that head,
I think his Grace would fufficiently underftand the
merits of the caufe.

I am very much obliged to your Grace, and moft
heartily thank you for beginning a correfpondence
between my Lord Lieutenant and me, and your kind
intentions to cultivate it : and I hope my behaviour to
my Lord Lieutenant will be fuch as to anfwer what
you are pleafed to reprefent to him he may expect
from me.

I cannot conclude without acquainting your Grace,
that notwithftanding all the oppofition and clamour of
Dean *Swift*, the papifts, and other difcontented or
whimfical perfons, our new copper half-pence circulate, and indeed are moft greedily received.

I am, my Lord, &c.

To

To the Duke of Devonſhire.

My Lord,   *Dublin, May* 16, 1737.

YOUR Grace will be ſo good as to excuſe my putting you in mind of an affair now depending in the Treaſury, relating to the reduction of our gold. We are in the laſt diſtreſs for want of ſilver in all the lower parts of buſineſs, there being a profit of 2 ½ *per cent.* by bringing *Portugal* gold here rather than ſilver, and the ſame loſs by carrying gold from hence rather than ſilver, ſo that what ſilver we had has been ſtill exporting, and the return of our exports have been ſtill made in gold : this our condition we repreſented to his Majeſty from the government and council, when his Grace the Duke of *Dorſet* was here laſt, and our repreſentation was referred to the council, and from thence to the Treaſury, and ſo to the officers of the mint, where it has reſted by the ſickneſs of Mr. *Conduit* ; but as he is now well, as I am told, and has a report ready when called for, I muſt deſire of your Grace to ſet that affair on foot again, and to get the Treaſury to call for that report, and make the report to the council, that we may receive his Majeſty's orders for a proclamation for ſuch reduction as he ſhall pleaſe to fix upon.

This is an affair of great conſequence to this nation, and the ſooner it is done before the ſeſſion of our parliament, that the little ferment ſuch a reduction muſt cauſe whenever it is made, may be quite over, I think the better. If your Grace will be ſo good as to enquire of the Duke of *Dorſet*, he will acquaint you how this affair ſtands, and of what importance it is to this nation to have it ſoon ſettled. I muſt beg that his Majeſty's commands on this occaſion, be very expreſs and poſitive, that there may be no difficulty or delay here when they are ſent us*.

* His Grace of *Devonſhire* had the honour of carrying this moſt deſirable ſcheme into execution.

There

There is another affair which I formerly troubled the Duke of *Dorset* about, and which I beg leave to lay before your Grace, which is the making Mr. *Gardiner* a privy counsellor. He is deputy to the Vice-Treasurers of this kingdom, and one of the most useful of his Majesty's servants here; as your Grace will be fully satisfied, when you do us the honour to be with us.

There is nobody here more against increasing the number of privy-counsellors than I am, who think they are by much too numerous; but it is because many have been brought in there without any knowledge of business, or particular attachment to his Majesty's service, merely for being members of either House of Parliament; but we want such an one as Mr. *Gardiner* there, to help to keep others in order, as he is most zealously attached to his Majesty by affection as well as by interest, and is a thorough man of business, and of great weight in this country; and I find he will not be the first in his post of deputy that has been a member of the privy council. And if your Grace pleases, I should be glad the King's letter were sent as soon as you think proper, for his admission, that he may be of the council when the reduction of the gold comes on; though I think, if his Majesty's commands are very express on that occasion, none will presume to make the least opposition.

I have formerly troubled the Duke of *Dorset* about Mr. *Gardiner*'s affair, and to his Grace I refer your Lordship to be more fully informed of Mr. *Gardiner*'s character, and of what service he may be to his Majesty in the council.

I beg pardon for having trespassed so long on your Grace's patiece, but I hope from your own goodness and from my sincere intention to serve his Majesty in what I have written, I may obtain your Grace's excuse. I am,

My Lord, &c.

To

To Mrs. Wall.

MADAM,   *Dublin, May* 17, 1737.

I Have received yours of the 10th, and have by this poft written to the Bifhop of *Peterborough**, to fecure his favour for your fon†. There has for fome time been very little correfpondence between the Duke of *Newcaftle* and me, fo that I did not think it proper to write to him on this occafion. I heartily wifh your fon good fuccefs. I am glad to hear your daughter is better than fhe has been. My fpoufe and I are well, God be thanked, and give our fervice to you and your family.

I am, Madam, &c.

To the Duke of Dorfet.

My Lord,   *Dublin, May* 24, 1737.

AS your Grace was pleafed to honour us with your prefence at the firft opening of our charter fociety, and accept of being our prefident, and encourage us by your generous benefaction, you will pardon my defiring one favour more of your Grace, which is to recommend us to the favour and protection of our new Lord Lieutenant, and to join with his Grace in recommending us to his Majefty's bounty. His Lordfhip has already been fpoke to on that fubject, and is well difpofed to affift us, but your Grace's interpofition with him will have a weight much fuperior to any application that has already been made to

---

* Dr. *Clavering*, at the fame time Canon of *Chrift Church*.

† This was for a Law Faculty Place in *Chrift Church, Oxford*. This Gentleman is fuppofed to have been a Mafter in Chancery in *Ireland* fome time after this date, which employment he fold, and returned to *England*.

him.

him. And your joint recommendations to his Majesty cannot fail of procuring us his bounty.

His Majesty has been formerly acquainted with our intentions, and expressed his approbation of our design. Her Majesty has likewise been applied to, and is disposed to assist us with her bounty, but as I am informed, is willing rather to follow his Majesty's example than to be before hand with him. And there are several persons of quality and worth about the court, who have expressed their readiness to follow the royal example.

Your Grace most thoroughly knows the unhappy ignorance and bigotry to popery under which the greatest part of this nation labours ; and the excessive idleness they are addicted to. And I am sure the push now made by this society in erecting working schools for the education of the children of poor papists, as well as of the meanest of the protestants, both in christian knowledge and some useful business, is the most rational method that has yet been attempted to bring about any reformation in this nation.

And we find that as our design is more known here and our fund increases, gentlemen from the several parts of the kingdom are daily making proposals of giving us land and other assistance to settle such working schools on their estates.

And I make no doubt but when we are once fallen into a well settled method of managing these schools, and have so far multiplied them that the good effects of them are visible in the several parts of the kingdom, the Commons here will very readily assist the good design with an annual fund.

But this must be a work of time, and will require the assistance of voluntary contributions to bring about, which cannot be better promoted than by his Majesty's gracious example ; which I hope will not be be wanting upon your Grace's and our new Lord Lieutenant's interceſſion.

We are printing an account of our proceedings from our firſt eſtabliſhment, which as ſoon as finiſhed ſhall wait on your Grace. I am,

My Lord, &c.

To the Duke of Devonſhire.

My Lord,   *Dublin, Jun.* 7, 1737.

I Have had the honour of your Grace's of the 14th paſt, encouraging me to give your Lordſhip my particular ſenſe of any affair that may occur here.

I am very much obliged to your Grace for this liberty, which I aſſure your Grace I ſhall not make uſe of but in what I apprehend may be for his Majeſty's ſervice, and for your Grace's eaſe and honour. Upon the aſſurances his Grace the Duke of *Dorſet* gave me, that your Lordſhip would not be offended, if I offered my beſt advice on occaſion, I made bold to trouble your Grace about Mr. *Gardiner's* being made privy counſellor here, and about obtaining his Majeſty's commands relating to the lowering the value of the gold coins here current, which I hope your Grace will think of when you find a proper ſeaſon.

I have been applied to by Dr. *St. George* who was chaplain to the Duke of *Dorſet,* to ſerve in the ſame capacity to your Grace. He has always been well affected to his Majeſty and his family. And I hope your Grace will not fill up the liſt of chaplains before your arrival here, that there may be room for him and ſeveral other worthy clergymen who have not yet applied, but I am confident will, when we have the pleaſure to ſee your Grace here.

VOL. II.   N   We

We have in a publick letter given your Grace an account how the affair of * Mr. *Nugent* and Capt. *Macguire* ſtands.   As for the latter, I believe things may be ſo managed as to prevent any farther proceedings againſt him, but the papiſts here have for ſome time been ſo inſolent, and there is ſo general a diſpoſition among proteſtants and papiſts to inſult magiſtrates for doing their duty, that we think it proper for preſerving the peace of the country, to proſecute any perſons indifferently that demand ſatisfaction of any magiſtrate for putting the laws in execution.   I am,

My Lord, &c.

To the Duke of Devonſhire.

My Lord,   *Dublin, Jun.* 18, 1737.

I Have had the honour of your Grace's of the 7th paſt, and thank your Lordſhip for your enquiry about our coin, and recommending it to Sir *Robert Walpole.*   As the ſpeaker is now in the country, and I find my Lord Chancellor is unwilling to do any thing in that affair without Mr. *Boyle's* name being to it as well as ours, if his Majeſty's commands on that ſubject come to us a little after the middle of next month, it will be time enough; for it will be of ſervice to have a proclamation iſſued here at once, without giving the diſaffected any previous time for clamour.

I thank your Grace likewiſe for your kindneſs to Mr. *Gardiner.*   I am,

My Lord, &c.

* Theſe Gentlemen being Roman Catholicks, were indicted at the aſſizes for wearing ſwords contrary to law.

To

To the Duke of Newcaftle.

My Lord,   *Dublin, Jun.* 18, 1737.

IT is always with great pleafure that I have the honour of your Grace's commands. We here were very well pleafed with the Duke of *Dorfet* for our governor, upon repeated experience of his behaviour amongft us: but we receive from all hands fo good a character of the Duke of *Devonfhire*, whom his Majefty has pleafed to appoint to fucceed him, that we have no doubt of our being equally happy under his adminiftration: and I am the more confirmed in it by your Grace's authority from your perfonal knowledge of his Lordfhip.

I am very much obliged to your Lordfhip for the good impreffions you and other my friends in *England* have been pleafed to make on his Grace in my favour. And I can undertake to affure your Grace, that whatever affurances you may have given his Lordfhip of my hearty zeal for his Majefty's fervice, and readinefs to make his adminiftration here eafy, by the beft advice and affiftance I can give him, fhall be fully anfwered to the utmoft of my power. And it is a great pleafure to me to know on what footing I ftand with our new governor.

I lye under thofe repeated obligations to your Grace, that it is the utmoft fatisfaction to me that you are pleafed to think that I have conftantly acted here for his Majefty's fervice and the publick good, fince I am fure it would give your Grace a great deal of uneafinefs if I failed of my duty in thofe points; and there is no perfon by whom I more defire my conduct here fhould be approved than by your Grace. I am,

My Lord, &c.

To

To the Duke of Devonshire.

My Lord,   *Dublin, July* 22, 1737.

WHEN *Dunleer*, &c. was laſt vacant, I took the liberty to recommend for it, Dr. *St. Paul*, a very worthy man of learning, and well affected to his Majeſty, and of ſome ſtanding in the Church. It was then beſtowed on * Mr. *Molloy*, who is ſince dead. I beg leave to renew my recommendations in favour of Dr. *St. Paul*, whom if your Excellency ſhall prefer, it will make a vacancy in the vicarage of *Carlingford*, which is in my gift, and which I am ready to beſtow as your Grace pleaſes to command. But if it be not taking too much upon me, I would in that caſe recommend for the vicarage of *Carlingford* Mr. *Hanover Sterling*, who is tutor to the † Maſter of Rolls children, and one whom he would gladly provide for, and who is a young man of worth and good principles. Your Grace's favour on this occaſion, will be eſteemed a great obligation on,

My Lord, &c.

P. S. I think it proper to acquaint your Grace that Mr. *Molloy* was poſſeſſed of the treaſurerſhip of *Chriſt Church* as well as *Dunleer*, yet they have no relation to one another, and probably never were poſſeſſed by the ſame perſon before.

* Mr. *Edward Molloy*, a gentleman of exceeding good character and great learning, was a Fellow of the Univerſity of *Dublin*, and preceptor to Lord *George Sackville*, third ſon of the Duke of *Dorſet*.

† The Rt. Hon. *Thomas Carter*, diſplaced in the Year 1754.

To

To the Reverend Mr. Bowes.

SIR,   *Dublin, July* 23, 1737.

WHereas * Mr. *Woolſey* informs me his perſon is in danger in the neighbourhood of *Dundalk*, where he is obliged to go to let his tythes, I deſire you would to the utmoſt of your power protect his perſon, whilſt he behaves himſelf harmleſsly and prudently.

I am, Sir, &c.

To Sir Robert Walpole.

SIR,   *Dublin, Aug.* 9, 1737.

I Am very ſorry for the occaſion I have to trouble you. But as it is what the King's intereſt and the peace of the publick here are very much concerned in, I doubt not of your excuſe for my ſo doing.

You have heard from others of the warmth of the Houſe of Commons laſt ſeſſion againſt the demands made by the clergy of agiſtment, and probably may have read the votes paſſed there on that occaſion. —

Several of the clergy had ſued for agiſtment, and the courts of juſtice here had determined in their favour, and the claim in general was ſo eſtabliſhed, that the only controverſy in the ſeveral ſuits for ſome time, had been about the number of cattle, and the quota to be paid for them : it has been decided to be due by common law ; it has indeed been ſaid on the other ſide, that the claim is new, and ſo it is in

* This gentleman was thought to be a little crazy at ſome certain periods.

N 3   ſome

some parts of the kingdom, but has been regularly paid in the north, where things have been best and soonest settled. But the case of the clergy here is very different from that in *England*, which has been the very antient usage is hard to say; but since the reformation, whilst the lands were mostly in popish hands, the clergy took what they could get thankfully, and very few ever went near their livings to do duty. That I do not look upon law to have had a free course here till since the reformation, and from thence to have gradually come to the knowledge of people. Without this tythe there are whole parishes where there is no provision for the minister : but we do not desire to be judges, but that our rights may stand on the same bottom as those of other subjects, and the judges not be intimidated by votes of either House of Parliament from doing us justice, if we seek for it.

As a great part of the gentry entered into associations not to pay for agistment to the clergy, and to make a common purse in each county to support any one there that should be sued for agistment, and were understood by the common people every where to be ready to distress the clergy all manner of ways, in their other rights, if they offered to sue for agistment, it was thought adviseable to hinder as much as we Bishops could, any of the clergy from carrying on or commencing any suits on that head for a time ; and the more so, as several persons among the Commons of more wisdom and temper, promised to think of some reasonable accommodation in this affair against another session.

But though the clergy have been quiet, and behaved themselves during this interval with a temper that has surprised their adversaries, yet I cannot find any of the laity have thought of any the least reasonable method of compounding matters, but the bulk of them reckon they have by the votes made last session
carried

carried this point, and are thereby animated to make new attacks on other rights of the clergy. I have in vain reprefented to feveral of them that in the fouth and weft of *Ireland* by deftroying the tithe of agiftment, they naturally difcourage tillage, and thereby leffen the number of people, and raife the price of provifions, and render thofe provinces incapable of carrying on the linnen manufacture, for which they fo much envy the north of this kingdom.

It is certain that by running into cattle the numbers of people are decreafing in thofe parts, and moft of their youth out of bufinefs, and difpofed to lift in foreign fervice for bread, as there is no employment for them at home, where two or three hands can look after fome hundreds of acres ftocked with cattle, and by this means a great part of our churches are neglected, in many places five, fix, or feven parifhes (denominations we commonly call them) beftowed on one incumbent, who perhaps with all his tithes fcarce gets an hundred a year.

I muft on this occafion not only obferve the illegality of thefe affociations, but the danger of them to the government, and efpecially to any acts of parliament paffed in *England* relating to this country, which may be efteemed hardfhips here, fince I do not well fee, if this humour goes on, how fuch acts can be put in execution here. And how far and to what other purpofes fuch affociations may in time extend, I do not pretend to judge, but I find in fome counties they already begin to form affociations againft what they own due to the clergy, but they are encouraged by the fuccefs of this firft attempt to go on to further fteps. The humour of clans and confederacies is neither fo well underftood nor felt in *England* as it is here.

But by difcourfes dropt among people and by fome papers handed about, there are other undoubted rights of the clergy, that are defigned to be voted away one

after

after another, or taken away by new laws, if they are permitted to go on, and I find we Bishops are threatened to have our fines if not part of our estates taken from us. I need not on this occasion observe what a support the Bishops with the weight of their estates and power are to the crown, both here and in *England*; but I must observe that they are of more immediate consequence here, to keep up the just dependence of this nation on the crown and kingdom of *England*, which too many here are disposed, if possible, to throw off, daily complaining of it as an almost insupportable burthen.

I cannot accuse the bulk of the protestants except the *Scots* in the north here, of being enemies to episcopacy and the established clergy as such, but some gentlemen have let their lands so high, that without robbing the clergy of their just dues, they are satisfied their rents can hardly be paid; and others fall in with them, that they may be able to raise their lands as high; and the controversy here is, not whether the farmer shall be eased of an unreasonable burthen, but whether the parson shall have his due, or the landlord a greater rent. Some hope they might come in for plunder, if the Bishops were stripped, and most of the needy gentry here envy to see the Bishops by a proper frugality, though not without a decent hospitality easy in their circumstances.

Against any attacks of this nature we shall prepare to make as good a provision for defence as we can; we shall not be wanting in our endeavours with those of weight in the House, and that are capable of any moderation, to prevent any new attempts on the rights of the clergy, without bringing on an attack by hastily raising a clamour that we are going to be attacked. But our great and only powerful defence under the divine providence, is from the protection of his Majesty, from whose goodness we would hope

to

to be defended in our juft rights in common with our fellow fubjects.

And I would hope that if fome difcouragement from the crown were given to what is fo unreafonable and unjuft itfelf, and muft raife the greateft heats and animofities amongft us, and give the utmoft encouragement to the papifts to fee proteftants fo violently attacking their own clergy ; and that paffing the next feffions quietly would with fuch difcountenances very much cool and balk the defigns of the ill intentioned, I cannot but make it my requeft, that you would be fo kind. as to recommend us to his Majefty's protection, which he has gracioufly declared in his fpeeches to parliament he would afford our brethren of *England*, and that when my Lord Lieutenant comes to receive his inftructions from his. Majefty before his fetting out for his government here, he may be directed by his Majefty to fignify in what way fhall be thought moft proper, that the clergy may enjoy their legal rights, and that his Majefty will be gracioufly difpofed to protect them therein from all unjuft attacks.

By a paper of queries handed about it looks as if fome gentlemen defigned to have a committee appointed to examine into the behaviour of the Bifhops and clergy in their paftoral cures : I muft own we are not faints, nor are we the greateft of finners ; but what a committee fet on foot by fuch as have the views there is reafon to fear too many have, may vote concerning our conduct, is eafily gueffed in general ; and I hope will make no bad impreffion againft us with the unprejudiced. But at the fame time I cannot but heartily wifh that thefe meafures may be prevented, which I have great reafon to believe are fet on foot from *England*, and defigned to be followed there, if they meet with fuccefs and encouragement here. I am,

Sir, your humble fervant, &c.

To

To the *Archbishop of* Canterbury.

My Lord,   *Dublin, Aug.* 9, 1737.

I Am fatisfied there is no occafion of fuggefting to your Grace, that the Church of *England* and *Ireland* are fo interwoven in point of intereft, that one cannot fuffer, but the other will foon fall into the fame diftrefs. Your own goodnefs and concern for a fifter church, would fufficiently engage you to help us in our diftrefs, though we were fure the example would not be followed on your fide of the water.

This makes me apply to your Lordfhip in our prefent and our apprehended diftrefs. The Houfe of Commons here attacked the tithe of agiftment laft feffion, and by their votes have fo far intimidated the Judges and the Clergy, that they have carried on no fuits fince, and efpecially to prevent any further ill confequences; as the gentry here have almoft univerfally entered into an affociation to fupport any perfon fued on that account by a common purfe in every county; and as they threatened to diftrefs the clergy in all their other rights, if they offered to fue for agiftment. But though fome were for venturing all this, and fuing for what in the courts here has been declared to be their right, yet as fome grave men in that Houfe promifed to think of fome temper to reconcile the laity and clergy on that point by fome reafonable compofition to be enacted this feffion, we prevailed on all the clergy to fit quiet. But inftead of any fuch propofal, the generality of the laity are encouraged to make farther attempts on the rights of the clergy; and feveral in their difcourfes and fome queries that are handed about in writing feem to defign taking away fome undoubted rights of the clergy, fuppofing the tithe of agiftment not due in fome parts of the kingdom where it has not been demanded till

lately,

lately, and among other things they feem to defign taking away from Bifhops, if not part of their lands, yet at leaft all fines. How much the crown would fuffer, if fuch things go on, by lofing the weight the Bifhops muft have, by their eftates and authority at prefent, I need only fuggeft; what I have to defire in behalf of myfelf and brethren, both on the bench and off of it, is that you would reprefent our prefent ftate to his Majefty and the miniftry, that my Lord Lieutenant when he comes foon to receive his inftructions from his Majefty before his coming hither, may be directed to let it be known here to his Majefty's fervants and others, that it is his Majefty's intention to fupport the clergy in their juft rights, as he has been gracioufly pleafed to intimate in fome of his fpeeches in *England*, and that he will take it ill of thofe who fhall attempt to raife heats and animofities here between the laity and the clergy. I have wrote to the fame purpofe to Sir *Robert Walpole*, but I make no doubt but your Grace's reprefentations on our behalf will have a much greater weight than any fuggeftions of mine.

My Lord Lieutenant will come to *London* foon after the 20th inftant, to receive his Majefty's inftructions. I am,

My Lord, &c.

To the Duke of Newcaftle.

My Lord,   *Dublin, Aug.* 16, 1737.

THE countenance and friendfhip I have met with from your Grace ever fince I came hither, makes me give you this new trouble.

The clergy here were laft feffion of parliament attacked in their rights by the Houfe of Commons, who paffed feveral votes againft them and their right to tithe of agiftment. At the fame time feveral ferious
men

men of that House gave us hopes that against the next session some temper might be found out to make that affair easy between the clergy and laity; but instead of any hopes of doing so, evil intentioned persons have raised a worse spirit against the clergy than had been raised then; and if one may guess by some words dropt by some persons, and by a paper privately handed about, some of them are disposed to strip the Bishops of some of their lands, and the rest if not all the clergy, of several of their uncontroverted rights. And till this spirit is laid, it is impossible to hope for any compromise about the affair of agistment. I am sure the oppressing the Bishops and Clergy here, will be very much to the damage of the Crown, and we hope it is his Majesty's intention to defend us and our rights as well as our brethren in *England*. And though I hope it will not be found so easy a work here to run down the Clergy, as some imagine, yet I must own their great security, next under the Divine Providence, to be in his Majesty's protection; but it would be much better to prevent any such attempts and the heats they must occasion, than finally to defeat them.

I wrote to Sir *Robert Walpole* on this subject, and desired that our Lord Lieutenant might be instructed to let it be known here that it was his Majesty's full intention to protect the Clergy here in their present just rights, and that he should be offended with such as attempted to invade them. My request to your Grace is that you would join with Sir *Robert Walpole* in representing these matters to his Majesty, and obtaining such instructions to my Lord Lieutenant; and that you would in virtue of your particular friendship with my Lord Lieutenant, dispose him to be the patron of the Clergy here in their present unhappy situation, and engage him to let me from time to time apply to him in their behalf, as things shall occur. I

can

can affure your Grace I fhall make no other ufe of fuch liberty and encouragement, than to promote peace and quiet, and his Majefty's fervice in this kingdom.

I am, my Lord, &c.

To the Duke of Newcaftle.

My Lord,   *Dublin, Sept.* 29, 1737.

I Have had the honour of your Grace's letter relating to the addrefs to his Majefty delivered by the Lord Mayor and city of *Dublin.* I communicated the matter to my Lord Chancellor and Mr. Speaker, who agreed that it was moft proper for my Lord Lieutenant to acquaint them that you had been fo kind as immediately to deliver their addrefs to the King, and that his Majefty received it very gracioufly, fince we had fent it as the government, and that we could not now return the anfwer in that capacity. I therefore delivered your Lordfhip's letter to my Lord Lieutenant, who fent for the Lord Mayor and Sheriffs, and acquainted them with the contents of your Grace's letter, of which probably he may have fent your Grace advice.

The affair of reducing the gold has by the management of the bankers and remitters, and the whole popifh party here, occafioned a great deal of heat. The former are very unwilling to part with fo confiderable a part of their profit, though it vifibly tended to the ruin of the country, by running all our money into * 4 *l.* pieces. I have in a particular manner been ill ufed on this occafion, and monftrous ftories have been fpread about to enrage the people.

* Which then paffed in *England* as they do now for 3 *l.* 12 *s.* and the other *Portuguefe* Gold coins in the fame Proportion, to which Standard the Currency was reduced in *Ireland,* which is now 3 *l.* 17 *s.* 8 *d.*

It

It is poffible fome difcontented people may endeavour to bring the affair into parliament, and make fome reflecting votes on the council here, which by our conftitution has a power to check the proceedings of both Lords and Commons. I think they will not be able to carry any vote on that point; but if they do, I am fure the only check here on their heat at any time will be taken away, except his Majefty is pleafed to fupport the council. In the whole affair I am fatisfied, the aim of feveral is to deprefs the *Englifh* intereft here, which the more fome labour to deprefs, the more neceffary will it be to fupport it here by his Majefty's authority.

As for myfelf, I make no difficulty of retiring if it may be of any ufe, and indeed have of late been fo ill ufed in this affair, that nothing but his Majefty's fervice fhould hinder me from retiring.

The heats in this town begin to cool, and would have been over by this time, if they had not been artfully kept up for a handle in another place *.

I am, my Lord, &c.

To the Bifhop of London.

My Lord,   *Dublin, Feb.* 10, 1737.

I Heartily beg your Lordfhip's pardon for not having anfwered your Lordfhip's laft favour fooner, but I have for fome weeks been fo conftantly em-

---

* Such a fpirit of oppofition had been raifed on this occafion by Dean *Swift* and the bankers, that it was thought proper to lodge at the Primate's houfe an extraordinary guard of foldiers; but truth foon got the better of this delufion, and the people returned again to their fenfes. Dean *Swift* not long after this feeble effort, this *telum imbelle fine ictu*, became one of his own meer doting *Struldbrugs*; an event which he was always apprehenfive of, in his more melancholy moments; and this way of thinking was the principal motive to that noble charity, which to his great honour he founded in *Dublin* for lunatics and idiots. *London* Edition.

ployed

ployed about our bills here, to prepare them for the council in *England*, or reject them in our council, that it has put all other business out of my head. I am very glad the popery tracts are at last finished, and as I had 50 receipts for the first payment of the subscriptions, I thought it most proper to return the money to your Lordship to pay the bookfellers, and accordingly I have here sent you a bill on my brother Mr. *Savage* for 52*l.* 10*s.* I believe there are about 15*l.* of the money I have not received, though I have given out the receipts, but that is an affair I am to look after. It is expected here that the books should be sent to some correspondent of the bookfellers in *Dublin*, where they may be had by the subscribers, on delivering in their receipts and the other guinea; and I guess no subscriber will fail taking out his book, as many of them have been very earnestly enquiring after the books.

I took care to have Dr. *Jenney* made one of the Lord Lieutenant's chaplains, and shall serve him according to your Lordship's desire as occasion offers.

We have got pretty well through the attacks on the Church here in bills; but I cannot answer but the Commons may make some angry votes before their rising, particularly about agiftment, on occasion of a clergyman having imprudently given notice to his parishioners to pay it on pain of being prosecuted. He is sensible of his error in not staying till the session was over, before giving notice; but the affair having made a noise, may probably produce some votes.

I am satisfied our people are set on here by some correspondents in *England*; we shall defend ourselves here as well as we can, but our last dependance is on the King and council in *England*.

We entertain great hopes here of an accommodation being concluded with you.

I heartily

I heartily wifh the Church may efcape all attacks this feffion; for I think every day it muft be feen, that the Church is not attacked purely on its own account.

I am, my Lord, &c.

To the Duke of Dorfet.

My Lord,   *Dublin, Feb.* 11, 1737.

I Have very lately received your Grace's commands in favour of Mr. *Darcey,* to whom I fhall very readily do all good offices in my power.

I take this occafion to thank your Lordfhip in my own name, and that of every honeft and underftanding perfon in this nation, for having at laft brought about the lowering our gold here. Your Grace has no doubt been fully informed of the clamours raifed againft it, and the infult on the government by * Dean *Swift* on that occafion; together with the petitions of the Houfe of Commons, and the warm debates there on that fubject.

I have had a great fhare of fuffering on this account, as far as the moft virulent papers, and the curfers of a deluded and enraged multitude could go: but God be thanked, I am got fafe through all. There had been no fuch ufage of me, or oppofition to fo neceffary a ftep, or infult of the populace, if thofe joined in power had acted with that courage that became governors. Though I muft do them juftice, that when it came to be debated in the Houfe of Commons, they were not wanting in engaging their friends to ftand by what the government had done.

The

* On this occafion a black flag was difplayed on the top of St. *Patrick's,* and a dumb peal as they call it, was rung, with the clappers of the bells muffled.

The effect of this alteration is already felt in having guineas, half-guineas, and piftoles very common, inftead of 4 l. pieces: and filver is in much greater plenty than it was; and the clamour that had been raifed is very near over.

I cannot conclude without thanking your Lordfhip for all the favours received during your government, and of ftill recommending myfelf to your protection.

I am, my Lord, &c.

To the Bifhop of London.

My Lord,   *Dublin, Apr.* 12, 1738.

THE bearer is Mr. *Strain*, who has ferved two cures in my diocefe, in the firft I found him placed by my predeceffor, the fecond I removed him to. He behaved himfelf very well in both cures, without any reproach either as to his morals or prudence; but as there were reports fpread about the country, that he was not in prieft's orders, and as when called upon he was not able to give a fatisfactory proof of his having been ordained by a deprived Bifhop in *Scotland,* as he afferted he was, and that the inftrument he produced of his being fo ordained was not fufficiently fupported, there was a neceffity of difmiffing him from his cure.

But he fays, one Mr. *Cockbourn,* who was a non-juror, but fince has taken the oaths, was prefent at his ordination, and can prove it; if at *London,* or if not, yet he thinks he can find thofe at *London,* that by their correfpondence at *Edinburgh,* will be able to atteft thofe proofs he can have from *Edinburgh.* As he has thoughts of feeking his fortune in the *Weft Indies,* and is pofitive he can clear the imputation he lies under here, he begged me to write to your Lordfhip to give him an opportunity of vindicating his innocency before your Lordfhip; and if he does so, to recommend him to your Lordship to put him in a way of getting bread in some of our plantations. And as he has no crime laid to his charge, but pretending falsely to be in orders, if he is able to prove he is unjustly accused on that head, I cannot but in compassion desire your Lordship to be assistant to him. I am very tender of giving your Lordship any trouble of this nature, but as the case is uncommon, I hope you will have the goodness to excuse my writing to your Lordship in his behalf, if he appears innocent.

I am, my Lord, &c.

To the Duke of Devonshire.

My Lord, Dublin, Apr. 18, 1738.

THE bearer is Mr. *Norris*, who married a * sister of my wife's; he is agent to Sir *James Wood*, and comes over to wait upon your Grace to solicit about a vacancy in Sir *James Wood*'s regiment. I do not take upon me to meddle in that affair, but desire your Grace will be pleased to give him a favourable reception, and to do what you shall think most proper.

I am, my Lord, &c.

To Dr. Butler †.

SIR, Dublin, Apr. 29, 1738.

OUR old friend Mr. *Morgan* was taken ill with a dozing this day se'nnight, and continued pretty much so till he died on *Wednesday* night. Last night he was buried. He left a scrap of a will written in his own hand, by which he leaves to his sister *Catharine Wynn*, alias *Gunn*, living near *Henley* in Ox-

---

* Miss *Savage*, a Lady of Fortune.
† President of *Magdalen* college, *Oxford*, and Member of Parliament for that University.

fordshire,

fordfbire, 100 guineas, to her heirs 100 guineas; for new cafting two bells at *Chrift Church* 100*l.* to the new buildings at *Magdalen* college 100*l.*

As I know nothing where his fifter lives, I defire you would be fo kind as to learn where fhe lives, and acquaint her with it. But befides what he has left her in this will, as I never heard him talk of any other relation he had, fhe will be entitled, I fuppofe, to the reft of his eftate; which in the whole may amount to 1200*l.* or better.

His papers have not yet been fearched, when they have I fhall acquaint you whether any other will is found; and fend you a more exact account of his effects.

I fhall take care to difpofe of what few effects in goods he has left. What cloaths he has I believe may be given to the fervants that attended him, if his fifter thinks proper.

His funeral expences, doctor, furgeon, apothecary, &c. I fhall difcharge out of his effects, and any thing that appears due from him, which can be very little. I believe it will not be worth while to come over hither about his effects, fince I fhall take care to have his affairs as well looked after as any one from *England* can do; and the ballance fhall be faithfully returned.

Any thing his fifter thinks proper to order on this occafion, had better be fent to * Mr. *Philips* under cover to me.

                              I am, Sir, &c.

To the Bifhop of London.

My Lord,   *Dublin, Apr.* 28, 1738.

THE trouble I give your Lordfhip is in favour of the bearer, Mr. *Norris,* a Batchelor of Arts, of this college.   It feems he went over to *England* in ex-

---

* *Ambrofe Philips,* Efq. Secretary to his Grace.

pectation

pectation of some preferment, but has met with a disappointment; but could, if he was ordained, be provided with a chaplainship in one of the men of war designed for the *West Indies*, which he is willing to accept of. But as he is wholly a stranger to any of the Bishops of *England*, and to any one there to recommend him for orders, he has wrote to his friends here to obtain a letter, setting forth his character, that he may have the favour of being ordained. His tutor, Mr. * *Cartwright*, who is a person of worth and honour, gives the following account of him under his hand :

Mr. *Norris* was my pupil, he has taken the degree of Bachelor, and has a testimonium to certify it : he behaved himself with diligence and virtue, during his residence in the college ; and since he left it, I am well assured his life has been innocent and industrious.

I find it is not many months since he left the college, and as his character is so well supported, and if he misses this opportunity, it may possibly be a long time before he finds any employment, I take the liberty to recommend him to your Lordship for orders, if you think it proper, and find him as well qualified as I believe you will.

I am, my Lord, &c.

To the Duke of Devonshire.

My Lord, *Dublin, May* 1, 1738.

AS it is taken for granted here that Col. *Pyot* is dying or dead, Capt. *Vernon* is very desirous that if the Major of the regiment is made Lieutenant Colonel, and the eldest Captain is made Major, he may succeed to the troop that will become vacant.

* A Senior Fellow of the University of *Dublin*.

I am

I am very tender in meddling with affairs so much out of my province, but I beg leave just to hint to your Grace how hearty he has shewn himself on all occasions for his Majesty's family, and how much he is attached to your Grace : and such a post I believe would fix him amongst us to spend his pay and his own estate in this country. But I submit the whole to your Lordship's pleasure. I am,

My Lord, &c.

To the Earl of Granard.

My Lord,   *Dublin, May* 4, 1738.

I Most heartily congratulate your Lordship on your new * government, and make no doubt but it is on those honourable terms as make it agreeable to your Lordship. I thought I could hardly have had occasion to trouble your Lordship about any thing in so remote a part of the world ; but it happens that my Chaplain Mr. *Congreve*, who is of a good family in *Staffordshire*, has an uncle in *New York*, in the service of the government, whose circumstances are somewhat particular. The person is Capt. *Charles Congreve*, who about thirty years ago was going for *New York*, Lieutenant and Adjutant, with his wife, family, and all his effects, and a number of recruits, and a brevet for a Captain's commission in one of the independent companies. In their passage they met a privateer, whom they engaged, and hoped to have got off in the night, but were betrayed by the master of the ship, who had insured the vessel. In the engagement the Captain lost his arm, and was obliged at his return to *New York*, by the expences of supporting himself, his family, and recruits, and other misfortunes to sell his commissions of Lieutenant and Adjutant, by which he lost the benefit of his

* Governor of the Counties of *Westmeath* and *Longford*.

brevet,

brevet, and remained there without any commission till eight or nine years ago, when he was made Lieutenant by the recommendation of the Earl of *Essex*, and is now upon duty in a very remote part of that province.

The favour I have to beg of your Lordship is that you would shew him your countenance, and as your Lordship shall find it confistent with the service, to remove him to a more comfortable situation.

I am, My Lord, &c.

To *Mrs.* Wall.

MADAM, *Dublin, Dec.* 19, 1738.

I Am glad to hear your son has behaved himself so well at the college as to have so many votes for a faculty place.

I am pretty well satisfied I am not so much behind hand in anfwering your letters as you seem to think in your laft; and I believe few or none of your letters have mifcarried. I laft week sent a bill to Mr. *Gell* for your ufe. I am sorry to hear you are in so indifferent a ftate of health, and that your hufband is as unkind as ever. It is with great pleafure that I hear your son minds his ftudies. I underftand by you and others, that Mrs. *Sparks* is returned safe to *London*, but neither I nor any of my family have heard from her since she left this place.

My service with my spoufe's to you and your family, wifhing you all a happy *Chriftmas*.

I am, Madam, &c.

F I N I S.

I N D E X.

☞ Where the firſt Volume is referred to, the number of the Volume is not mentioned.

I N D E X.

Cox's

Echlin's

INDEX.

I N D E X.

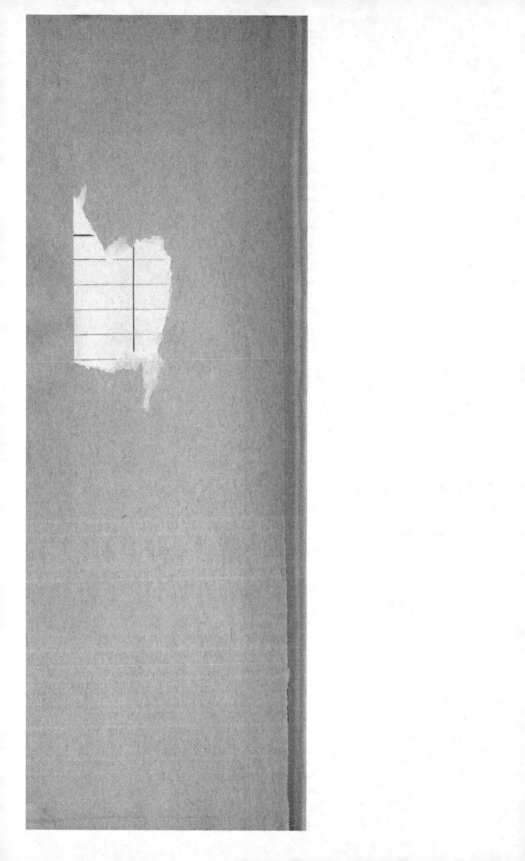

CPSIA information can be obtained
at www.ICGtesting.com
Printed in the USA
BVHW082309190819
556223BV00020B/2480/P